Lecture Notes in Computer Science   8604

Commenced Publication in 1973
Founding and Former Series Editors:
Gerhard Goos, Juris Hartmanis, and Jan van Leeuwen

T0212683

Alessandro Aldini   Javier Lopez
Fabio Martinelli (Eds.)

Foundations
of Security Analysis
and Design VII

FOSAD 2012/2013 Tutorial Lectures

 Springer

Volume Editors

Alessandro Aldini
University of Urbino "Carlo Bo"
Dipartimento di Scienze di Base e Fondamenti
Piazza della Repubblica 13, 61029 Urbino, Italy
E-mail: alessandro.aldini@uniurb.it

Javier Lopez
University of Malaga, Department of Computer Science
Network, Information and Computer Security Lab
Campus de Teatinos s/n, 29071 Malaga, Spain
E-mail: jlm@lcc.uma.es

Fabio Martinelli
National Research Council - CNR
Istituto di Informatica e Telematica - IIT
Via G. Moruzzi 1, 56124 Pisa, Italy
E-mail: fabio.martinelli@iit.cnr.it

ISSN 0302-9743   e-ISSN 1611-3349
ISBN 978-3-319-10081-4   e-ISBN 978-3-319-10082-1
DOI 10.1007/978-3-319-10082-1
Springer Cham Heidelberg New York Dordrecht London

Library of Congress Control Number: 2014945357

LNCS Sublibrary: SL 4 – Security and Cryptology

Typesetting: Camera-ready by author, data conversion by Scientific Publishing Services, Chennai, India

Printed on acid-free paper

Springer is part of Springer Science+Business Media (www.springer.com)

International School on
Foundations of Security Analysis and Design

The LNCS series entitled *Foundations of Security Analysis and Design* (FOSAD) began on 2001 with the aim of proposing a collection of tutorial papers accompanying lectures given at the FOSAD summer school. This year we present the 7th volume in the series, which is dedicated to FOSAD 2012 and 2013. FOSAD has been one of the foremost educational events established to disseminate knowledge in the area of security for computer systems and networks. Over the years, both the summer school and the book series have represented a reference point for graduate students and young researchers from academia or industry interested in approaching the field, investigating open problems, and following priority lines of research. The topics covered in this book include model-based security, automatic verification of secure applications, information flow analysis, cryptographic voting systems, encryption in the cloud, and privacy preservation.

The opening paper by Fabrice Bouquet, Fabien Peureux, and Fabrice Ambert presents a survey of model-based approaches for security testing, by discussing existing techniques, the state of the art, and deployment. A specific model-based tool-supported technique is presented in the contribution by Jan Jürjens et al., who describe a dynamic approach to security engineering using UMLsec.

Automatic verification through formal methods is the main topic of the paper by Bruno Blanchet, who introduces the specific case of ProVerif, an automatic protocol verifier that relies on the symbolic model of cryptography, a process algebraic specification language, and resolution-based proof techniques. Karthikeyan Bhargavan, Antoine Delignat-Lavaud, and Sergio Maffeis present a tutorial of the Defensive JavaScript language, which is a typed subset of JavaScript with specific security guarantees. In particular, they show how to use it to program secure applications and analyze them automatically through ProVerif. Willem De Groef, Dominique Devriese, Mathy Vanhoef, and Frank Piessens discuss information flow control mechanisms for the security analysis and control of Web scripts. To this aim, they formalize both a static type-system and a dynamic enforcement mechanism. The paper by Gilles Barthe et al. introduces a machine-checked framework, called EasyCrypt, supporting the construction and automated verification of cryptographic systems in the computational model.

David Bernhard and Bogdan Warinschi propose a survey of the main ideas and techniques used in cryptographic voting systems. As a real-world example, they describe the security properties of the Helios voting system. In their paper, Samarati et al. address the issue of protecting sensitive information from uncontrolled access in the cloud. In order to preserve confidentiality and integrity in this setting, they discuss the benefits of data encryption and data fragmentation.

Finally, Ruben Rios, Javier Lopez, and Jorge Cuellar describe location privacy issues in wireless sensor networks, by categorizing solutions and open problems.

We would like to thank all the institutions that have promoted and funded FOSAD in the last few years. We are particularly grateful to the IFIP Working Groups 1.7 on Theoretical Foundations of Security Analysis and Design and 11.14 on Secure Engineering (NESSoS), the ERCIM Working Group in Security and Trust Management (STM), and the EPSRC CryptoForma network.

To conclude, we also wish to thank all the staff of the University Residential Centre of Bertinoro for the organizational and administrative support.

June 2014

Alessandro Aldini
Javier Lopez
Fabio Martinelli

Table of Contents

Model-Based Testing
for Functional and Security Test Generation

Fabrice Bouquet[1,2], Fabien Peureux[2], and Fabrice Ambert[2]

[1] Inria Nancy Grand Est – CASSIS Project
Campus Scientifique, BP 239, 54506 Vandœuvre-lès-Nancy Cedex, France
fabrice.bouquet@inria.fr
[2] Institut FEMTO-ST – UMR CNRS 6174, University of Franche-Comté
16, route de Gray, 25030 Besançon, France
{fbouquet,fpeureux,fambert}@femto-st.fr

Abstract. With testing, a system is executed with a set of selected stimuli, and observed to determine whether its behavior conforms to the specification. Therefore, testing is a strategic activity at the heart of software quality assurance, and is today the principal validation activity in industrial context to increase the confidence in the quality of systems. This paper, summarizing the six hours lesson taught during the Summer School FOSAD'12, gives an overview of the test data selection techniques and provides a state-of-the-art about Model-Based approaches for security testing.

1 Testing and Software Engineering

One major issue, regarding the engineering in general and the software domain in particular, concerns the conformity of the realization in regards of the stakeholder specification. To tackle this issue, software engineering relies on two kinds of approaches: Validation and Verification, usually called *V&V*.

1.1 Software Engineering

The approaches proposed by Software engineering to ensure software conformity are the validation and the verification. There are many definitions of these two words but we propose to explain them in regards of the usage. The **validation** addresses the question *"Are we building the right product?"*, which aims to validate that the software should do what the end users really requires, i.e. that the developed software conforms to the requirements of its specification. The **verification** addresses the question *"Are we building the product right?"*, which aims to verify that all the artifacts defined during the development stages to produce the software conform to the requirements of its specification, i.e. that the requirements and design specifications has been correctly integrated in development stuff (model, code, etc.). It should be noted that another variants or interpretations of these definitions can be found in the literature, mainly depending of the engineering domain they are applied.

A. Aldini et al. (Eds.): FOSAD VII, LNCS 8604, pp. 1–33, 2014.
© Springer International Publishing Switzerland 2014

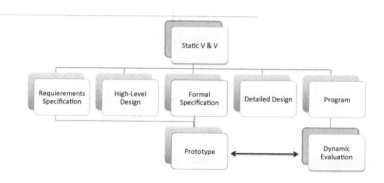

Fig. 1. Validation and verification

Figure 1 describes the different steps used by the methods of Verification and Validation. For each step, different techniques can be used:

- **Static Test** for the reviews of code, of specification, of design documentation.
- **Dynamic Test** for the execution of program to ensure the correctness of its functionalities.
- **Symbolic Verification** for run-time checking, symbolic execution (of model or code).
- **Formal Verification** for proof, model-checking from formal model.

The rest of this presentation focuses on dynamic test approach, which is today the principal validation activity in industrial context to increase the confidence in the quality of software.

1.2   What Is Testing?

Naturally, the next question is *"what is testing?"*. Since the first and the second techniques proposed in the previous part concern the Static Test and Dynamic Test, we propose three definitions of testing from the state of the art:

- IEEE Std 829 [1]: "The process of analyzing (execution or evaluation) a software item to detect the differences between existing and required conditions (that is, bugs), and to evaluate the features of the software item."
- G.J. Myers (The Art of Software testing [2]): "Test is the process of executing a program (or part of a program) with the intention of finding errors."
- E.W. Dijkstra (Notes on Structured Programming [3]): "Testing can reveal the presence of errors but never their absence."

Three major features can be underlined in these definitions. The first one concerns the capacity to compare the results, provided by the real system, to the expected value, defined in the specifications. It implies to have a referential to ensure the confidence in testing activity. The second one concerns the testing process itself, and the way to find bugs. Therefore, we need to define a coverage strategy of the referential element to be tested (such as code, requirements or any artifact like models). Finally, the third issue is the uncompletion of testing because, in general, we cannot explore all possibilities. Indeed, due to combinatorial explosion of reachable states, exhaustive testing is unfeasible in practice, and dedicated strategies are needed to manage this explosion and to keep a relevant quality assessment.

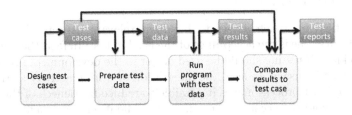

Fig. 2. Activities of dynamic test

As shown in Fig. 2, testing process can be decomposed in five main activities:

1. Select or design test cases: choose a subset of all possible features of the System Under Test (SUT). This information is provided by the validation and test plan. This step aims to produce the abstract test cases, i.e. scenarios that have still to be concretized using concrete values and function calls.
2. Identify the data for test cases: the test cases, defined in the previous step, can be used with several data. Then, it is important to choice a relevant subset of data. The number of test cases execution is equal to the number of chosen data.
3. Execute the test cases with the data: the test cases with data are executed on the SUT and test results are gathered using manual or automatic execution environment.
4. Analyze the results of the executed test. This step consists to assign a verdict to each executed test case by deciding if the test is in success or not:
   - Pass: the obtained results conform to the expected values.
   - Fail: the obtained results do not conform to the expected values.
   - Inconclusive: it is not possible to conclude.
5. Reporting: it is the evaluation of the quality and the relevance of the tests (to determine the need and effort to correct discovered bugs, to decide to stop testing phase, etc.).

Beyond this theoretical point of view, regarding the reality and practices of the industrial development context, the maturity of the Quality Assurance or Test function shift from theoretical ad hoc process to a more strategic and centralized approach. Moreover, the testing activity often concerns areas of IT organizations from western Europe Enterprise, which mainly promote and apply the following process steps[1]:

---

[1] Source IDC - European Services, Enterprise Application Testing Survey, March 2011.

1. Choose a testing methodology to address **agile/component** based development life cycle.
2. Provide **automated test coverage** that makes it possible to apply agility in testing.
3. Focus on the **non-functional aspects** like performance, availability, security, etc.
4. Refine the test strategy to **optimize the use of testing services** (traditional and cloud based).

This practical approach allows to highlight relevant aspects about testing activity. The first one is the acceptance of the need to test. In fact, the question is no more to know if testing should be used or not in the development process, but how to enhance its usage. Indeed, the integration of testing activity at the heart of the development process makes it possible to reduce bottleneck of the project deadline and avoid the crushing tension of the validation phase before releasing the product. Therefore, optimization issues are studied and generalization are discussed to generalize it for other aspects (up to unit and/or functional for example). The automation of the testing activity and the improvement of the confidence level are thus today the main issues about testing.

1.3   Kinds of Test

"Testing" is a very generic term. In reality, as suggested in previous IDC survey, thus we need to refine it. J. Tretmans in [4] proposed to decompose the testing approaches regarding three dimensions. This representation is shown in Fig. 3.

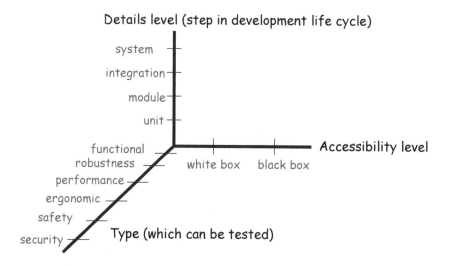

Fig. 3. Kind of testing approaches as proposed by J. Tretmans

The first dimension (horizontal axis) concerns the accessibility of the code to be tested. *White box* defines an open box in which all the information about the code are accessible. *Black box* defines a closed box and only the binaries are available to execute the test. The second dimension (vertical axis) is the architecture level of the system to be tested, i.e. the development phase from the software life cycle point of view. An example of the development life cycle and validation steps is proposed in Fig. 4. The figure depicts four phases from the specification, provided by the client, to the code implementation. Each described phase has four specific level or context, which are addressed by dedicated test objectives. For example, Unit testing focuses on the coverage of the code to separately validate the computation of each implemented functions or procedures, while Acceptance testing focuses on the end-user features and thus addresses only the functional (or domain) requirements.

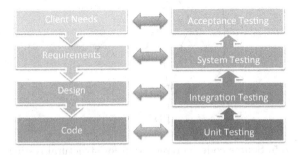

Fig. 4. Development life cycle & testing levels

Finally, the third dimension (plan axis) is the usage or targeted aspects to be validated by the tests. So, each test is an element that can be located in this 3D space representation.

White Box. White box testing, also called Structural Testing, instantiates the four activities of the Fig. 2 as follows:

- Test cases: they cover all the functions of the source code to be tested.
  - Deriving from the internal design of the program.
  - Requiring detailed knowledge of its structure.
- Data: test data are produced from the source code analysis in order to ensure some given coverage criteria. The most common coverage criteria are based on the analysis and coverage of the flow graph associated to a function of the source code as illustrated in Fig. 5.
  - Statement: node or block of instructions,
  - Branch: condition,

- Path: a problem regarding the path coverage is the number of loops (for example between B and A in Fig. 5), so there exist more restrictive criteria as *independent path* or *k-path* (where k defines the maximum number of loops to be tested). A comparison and a hierarchy of all such structural criteria are proposed in [5].
- Execution: the test scripts take the form of a suite of function calls (with data) of the source code.
- Reporting and end of the testing phase: it directly depends on the completion of the given targeted coverage criteria.

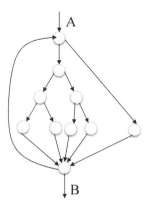

Fig. 5. Source code representation for structural testing

Black Box. Black box testing, also called Functional Testing, instantiates the four activities of the fig. 2 as follows (the overall black box testing process is also depicted in Fig. 6):

- Test cases are derived from the functional specification.
  - Designed without knowledge of the source code internal structure and design.
  - Based only on functional requirements.
- Test data are also derived from the functional specification by applying dedicated test coverage criteria on the related specification in order to identify and target some requirements or functionalities as test objectives.
- Execution: the test scripts take the form of a suite of API call or implemented user actions (with concrete data) of user or software interfaces of the program.
- Reporting and end of the testing phase: it directly depends on the completion of the given targeted coverage criteria.

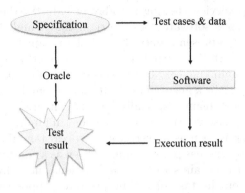

Fig. 6. Functional testing process

1.4 Testing Universe

In fact, testing is in the middle of many artifacts, called test universe. For instance, the specification explains, in term of needs and requirements, the features that have to be developed, and also what the tests have to validate. It also identifies the defects to be avoided (from which associated test can be derived). A same test can be used to validate that a requirement is correctly implemented (at its first execution), but it can also be used to ensure this requirement remains correctly implemented in future versions (this kind of test is called *non regression test*). It is also possible to create or derive test from specific artifacts such as contracts or models, which provide an abstraction level to help and ease the design of the tests. Finally, as depicted in Fig. 7, some tooling and environment are now available to manage, in an automated manner, all these artifacts related to requirements, models, defects, test scripts and test definition repository. Those make it possible to offer a scalable and reliable automation of the testing process, and ease its usage in the industrial development and validation team.

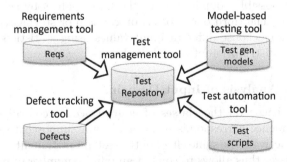

Fig. 7. Sphere of testing tools

To conclude this overview, testing is today in industry the main activity to determine if a developed software does the right things and things right (using each level of test). It represents until 60% of the complete effort for software development. This effort is reported in 1/3 during software development and 2/3 during software maintenance. Nevertheless, in current software development, testing is still often seen as a necessary evil. It indeed remains a not very popular activity in development teams especially because integrating testing activities during development phase give rise to a psychological hindrance and/or cultural brake because testing is seen as a destructive process (an efficient test is a test that reveals an error), whereas programming is seen as a constructive and helpful process (each line of code aims to fulfill a functional need for the end users). Moreover, teams given the task of testing are often appointed by default and have no professional skills in testing activities, although specific knowledge and competences are required for the task. This paper precisely aims to fill in the gaps on testing knowledge by introducing practical testing approaches focusing on functional testing and security test design.

The paper is organized as follows. Techniques for test data selection are introduced in Section 2, functional Model-Based Testing approaches are described in Section 3, and specificities about Model-Based Testing to address security features are presented in Section 4. Finally, Section 5 concludes the paper and gives several tooling references to look at practical Model-Based Testing in more depth.

2   Test Data Selection

The previous section introduced the testing steps to design test cases. This section deals with the strategic activity concerning the selection of the data that will be used to build executable test cases. Three main techniques are used to choice the test data. The first one uses a partition analysis based on the input domains. This approach reduces the number of possible values by selecting a representative value (bound, middle, random...) for each identified partition. The second one consists to apply a combinatorial testing strategy. This approach can also restrict the possible combination of the input values by selecting specific n-uplets of values. The third one is based on random or stochastic testing. This approach enables to choose different input values using statistic strategies that allow an uniform distribution of the selected data.

2.1   Partition Analysis of Input Domains

This technique, based on the classes of equivalence, is control flow oriented. A class of equivalence corresponds to a set of data supposed to test the same behavior, i.e. to activate the same effect of the tested functionality. The definition of equivalent classes thus allows to convert an infinite number of input data into a finite number of test data. The computation of the test data are performed in order to cover each identified behaviors. For example, let a given function defined by:

Domain: $x \in -1000..1000$
Precondition: $x \leq 100$
Postcondition:
IF $x \leq 0$ **THEN** $y \leftarrow$ default
ELSE IF $x \leq 40$
    THEN $y \leftarrow$ low
    ELSE $y \leftarrow$ high
    END
END

The partition analysis of this function gives rise to identify three behaviors P_i in regards to Pre and Postcondition:

1. P_1: $x \leq 0$
2. P_2: $x > 0 \wedge x \leq 40$
3. P_3: $x > 40 \wedge x \leq 100$

We can then derive the corresponding constraints about the domain of the variable x and define four classes of equivalence C_i:

1. C_1: $x \in [-1000, 0]$
2. C_2: $x \in [1, 40]$
3. C_3: $x \in [41, 100]$
4. C_4: $x \in [101, 1000]$

This technique thus aims to select data in order to cover each behavior of the tested function. Such function often includes control points, which are usually (such as the previous example) represented by IF-THEN-ELSE construct in programming languages. The executed effects of a given execution depend on the evaluation of the boolean formula, called *decision*, which is expressed in the IF statement and gives rise to two equivalent classes : one makes true the evaluation of the decision, the other makes it false. In the previous example, this decision is an atomic expression ($x \leq 0$), but in practice decisions are complex predicates constructed with $\wedge$, $\vee$ and $\neg$ operators, combining elementary boolean expressions, called *conditions*, that cannot be divided into further boolean expressions. Exposing the internal structure of a decision can lead to extend the number of equivalence classes if each evaluation of each condition is considered. This issue of how to treat multiple conditions without exponential test case explosion is a key point for test generation. Several structural coverage criteria for decisions with multiple conditions have thus been defined in the testing literature. Brief informal definitions and hierarchy (see Fig. 8) are given here, but more details including formal definitions in Z are available elsewhere [6,7]. Note the terminology: a *decision* contains one or more primitive *conditions*, combined by disjunction, conjunction and negation operators.

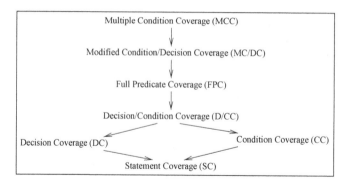

Fig. 8. The Hierarchy of control-flow coverage criteria for multiple conditions. $C_1 \longrightarrow C_2$ means that criterion C_1 is stronger than criterion C_2.

Statement Coverage (SC). The test set must execute every reachable statement of the program.

Condition Coverage (CC). A test set achieves CC when each condition in the program is tested with a true result, and also with a false result. For a decision containing N conditions, two tests can be sufficient to achieve CC (one test with all conditions true, one with them all false), but dependencies between the conditions typically require several more tests.

Decision/Condition Coverage (D/CC). A test set achieves D/CC when it achieves both decision coverage (DC) and CC.

Full Predicate Coverage (FPC). A test set achieves FPC when each condition in the program is forced to true and to false, in a scenario where that condition is *directly correlated* with the outcome of the decision. A condition c is directly correlated with its decision d when either $d \iff c$ holds, or $d \iff \neg c$ holds [8]. For a decision containing N conditions, a maximum of $2N$ tests are required to achieve FPC.

Modified Condition/Decision Coverage (MC/DC). This strengthens the *directly correlated* requirement of FPC by requiring the condition c to *independently affect* the outcome of the decision d. A condition is shown to independently affect a decision's outcome by varying just that condition while holding fixed all other possible conditions [9,10]. Achieving MC/DC may require more tests than FPC, but the number of tests generated is generally linear in the number of conditions.

Multiple Condition Coverage (MCC). A test set achieves MCC if it exercises all possible combinations of condition outcomes in each decision. This requires up to 2^N tests for a decision with N conditions, so is practical only for simple decisions.

These different coverage criteria can also be used to as data selection criteria by rewriting the decision into several predicates. Each predicate defines a specific equivalent class in which data have to be derived. To achieve it, a simplistic way is to consider a single disjunction $A \vee B$ nested somewhere inside a decision.

We propose four possible rewriting rules to transform the disjunction into a set of predicates defining data equivalent classes:

- $A \vee B \rightsquigarrow \{\,A \vee B\,\}$. This generates just one equivalent class for the whole disjunct, resulting in one test for the whole decision. This corresponds to decision coverage (because the negated decision is achieved by another equivalent class, e.g., corresponding to the ELSE branch).
- $A \vee B \rightsquigarrow \{\,A, B\,\}$. This ensures D/CC, because there is one equivalent class defined by A true, and one by B true, and another one with the negated decision that will cover $\neg A \wedge \neg B$. In fact, a single equivalent class, $A \wedge B$, would in theory be enough to ensure D/CC, but $A \wedge B$ is often not satisfiable, so two weaker tests are generated instead.
- $A \vee B \rightsquigarrow \{\,A \wedge \neg B, \neg A \wedge B\,\}$. This is similar to FPC, because the result of the true disjunct is directly correlated with the result of the whole disjunction, since it cannot be masked by the other disjunct becoming true.
- $A \vee B \rightsquigarrow \{\,A \wedge \neg B, \neg A \wedge B, A \wedge B\,\}$. This corresponds to MCC, because it defines an specific equivalent class for each combinations of A and B (the $\neg A \wedge \neg B$ combination is covered by the negated decision). This usually becomes unmanageable even for moderate values of N conditions.

Figure 9 depicts these rewriting rules by showing the different equivalent classes: the regions A and B identify the data domain of the two conditions A and B of the decision $A \vee B$.

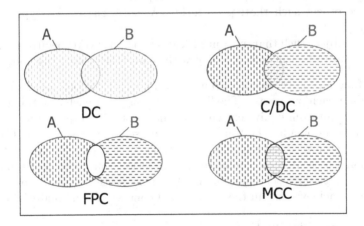

Fig. 9. Decision coverage

Finally, selecting data from obtained equivalent classes can be performed non-deterministically, but also by applying a boundary/domain approach [11]. This boundary values approach is known to be an efficient strategy to select test data and is currently used as the basis for test generation algorithms [12], but it has not generally been formalized as coverage criteria.

To achieve this approach, some simple rules, based on the type of the parameter, can be applied to choice the values of data. Basically, for each equivalent class, it consists to take the data value at an extremum – minimum or maximum – of its domain. It should be noted that this approach can only be performed if an evaluation function can discriminate each value of the domain (minimum or maximum of integers, minimum or maximum of the cardinality of sets, etc.), else an arbitrary value can be selected by default as usual. Some examples illustrating this approach are given below:

- for each interval of integer described by an equivalent class, we select 2 values corresponding to the extrema (minimum and maximum), and 4 values corresponding to the values of the extrema with minus/plus delta:
  $n \in 3..15 \Rightarrow v1 = 3, v2 = 15, v3 = 2, v4 = 4, v5 = 14, v6 = 16$
- if the variable takes its value in an ordered set of values, we select the first, the second, before the last and the last data and one data outside the definition set:
  $n \in \{-7, 2, 3, 157, 200\} \Rightarrow v1 = -7, v2 = 2, v3 = 157, v4 = 200, v5 = 300$
- for the data defining an object, we can minimize or maximize some feature of its format, by selecting valid extremum values
- for an input file containing 1 to 255 records, we can select files with: 0, 1, 255 and 256 records
- for an object p typed by a static type C:
  - `null` reference
  - `this` reference (if \typeof(this) <: \type(C))
  - One object such that: p != `null` && p != `this` && \typeof(p) == \type(c)
  - One object such that: p != `null` && p != `this` && \typeof(p) ∈ \type(c)
  - One object such that: p == p' with p' an other compatible object

When functions have several parameters (inputs), the global approach has to be applied for each parameter. The first step consists, for each input, in calculating their domain from equivalent classes. The second is to select representative value(s) of each domain. The third consists to use a composition (by Cartesian product as instance) of all selected input values to generate the test data. This composition can lead to a combinatorial explosion that need to be mastered to make the test data set manageable. The next section gives an overview of techniques to achieve that in the more global context of combinatorial testing.

2.2   Combinatorial Testing

The combination of all possible (or selected) input values can give rise to combinatorial explosion of the configurations. For example, from two inputs defined as integer, we obtain: $2^{32} * 2^{32} = 2^{64} = 18\ 000\ 000\ 000\ 000\ 000\ 000$ possible configurations. Another concrete example concerns the preference parameter to fix a character styles (see Fig. 10). The form is composed by seven check boxes and one pull-down menu with four entries: it thus defines $2^7 * 4 = 512$ data possible combinations.

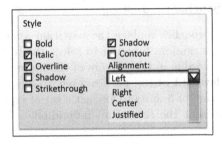

Fig. 10. GUI example for combinatorial testing

To control this combination, a classic approach is the Pair-Wise strategy. It aims to test a fragment of the value combinations such that they guarantee that each combination of two variables is tested. Indeed, practice shows that a majority of bugs can be detected by only covering the combinations of two data. For example, given the four following inputs representing:

- the operating System (OS): Windows, Mac Os, Linux,
- the Network connection: Cable, Wifi, Bluetooth,
- the file format: text, picture, mixed text picture,
- the printer technology: laser, liquid inkjet and Solid ink.

To cover all the possible configurations for the four inputs with a domain of 3 values, we must generate: $3^4 = 81$ test data. The Pair-Wise approach makes it possible to cover all the combinations of two values with only nine test data as shown in Tab. 1.

Table 1. Pair-Wise results

Case	OS	Network	Format	Printer
1	Windows	Bluetooth	laser	Text
2	Mac OS	Cable	Liquid	Text
3	Mac OS	Wifi	laser	Picture
4	Windows	Cable	Solid	Picture
5	Windows	Wifi	Liquid	Mixed
6	Linux	Bluetooth	Liquid	Picture
7	Linux	Cable	laser	Mixed
8	Mac OS	Bluetooth	Solid	Mixed
9	Linux	Wifi	Solid	Text

It is also possible to combine more values using a N-wise approach, in which N defines the number of data value to be associated (N=2 for Pair-wise, N=3 for Triplet-Wise, N=4 for Quadruplet-Wise, etc.). However, it should be noted that the number of test cases can quickly increase. More details (various articles and tools) about this kind of strategies can be found at the following website: http://www.pairwise.org/default.html.

2.3   Random and Stochastic Testing

This kind of testing approaches replace the partition analysis. Basically, their principles are to apply a random function to select the test data. The random function allows to take a value in the domain of the input in a nondeterministic way or using statistic laws [13,14,15]. For example, to select a data representing a distance, a sampling rate of 5 units to extract a set of input data to be tested; to choose data to represent the size of an individual, a law of Gauss can be applied.

The interest of such approaches concerns the simple way of automation to perform the test data selection, even if the expected result can be more difficult to predict. The objectivity of the test data is assumed by the blinding research. However, the blinding research could be a problem because it is difficult to generate real-life use case with arbitrary automated process.

The case studies show that the statistical testing approaches make it possible to quickly achieve 50% of the testing objective, but, as described in Fig. 11, it has a tendency to stagnate at this rate.

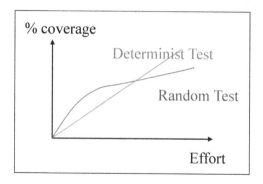

Fig. 11. Random testing achievement

3   Functional and Model-Based Testing

Functional testing aims to validate the system under test from a behavioral point of view, i.e. to ensure it conforms to the required functional requirements of its specification. It requires that the system under test is checked according to predetermined and expected behavior under specific circumstances. As shown in Fig. 3, this kind of test is therefore performed to an upper level since it involves the system as a product ready to be used (black box approach), and not pieces of code as structural testing does (white box approach). However, regarding test generation techniques, both domain are close since the strategies to select test data, introduced in previous Section 2, have been adapted to be applied to functional approaches [11,16]. Next subsection illustrates the application of the test data selection based on equivalent classes (introduced in Section 2.1) in the context of functional testing.

3.1 Example of Data Selection for Functional Testing

This use-case example deals with a secure register form of a web site. The goal of this use-case is to provide the test cases to validate this application. Figure 12 provides a simple version (V_1) of the form.

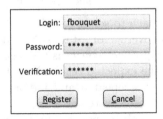

Fig. 12. GUI of the register form (version V_1)

From the interface of the Fig. 12, we can define five test objectives expanded (with data) into twelve test cases:

1. The Login field is kept empty or not. For non empty scenario, we can decide to fill with one character (minimal size), 8 characters (classical size) and 256 characters (huge size). Therefore, 4 different test data can be derived.
2. The Login exists in the system or not (2 test data).
3. The Password field is kept empty or not (2 test data).
4. The Password and Verification (to enter again the password) fields are the same or not (2 test data).
5. The security aspect is assumed by the protocol to be used: HTTP or HTTPS (2 test data).

Possible extensions of the form can also be handled by considering a greater level of robustness regarding password security (as proposed in version V_1 of Fig. 13(a)), and by increasing the protection against robot using captcha technique (as proposed in version V_2 of Fig. 13(b)).

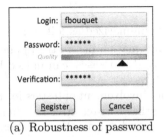
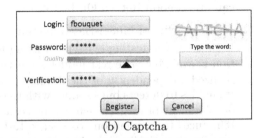

(a) Robustness of password   (b) Captcha

Fig. 13. GUI of the register form (version V_1 and V_2)

To derive test cases from the aggregating version V_2, we can reuse the 12 test data of the previous version, and complete them using two additional test objectives that can be expanded into 5 test data (so 17 test data in all):

- Verification of the quality / robustness of the entered password (3 data - one by level: poor, average, good).
- Verification of the captcha word by succeeding or not the challenge (2 data).

The equivalent class approach to select test data is therefore an efficient way to maximize the functional coverage of a test suite with a minimal set of data. The major weakness of this approach concerns the lack of automation: test data are manually designed and the expected results have to be empirically checked. This lack of automation makes repeated and tedious the activity of test case design and verdict assignment. To overcome this problem, Model-based Testing provides an automated approach by using a formal test model to derive test cases, predict the test results, and compare obtained results with expected ones to assign the verdict [17]. The automation of such test generation process is a strategic issue, since it can replace the (so current) manual development of test cases, which is known as costly and error-prone [18]. The next subsection introduces this functional testing approach.

3.2   Model-Based Testing Overview

Model-based testing (MBT) is an increasingly widely-used technique, relying on (semi) formal models called test models, for automating the generation of tests [19]. There are several reasons for the growing interest in MBT approach:

- The complexity of software applications continues to increase, and the user aversion to software defects is greater than ever, so the testing process has to become more and more effective at detecting bugs.
- The cost and time of testing is already a major proportion of many projects (sometimes exceeding the costs of development), so there is a strong push to investigate methods like MBT that can decrease the overall cost of test by designing tests automatically as well as executing them automatically.
- The MBT approach and the associated tools are now mature enough to be applied in many application areas, and empirical evidence is showing that it can give a good Return On Investment.

The main benefits of Model-Based Testing can be summarized as follows:
- It shortens the testing cycle by starting test automation before the application is available. The test models, and the derived test cases, can indeed be realized independently of the development progress.
- It enables to detects bugs sooner with the earlier involvement of testers in the development process (which can be seen as another cost-effective benefit).
- It reduces test execution costs since test cases can be concretized and executed automatically. Execution of automated tests can also be done overnight.
- It improves the overall quality of the test cases: test case generation is computed in an automated manner and is therefore more predictive and less error-prone than manual processes.

- It increases the scope and the value of regression testing: the test cases, based on the same model, can be generated for various implementations, releases, and versions of a single application, which ensures efficient regression testing.
- It reduces test maintenance effort since the test model becomes the single reference source of the testing process, and it is usually easier to manage this model rather than to directly update the test cases (it is a key item when features change constantly).

In this way, MBT approach renews the whole process of software testing from business requirements to the test repository, with manual or automated test execution by supporting the phases of designing and generating tests, documenting the test repository, producing and maintaining a bidirectional traceability matrix between tests and requirements, automating test verdict assignment and finally accelerating test automation [20]. The global picture of the MBT process is shown in Figure 14. The first step of this approach consists to specify a test model that captures the functional behavior of the system under test. From this model, test cases can be automatically computed using algorithms or designed manually to feed a test repository. The computed test cases are often abstract because they are defined at the same abstraction level than the test model: a dedicated publisher makes it possible to produce, from the abstract test cases, executable test scripts. Afterwards, executable scripts or informal scenarios can be executed on the concrete system to be tested. The test results and verdicts can then be saved to be used as test report. It should be noted that some artifacts of this process have already been introduced in Fig. 7 regarding test universe.

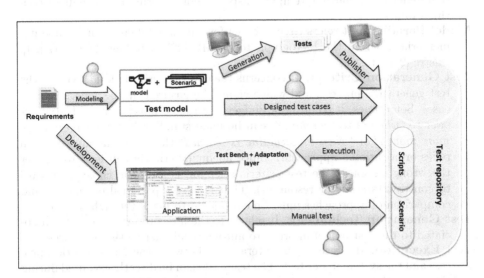

Fig. 14. Model-Based Testing architecture

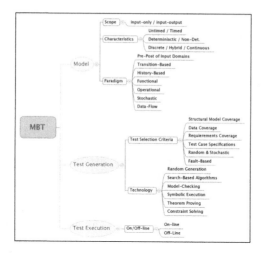

Fig. 15. Model-Based Testing taxonomy

Many approaches and techniques can be used to apply MBT process. In [21], the authors propose a taxonomy based on the modeling, test generation and execution paradigm. Figure 15 summarizes each of the paradigms identified by the authors to provide this taxonomy:

Model Scope. The test model can be based on the requirements associated to the inputs only or both to inputs and outputs.

Model Characteristics. The test model can capture some features of the system under test regarding temporal aspects, non determinism, events or continue values,...

Model Paradigm. It refers to all (semi-) formal model defined since time immemorial ... from the hieroglyph to SysML [22] including Z [23], B [24], Lustre [25], etc.

Test Generation Criteria. It concerns the coverage criteria used to drive the test generation process, and which should be ensured by the generated test cases. Sometimes, it could be a budget coverage criterion: the industry answer to *"when is testing done?"* can be understanding by *"when there is no more money"* or *"when the deadline is reached"* (however, the answer often relies on a rational approach!). Since adequacy criteria can lead to answer the wrong response, the test criteria selection is a crucial choice in regard to constraints (time or resources). That is why a practical evaluation and comparison of approaches must be considered to make the right choice.

Test Generation Technology. It relates to the interpretative semantics associated to the test model in order to automatically derive the test cases.

Test Execution. It concerns the interactions between the test execution process and the system under test. The test cases can be directly executed during the generation process (on-line approach) or not (off-line approach). Using on-line approaches makes it possible to interact with the system under test, and to dynamically use its outputs to adapt the test generation algorithms (to choose the inputs of the next stimuli as instance).

3.3   Example of MBT Approach for Functional Testing

This section illustrates a such MBT approach, based on a UML test model, using a simple example of Web application, namely eCinema. Basically, eCinema is a simple web-application that allows a customer to buy tickets on line before to go to his favorite cinema. The main screen of the application displays the list of available movies and show times. Before selecting tickets, a user should be logged to the system. This requires a registration. A registration is valid when a user gives a name (not already used) and a valid password. A valid new registration implies that the user is automatically logged in. When logged in, the user can buy tickets. If there are available tickets he can see his basket to verify his selection. When checking his selection, the user can delete tickets and then the number of available tickets for the session is automatically updated. The functional requirements of the application are described in Table 2.

Table 2. Requirements of eCinema website example

#	Requirements	Description
1	ACCOUNT_MNGT/LOG	The system must be able to manage the login process and allow only registered user to login.
2	ACCOUNT_MNGT/ REGISTRATION	The system must be able to manage the user's accounts.
3	BASKET_MNGT/ BUY_TICKETS	The system must be able to allow users to buy available tickets.
4	BASKET_MNGT/ DISPLAY_BASKET DISPLAY_BASKET_PRICE	The system must be able to display booked tickets and the total basket's price for a connected user.
5	BASKET_MNGT/ REMOVE_TICKETS	The system must be able to allow deletion of all tickets for a given user.
6	CLOSE_APPLICATION	The system can be shut down.
7	NAVIGATION	It is possible to navigate from one state to another.

The requirements are translated into a UML test model written with a subset of UML/OCL (called UML4MBT [26]). Concretely, a UML4MBT model consists of (i) UML class diagrams to represent the static view of the system (with classes, associations, enumerations, class attributes and operations), (ii) UML Object diagrams to list the concrete objects used to compute test cases and to define the initial state of the SUT, and (iii) state diagrams (annotated with OCL constraints) to specify the dynamic view of the SUT.

Figures 16, 17 and 18 respectively show the UML class diagram, Object diagram and state diagrams with an excerpt of OCL constraints that describe the eCinema example.

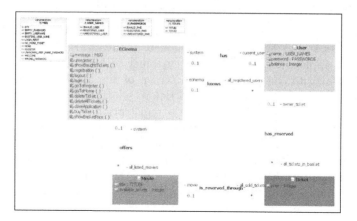

Fig. 16. eCinema class diagram

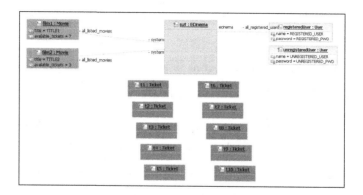

Fig. 17. eCinema object diagram

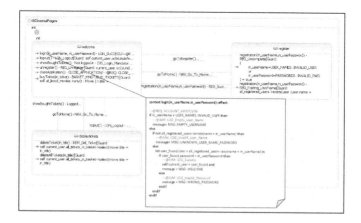

Fig. 18. eCinema state diagram with OCL constraints

These three diagrams enable to simulate the execution of the eCinema application and to automatically generate test cases by applying predefined coverage strategies (such as D/CC) on OCL constraints. The generated test cases and expected outputs are then published into a test repository, namely Testlink[2], as depicted in Fig. 19. During this step, a manually-designed mapping table concretizes the abstract generated test cases into executable scripts by translating the UML data into concrete ones. More details about this MBT testing approach can be found in [27].

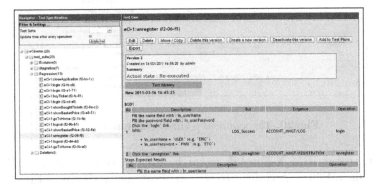

Fig. 19. Management of generated test cases using Testlink

The next section introduces the features of security testing and shows how such MBT processes can be efficiently used for this specific testing domain.

4   MBT Approach within Security Testing

Software security testing aims at validating and verifying that a software system meets its security requirements [28]. It targets two principal testing domain: functional security testing and security vulnerability testing [29]. Functional security testing is used to check the functionality, efficiency and availability of the designed security functionalities and/or security systems (e.g. firewalls, authentication and authorization subsystems, access control). Security vulnerability testing (or penetration testing, often called pentesting) directly addresses the identification and discovery of system vulnerabilities, which are introduced by security design flaws or by software defects, using simulation of attacks and other kinds of penetration attempts.

The security testing techniques can be divided into four families as shown in Fig. 20. The first one is the network security toolkit, with the network scanners to check active ports and (characteristics of) computers on the network. The second one concerns the Static Application Security Testing (SAST), which aims to analyse application regarding known security threats using tools such as

---

[2] http://testlink.org/

HP/Fortify, Veracode, Checkmarx, Parasoft... The third family focuses on monitoring approach, which consists to capture and analyse the behaviors and events on the network using tools like Syslog, Nagios or IBM Tivoli... Finally, the fourth family relates to Dynamic Application Security Testing (DAST) that consists to dynamically check the security requirements. Typically, DAST techniques can be performed using model-based testing approach dedicated to security features.

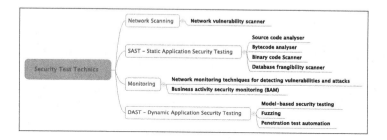

Fig. 20. Taxonomy of security software testing

In fact, recent IBM X-Force© research revealed that, in 2012, 41% of all security vulnerabilities pertained to web applications as shown in Fig. 21. This kind of attacks is more and more complex and can be usually discovered only using a dynamic approach. The rest of this section thus deals with on DAST techniques, with a specific focus on MBT security testing approaches.

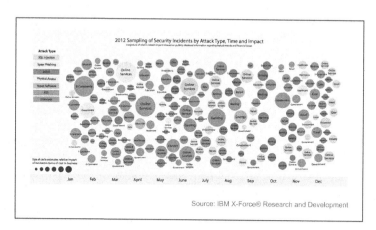

Fig. 21. Attack evolution from IBM X-Force

For further details about Web application security attacks, the Open Web Application Security Project (OWASP) proposes some documentation including a current Top Ten of the current threats [30]. The most prevalent and dangerous cyber-attacks against Web Applications are also reported and available in CWE/SANS 25 [31] and WhiteHat Website Security Statistic Report 2013 [32].

4.1   Model for Security Testing

M. Felderer et al. propose in [33] a classification for Model-Based Security Testing decomposed into five families:

Individual Knowledge. The individual knowledge determines the design of security tests. It is also used to select function and data to be tested.
(Adapted) Risk-Based Testing. These techniques are based on threat models and enable the prioritization of test concept or execution.
Scenario-Based MBT. It concerns techniques to complete test models (of MBT approach) using scenarios dedicated to security aspects.
Risk Enhanced Scenario-Based MBT. This kind of approaches completes the (MBT) test models using risk information in addition to the scenarios.
Adapted MBT. It relates to all other MBT approaches that use a dedicated test model for security.

In many families presented for security testing, the link between risk and testing is very important. As described in Fig. 22, risk assessment activity can drive the MBT approach. In fact, each step of the MBT approach (modeling, criteria to drive test generation and prioritization of the test execution) are driven by the results of risk analysis and assessment. One of the more mature approach addressing Model-Driven Risk Analysis is CORAS [34], which provides a customized language for threat and risk modeling. More precisely, CORAS is a model-driven method for risk analysis featuring a tool-supported modelling language specially designed to model risks that are common for a large number of systems. Such model serves as a basis to perform risk identification and prioritization.

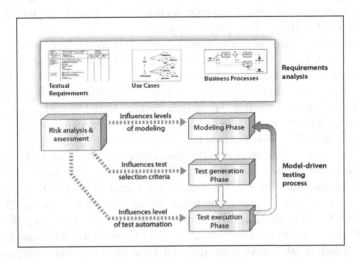

Fig. 22. Link between MBT and risk assessment

4.2   Security Test Objectives

To define security test objectives, two main approaches have been defined during the last decade. The first approach is based on dedicated security test models as proposed in [35,36] with UMLSec, or as previously proposed with SecureUML in [37]. These approaches can have a specific focus on protocols as proposed in [38] using finite state machine, or using networks rules [39], or using protocol mutation as described in [40]. In parallel, some other techniques are emerging to help analysis like Threat or Risk model like CORAS [34].

We can also find specific testing techniques such as Fuzz testing (or Fuzzing) as proposed in [41], which was used by Microsoft company to validate the layer that manages the data and files acquired from network [42]. Fuzz testing, originated from B.Miller at the University of Wisconsin [43], involves providing invalid, unexpected, or random data to the inputs of a system under test. Although its origin is based on a complete randomized approach, more systematic approaches have been recently proposed: model-based fuzzers use their knowledge about the message structure to systematically generate messages containing invalid data among valid data [44]. It can also use a model describing the behavior of an attacker to drive the test generation process [45]. Some tooling are now available to compute fuzzing strategies such as the fuzz test data generator Fuzzino[3], which determines fuzzed test data by applying security test strategies to message arguments from a given correct communication sequence [46,47].

The second main approach is based on properties or schema languages. Many formalisms have already been used to drive the test generation from a property, or by means of a test purpose. By using this kind of formalisms, the test objectives are expressed either as a particular sequencing of the actions (temporal view) or as properties that the data of the system have to verify (spatial view). Such formalism can address a specific security aspect such as access control domain like OrBac [48] or SPL [49] languages.

Temporal logics, such as the Linear Temporal Logic (LTL) [50,51] allow to specify properties on the state of the system under test w.r.t. several successive moments in its life. Tests can then be obtained using a model-checker in the shape of traces from a model that contradicts the required properties (see [52,53] for example). Input/Output Labelled Transition System (IOLTS) and Input/Output Symbolic Transition System (IOSTS) have been also frequently used to specify test purposes [54,55]. These formalisms enable to specify sequencing of actions by using the actions of the model, and possess two trap states named *Accept* and *Refuse*. The *Accept* states are used as end states for the test generation, while the *Refuse* states allow to cut the traces not targeted by the test generation objectives. For example, these formalisms are used in tools such as TGV [54], STG [56], TorX [57] or Agatha [58]. Another approach, described in [59], consists to generate traces using model-checking techniques from a model specified as an IOLTS, in which a fault have been injected by a mutation operator, according to a fault model. The trace is then used as a test objective for the TGV tool.

---

[3] https://github.com/fraunhoferfokus/Fuzzino

Some security testing approaches are indeed based on the definition of scenarios as test objectives. In [60,61], test cases are issued from UML diagrams as a set of trees. The scenarios are extracted by a breadth-first search on the trees. A similar approach is implemented in the tool *Telling TestStories* [62], which defines a test model from elementary test sequences composed of an initial state, a *test story* and test data. An operational language to describe test schemas in a "textual" way is proposed in [63]. Let us also cite Tobias tool [64,65] that provides a combinatorial unfolding of some given test schemas. The schemas are sequences of patterns composed of operation calls and parameter constraints. The schemas are unfolded independently from any model, therefore the obtained test cases have to be instantiated on a model. In [66], a connection between Tobias and the UCASTING tool is studied to produce instantiated test cases. UCASTING [67] aims to concretize sequences of operations that are derived from a UML model, and thus are not, or only partially, instantiated.

It should also be noted that Advanced Open Standards of the Information Society[4] (OASIS) proposes some works to normalize the description as eXtensible Access Control Markup Language (XACML) or the Security Assertion Markup Language (SML).

4.3   Example of Properties Description Language

To facilitate the use of temporal properties by validation engineers, M. Dwyer et al. have identified in [68] a set of design patterns that allow to express a set of temporal requirements frequently met in industrial studies as temporal properties. A web version of the evolution of this works can be found at `http://patterns.projects.cis.ksu.edu/`. As depicted in Figure 23, a property pattern can be defined by the one way using occurrence patterns. This family is composed of (i) Absence: an event never occurs, (ii) Existence: an event occurs at least once, (iii) Bounded Existence has 3 variants: an event occurs k times, at least k times or at most k times, and (iv) Universality: an event/state is permanent. The second way concerns the order patterns: (v) Precedence: an event P is always preceded by an event Q, (vi) Response: an event P is always followed by an event Q, (vii) Chain Precedence: a sequence of events $P_1, \ldots,$ P_n is always preceded by a sequence $Q_1, \ldots, Q_m$ (it is a generalization of the Precedence pattern), (viii) Chain Response: a sequence of events $P_1, \ldots, P_n$ is always followed by a sequence $Q_1, \ldots, Q_m$ (it defines a generalization of the Response pattern).

From this work, an extension is proposed in [69] to add five scopes. Basically, a scope concerns the pattern observation and is composed of events. Events corresponds to all methods specified in the test model. The interest of the method is that the properties are translated into automata and coverage criteria are proposed to drive the test generation to derive test cases that target the related security patterns.

---

[4] `http://www.oasis-open.org`

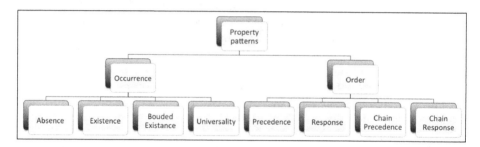

Fig. 23. Pattern expressiveness by M. Dwyer

4.4 Example of Pattern-Driven Security Testing Approach

The purpose of this section is to present an example of Model-Based Testing approach driven by security test pattern [70]. This example aims to validate the detection of SBS-1 malicious signals, formatted according to the ADS-B air-traffic control standard[5], which could be received by the control tower from the aircraft. The ADS-B air-traffic control standard is all about communications between aircraft, and also between aircraft and ground by providing every second a broadcast of the aircraft status (including position, identity, velocity,... calculated using a Global Navigation Satellite System) and make it possible to generate a precise air picture for air traffic management. However, the ADS-B standard is public and all the transmitted information are unencrypted, and decoding them is not difficult (see Figure 24 in which each line defines a separate message that have been sent by a single aircraft).

```
 1  "2013/09/16","10:54:09.250","3951363","3C4B03","BER28N","Germany","0","39850","39950","48.21606","6.31798","0","0","466.3","356.7","21300","5334"
 2  "2013/09/16","10:54:09.296","4494058","4492EA","BEL8LS","Belgium","0","27000","27000","47.21593","6.40017","0","0","374.3","189.7","273","0111"
 3  "2013/09/16","10:54:09.296","172462","02A1AE","LBT5125","Tunisia","0","39000","39000","47.10008","6.34110","64","64","396.4","191.8","274","0112"
 4  "2013/09/16","10:54:09.703","3956993","3C6101","HAY2213","Germany","0","38050","38050","47.86545","6.19537","-64","-64","451.1","389.0","21301","5335"
 5  "2013/09/16","10:54:09.703","172462","02A1AE","LBT5128","Tunisia","0","39000","39000","47.09935","6.34290","64","64","396.4","191.8","274","0112"
 6  "2013/09/16","10:54:09.703","9746549","392AF5","AFR1127","France","0","34400","34400","47.51651","5.61964","-896","-896","407.0","309.5","563","0233"
 7  "2013/09/16","10:54:09.906","4738137","484C59","TRA772","Netherlands","0","38000","38000","48.36003","6.21298","-64","-64","464.3","358.0","4423","1147"
 8  "2013/09/16","10:54:09.906","3951073","3C49E1","CFG011","Germany","0","36000","36000","47.29768","6.40454","-64","-64","453.1","356.0","21328","5350"
 9  "2013/09/16","10:54:09.906","172497","02A1D1","TAR546","Tunisia","0","34380","34580","48.66818","6.18162","-1984","-1984","480.2","388.2","26465","6761"
10  "2013/09/16","10:54:10.187","4921467","4B187B","","Switzerland","0","31000","31000","48.11934","5.62534","64","64","486.7","109.4","0","    "
```

Fig. 24. Excerpt of ADS-B/SBS-1 data stream

In this context, the Model-Based Security Testing generation process aims to produce communication sequences including malicious data. The objective of these generated sequences is to evaluate the vulnerability detection rate of automated air-control system, and the corresponding human attitude during monitoring. It also can be relevant to develop and elaborate new warning protocol, and to improve existing countermeasures, which are today mainly based on data comparison between ADS-B and radar information, and to a latter extent visual inspection. The global process of the approach is depicted in Figure 25.

---

[5] http://adsb.tc.faa.gov/ADS-B.htm

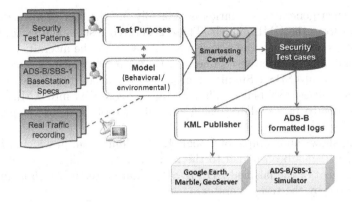

Fig. 25. Security testing process overview

The proposed process is based on the Smartesting Model-Based Testing tool (namely CertifyIt) [27] provided by the company Smartesting[6], which allows to generate test sequences from UML behavioural models and security test purposes, which are described in a language formalizing textual test patterns.

The behavioural model (UML class diagram, object diagram and state diagram with OCL constraints as introduced in the eCinema example in Sect. 3.3) defines the environmental aspects of the domain to be tested in order to generate consistent (from a functional point of view) sequences of ADS-B signals. On the one hand, it includes the communication format of the SBS-1 message of the ADS-B standard (static aspect), and on the other hand, it captures real (or realistic) air-traffic scenarios (dynamic aspect).

A test purpose is here a high-level expression that formalizes a test intention linked to a testing objective to drive the automated test generation on the behavioral model. This is a textual language, which has been originally designed to drive model-based test generation for security components, typically Smart card applications and cryptographic components [71]. This test purpose language has also been extended to be able to formalize typical vulnerability test patterns for Web applications [72]. In the context of this case-study, this test purpose language allows the formalization of attack patterns in terms of states to be reached and SBS-1 messages to be sent. It relies on combining keywords and instructions allowing updating and/or falsifying the real air-traffic scenarios described in the UML behavioural model. The test generation algorithm, computed by the Smartesting CertifyIt tool, enables then to produce mutated real air-traffic scenarios (sequences of transmitted ADS-B signals) by changing and/or adding communication data, which simulate a malicious aircraft broadcast. As example, from a real air-traffic configuration, test patterns and corresponding test purposes can give rise to the production of vulnerability air-traffic scenarios including injection of fake aircrafts into a real configuration, injection of cancelled flights into a real configuration, introduction of (slight) variations in real flights, change of an apparent airliner into fighter(s),...

---

[6] http://www.smartesting.com

Each of such generated scenarios is typically an abstract sequence of high-level actions from the UML models. These generated test sequences contain the sequence of stimuli, i.e. all the SBS-1 messages sent by the aircrafts concerning their position. These generated sequences, that constitute attack scenarios, are next translated into SBS-1 Simulator using ADS-B formatted signals to be executed on a realistic test bench. They are also concretized into KML language scripts in order to be simulated using simulation tools such as Google Earth, Marble or GeoServer.

Figure 26 shows an example of Google Earth simulation, in which a fake aircraft (red path) has been added to the real air-traffic configuration. Figure 27 shows an excerpt of the falsified ADS-B/SBS-1 data stream, which is automatically generated by the test generator.

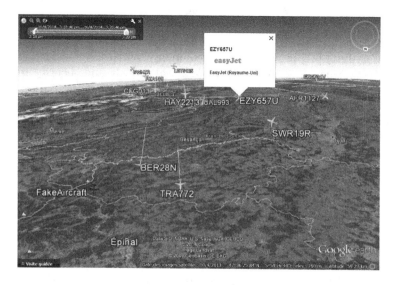

Fig. 26. Simulation of a falsified air-traffic scenario using Google Earth

```
1   "2013/09/16","10:54:09.250","3951363","3C4B03","BER28N","Germany","0","39950","39950","48.21606","6.31798","0"
2   "2013/09/16","10:54:09.250","3951364","3C4B04","FAK123","France","0","34400","34400","47.51651","5.61964","0",
3   "2013/09/16","10:54:09.296","4494058","4492EA","BEL8LS","Belgium","0","27000","27000","47.21593","6.40017","0"
4   "2013/09/16","10:54:09.296","172462","02A1AE","LBT5125","Tunisia","0","39000","39000","47.10008","6.34110","64
5   "2013/09/16","10:54:09.703","3956993","3C6101","HAY2213","Germany","0","38050","38050","47.56545","6.19537","-
```

Fig. 27. Excerpt of a falsified ADS-B/SBS-1 data stream

5   Conclusion

Testing is nowadays a strategic activity at the heart of software quality assurance, no matter the type of software development: all developments undergo some testing, and effort as well as budget are allocated to this task. This paper gave an overview of existing techniques and state-of-the-art about Model-Based Testing and its deployment to address both functional and security testing.

The idea of Model-Based Testing is to use an explicit abstract model of the system under test and/or of its environment to automatically derive test cases: the behavior of the model is interpreted as the intended behavior of the system under test. The algorithms, driving the test generation process and selecting the test data, enable to ensure a given coverage of the model entities, and so of the functional features of the system. It should be noted that these algorithms mainly originate from structural testing strategies: they are no more applied to the code of the system, but to models specifying its expected functional behavior.

Therefore, Model-Based Testing promises higher quality and conformance to the respective functional safety and quality standards at a reduced cost through increased coverage, advanced test generation techniques, increased automation of the process, eased regression testing management, and finally decreased test maintenance effort. The technology of automated model-based test case generation has matured to the point where large-scale deployments of this technology are becoming commonplace, and a wide range of commercial and open-source tools are now available (this list is not exhaustive !):

- CertifyIt (Smartesting)
- Fokus!MBT (Fraunhofer Fokus)
- MaTeLo (All4Tec)
- ModelJUnit (CSZ)
- Conformiq Designer (Conformiq)
- Reactis (Reactive System)
- Scade (Esterel Technologies)
- Spec Explorer (Microsoft)
- STG - TGV (IRISA)
- UPPAAL Cover (UP4ALL)

Even if Model-Based testing approach is an effective and useful technique, which brings significant progress in the current practice of functional software testing, it does not solve all testing problems. This weakness especially occurs when addressing non functional testing such as security testing that aims at validating and verifying that a software system meets its security requirements. Indeed, contrary to behavioral features, test objectives targeting security requirements cannot be easily derived from the structure of the test model, and the expertise of the security engineers is clearly missing. To tackle this weakness, especially regarding security issues, dedicated test model targeting security aspects (including risk assessment results) and specific testing strategies have been created. These strategies are mainly based on fuzzing algorithms and security test patterns languages. These artefacts drive the security test generation process, and therefore replace the coverage criteria traditionally used to address functional purposes. Although model-based approaches for security testing are not yet so advanced and so popular compared to functional Model-Based Testing approaches, this research direction gives rise, from several years, to efficient and emerging approaches and technologies, especially concerning fuzzing techniques.

References

1. IEEE: IEEE Standard for Software and System Test Documentation. IEEE Std 829-2008 (2008)
2. Myers, G., Sandler, C., Badgett, T., Thomas, T.: The Art of Software Testing, 2nd edn. Wiley (2004) ISBN: 978-0-4714-6912-4
3. Dijkstra, E.: Notes on structured programming. Technical Report EWD249, Eindhoven University of Technology (1970)
4. Tretmans, J.: Model Based Testing with Labelled Transition Systems. In: Hierons, R.M., Bowen, J.P., Harman, M. (eds.) Formal Methods and Testing. LNCS, vol. 4949, pp. 1–38. Springer, Heidelberg (2008)
5. Clarke, L.A., Podgurski, A., Richardson, D.J., Zeil, S.J.: A formal evaluation of data flow path selection criteria. IEEE Transactions on Software Engineering 15(11), 1318–1332 (1989)
6. Zhu, H., Hall, P., May, J.: Software Unit Test Coverage and Adequacy. ACM Computing Surveys 29(4), 366–427 (1997)
7. Vilkomir, S., Bowen, J.: Formalization of software testing criteria using the Z notation. In: Proceedings of the 25th International Conference on Computer Software and Applications (COMPSAC 2001), Chicago, USA. IEEE Computer Society Press (October 2001)
8. Offutt, A., Xiong, Y., Liu, S.: Criteria for generating specification-based tests. In: Proceedings of the 5th IEEE International Conference on Engineering of Complex Computer Systems (ICECCS 1999), pp. 119–131. IEEE Computer Society Press, Las Vegas (1999)
9. Chilenski, J., Miller, S.: Applicability of modified condition/decision coverage to software testing. Software Engineering Journal 9(5), 193–200 (1994)
10. RTCA Committee SC-167: Software considerations in airborne systems and equipment certification, 7th draft to Do-178B/ED-12A (July 1992)
11. Beizer, B.: Black-Box Testing: Techniques for Functional Testing of Software and Systems, 2nd edn. John Wiley & Sons, New York (1995)
12. Legeard, B., Kosmatov, N., Peureux, F., Utting, M.: Boundary Coverage Criteria for Test Generation from Formal Models. In: Proceedings of the 15th International Symposium on Software Reliability Engineering (ISSRE 2004), Saint-Malo, France, pp. 139–150. IEEE Computer Society Press (November 2004)
13. Prowell, S.J.: Jumbl: A tool for model-based statistical testing. In: HICSS, p. 337 (2003)
14. Bauer, T., Bohr, F., Landmann, D., Beletski, T., Eschbach, R., Poore, J.: From requirements to statistical testing of embedded systems. In: SEAS 2007: Proceedings of the 4th International Workshop on Software Engineering for Automotive Systems, p. 3. IEEE Computer Society, Washington, DC (2007)
15. le Guen, H., Marie, R.A., Thelin, T.: Reliability estimation for statistical usage testing using markov chains. In: ISSRE, pp. 54–65. Computer Society (2004)
16. Offutt, A., Liu, S., Abdurazik, A., Ammann, P.: Generating test data from state-based specifications. The Journal of Software Testing, Verification and Reliability 13(1), 25–53 (2003)
17. Bernard, E., Legeard, B., Luck, X., Peureux, F.: Generation of test sequences from formal specifications: GSM 11-11 standard case study. Software: Practice and Experience 34(10), 915–948 (2004)
18. Zhu, H., Belli, F.: Advancing test automation technology to meet the challenges of model-based software testing. Journal of Information and Software Technology 51(11), 1485–1486 (2009)

19. Utting, M., Legeard, B.: Practical Model-Based Testing - A tools approach. Elsevier Science (2006) ISBN 0 12 372501 1

20. Dias-Neto, A., Travassos, G.: A Picture from the Model-Based Testing Area: Concepts, Techniques, and Challenges. Advances in Computers 80, 45–120 (2010) ISSN: 0065-2458

21. Utting, M., Pretschner, A., Legeard, B.: A taxonomy of model-based testing approaches. Software Testing, Verification and Reliability 22(5), 297–312 (2012)

22. OMG: Sysml documentation, http://www.omgsysml.org/

23. Spivey, J.M.: The Z notation: a reference manual. Prentice Hall International (UK) Ltd., Hertfordshire (1992)

24. Abrial, J.R.: The B-Book. Cambridge University Press (1996)

25. Halbwachs, N., Caspi, P., Raymond, P., Pilaud, D.: The synchronous data flow programming language lustre. Proceedings of the IEEE 79(9), 1305–1320 (1991)

26. Bouquet, F., Grandpierre, C., Legeard, B., Peureux, F., Vacelet, N., Utting, M.: A subset of precise UML for model-based testing. In: A-MOST 2007, 3rd Int. Workshop on Advances in Model Based Testing, pp. 95–104. ACM Press (2007)

27. Bouquet, F., Grandpierre, C., Legeard, B., Peureux, F.: A test generation solution to automate software testing. In: 3rd Int. Workshop on Automation of Software Test, AST 2008, Leipzig, Germany, pp. 45–48. ACM Press (May 2008)

28. Schieferdecker, I., Großmann, J., Schneider, M.: Model-Based Security Testing. In: Proceedings of the 7th Int. Workshop on Model-Based Testing (MBT 2012), Tallinn, Estonia. EPTCS, vol. 80, pp. 1–12 (March 2012)

29. Tian-yang, G., Yin-sheng, S., You-yuan, F.: Research on Software Security Testing. World Academy of Science, Engineering and Technology 4(9), 572–576 (2010)

30. Wichers, D.: Owasp top 10 (October 2013), https://www.owasp.org/index.php/Category:OWASP_Top_Ten_Project (last visited: May 2014)

31. MITRE: Common weakness enumeration (October 2013), http://cwe.mitre.org/ (last visited: May 2014)

32. Whitehat: Website security statistics report (October 2013), https://www.whitehatsec.com/assets/WPstatsReport_052013.pdf (last visited: May 2014)

33. Felderer, M., Agreiter, B., Zech, P., Breu, R.: A classification for model-based security testing. In: The Third International Conference on Advances in System Testing and Validation Lifecycle, VALID 2011, pp. 109–114 (2011)

34. Lund, M.S., Solhaug, B., Stølen, K.: Model-Driven Risk Analysis: The CORAS Approach, 1st edn. Springer Publishing Company, Incorporated (2010)

35. Jürjens, J.: UMLsec: Extending UML for secure systems development. In: Jézéquel, J.-M., Hussmann, H., Cook, S. (eds.) UML 2002. LNCS, vol. 2460, pp. 412–425. Springer, Heidelberg (2002)

36. Jürjens, J.: Model-based security testing using UMLsec. Electron. Notes Theor. Comput. Sci. 220(1), 93–104 (2008)

37. Lodderstedt, T., Basin, D., Doser, J.: SecureUML: A UML-based modeling language for model-driven security. In: Jézéquel, J.-M., Hussmann, H., Cook, S. (eds.) UML 2002. LNCS, vol. 2460, pp. 426–441. Springer, Heidelberg (2002)

38. Bosik, B.S., Uyar, M.U.: Finite state machine based formal methods in protocol conformance testing: from theory to implementation. Computer Networks and ISDN Systems 22(1), 7–33 (1991); 9th IFIP TC-6 International Symposium on Protocol Specification, Testing and Verification

39. Fernandez, J.-C., Jard, C., Jeron, T., Viho, C.: An experiment in automatic generation of test suites for protocols with verification technology. Science of Computer Programming 29(1), 123–146 (1997)
40. Dadeau, F., Héam, P.C., Kheddam, R.: Mutation-based test generation from security protocols in HLPSL. In: Harman, M., Korel, B. (eds.) 4th Int. Conf. on Software Testing, Verification and Validation, ICST 2011, Berlin, Germany, pp. 240–248. IEEE Computer Society Press (March 2011)
41. Sutton, M., Greene, A., Amini, P.: Fuzzing: brute force vulnerability discovery. Pearson Education (2007)
42. Godefroid, P.: Random testing for security: blackbox vs. whitebox fuzzing. In: Proceedings of the 2nd International Workshop on Random Testing: Co-located with the 22nd IEEE/ACM International Conference on Automated Software Engineering (ASE 2007), pp. 1. ACM (2007)
43. Miller, B.P., Fredriksen, L., So, B.: An Empirical Study of the Reliability of UNIX Utilities. Commun. ACM 33(12), 32–44 (1990)
44. Takanen, A., DeMott, J., Miller, C.: Fuzzing for Software Security Testing and Quality Assurance. Artech House, Inc., Norwood (2008)
45. Duchene, F., Groz, R., Rawat, S., Richier, J.L.: XSS Vulnerability Detection Using Model Inference Assisted Evolutionary Fuzzing. In: Proc. of the 5th Int. Conference on Software Testing, Verification and Validation (ICST 2012), Montreal, Canada, pp. 815–817. IEEE CS (April 2012)
46. Schieferdecker, I.: Model-Based Fuzzing for Security Testing. Keynote talk at the 3rd International Workshop on Security Testing (SECTEST 2012), Montreal, Canada (April 2012)
47. Schneider, M., Großmann, J., Tcholtchev, N., Schieferdecker, I., Pietschker, A.: Behavioral Fuzzing Operators for UML Sequence Diagrams. In: Haugen, Ø., Reed, R., Gotzhein, R. (eds.) SAM 2012. LNCS, vol. 7744, pp. 88–104. Springer, Heidelberg (2013)
48. Abou El Kalam, A., El Baida, R., Balbiani, P., Benferhat, S., et al.: Organization based access control. In: Lutfiyya, H., Moffett, J., Garcia, F. (eds.) Policies for Distributed Systems and Networks (POLICY 2003), Como, January 01-December 31, pp. 120–131. Institute of Electrical and Electronics Engineers (2003)
49. Ribeiro, C., Zuquete, A., Ferreira, P., Guedes, P.: Spl: An access control language for security policies and complex constraints. In: NDSS, vol. 1 (2001)
50. Pnueli, A.: The temporal semantics of concurrent programs. Theoretical Computer Science 13, 45–60 (1981)
51. Tan, L., Sokolsky, O., Lee, I.: Specification-based testing with linear temporal logic. In: IEEE Int. Conf. on Information Reuse and Integration, IRI 2004, pp. 413–498 (November 2004)
52. Gargantini, A., Heitmeyer, C.: Using model checking to generate tests from requirements specifications. SIGSOFT Softw. Eng. Notes 24(6), 146–162 (1999)
53. Ammann, P.E., Black, P.E., Majurski, W.: Using model checking to generate tests from specifications. In: 2nd IEEE Int. Conf. on Formal Engineering Methods, ICFEM 1998, pp. 46–54. IEEE Computer Society Press (December 1998)
54. Jard, C., Jéron, T.: Tgv: theory, principles and algorithms: A tool for the automatic synthesis of conformance test cases for non-deterministic reactive systems. Int. J. Softw. Tools Technol. Transf. 7(4), 297–315 (2005)
55. Frantzen, L., Tretmans, J., Willemse, T.A.C.: Test generation based on symbolic specifications. In: Grabowski, J., Nielsen, B. (eds.) FATES 2004. LNCS, vol. 3395, pp. 1–15. Springer, Heidelberg (2005)

56. Clarke, D., Jéron, T., Rusu, V., Zinovieva, E.: STG: A symbolic test generation tool. In: Katoen, J.-P., Stevens, P. (eds.) TACAS 2002. LNCS, vol. 2280, pp. 151–173. Springer, Heidelberg (2002)

57. Tretmans, G.J., Brinksma, H.: TorX: Automated model-based testing. In: First European Conference on Model-Driven Software Engineering, Nuremberg, Germany, pp. 31–43 (December 2003)

58. Bigot, C., Faivre, A., Gallois, J.-P., Lapitre, A., Lugato, D., Pierron, J.-Y., Rapin, N.: Automatic test generation with AGATHA. In: Garavel, H., Hatcliff, J. (eds.) TACAS 2003. LNCS, vol. 2619, pp. 591–596. Springer, Heidelberg (2003)

59. Aichernig, B.K., Weiglhofer, M., Wotawa, F.: Improving fault-based conformance testing. Electron. Notes Theor. Comput. Sci. 220, 63–77 (2008)

60. Bertolino, A., Marchetti, E., Muccini, H.: Introducing a reasonably complete and coherent approach for model-based testing. Electron. Notes Theor. Comput. Sci. 116, 85–97 (2005)

61. Basanieri, F., Bertolino, A., Marchetti, E.: The Cow_Suite approach to planning and deriving test suites in UML projects. In: Jézéquel, J.-M., Hussmann, H., Cook, S. (eds.) UML 2002. LNCS, vol. 2460, pp. 383–397. Springer, Heidelberg (2002)

62. Felderer, M., Breu, R., Chimiak-Opoka, J., Breu, M., Schupp, F.: Concepts for Model-based Requirements Testing of Service Oriented Systems. In: Proceedings of the IASTED International Conference, vol. 642, p. 018 (2009)

63. Fourneret, E., Ochoa, M., Bouquet, F., Botella, J., Jurjens, J., Yousefi, P.: Model-based security verification and testing for smart-cards. In: 6th International Conference on Availability, Reliability and Security, ARES 2011, pp. 272–279. IEEE (2011)

64. Ledru, Y., du Bousquet, L., Maury, O., Bontron, P.: Filtering TOBIAS combinatorial test suites. In: Wermelinger, M., Margaria-Steffen, T. (eds.) FASE 2004. LNCS, vol. 2984, pp. 281–294. Springer, Heidelberg (2004)

65. Ledru, Y., Dadeau, F., Du Bousquet, L., Ville, S., Rose, E.: Mastering combinatorial explosion with the TOBIAS-2 test generator. In: ASE 2007: Procs of the 22nd IEEE/ACM Int. Conf. on Automated Software Engineering, pp. 535–536 (2007)

66. Maury, O., Ledru, Y., du Bousquet, L.: Intégration de TOBIAS et UCASTING pour la génération des tests. In: 16th Int. Conf. on Software and Systems Engineering and their Applications, ICSSEA 2003, Paris, France (2003)

67. Van Aertryck, L., Jensen, T.: UML-CASTING: Test synthesis from UML models using constraint resolution. In: AFADL 2003 (2003)

68. Dwyer, M.B., Avrunin, G.S., Corbett, J.C.: Patterns in property specifications for finite-state verification. In: 21st International Conference on Software Engineering, ICSE 1999, Los Angeles, California, United States, pp. 411–420 (1999)

69. Castillos, K.C., Dadeau, F., Julliand, J., Kanso, B., Taha, S.: A compositional automata-based semantics for property patterns. In: Johnsen, E.B., Petre, L. (eds.) IFM 2013. LNCS, vol. 7940, pp. 316–330. Springer, Heidelberg (2013)

70. Botella, J., Cao, P., Civeit, C., Gidoin, D., Peureux, F.: Model-Based Test Generation of Aircraft Traffic Attack Scenarios using ADS-B Standard Signals. In: 1-st User Conference on Advanced Automated Testing, UCAAT 2013, Paris, France (October 2013)

71. Botella, J., Bouquet, F., Capuron, J.F., Lebeau, F., Legeard, B., Schadle, F.: Model-Based Testing of Cryptographic Components – Lessons Learned from Experience. In: Proc. of the 6th Int. Conference on Software Testing, Verification and Validation (ICST 2013), Luxembourg, pp. 192–201. IEEE CS (March 2013)

72. Lebeau, F., Legeard, B., Peureux, F., Vernotte, A.: Model-Based Vulnerability Testing for Web Applications. In: Proc. of the 4th Int. Workshop on Security Testing (SECTEST 2013), Luxembourg, pp. 445–452. IEEE CS Press (March 2013)

Model-Based Security Engineering: Managed Co-evolution of Security Knowledge and Software Models*

Jens Bürger[1], Jan Jürjens[3], Thomas Ruhroth[1],
Stefan Gärtner[2], and Kurt Schneider[2]

[1] Technische Universität Dortmund, Germany
`{thomas.ruhroth,jens.buerger}@cs.tu-dortmund.de`
[2] Leibniz Universität Hannover, Germany
`{stefan.gaertner,kurt.schneider}@inf.uni-hannover.de`
[3] Technische Universität Dortmund and Fraunhofer ISST, Germany
`jan.jurjens@cs.tu-dortmund.de`

Abstract. We explain UMLsec and associated techniques to incorporate security aspects in model-based development. Additionally, we show how UMLsec can be used in the context of software evolution. More precisely, we present the SecVolution approach which supports monitoring changes in external security knowledge sources (such as compliance regulations or security databases) in order to react to security related modification and to support the associated co-evolution of the UMLsec models.

1 Introduction

Security modeling allows one to consider security issues at an early stage in the development process [15]. Many security problems are induced by design flaws which leads to problems in the developed software. A software design which is augmented by security information helps the developer to avoid vulnerabilities in the software design.

Although several approaches for model-based secure software engineering exist, few of these include automated tools for formally verifying the models against the security requirements. Here, we focus on one such approach called *UMLsec* [26]. It extends the Unified Modeling Language (UML) and offers automated tools to verify UML models against security requirements [19] (cf. Fig. 1). The *UMLsec tool* as well as its successor *CARiSMA* [11] support the analysis of the security aspects expressed in the security extension UMLsec [26] (cf. Fig. 2). CARiSMA is a reimplementation of the UMLsec tool and build upon the Eclipse Modeling Framework (EMF). It thus supports UML and UMLsec models but is especially extensible to support further modeling languages (e.g. BPMN as

---

* Funded by the DFG project SecVolution (JU 2734/2-1, SCHN 1072/4-1), part of the priority programe SPP 1593 "Design For Future - Managed Software Evolution".

A. Aldini et al. (Eds.): FOSAD VII, LNCS 8604, pp. 34–53, 2014.

domain-specific language). Moreover, CARiSMA ist designed highly modular and offering a flexible plugin-structure. CARiSMA as well as the UMLsec tool mainly focus on the verification of the most important security requirements, which can be directly used in the model, together with their formal definitions.

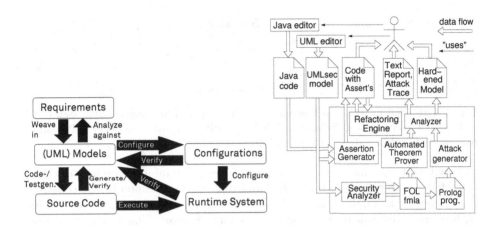

Fig. 1. Model-based Security Engineering   **Fig. 2.** UMLsec Tool Suite

Security Decay in Ageing Information Systems: Information systems are exposed to constantly changing environments which require constant updating. Software "ages" not by wearing out, but by failing to keep up-to-date with its environment [32]. New technology, changing customer requirements, and new knowledge on various software development issues require constant updating. An information system that does not react to changes in its environment will soon be outdated. This is especially true for security and secure development [12]. When an information system handles assets of a company or an organization, any security loophole can be exploited by attackers. Advances in knowledge and technology of attackers are part of the environment of a security-relevant information system. Outdated security precautions can, therefore, permit sudden and substantial losses [3]. Security in long-living information systems, thus, requires an on-going and systematic evolution of knowledge and software for its protection. Thus, techniques, tools and processes are desired to support security requirements and design analysis techniques for evolving information systems in order to ensure "lifelong" compliance to security requirements.

SecVolution. We therefore introduce the SecVolution approach for demonstrating how to cope with (co-)evolution of UMLsec models. The ultimate goal of SecVolution is to preserve the security of an information system by adapting software models through the use of external and internal knowledge sources. As presented in the workflow in Fig. 3, our approach supports reusing security engineering knowledge gained during the development of security-critical software

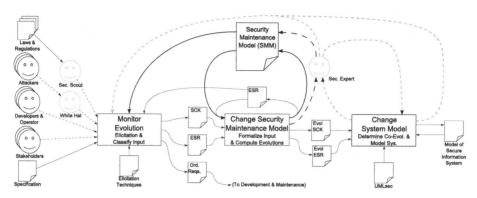

Fig. 3. Extended information flow model of the proposed *SecVolution* approach (ESR = Essential Security Requirements; SCK = Security Context Knowledge). The information flow syntax is described in [43,42].

and feeding it back into the development process. The information flow interface of UMLsec is depicted on the right hand side. UMLsec supports the construction activity. The input of that activity is an improved requirements specification with security-relevant parts being identified and marked. The ultimate outcome is supposed to be a secure system, by making use of a set of security-enhanced UMLsec models.

Since changes in the environment are the reason for updating an information system, a knowledge model, namely the *Security Maintenance Model* (SMM), plays an intermediary role. Incoming information on changes is represented in that model. For this purpose, heuristic tools and techniques are used to support elicitation of relevant changes in the environment. Then, findings are formalized for semi-automatic security updates and stored in the SMM. Therefore, it is essential to stay aware of potential sources for relevant changes and to prepare for eliciting new knowledge. On the back-end, represented changes trigger respective changes in the software models and their security aspects by means of co-evolution. This leads to fast reactions and security updates in order to keep information systems secure and "young at heart".

CoCoME Case Study: To illustrate the usage of UMLsec regarding secure information flow as well as (co-)evolution, we introduce the *Common Component Modeling Example (CoCoME)* as running case study. CoCoME represents a point-of-sale system as it can be found in most supermarkets. The system consists of a number of cash desk PCs connected to a store server in a hierarchical manner. A number of store servers again is connected to a central enterprise server. As the communication paths between these systems are used to transmit business as well as personal data (e.g. when processing EC transactions), communication between the systems has to satisfy given security requirements. Moreover, a lot of additional hardware is plugged into the cash desk PC providing various entry points to the whole trading system. For additional information and models of CoCoME, we refer to [18].

The remainder of this paper is organized as follows: In Sec. 2, we shortly recall some relevant background on the UMLsec approach. In Sec. 3, we explain how to model security knowledge and how to deal with its evolution. In Sec. 4, we explain how, in reaction to changes in the security knowledge, the security models can be co-evolved accordingly to deal with these changes appropriately. After a discussion of further reading in Sec. 5, we end with a conclusion.

2   Model-Based Security Engineering Using UMLsec

In the UML extension UMLsec [26], recurring security requirements (such as secrecy, integrity, authenticity and others) and security assumptions on the system environment can be specified within a UML specification as annotations. This way we can encapsulate knowledge on prudent security engineering and make it available to developers who may not be security experts. The UMLsec extension is given in form of a UML profile using the standard UML extension mechanisms. *Stereotypes* are used together with *tags* to formulate the security requirements and assumptions. *Constraints* give criteria that determine whether the requirements are met by the system design, by referring to a precise semantics of the used fragment of UML. The security-relevant information added using stereotypes includes security assumptions on the physical level of the system, security requirements related to the secure handling and communication of data and security policies that system parts are supposed to obey.

More information about the UMLsec approach and its notation can be found in [26,25]. Some applications are reported in [29,23,28,24,21,20,27].

2.1   Secure Information Flow

Secure Information Flow (SIF) describes techniques to analyze and prevent the flow of confidential information from a trusted ("high") to an untrusted ("low") domain [17,35]. While dealing with SIF, a direct and an indirect flow can be distinguished. Figure 4 shows both of them. In the left part a boolean variable l in an untrusted environment is assigned a value from a high domain (h). Here, the confidential information flows directly to the untrusted domain. The right

```
                if (h)
                    l = false ;
l = h;          else
                    l = true ;
                fi
```

storeAdmin

|

storeManager

|

cashier

Fig. 4. Direct and indirect information flow: h is a variable containing confidential (high) data and l is a variable containing normal data (low) data. For simplicity both variables are booleans.

Fig. 5. Hasse-Digram for the security levels used in the running case study

side shows an indirect information flow. Through the if statement the information in the low domain is influenced in a way that the high value can be simply computed. This easy example shows that secure information flow is not easily analyzed using dataflow in program, furthermore all side-effects from the program logic need to be considered. In the literature, therefore, an approach using observations of an program is often used. A program interacts with its environment and events can be observed. These events are categorized like the data into high and low data, which are used to describe the SIF properties in terms of program observations. One of these approaches, which covers many others, is the *Modular Assembly Kit for Security* (MAKS) [34,33]. It can be used to express secure information flow properties in a modular and uniform way. The fundamental elements are *Basic Security Predicates* (BSP). All BSPs are parameterized with a view $\mathcal{V}$, denoting the elements which are confidential. A MAKS *view* $\mathcal{V} = (V, N, C)$ [34] is a disjoint partition of the event set E into three sets V, N, C.

	visible	invisible
confidential	$\emptyset$	C
not confidential	V	N

The set C collects confidential events which should not be seen. The events of V are visible and hold non confidential data. Events which cannot be observed and are not confidential are collected in the set N. The combination of visible but confidential events makes no sense, because visibility and confidentiality are contradicting.

The system model is given as a prefix closed set Tr of all system traces where a trace is a sequence of events E. The system traces Tr are prefix closed if for all traces all prefixes are in Tr also. For example, if the sequence $\langle abc \rangle$ is in Tr then the traces $\langle ab \rangle$, $\langle a \rangle$ and $\langle \rangle$ need to be in Tr also.

Using a view $\mathcal{V}$ we can define BSPs. One example for such a BSP is *strict removal* (SR):

$$SR_{V,N,C}(Tr) := \forall \tau \in Tr : \tau|_{V \cup N} \in Tr$$

Strict removal describes that all "confidential" events C are independent of the "visible" V and "neither-nor" events N and thus no information about confidential events can be inferred from the others.

BSPs can be combined and parameterized by views. By using BSPs many SIF properties can be expressed, including many traditional notions. For example, non-interference ($NF_{H,L}(Tr) := \forall \tau \in Tr : \tau|_L \in Tr$) can be modeled using SR [34]:

Let L be a set of low events and H be a set of high events with $L \cup H = E$. Then the following equality holds:

$$SR_{H,\emptyset,L}(Tr) = NF_{H,L}(Tr)$$

In many applications the distinction in two security levels (high and low) is too simple. A common used approach using partially ordered sets (poset) can be used to reduce a multi-level problem. For example, a widely known system using this approach is the linear system of the NATO defining the security levels unclassified, classified, secret and top secret. In general, the security level structure is described by a *partially ordered set* $(A, \leq)$ with the set A containing the security levels and an partial order $\leq$ between the levels. If P denotes the set of all permissions, then a security level can be described as a subset of P. The family of security levels together with the operation subset $\subset$ builds a poset. This can be depicted as a Hasse Diagram (cf. Figure 5). Each connection from a higher node x to a lower node y means $x \leq y$. In security analysis, the poset approach can be analyzed in terms of the high/low-approach. For each security level S we define two sets H and L. H contains all permissions of S and all greater sets of the poset. The set L holds all other permissions. This translation is the input for high/low-analysis. If the analysis for all security levels fulfilled the poset holds the SIF property.

In this tutorial, the security levels are modeled as sets of events that are allowed to be seen by users holding this permission. Therefore, the relation between the security levels is modeled as a poset.

2.2   CoCoME Case Study: Modeling Secure Information Flow

In this section, we illustrate the use of UMLsec and the extension to its core to model secure information flow as introduced above. For this purpose, we extend particular models of the CoCoME system.

Figure 6 shows a class diagram that depicts the components and interfaces defined to handle inventory data of a specific store. Some details are omitted in the figure due to the sake of readability. We only show the elements that are relevant for the example. The operations defined as part of the interfaces model the information flow and data handling inside the store.

According to the requirements [18], it seems reasonable to define three roles and arrange their rights as a poset as part of the $\langle\langle DefSecurityLevels\rangle\rangle$ stereotype (cf. Figure 5). The lowest level is set to the *cashier* as he only needs limited access to the system and only uses few operations respectively. In fact, the cashier needs to book sales, query stock items and specific products. The next level is defined by the role *manager*. This role resembles the one of the store's manager. In consequence, the manager needs to access a number of administrative operations such as `queryLowStockItems`. The third role necessary to model the secure information flow of this example is the administrator who maintains the IT of the store. This role, called *storeAdmin*, is the only one to be able to set the store's ID of the shop system (`setStoreId`).

3   Modeling and Evolution of Security Knowledge

Challenges in the evolution of an information system are driven by unforeseeable changes in the environment of a security-relevant information system:

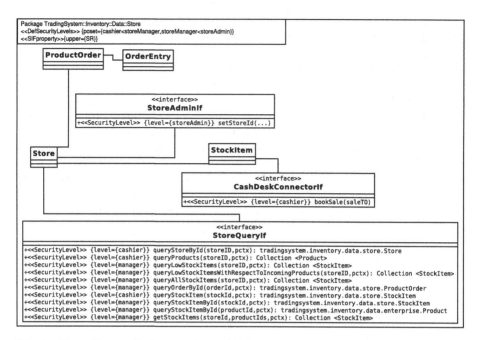

```
Package TradingSystem::Inventory::Data::Store
<<DefSecurityLevels>> {poset={cashier<storeManager,storeManager<storeAdmin}}
<<SIFproperty>>{upper={SR}}
```

Fig. 6. Class diagram reflecting data handling of a single CoCoME store featuring UMLsec SIF

New regulations require compliance; the source of new regulations (e.g. standards organizations, law-makers, interest groups etc.) are usually well-known. Moreover, failures will be detected in the construction of the information system itself. When it comes to new or changing technologies and knowledge, it is difficult to determine the impact on security of the information system. For example, faster computers can make it easier to decode simplistic encodings. New approaches like rainbow tables [37] can compromise password encoding schemes that were considered sufficient before. A rainbow table is a preprocessed table for reversing cryptographic hash functions. This technique, published in 2003, is used for cracking password hashes and has be successfully applied to various systems.

Knowledge management is an essential part of our SecVolution approach to cope with security issues properly. In this section, we therefore focus on organizing security knowledge and its evolution. Whenever security knowledge changes, software engineers need to know how to adapt the regarded information system, so that a certain level of security is retained.

3.1 Modeling Security Context Knowledge

Security knowledge generally contains essential axioms, concepts and their relations including all important hierarchies and constraints. Additionally, *Security Context Knowledge* (SCK) is defined as security-relevant knowledge of the environment of an information system, including but not limited to attacker types and their abilities, encryption protocols and their robustness against different attacks, etc. It is contained in information sources of various kind (e.g. security guidelines and obligations [9] or attack and vulnerability reports [47]). In SecVolution, security context knowledge is part of the *Security Maintenance Model* (SMM) as presented in Figure 3. Since this knowledge is not necessarily limited and cannot guarantee that we will discover complete information about security, the knowledge must be extended at any time.

In recent years, different ontologies and meta-models for security knowledge have been proposed. One can distinguish between asset-centric modeling, which focuses on the values that are threatened, and system-centric modeling, which depicts systems and their vulnerabilities. Since SecVolution should deal with versatile security knowledge on the one hand and an actual information system that is to be maintained on the other hand, we need an integrated view that incorporates security- and system-specific aspects.

In [36], a generic meta-model for IT security obtained from an extensive literature review is presented. It provides common security concepts and properties that are the same across different domains. It has an asset-centric view and distinguishes between the different properties of attacks and countermeasures on a conceptual level (e.g. is an attack taking place in public or in private, using legal or criminal means; or whether it is detected by audits or by prediction). Further relevant meta-models and ontologies are proposed in [7,48,14]. A widely accepted meta-model considering security-relevant system properties is introduced in [45]. Further publications about security knowledge modeling can be found in [16].

In this tutorial, we use a minimal knowledge structure to model SCK, which can be found in each of the abovementioned meta-models and ontologies in one or the other way. It is shown in Figure 7.

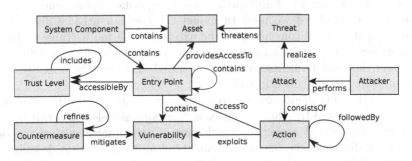

Fig. 7. Minimal core of our knowledge structure [16]

To model an actual system from a security perspective, following concepts are defined. An *asset* is an item of interest worth being protected. This generally includes hardware (e.g. server, switches) and software (e.g. critical applications, services) components. Regarding information systems, assets are also sensitive or confidential information (e.g. passwords, user data, financial data and reports). To provide access to assets, an *entry point* is defined as the interface to interact with the system (e.g. login website, email, input field). Thus, each asset has at

Table 1. Extension of the used knowledge structure to model privacy

Class	Subclasses
Trust Level	Agent (Person Affected, Third Party, Recipient)
Asset	Data (Personal Data)
Action	Anonymization, Data Usage, Data Processing, Pseudonymization, Approval, Notification, Allowed Action, Critical Action
System Component	Data Storage Device (File, Database), Data Processing Unit
Countermeasure	Access Control, Physical Access Control, Encryption, Availability Check

least one entry point. A *trust level* describes which role has access to an asset using a specific entry point (e.g. customer, manager, administrator). *System components* model the regarded information system focusing on assets and entry points.

To model security knowledge from an attacker perspective, the following concepts are defined. A *threat* is the possibility to perform a successful attack on a specific asset (e.g. execute unauthorized code or commands, expose sensitive data). Here, an *attack* is a sequence of malicious *actions* that are performed by an attacker (e.g. cross-site scripting, denial-of-service attack). To perform a successful attack, the attacker uses vulnerable entry points. Here, a *vulnerability* is a system property that violates an explicit or implicit security policy (e.g. improper neutralization of input, missing encryption of sensitive data). Thus, it facilitates unintended access or modification of assets. To mitigate a certain threat, *countermeasures* are used to fix the respective vulnerability (e.g. input validation, encryption of sensitive data).

Note that this knowledge structure is not limited to the concepts depicted here. It can be extended to fulfill further domain-specific requirements and constraints. For example, if we need to model the German privacy directive as declared in [10], several concepts must be extended as listed in Table 1. To use the knowledge structure for an actual system, system components, assets, entry points and their relationships must be identified. This can be done by using threat modeling as explained in [45].

To realize our knowledge base in practice, we decided to use the Web Ontology Language (OWL) [38]. The SCK is therefore modeled in terms of *concepts* and *individuals*. A concept is a collection of individuals, which share some properties. Individuals are the basic elements of an ontology that describe the actual knowledge. One advantage is that we are able to use standard OWL tools such as Protégé [39] to edit knowledge elements. Moreover, reasoning and query languages exists and allow to have unified access to knowledge. To extend the knowledge structure as mentioned, OWL provides a mechanism to import knowledge elements from other ontologies.

3.2   Managing Evolving Security Knowledge

Security knowledge must be up-to-date in order to preserve security sustainably. The problem is to determine which security information remains valid, which information changes, how it changes, and why it changes. Moreover, information systems are complex due to various technologies and frameworks used for implementation.

To cope with security issues in long-living information systems, software engineers need to overview numerous knowledge sources during maintenance. As a consequence, they need methods to support identification and analysis of security loopholes and design flaws in development artifacts based on security-relevant knowledge. In particular, the evaluation whether a vulnerability can be exploited by an attack may alter with each change of the system itself or of the system context represented in the SMM. For example, encryption of a data connection might become vulnerable due to change in configuration or due to the development of more powerful algorithms for cracking passwords. To describe evolution of SCK, knowledge elements can be added, modified and deleted (atomic edit operations). If a change is reported by a knowledge source, the information must be classified in either ordinary requirements, essential security requirements, or security context knowledge.

SecVolution is not intended to detect or even to forecast new security issues or to mitigate known exploits automatically. It is rather meant as a methodology to systematically describe and share security knowledge and to make it usable for non-security experts. For this purpose, we developed heuristic tools and techniques to support security analysis of development artifacts and monitoring of relevant changes in the environment. In [16], a security assessment of natural-language requirements based on heuristics and reported security incidents is proposed.

3.3   CoCoME Case Study: Managing Security Knowledge

In this section, we illustrate the use of our knowledge structure to model security problems. Regarding the CoCoME case study, we consider an extension of the trading system which enables customers to order goods online and to come to the shop to pick their order up (pick-up shop). The pick-up shop makes use of hidden fields to pass values from one page-call to another. This simplifies the server component, since it can be implemented stateless. Stateless in this case means that every HTTP request happens in isolation. Thus, each HTTP request must include all information necessary for the server to process the request successfully. By doing so, the server does not need to store the data and neither to cope with many special cases like session aborts. Statelessness also corresponds to the resource-oriented architecture of the web.

In this example, we assume that an attacker exploited hidden fields to change the price of an order in our pick-up shop. Here, the price is stored in a hidden field to allow calculations, like the total over all items. It is forwarded using a HTTP request to submit the order. On the server side, the integrity of the hidden values is not checked explicitly. Therefore, the prices in the request can be altered and used in the subsequent delivery process.

A similar vulnerability has been reported as CVE-2000-1001 [46] in the Common Vulnerabilities and Exposures (CVE) database [47]. The CVE database provides security information about known vulnerabilities and exposures. The goal is to standardize the identification of publicly known vulnerabilities. The CVE database serves as a reference by software engineers for identifying and mitigating known vulnerabilities.

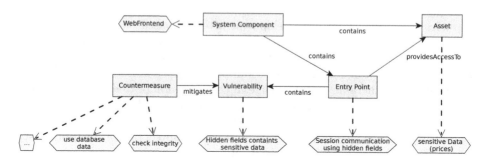

Fig. 8. Elements that are added to the SCK to reflect knowledge about a new attack and countermeasures

The knowledge about the vulnerability, the attack, and its entry points as introduced in the preceding section needs to be added into the SMM. For this, we need to modify the SCK. In this case, we add the notion of sensible data (e.g. the price in the attack), the skills of the attacker and the countermeasures for the attack. Possible countermeasures include using the price of the product in the price database and not using the price in the HTTP request, or the integrity check of the HTTP request that is transmitted. For simplicity, we show only the addition of the countermeasure integrity check of the HTTP request. In Figure 8, we see a fraction of a SCK that is already extended by new countermeasures. The system component affected is the web front-end which exposes an entry point by the definition and use of hidden fields for state communication between the HTTP requests. When these hidden fields contain sensible data (*asset*) this leads to the corresponding vulnerability.

4   Co-evolving Security Models

The ongoing change through modified requirements, corrections of discovered problems etc. is often referenced as software evolution. A change occurs when certain facts that are true in a situation are no longer true in a later situation [44]. Additionally, software evolution describes the process in the maintenance phase which precedes the servicing and decommission phase. Since the evolution should not depend on ad-hoc change, we also need a notion of evolution in the area of software and security knowledge modeling. Here, evolution is often characterized as ongoing change to the model.

In the remainder we show how knowledge evolution affects co-evolution of security models. Moreover, we present an approach to model co-evolution of UMLsec models based on security knowledge stored in the SMM.

4.1   Evolution of Knowledge and Co-evolution of Security Models

If the information system was developed in a model-driven way, the adaptations with respect to changed security knowledge or requirements can even be automatized with co-evolution expressed as model transformations. For this purpose, adaption information describing potential changes and how to deal with such changes if they appear must also be stored in the SMM.

Since knowledge evolution and the corresponding co-evolution of the system model are manifold, we designed the SMM consisting of three parts. Firstly, the *Security Context Knowledge* (SCK) incorporates security-relevant knowledge of the environment of the regarded system. Secondly, the *Catalog of Reactions* (CoRe) bridges the gap between changes in the knowledge (i.e. evolutions of the SCK) and consequent changes that have to be applied to the system model (i.e. co-evolution). Thirdly, the *History of Evolutions* (HoE) is a supportive element that is used to determine changes happened to the SMM so far.

When knowledge sources are identified, information on new knowledge and its potential impact on security must be elicited. This analysis needs to reach a level of detail that allows conceiving countermeasures and updating of models during co-evolution. Therefore, each change in the elicited knowledge needs to be reflected in the models, such that the security knowledge and the models evolve together. Thus, a side by side evolution is referenced to as co-evolution.

Figure 9 shows the interrelationship between knowledge evolution and co-evolution of the system model. First, a security analysis evaluates whether the system model is secure in terms of the knowledge represented in the SMM at design-time. This can be achieved by using our tool-support CARiSMA[11]. Changes in the SCK may trigger respective changes in the system model and their security aspects as described by the CoRe. Evolution of the SCK

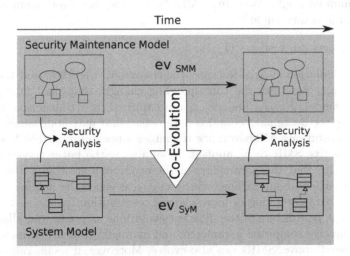

Fig. 9. Interrelationship between security knowledge evolution and co-evolution of the system model built upon this knowledge

contained in the SMM is described in terms of atomic evolution steps. Depending on the parameters of all evolutions that took place, it has to be checked whether security is retained. Unfortunately, the changes to the SMM cannot be fully automatically used to adapt the system model, since these changes require design decisions as well as that they depend on the language of the model. Thus, we use a flexible approach that allows explicit modeling of different adaption options.

4.2   Modeling Security Maintenance Rules

To adapt the system model sufficiently, a sequence of evolution operations on the system model is necessary. The pairing of the evolution of two different artifacts (here SMM and system model) is referred to as co-evolution. These co-evolutions are derived from the sequence of applied edit operations which have been used to change the SCK. This interrelationship is modeled in the SMM using the *Security Maintenance Rules* (SMR). They are a part of the CoRe and build the connecting link between ev_{SMM} and possible corrective actions that have to take place at the system model. Since these rules depend on the security information in the SMM and are themselves part of the SMM, they can also evolve. The SMRs are to trigger reactions upon the security knowledge that has changed. Regarding the kinds of possible reaction types, an appropiate reaction can be the direct manipulation of the *System Model* (SyM). This can for example be achieved by making use of graph transformation techniques. Moreover, displaying instructions to the maintainer is also an important kind of reaction to security knowledge evolution. For example, a newly discovered attack that can be performed if the passwords used in the system underrun a certain length does not require changes at the model level. In fact, the countermeasure is to instruct the maintainer to ensure that all passwords used in the systems exceed a (new) minimum length. We define SMRs to describe the adaption opportunities for the SyM as a quadruple

$$(ev_{\text{SMM}}, ev_{\text{SyM}}, pars, pre). \quad (1)$$

The first evolution ev_{SMM} describes the changes to the SMM and the second evolution ev_{SyM} describes the corresponding changes that shall take place at the system model. Ev_{SMM} and ev_{SyM} are captured in a transformation-based manner. The predicate *pars* contains parameters that may additionally characterize both evolutions. Moreover, *pre* resembles a precondition that has to hold for the respective SMR to be applied. In summary, the latter two elements of an SMR ensure that the parameters of the evolutions are compatible to each other. Information about parameterizing ev_{SMM} is especially helpful because it can support parameterizing of more generic co-evolution functions. Seeing the relation of the parameters of the different evolutions as predicated allows us to deal with directly computed parameters and manually chosen parameters.

As discussed above, SMRs can also evolve. Moreover, it seems reasonable to not have any duplicates and detect variants of the same SMRs. We thus do not let SMRs be created or modified directly but provide editing operations. Using editing operations, we can attach operations that check certain conditions prior to modifying the set of SMRs. For example, adding a new countermeasure can be performed by an operation formally denoted as

$$add.countermeasure.type(countermeasure, vulnerability, pars, pre)$$

where the *countermeasure* is the countermeasure and *vulnerability* the vulnerability to be mitigated. *pars* and *pre* are used to parameterize the countermeasure and define a precondition prior to applying the corrective actions. *type* denotes the reaction's type. For example, *instructions* to the maintainer or requesting a (sequence of) model alterations through graph *transformation* steps are possible values.

It is difficult to describe evolutions for a general system model. Thus, the second part of the rules is described in terms of the regarded model language. Here, we choose UMLsec as introduced in Section 2, because it provides lightweight annotations of security properties and requirements. These annotations are used to ensure the security in the code.

The mapping between the SMM and the system model need not to be one-to-one. For each SMM evolution, we can define an arbitrary number of system model co-evolutions. In this case, the maintainer can choose between different solutions. This allows the modeling of different solutions for one given adaption. For example, the integrity of data communicated can be obtained by different adaptions. One possibility is to use digital signatures over the value. Another possibility is to check the value when it is communicated back to the issuer.

After describing the parts of the SMM including SCK and SMRs, we show an application of our approach by continuing our case study in the next section.

4.3   CoCoME Case Study: Adapting UMLsec Models

In this section, we illustrate the use of security maintenance rules to adapt UMLsec models. For this purpose, we consider the pick-up shop extension as introduced in Section 3.3. We use UMLsec to annotate security related annotations into the models. In detail, the security requirement of data integrity as resembled by the stereotype ⟨⟨integrity⟩⟩ .

At design-time, there is no integrity check of the hidden fields data transmitted between browser and the server component. Later, the analysis of the reported vulnerability leads to new knowledge about the use of hidden fields in a web page and data in our pick-up shop. In this example, this leads to the perception that the integrity of sensitive data needs to be checked and the prices need to be treated as sensitive data. Therefore, respective model elements need to be annotated with appropriate UMLsec stereotypes (e.g. ⟨⟨integrity⟩⟩) to enforce respective security checks as part of the implementation.

The compliance of security requirements annotated using UMLsec can be easily checked using our tools support. In the following, we focus on the integrity of sensitive data in hidden fields as introduced in Section 3.3. Here, we explain how the modified knowledge facilitates changes to the model such that the security of the information system under consideration is preserved.

Modeling Security Maintenance Rules. As explained in Section 3.3, the SCK must be updated to reflect the new knowledge. After that, it is necessary to model SMRs that are used to react upon security issues. On this account, we need to define SMRs for every possible evolution of the SCK. Regarding the reported vulnerability, the countermeasure *integrity check* needs to be described as an evolution of a software model. Because an integrity check can be directly annotated in UMLsec, this rule mainly has to describe the location where to add the tag $\langle\langle$integrity$\rangle\rangle$ and some parameters (what to check and where the integrity should be ensured). There are often several possible modifications, thus more co-evolutions can be added (see [22]). For example, the operation call following the formalization as introduced above to add a SMR for this countermeasure is as follows:

$$add.countermeasure.transformation(\text{"add integrity check"},$$
$$\text{"hidden fields manipulation"}, pars, pre)$$

with

$$pre = \emptyset$$
$$pars = (\text{fields} = \text{getFieldsMarked}(\text{"integrity"})) \tag{2}$$

For simplicity, we assume an auxiliary function to query the model. We use `getFieldsMarked` to get all fields which need to be secured by the SyM evolution. such functions can be realized, for example by using existing tool frameworks (e.g. CARiSMA).

Modifying the Model. After the SCK is updated and SMRs are added (ev_{SMM}), the co-evolution (ev_{SyM}) as introduced in Figure 9 takes place. Here, the SMR chosen to be applied is the one created through (2) and realizes the countermeasure *check integrity*. It thus leads to application of model transformations of the models that for example realize the addition of $\langle\langle$integrity$\rangle\rangle$ stereotype. In

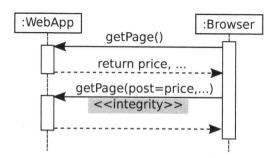

Fig. 10. One of the model changes modeling the use of the new countermeasure *check integrity* in the model. Here, the state-chart communication is annotated requiring that the integrity of the communicated data is checked. For simplicity the parameter tags of the stereotype are omitted.

summary, the resulting model is annotated with new security requirements. For example, the *check integrity* countermeasure leads to the requirement of checking the integrity of some post variables (see Figure 10).

5 Further Reading

Our approach combines methods and concepts from the field of secure software development as well as information security management. In the next subsection we give some further literature to other or connected approaches.

5.1 Model-Based Security Engineering Using UMLsec

Today, several approaches for model-based secure software engineering exist: Ray et al. [41] propose to use aspect-oriented modeling for addressing access control concerns. Functionality that addresses a pervasive access control concern is defined in an aspect. The remaining functionality is specified in a so-called primary model. Composing access control aspects with a primary model then delivers a system model that addresses access control concerns. Basin et al. [5] show how UML can be used to specify access control in an application and how one can then generate access control mechanisms from the specifications. The approach is based on role-based access control and gives additional support for specifying authorization constraints. Brose et al. [8] demonstrate how to deal with access control policies in UML. The specification of access control policies is integrated into UML. A graph-based formal semantics for the UML access control specification permits one to reason about the coherence of the access control specification. The SECTET framework for Model Driven Security as proposed by Alam et al. [1] is applied for example towards a domain-specific approach for health care scenarios, including the modeling of access control policies, a target architecture for their enforcement, and model-to-code transformations. In the above-mentioned work, extensive security expertise is required to implement the proposed methods or to operate relevant tools. Moreover, several approaches are focused on a specific aspect of software systems such as access control.

5.2 Modeling and Evolution of Security Knowledge

A significant amount of work has been carried out on security knowledge management for information system. Belsis and Kokolakis [6] state that successful security knowledge management of information systems largely depends on the involvement of various stakeholders in security analysis, design, and implementation. However, they also found out in their field research that most stakeholders lack relevant security knowledge. To overcome this knowledge gap, Raskin et al. [40] present an ontology-driven security approach. Ontology organizes security knowledge (e.g. attacks and countermeasures, etc.) retrieved from natural language data sources. This approach can be seen as an interface of natural language processing and information security. Eloff and Solms [13] present a

hierarchical framework for information security management. It is an early attempt to clarify security terminology and its interrelationships. The result is
used to build up a hierarchical framework made available to the information
system industry. Tsoumas and Gritzalis [48] suggest a security management approach for information systems which builds upon security knowledge gathered
from various information sources. Security knowledge is organized in an ontology based on an extension of the DMTF Common Information Model. Other
approaches dealing with similar ontologies to manage security knowledge properly are presented in [30,6,4]. In this approach the ontology is set up beforehand,
considering widely-accepted standards and information about the infrastructure
of the information system as well as established policy documents. Kritzinger
and Smith [31] present a conceptual view of an information security retrieval
and awareness model. The purpose of the model is to increase security awareness among employees of an organization. It ensures that technical aspects of
information security do not outweigh human-related issues. Moreover, the presented model considers measuring and monitoring the current level of security
awareness of each stakeholder in an organization. The measurement is mainly
based on an awareness test consisting of multiple choice questions. The approach
aims to link high-level policy statements and deployable security controls to support security expert's work. AlHogail and Berri [2] propose the development of
an architecture sustaining security knowledge within an organization. The architecture aims to manage tailored security processes, policies and solutions. The
goal of this approach is to capture and share security-related knowledge in order
to efficiently react on security incidents and decrease dependencies on security
experts. To capture security incidents as well as actions taken to mitigate the
issue, a pre-defined report template is used. Subsequently, reports are analyzed
manually to establish rules that are stored in an organization-wide knowledge
base.

6   Conclusion

We described how to use UMLsec and the SecVolution approach for the security
maintenance of evolving systems. UMLsec can be used to include different aspects
of security requirements and techniques into model driven development processes
build on UML. We demonstrated this by showing how to model secure information
flow properties in a webshop case study build on CoCoME. We then showed how to
model the evolution of security knowledge. We used an ontology to store security
knowledge related to webstores. Based on this we can use the security knowledge
to co-evolve the UMLsec model when the security knowledge changes.

References

1. Alam, M., Hafner, M., Breu, R.: Model-Driven Security Engineering for Trust
   Management in SECTET. Journal of Software 2(1) (February 2007)
2. AlHogail, A., Berri, J.: Enhancing it security in organizations through knowledge
   management. In: 2012 International Conference on Information Technology and
   e-Services (ICITeS), pp. 1–6. IEEE (2012)

3. Anderson, R.J.: Security engineering - a guide to building dependable distributed systems, 2nd edn. Wiley (2008)
4. Anquetil, N., de Oliveira, K.M., de Sousa, K.D., Batista Dias, M.G.: Software maintenance seen as a knowledge management issue. Information and Software Technology 49(5), 515–529 (2007)
5. Basin, D.A., Doser, J., Lodderstedt, T.: Model driven security: From UML models to access control infrastructures. ACM Trans. Softw. Eng. Methodol. 15(1), 39–91 (2006)
6. Belsis, P., Kokolakis, S., Kiountouzis, E.: Information systems security from a knowledge management perspective. Information Management & Computer Security 13(3), 189–202 (2005)
7. Blanco, C., Lasheras, J., Valencia-Garc, R., Fern, E., Toval, A., Piattini, M.: A Systematic Review and Comparison of Security Ontologies. In: 2008 Third International Conference on Availability, Reliability and Security, vol. 1(1), pp. 813–820 (March 2008)
8. Brose, G., Koch, M., Löhr, K.-P.: Integrating Access Control Design into the Software Development Process. In: Integrated Design and Process Technology, IDPT (2002)
9. Bundesamt für Sicherheit in der Informationstechnik (BSI). IT-Grundschutz-catalogues (2013), https://www.bsi.bund.de/EN/Topics/ITGrundschutz/ ITGrundschutzCatalogues/itgrundschutzcatalogues_node.html
10. Bundesministerium des Inneren. Bundesdatenschutzgesetz. Bundesgesetzblatt, http://www.bfdi.bund.de/DE/GesetzeUndRechtsprechung/BDSG/BDSG_node.html
11. CARiSMA project homepage, http://carisma.umlsec.de/
12. Dhillon, G., Torkzadeh, G.: Value-focused assessment of information system security in organizations. Information Systems Journal 16(3), 293–314 (2006)
13. Eloff, M.M., von Solms, S.H.: Information Security Management: A Hierarchical Framework for Various Approaches. Computers & Security 19(3), 243–256 (2000)
14. Fenz, S., Ekelhart, A.: Formalizing information security knowledge. In: Proceedings of the 4th International Symposium on Information, Computer, and Communications Security (ASIACCS), p. 183. ACM Press, New York (2009)
15. Fernández-Medina, E., Jürjens, J., Trujillo, J., Jajodia, S.: Model-driven development for secure information systems. Information & Software Technology 51(5), 809–814 (2009)
16. Gärtner, S., Ruhroth, T., Bürger, J., Schneider, K., Jürjens, J.: Maintaining Requirements for Long-Living Software Systems by Incorporating Security Knowledge. In: Proc. of the 22nd International Conference on Requirement Engineering (2014)
17. Graham-Cumming, J.: Some laws of non-interference (CSP algebra). In: Computer Security Foundations Workshop, pp. 22–33. IEEE Computer Society Press (1992)
18. Herold, S., et al.: CoCoME - the common component modeling example. In: Rausch, A., Reussner, R., Mirandola, R., Plášil, F. (eds.) The Common Component Modeling Example. LNCS, vol. 5153, pp. 16–53. Springer, Heidelberg (2008)
19. Höhn, S., Jürjens, J.: Rubacon: Automated support for model-based compliance engineering. In: International Conference on Software Engineering (ICSE), pp. 875–878. ACM (2008)
20. Houmb, S.H., Georg, G., Jürjens, J., France, R.B.: An integrated approach to security verification and security solution design trade-off analysis. In: Mouratidis, H. (ed.) Integrating Security and Software Engineering: Advances and Future Vision, pp. 190–219. Idea Group (August 2006), Invited chapter

21. Houmb, S.H., Georg, G., France, R.B., Bieman, J.M., Jürjens, J.: Cost-benefit trade-off analysis using BBN for aspect-oriented risk-driven development. In: 10th International Conference on Engineering of Complex Computer Systems (ICECCS 2005), Shanghai, China, June 16-20, pp. 195–204. IEEE Computer Society (2005)
22. Jayaraman, K., Lewandowski, G.: Enforcing request integrity in web applications. In: Data and Applications Security, vol. 14, pp. 225–240 (2010)
23. Jürjens, J.: Secure information flow for concurrent processes. In: Palamidessi, C. (ed.) CONCUR 2000. LNCS, vol. 1877, pp. 395–409. Springer, Heidelberg (2000)
24. Jürjens, J.: Modelling audit security for smart-card payment schemes with UMLsec. In: Dupuy, M., Paradinas, P. (eds.) Trusted Information: The New Decade Challenge. IFIP, vol. 65, pp. 93–108. Kluwer Academic Publishers (2001), Proceedings of the 16th International Conference on Information Security (SEC 2001)
25. Jürjens, J.: Model-based security engineering with UML. In: Aldini, A., Gorrieri, R., Martinelli, F. (eds.) FOSAD 2004/2005. LNCS, vol. 3655, pp. 42–77. Springer, Heidelberg (2005)
26. Jürjens, J.: Secure Systems Development with UML. Springer (2005)
27. Jürjens, J.: Model-based security testing using UMLsec. Electronic Notes in Theoretical Computer Science 220(1), 93–104 (2008)
28. Jürjens, J., Wimmel, G.: Formally testing fail-safety of electronic purse protocols. In: 16th International Conference on Automated Software Engineering (ASE 2001), pp. 408–411. IEEE Computer Society (2001)
29. Jürjens, J., Wimmel, G.: Security modelling for electronic commerce: The Common Electronic Purse Specifications. In: Schmid, B., Stanoevska-Slabeva, K., Tschammer, V. (eds.) Towards the E-Society: E-Commerce, E-Business, and E-Government. IFIP, vol. 74, pp. 489–506. Kluwer Academic Publishers (2001), First IFIP Conference on E-Commerce, E-Business, and E-Government (I3E 2001)
30. Kesh, S., Ratnasingam, P.: A knowledge architecture for IT security. Communications of the ACM 50(7) (2007)
31. Kritzinger, E., Smith, E.: Information security management: An information security retrieval and awareness model for industry. Computers & Security 27(5-6), 224–231 (2008)
32. Lehman, M.M.: Programs, life cycles, and laws of software evolution. Proceedings of the IEEE 68(9), 1060–1076 (1980)
33. Mantel, H.: Possibilistic definitions of security – an assembly kit. In: Proceedings of the IEEE Computer Security Foundations Workshop, Cambridge, UK, July 3-5, pp. 185–199. IEEE Computer Society (2000)
34. Mantel, H.: A Uniform Framework for the Formal Specification and Verification of Secure Information Flow. PhD thesis, Saarland University, Saarbrücken, Germany (2003)
35. McCullough, D.: Noninterference and the composability of security properties. In: IEEE Symposium on Security and Privacy, pp. 177–186 (April 1988)
36. Miede, A., Nedyalkov, N., Gottron, C., König, A., Repp, N., Steinmetz, R.: A Generic Metamodel for IT Security Attack Modeling for Distributed Systems. In: 2010 International Conference on Availability, Reliability and Security (ARES), pp. 430–437 (2010)
37. Oechslin, P.: Making a faster cryptanalytic time-memory trade-off. In: Boneh, D. (ed.) CRYPTO 2003. LNCS, vol. 2729, pp. 617–630. Springer, Heidelberg (2003)
38. W3C OWL Working Group. *OWL 2 Web Ontology Language: Document Overview.* W3C Recommendation (October 27, 2009), http://www.w3.org/TR/owl2-overview/

39. Protégé project homepage, http://protege.stanford.edu/
40. Raskin, V., Hempelmann, C.F., Triezenberg, K.E., Nirenburg, S.: Ontology in information security: a useful theoretical foundation and methodological tool. In: Proceedings of the 2001 Workshop on New Security Paradigms, pp. 53–59. ACM, New York (2001)
41. Ray, I., France, R.B., Li, N., Georg, G.: An aspect-based approach to modeling access control concerns. Information & Software Technology 46(9), 575–587 (2004)
42. Schneider, K., Knauss, E., Houmb, S., Islam, S., Jürjens, J.: Enhancing Security Requirements Engineering by Organizational Learning. Requirements Engineering Journal (REJ), Special Issue on REFSQ 2012 (2012)
43. Schneider, K., Stapel, K., Knauss, E.: Beyond Documents: Visualizing Informal Communication. In: Proceedings of Third International Workshop on Requirements Engineering Visualization (REV 2008), Barcelona, Spain (November 2008)
44. Sowa, J.F.: Knowledge representation: logical, philosophical, and computational foundations, vol. 3(1). MIT Press (2000)
45. Swiderski, F., Snyder, W.: Threat Modeling. Microsoft Press Corp. (2004)
46. The MITRE Corporation. Vulnerability Summary for CVE-2000-1001 (2001)
47. The MITRE Corporation. Common Vulnerabilities and Exposures (2013)
48. Tsoumas, B., Gritzalis, D.: Towards an Ontology-based Security Management. In: Proceedings of the 20th International Conference on Advanced Information Networking and Applications (AINA), vol. 1, pp. 985–992. IEEE (2006)

Automatic Verification of Security Protocols in the Symbolic Model: The Verifier ProVerif

Bruno Blanchet

INRIA Paris-Rocquencourt, France
`Bruno.Blanchet@inria.fr`

Abstract. After giving general context on the verification of security protocols, we focus on the automatic symbolic protocol verifier ProVerif. This verifier can prove secrecy, authentication, and observational equivalence properties of security protocols, for an unbounded number of sessions of the protocol. It supports a wide range of cryptographic primitives defined by rewrite rules or by equations. The tool takes as input a description of the protocol to verify in a process calculus, an extension of the pi calculus with cryptography. It automatically translates this protocol into an abstract representation of the protocol by Horn clauses, and determines whether the desired security properties hold by resolution on these clauses.

1 Introduction

The verification of security protocols has been a very active research area since the 1990s. The interest of this topic has several motivations. Security protocols are ubiquitous: they are used for e-commerce, wireless networks, credit cards, e-voting, among others. The design of security protocols is notoriously error-prone. This point can be illustrated by attacks found against many published protocols, including the famous attack found by Lowe [59] against the Needham-Schroeder public-key protocol [65] 17 years after its publication. Moreover, security errors cannot be detected by functional testing, since they appear only in the presence of a malicious adversary. These errors can also have serious consequences. Hence, the formal verification or proof of protocols is particularly desirable.

In order to verify protocols, two main models have been considered:

- In the *symbolic model*, often called Dolev-Yao model and due to Needham and Schroeder [65] and Dolev and Yao [46], cryptographic primitives are considered as perfect blackboxes, modeled by function symbols in an algebra of terms, possibly with equations. Messages are terms on these primitives and the adversary can compute only using these primitives.
- In contrast, in the *computational model*, messages are bitstrings, cryptographic primitives are functions from bitstrings to bitstrings, and the adversary is any probabilistic Turing machine. This is the model usually considered by cryptographers.

A. Aldini et al. (Eds.): FOSAD VII, LNCS 8604, pp. 54–87, 2014.

The symbolic model is an abstract model that makes it easier to build automatic verification tools, and many such tools exist: AVISPA [12], FDR [59], ProVerif [23], Scyther [42], Tamarin [70], for instance. The computational model is closer to the real execution of protocols, but the proofs are more difficult to automate; we refer the reader to [27] for some information on the mechanization of proofs in the computational model. Even though it is closer to reality than the symbolic model, we stress that the computational model is still a model. In particular, it does not take into account side channels, such as timing and power consumption, which may give additional information to an adversary and enable new attacks. Moreover, one often studies specifications of protocols. New attacks may appear when the protocol is implemented, either because the specification has not been faithfully implemented, or because the attacks rely on implementation details that do not appear at the specification level.

In this course, we focus on the verification of specifications of protocols in the symbolic model. Basically, to verify protocols in this case, one computes the set of terms (messages) that the adversary knows. If a message does not belong to this set, then this message is secret. The difficulty is that this set is infinite, for two reasons: the adversary can build terms as large as he wants, and the considered protocol can be executed any number of times. Several approaches can be considered to solve this problem:

- One can bound the size of messages and the number of executions of the protocols. In this case, the state space is finite, and one can apply standard model-checking techniques. This is the approach taken by FDR [59] and in the SATMC [13] back-end of AVISPA [12], for instance.
- If we bound only the number of executions of the protocol, the state space is infinite, but under reasonable assumptions, one can show that the problem of security protocol verification is decidable: protocol insecurity is NP-complete [69]. Basically, the non-deterministic Turing machine guesses an attack and polynomially checks that it is actually an attack against the protocol. There exist practical tools that can verify protocols in this case, using for instance constraint solving as in Cl-AtSe [38] or extensions of model checking as in OFMC [19]; both tools are back-ends of AVISPA [12].
- When the number of executions of the protocol is not bounded, the problem is undecidable [47] for a reasonable model of protocols. Hence, there exists no automatic tool that always terminates and solves this problem. However, there are several approaches that can tackle an undecidable problem:
  - One can rely on help from the user. This is done for example using the interactive theorem prover Isabelle [67], Tamarin [70], which just requires the user to give a few lemmas to help the tool, or Cryptyc [50], which relies on typing with type annotations.
  - One can have incomplete tools, which sometimes answer "I don't know" but succeed on many practical examples. For instance, one can use abstractions based on tree-automata to represent the knowledge of the adversary [64,33].
  - One can allow non-termination, as in Maude-NPA [62,48].

ProVerif uses an abstract representation of protocols by Horn clauses, in the line of ideas by Weidenbach [71], which is more precise than tree-automata because it keeps relational information on messages. However, using this approach, termination is not guaranteed in general.

In this chapter, we will focus on the tool ProVerif. We refer the reader to [28] for a more complete survey of security protocol verification.

2   Structure and Main Features of ProVerif

The structure of ProVerif is represented in Fig. 1. ProVerif takes as input a model of the protocol in an extension of the pi calculus with cryptography, similar to the applied pi calculus [5] and detailed in the next section. It supports a wide variety of cryptographic primitives, modeled by rewrite rules or by equations. ProVerif also takes as input the security properties that we want to prove. It can verify various security properties, including secrecy, authentication (correspondences), and some observational equivalence properties. It automatically translates this information into an internal representation by Horn clauses: the protocol is translated into a set of Horn clauses, the security properties to prove are translated into derivability queries on these clauses. ProVerif uses an algorithm based on resolution with free selection to determine whether a fact is derivable from the clauses. If the fact is *not* derivable, then the desired security property is proved. If the fact is derivable, then there may be an attack against the considered property: the derivation may correspond to an attack, but it may also correspond to a "false attack", because the Horn clause representation makes some abstractions. These abstractions are key to the verification of an unbounded number of sessions of protocols.

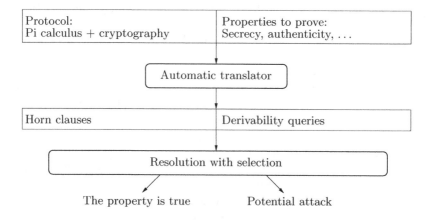

Fig. 1. Structure of ProVerif

$$M, N ::= \qquad\qquad\qquad \text{terms}$$

x, y, z	variable
a, b, c, k, s	name
$f(M_1, \ldots, M_n)$	constructor application

$$P, Q ::= \qquad\qquad\qquad \text{processes}$$

$\overline{M}\langle N \rangle.P$	output
$M(x).P$	input
$\mathbf{0}$	nil
$P \mid Q$	parallel composition
$!P$	replication
$(\nu a)P$	restriction
let $x = g(M_1, \ldots, M_n)$ in P else Q	destructor application
let $x = M$ in P	local definition
if $M = N$ then P else Q	conditional

Fig. 2. Syntax of the process calculus

Section 3 presents the model of protocols. Section 4 presents the Horn clause representation of protocols and the resolution algorithm. Section 5 gives the translation from the pi calculus model to Horn clauses for secrecy properties. Finally, Sect. 6 summarizes some applications of ProVerif and Sect. 7 concludes.

3 A Formal Model of Security Protocols

This section details the model of protocols used by ProVerif. This calculus was presented in [2]; we adapt that presentation.

3.1 Syntax and Informal Semantics

Figure 2 gives the syntax of terms (data) and processes (programs) of ProVerif's input language. The identifiers a, b, c, k, and similar ones range over names, and x, y, and z range over variables. Names represent atomic data, such as keys and nonces (random numbers). The syntax also assumes a set of symbols for constructors and destructors; we often use f for a constructor and g for a destructor.

Constructors are used to build terms. Therefore, the terms are variables, names, and constructor applications of the form $f(M_1, \ldots, M_n)$; the terms are untyped. On the other hand, destructors do not appear in terms, but only manipulate terms in processes. They are partial functions on terms that processes can apply. The process let $x = g(M_1, \ldots, M_n)$ in P else Q tries to evaluate $g(M_1, \ldots, M_n)$; if this succeeds, then x is bound to the result and P is executed, else Q is executed. More precisely, the semantics of a destructor g of arity n is given by a set $\text{def}(g)$ of rewrite rules of the form $g(M_1, \ldots, M_n) \to M$ where $M_1, \ldots, M_n, M$ are terms without names, and the variables of M also occur in

$M_1, \ldots, M_n$. We extend these rules by $g(M_1', \ldots, M_n') \to M'$ if and only if there exist a substitution σ and a rewrite rule $g(M_1, \ldots, M_n) \to M$ in $\text{def}(g)$ such that $M_i' = \sigma M_i$ for all $i \in \{1, \ldots, n\}$, and $M' = \sigma M$. We assume that the set $\text{def}(g)$ is finite. (It usually contains one or two rules in examples.)

Using these constructors and destructors, we can represent data structures, such as tuples, and cryptographic operations, for instance as follows:

- $\text{ntuple}(M_1, \ldots, M_n)$ is the tuple of the terms $M_1, \ldots, M_n$, where ntuple is a constructor. (We sometimes abbreviate $\text{ntuple}(M_1, \ldots, M_n)$ to $(M_1, \ldots, M_n)$.) The n projections are destructors ith_n for $i \in \{1, \ldots, n\}$, defined by

$$\text{ith}_n(\text{ntuple}(x_1, \ldots, x_n)) \to x_i$$

- $\text{senc}(M, N)$ is the symmetric (shared-key) encryption of the message M under the key N, where senc is a constructor. The corresponding destructor sdec is defined by

$$\text{sdec}(\text{senc}(x, y), y) \to x$$

Thus, $\text{sdec}(M', N)$ returns the decryption of M' if M' is a message encrypted under N.
- In order to represent asymmetric (public-key) encryption, we may use two constructors pk and aenc: $\text{pk}(M)$ builds a public key from a secret key M and $\text{aenc}(M, N)$ encrypts M under the public key N. The corresponding destructor adec is defined by

$$\text{adec}(\text{aenc}(x, \text{pk}(y)), y) \to x$$

It decrypts the ciphertext $\text{aenc}(x, \text{pk}(y))$ using the secret key y corresponding to the public $\text{pk}(y)$ used to encrypt this ciphertext.
- As for digital signatures, we may use a constructor sign, and write $\text{sign}(M, N)$ for M signed with the signature key N, and the two destructors check and getmess with the rewrite rules:

$$\text{check}(\text{sign}(x, y), \text{pk}(y)) \to x$$
$$\text{getmess}(\text{sign}(x, y)) \to x$$

The destructor check verifies that the signature $\text{sign}(x, y)$ is a correct signature under the secret key y, using the public key $\text{pk}(y)$. When the signature is correct, it returns the signed message. The destructor getmess always returns the signed message. (This encoding of signatures assumes that the signature contains the signed message in the clear.)
- We may represent a one-way hash function by the constructor h. There is no corresponding destructor; so we model that the term M cannot be retrieved from its hash $h(M)$.

Thus, the process calculus supports many of the operations common in security protocols. It has limitations, though: for example, modular exponentiation or XOR cannot be directly represented by a constructor or by a destructor. We explain how we can treat some of these primitives in Sect. 5.4.

The other constructs in the syntax of Fig. 2 are standard; most of them come from the pi calculus.

- The input process $M(x).P$ inputs a message on channel M, and executes P with x bound to the input message. The output process $\overline{M}\langle N\rangle.P$ outputs the message N on the channel M and then executes P. Here, we use an arbitrary term M to represent a channel: M can be a name, a variable, or a constructor application. The calculus is monadic (in that the messages are terms rather than tuples of terms), but a polyadic calculus can be simulated since tuples are terms. It is also synchronous (in that a process P is executed after the output of a message). As usual, we may omit P when it is 0.
- The nil process 0 does nothing.
- The process $P \mid Q$ is the parallel composition of P and Q.
- The replication $!P$ represents an unbounded number of copies of P in parallel. It makes it possible to represent an unbounded number of executions of the protocol.
- The restriction $(\nu a)P$ creates a new name a, and then executes P. It can model the creation of a fresh key or nonce.
- The local definition let $x = M$ in P executes P with x bound to the term M.
- The conditional if $M = N$ then P else Q executes P if M and N reduce to the same term at runtime; otherwise, it executes Q. As usual, we may omit an else branch when it consists of 0.

The name a is bound in the process $(\nu a)P$. The variable x is bound in P in the processes $M(x).P$, let $x = g(M_1, \ldots, M_n)$ in P else Q, and let $x = M$ in P. We write $fn(P)$ and $fv(P)$ for the sets of names and variables free in P, respectively. A process is closed if it has no free variables; it may have free names. We write $\{M_1/x_1, \ldots, M_n/x_n\}$ for the substitution that replaces $x_1, \ldots, x_n$ with $M_1, \ldots, M_n$, respectively. When D is some expression, we write $D\{M_1/x_1, \ldots, M_n/x_n\}$ for the result of applying this substitution to D, but we write σD when the substitution is simply denoted σ. Except when stated otherwise, substitutions always map variables (not names) to expressions.

ProVerif's calculus resembles the applied pi calculus [5]. Both calculi are extensions of the pi calculus with (fairly arbitrary) functions on terms. However, there are also important differences between these calculi. The first one is that ProVerif uses destructors instead of the equational theories of the applied pi calculus. (Section 5.4 contains further material on equational theories.) The second difference is that ProVerif has a built-in error-handling construct (the else branch of the destructor application), whereas in the applied pi calculus the error-handling must be done "by hand".

3.2 Example

We use as a running example a simplified version of the Denning-Sacco key distribution protocol [44], omitting certificates and timestamps:

$$\text{Message 1. } A \to B : \{\{k\}_{sk_A}\}_{pk_B}$$
$$\text{Message 2. } B \to A : \{s\}_k$$

This protocol involves two principals A and B. The key sk_A is the secret key of A, pk_A its public key. Similarly, sk_B and pk_B are the secret and public keys of B, respectively. The key k is a fresh session key created by A. A sends this key signed with its private key sk_A and encrypted under the public key of B, pk_B. When B receives this message, B decrypts it and assumes, seeing the signature, that the key k has been generated by A. Then B sends a secret s encrypted under k. Only A should be able to decrypt the message and get the secret s. (The second message is not really part of the protocol, we use it to check if the key k can really be used to exchange secrets between A and B. In fact, there is an attack against this protocol [7], so s will not remain secret.)

This protocol can be encoded by the following process:

$$P_0 = (\nu sk_A)(\nu sk_B)\text{let } pk_A = \text{pk}(sk_A) \text{ in let } pk_B = \text{pk}(sk_B) \text{ in } \overline{c}\langle pk_A \rangle.\overline{c}\langle pk_B \rangle.$$
$$(P_A(pk_A, sk_A) \mid P_B(pk_B, sk_B, pk_A))$$
$$P_A(pk_A, sk_A) = \ !\ c(x\_pk_B).(\nu k)\overline{c}\langle \text{aenc}(\text{sign}(k, sk_A), x\_pk_B)\rangle.$$
$$c(x).\text{let } z = \text{sdec}(x, k) \text{ in } 0$$
$$P_B(pk_B, sk_B, pk_A) = \ !\ c(y).\text{let } y' = \text{adec}(y, sk_B) \text{ in}$$
$$\text{let } x\_k = \text{check}(y', pk_A) \text{ in } \overline{c}\langle \text{senc}(s, x\_k)\rangle$$

Such a process can be given as input to ProVerif, in an ASCII syntax. This process first creates the secret keys sk_A and sk_B, computes the corresponding public keys pk_A and pk_B, and sends these keys on the public channel c, so that the adversary has these public keys. Then, it runs the processes P_A and P_B in parallel. These processes correspond respectively to the roles of A and B in the protocol. They both start with a replication, which makes it possible to model an unbounded number of sessions of the protocol.

The process P_A first receives on the public channel c the key x_pk_B, which is the public key of A's interlocutor in the protocol. This message is not strictly speaking part of the protocol; it makes it possible for the adversary to choose with whom A is going to execute a session. In a standard session of the protocol, this key is pk_B, but the adversary can also choose another key, for instance one of his own keys. Then, P_A executes the role of A: it creates a fresh key k, signs it with its secret key sk_A, then encrypts this message under x_pk_B, and sends the obtained message on channel c. P_A then expects the second message of the protocol on channel c, stores it in x and decrypts it. If decryption succeeds, the result (normally the secret s) is stored in z.

The process P_B receives the first message of the protocol on channel c, stores it in y, decrypts it with sk_B, and verifies the signature with pk_A. (The signature is verified with the key pk_A of A and not with an arbitrary key chosen by the adversary since B sends the second message $\{s\}_k$ only if its interlocutor is the honest participant A.) If these verifications succeed, B believes that x_k is a key shared between A and B, and it sends the secret s encrypted under x_k. If the protocol is correct, s should remain secret.

In the above model, we have assumed for simplicity that A and B each play only one role of the protocol. One could easily write a more general model in which they play both roles, or one could even provide the adversary with an interface that allows it to dynamically create new protocol participants.

3.3   Formal Semantics

The formal semantics of this calculus can be defined in two ways. We can use a structural congruence and a reduction relation (Fig. 3), which is the most common approach, as in [5]. The main semantic rule is (Red I/O), which performs a communication: the message M is sent on channel N by $\overline{N}\langle M \rangle.Q$ and received by $N(x).P$. After the communication, the process Q remains in parallel with P, in which x is replaced with the received message M. In our calculus, one can communicate on channels that are any term.

However, the process is not always exactly of the form required to perform the communication. Therefore, we use the structural congruence relation $\equiv$ to prepare the process in order to perform reductions. The structural congruence says that the parallel composition is associative, commutative, has $\mathbf{0}$ as neutral element. It allows swapping restrictions and modifying the scope of the restriction. As the name says, structural congruence is a congruence, that is, it is an equivalence relation (reflexive, symmetric, and transitive) and it can be applied under parallel compositions and restrictions. The rule (Red $\equiv$) allows one to apply structural congruence before and after reduction.

The rules (Red Destr 1) and (Red Destr 2) correspond respectively to the success and failure of the destructor application. The rule (Red Let) allows one to evaluate a let binding. The rules (Red Cond 1) and (Red Cond 2) correspond respectively to the success or failure of a conditional. The rule (Red Repl) creates a new copy of a replicated process. Finally, the rules (Red Par) and (Red Res) allow one to apply reductions under parallel compositions and restrictions. We identify processes up to renaming of bound names and variables.

We can also define the semantics by a reduction relation on semantic configurations [26], as in Fig. 4. A semantic configuration is a pair $E, \mathcal{P}$ where the environment E is a finite set of names and $\mathcal{P}$ is a finite multiset of closed processes. The environment E must contain at least all free names of processes in $\mathcal{P}$. The configuration $\{a_1, \ldots, a_n\}, \{P_1, \ldots, P_n\}$ corresponds intuitively to the process $(\nu a_1)\ldots(\nu a_n)(P_1 \mid \ldots \mid P_n)$. The semantics of the calculus is defined by a reduction relation $\rightarrow$ on semantic configurations, shown in Fig. 4. The rule (Red Res) is the only one that uses renaming. This second semantics guides the reduction of the process more precisely, which simplifies the computation of the evaluation of a process as well as the proofs of some results on ProVerif. In this tutorial, we will focus on this second semantics.

3.4   Definition of Secrecy

We assume that the protocol is executed in the presence of an adversary that can listen to all messages, compute, and send all messages it has, following the so-called Dolev-Yao model [46]. Thus, an adversary can be represented by any process that has a set of public names S in its initial knowledge. (Although the

$$P \mid 0 \equiv P$$
$$P \mid Q \equiv Q \mid P$$
$$(P \mid Q) \mid R \equiv P \mid (Q \mid R)$$
$$(\nu a_1)(\nu a_2)P \equiv (\nu a_2)(\nu a_1)P$$
$$(\nu a)(P \mid Q) \equiv P \mid (\nu a)Q \text{ if } a \notin fn(P)$$

$$P \equiv Q \ \Rightarrow \ P \mid R \equiv Q \mid R$$
$$P \equiv Q \ \Rightarrow \ (\nu a)P \equiv (\nu a)Q$$
$$P \equiv P$$
$$Q \equiv P \ \Rightarrow \ P \equiv Q$$
$$P \equiv Q, Q \equiv R \ \Rightarrow \ P \equiv R$$

$$\overline{N}\langle M\rangle.Q \mid N(x).P \ \to \ Q \mid P\{M/x\} \qquad\qquad \text{(Red I/O)}$$

let $x = g(M_1, \ldots, M_n)$ in P else $Q \to P\{M'/x\}$ (Red Destr 1)
  if $g(M_1, \ldots, M_n) \to M'$

let $x = g(M_1, \ldots, M_n)$ in P else $Q \to Q$ (Red Destr 2)
  if there exists no M' such that $g(M_1, \ldots, M_n) \to M'$

let $x = M$ in $P \to P\{M/x\}$ (Red Let)

if $M = M$ then P else $Q \to P$ (Red Cond 1)
if $M = N$ then P else $Q \to Q$ if $M \neq N$ (Red Cond 2)

$!P \ \to \ P \mid !P$ (Red Repl)

$$P \to Q \ \Rightarrow \ P \mid R \to Q \mid R \qquad\qquad\qquad \text{(Red Par)}$$
$$P \to Q \ \Rightarrow \ (\nu a)P \to (\nu a)Q \qquad\qquad\qquad \text{(Red Res)}$$

$$P' \equiv P, P \to Q, Q \equiv Q' \ \Rightarrow \ P' \to Q' \qquad\quad \text{(Red $\equiv$)}$$

Fig. 3. Structural congruence and reduction

initial knowledge of the adversary contains only names in S, one can give any terms to the adversary by sending them on a channel in S.)

Definition 1. *Let S be a finite set of names. The closed process Q is an S-adversary if and only if $fn(Q) \subseteq S$.*

In this chapter, we only consider the property of secrecy. Intuitively, a process P preserves the secrecy of M when M cannot be output on a public channel, in a run of P with any adversary. Formally, we define that a trace outputs M as follows:

Definition 2. *We say that a trace $\mathcal{T} = E_0, \mathcal{P}_0 \to^* E', \mathcal{P}'$ outputs M if and only if $\mathcal{T}$ contains a reduction $E, \mathcal{P} \cup \{\, \overline{c}\langle M\rangle.Q, c(x).P \,\} \to E, \mathcal{P} \cup \{\, Q, P\{M/x\} \,\}$ for some $E, \mathcal{P}, x, P, Q,$ and $c \in S$.*

We can finally define secrecy:

Definition 3. *The closed process P preserves the secrecy of M from S if and only if for any S-adversary Q, for any E_0 containing $fn(P_0) \cup S \cup fn(M)$, for any trace $\mathcal{T} = E_0, \{P_0, Q\} \to^* E', \mathcal{P}'$, the trace $\mathcal{T}$ does not output M.*

This notion of secrecy is similar to that of [1,32,35]: a term M is secret if the adversary cannot get it by listening and sending messages, and performing computations.

$$E, \mathcal{P} \cup \{0\} \to E, \mathcal{P} \qquad \text{(Red Nil)}$$

$$E, \mathcal{P} \cup \{!P\} \to E, \mathcal{P} \cup \{P, !P\} \qquad \text{(Red Repl)}$$

$$E, \mathcal{P} \cup \{P \mid Q\} \to E, \mathcal{P} \cup \{P, Q\} \qquad \text{(Red Par)}$$

$$E, \mathcal{P} \cup \{(\nu a)P\} \to E \cup \{a'\}, \mathcal{P} \cup \{P\{a'/a\}\} \qquad \text{(Red Res)}$$
where $a' \notin E$.

$$E, \mathcal{P} \cup \{\overline{N}\langle M\rangle.Q, N(x).P\} \to E, \mathcal{P} \cup \{Q, P\{M/x\}\} \qquad \text{(Red I/O)}$$

$$E, \mathcal{P} \cup \{\text{let } x = g(M_1, \ldots, M_n) \text{ in } P \text{ else } Q\} \to E, \mathcal{P} \cup \{P\{M'/x\}\} \quad \text{(Red Destr 1)}$$
if $g(M_1, \ldots, M_n) \to M'$

$$E, \mathcal{P} \cup \{\text{let } x = g(M_1, \ldots, M_n) \text{ in } P \text{ else } Q\} \to E, \mathcal{P} \cup \{Q\} \qquad \text{(Red Destr 2)}$$
if there exists no M' such that $g(M_1, \ldots, M_n) \to M'$

$$E, \mathcal{P} \cup \{\text{let } x = M \text{ in } P\} \to E, \mathcal{P} \cup \{P\{M/x\}\} \qquad \text{(Red Let)}$$

$$E, \mathcal{P} \cup \{\text{if } M = M \text{ then } P \text{ else } Q\} \to E, \mathcal{P} \cup \{P\} \qquad \text{(Red Cond 1)}$$

$$E, \mathcal{P} \cup \{\text{if } M = N \text{ then } P \text{ else } Q\} \to E, \mathcal{P} \cup \{Q\} \qquad \text{(Red Cond 2)}$$
if $M \neq N$

Fig. 4. Operational semantics

4 The Horn Clause Representation of Protocols

In this section, we introduce the internal representation of protocols used by ProVerif, based on Horn clauses. We also give and prove a resolution algorithm on these clauses.

4.1 Definition of This Representation

Internally, ProVerif translates the protocol into a representation by a set of Horn clauses; the syntax of these clauses is given in Fig. 5. In this figure, x ranges over variables, a over names, f over function symbols, and *pred* over predicate symbols. The patterns p represent messages that are exchanged between participants of the protocol. (Patterns are terms; we use the word patterns to distinguish them

$p ::=$	patterns
$\quad x$	variable
$\quad a[p_1, \ldots, p_n]$	name
$\quad f(p_1, \ldots, p_n)$	constructor application
$F ::= pred(p_1, \ldots, p_n)$	fact
$R ::= F_1 \wedge \ldots \wedge F_n \Rightarrow F$	Horn clause

Fig. 5. Syntax of ProVerif's internal protocol representation

from terms of the process calculus.) A variable can represent any pattern. Names represent in particular random numbers. In the process calculus, each principal has the ability of creating new names: fresh names are created at each run of the protocol, and names created in different runs of the protocol are always distinct. In the Horn clause representation, the created names are considered as functions $a[p_1, \ldots, p_n]$ of the messages previously received by the principal that creates the name. Thus, names are distinguished only when the preceding messages are different. As noticed by Martín Abadi (personal communication), this approximation is in fact similar to the approximation done in some type systems (such as [1]): the type of the new name depends on the types in the environment. It is enough to handle many protocols, and can be enriched by adding other parameters to the name. The constructor applications $f(M_1, \ldots, M_n)$ build patterns. A fact $F = pred(p_1, \ldots, p_n)$ expresses a property of the messages $p_1, \ldots, p_n$. Several predicates $pred$ can be used but, for a first example, we are going to use a single predicate attacker, such that the fact attacker(p) means "the attacker may have the message p". A clause $R = F_1 \wedge \ldots \wedge F_n \Rightarrow F$ means that, if all facts $F_1, \ldots, F_n$ are true, then F is also true. A clause with no hypothesis $\Rightarrow F$ is written simply F.

We use illustrate the encoding of a protocol on the example of Sect. 3.2:

$$\text{Message 1. } A \to B : \{\{k\}_{sk_A}\}_{pk_B}$$
$$\text{Message 2. } B \to A : \{s\}_k$$

Representation of the Abilities of the Attacker. We first present the encoding of the computation abilities of the attacker. The encoding of the protocol itself will be detailed below.

During its computations, the attacker can apply all constructors and destructors. If f is a constructor of arity n, this leads to the clause:

$$\text{attacker}(x_1) \wedge \ldots \wedge \text{attacker}(x_n) \Rightarrow \text{attacker}(f(x_1, \ldots, x_n)).$$

If g is a destructor, for each rewrite rule $g(M_1, \ldots, M_n) \to M$ in def(g), we have the clause:

$$\text{attacker}(M_1) \wedge \ldots \wedge \text{attacker}(M_n) \Rightarrow \text{attacker}(M).$$

The destructors never appear in the clauses, they are coded by pattern-matching on their parameters (here $M_1, \ldots, M_n$) in the hypothesis of the clause and generating their result in the conclusion. In the particular case of public-key encryption, this yields:

$$\text{attacker}(m) \wedge \text{attacker}(pk) \Rightarrow \text{attacker}(\text{aenc}(m, pk)),$$
$$\text{attacker}(sk) \Rightarrow \text{attacker}(\text{pk}(sk)),$$
$$\text{attacker}(\text{aenc}(m, \text{pk}(sk))) \wedge \text{attacker}(sk) \Rightarrow \text{attacker}(m), \tag{1}$$

where the first two clauses correspond to the constructors aenc and pk, and the last clause corresponds to the destructor pdec. When the attacker has an encrypted message $\mathsf{aenc}(m, pk)$ and the decryption key sk, then it also has the cleartext m. (We assume that the cryptography is perfect, hence the attacker can obtain the cleartext from the encrypted message only if it has the key.)

Clauses for signatures (sign, getmess, check) and for shared-key encryption (senc, sdec) are given in Fig. 6.

The clauses above describe the computation abilities of the attacker. Moreover, the attacker initially has the public keys of the protocol participants. Therefore, we add the clauses $\mathsf{attacker}(\mathsf{pk}(sk_A[]))$ and $\mathsf{attacker}(\mathsf{pk}(sk_B[]))$. We also give a name a to the attacker, that will represent all names it can generate: $\mathsf{attacker}(a[])$. In particular, $a[]$ can represent the secret key of any dishonest participant, his public key being $\mathsf{pk}(a[])$, which the attacker can compute by the clause for constructor pk.

Representation of the Protocol Itself. Now, we describe how the protocol itself is represented. We consider that A and B are willing to talk to any principal, A, B but also malicious principals that are represented by the attacker. Therefore, the first message sent by A can be $\mathsf{aenc}(\mathsf{sign}(k, sk_A[]), \mathsf{pk}(x))$ for any x. We leave to the attacker the task of starting the protocol with the principal it wants, that is, the attacker will send a preliminary message to A, mentioning the public key of the principal with which A should talk. This principal can be B, or another principal represented by the attacker. Hence, if the attacker has some key $\mathsf{pk}(x)$, it can send $\mathsf{pk}(x)$ to A; A replies with his first message, which the attacker can intercept, so the attacker obtains $\mathsf{aenc}(\mathsf{sign}(k, sk_A[]), \mathsf{pk}(x))$. Therefore, we have a clause of the form

$$\mathsf{attacker}(\mathsf{pk}(x)) \Rightarrow \mathsf{attacker}(\mathsf{aenc}(\mathsf{sign}(k, sk_A[]), \mathsf{pk}(x))).$$

Moreover, a new key k is created each time the protocol is run. Hence, if two different keys $\mathsf{pk}(x)$ are received by A, the generated keys k are certainly different: k depends on $\mathsf{pk}(x)$. The clause becomes:

$$\mathsf{attacker}(\mathsf{pk}(x)) \Rightarrow \mathsf{attacker}(\mathsf{aenc}(\mathsf{sign}(k[\mathsf{pk}(x)], sk_A[]), \mathsf{pk}(x))). \tag{2}$$

When B receives a message, he decrypts it with his secret key sk_B, so B expects a message of the form $\mathsf{aenc}(x', \mathsf{pk}(sk_B[]))$. Next, B tests whether A has signed x', that is, B evaluates $\mathsf{check}(x', pk_A)$, and this succeeds only when $x' = \mathsf{sign}(y, sk_A[])$. If so, he assumes that the key y is only known by A, and sends a secret s (a constant that the attacker does not have a priori) encrypted under y. We assume that the attacker relays the message coming from A, and intercepts the message sent by B. Hence the clause:

$$\mathsf{attacker}(\mathsf{aenc}(\mathsf{sign}(y, sk_A[]), \mathsf{pk}(sk_B[]))) \Rightarrow \mathsf{attacker}(\mathsf{senc}(\mathsf{s}, y)).$$

Remark 1. With these clauses, A cannot play the role of B and vice-versa. In order to model a situation in which all principals play both roles, we can replace

Computation abilities of the attacker:

For each constructor f of arity n:

$$\mathsf{attacker}(x_1) \wedge \ldots \wedge \mathsf{attacker}(x_n) \Rightarrow \mathsf{attacker}(f(x_1, \ldots, x_n))$$

For each destructor g, for each rewrite rule $g(M_1, \ldots, M_n) \to M$ in def(g):

$$\mathsf{attacker}(M_1) \wedge \ldots \wedge \mathsf{attacker}(M_n) \Rightarrow \mathsf{attacker}(M)$$

that is

aenc	$\mathsf{attacker}(m) \wedge \mathsf{attacker}(pk) \Rightarrow \mathsf{attacker}(\mathsf{aenc}(m, pk))$
pk	$\mathsf{attacker}(sk) \Rightarrow \mathsf{attacker}(\mathsf{pk}(sk))$
pdec	$\mathsf{attacker}(\mathsf{aenc}(m, \mathsf{pk}(sk))) \wedge \mathsf{attacker}(sk) \Rightarrow \mathsf{attacker}(m)$
sign	$\mathsf{attacker}(m) \wedge \mathsf{attacker}(sk) \Rightarrow \mathsf{attacker}(\mathsf{sign}(m, sk))$
getmess	$\mathsf{attacker}(\mathsf{sign}(m, sk)) \Rightarrow \mathsf{attacker}(m)$
check	$\mathsf{attacker}(\mathsf{sign}(m, sk)) \wedge \mathsf{attacker}(\mathsf{pk}(sk)) \Rightarrow \mathsf{attacker}(m)$
senc	$\mathsf{attacker}(m) \wedge \mathsf{attacker}(k) \Rightarrow \mathsf{attacker}(\mathsf{senc}(m, k))$
sdec	$\mathsf{attacker}(\mathsf{senc}(m, k)) \wedge \mathsf{attacker}(k) \Rightarrow \mathsf{attacker}(m)$
Name generation:	$\mathsf{attacker}(a[\,])$

Initial knowledge: $\mathsf{attacker}(\mathsf{pk}(sk_A[\,])), \quad \mathsf{attacker}(\mathsf{pk}(sk_B[\,]))$

The protocol:

First message:	$\mathsf{attacker}(\mathsf{pk}(x)) \Rightarrow \mathsf{attacker}(\mathsf{aenc}(\mathsf{sign}(k[\mathsf{pk}(x)], sk_A[\,]), \mathsf{pk}(x)))$
Second message:	$\mathsf{attacker}(\mathsf{aenc}(\mathsf{sign}(y, sk_A[\,]), \mathsf{pk}(sk_B[\,]))) \Rightarrow \mathsf{attacker}(\mathsf{senc}(s, y))$

Fig. 6. Summary the Horn clause representation of the protocol of Sect. 3.2

all occurrences of $sk_B[\,]$ with $sk_A[\,]$ in the clauses above. Then A plays both roles, and is the only honest principal. A single honest principal is sufficient for proving secrecy properties by [40].

More generally, a protocol that contains n messages is encoded by n sets of clauses. If a principal X sends the ith message, the ith set of clauses contains clauses that have as hypotheses the patterns of the messages previously received by X in the protocol, and as conclusion the pattern of the ith message. There may be several possible patterns for the previous messages as well as for the sent message, in particular when the principal X uses a function defined by several rewrite rules, such as the function exp of Sect. 5.4. In this case, a clause must be generated for each combination of possible patterns. Moreover, the hypotheses of the clauses describe all messages previously received, not only the last one. This is important since in some protocols the fifth message for instance can contain elements received in the first message. The hypotheses summarize the history of the exchanged messages.

Summary. To sum up, a protocol can be represented by three sets of Horn clauses, as detailed in Fig. 6 for the protocol of Sect. 3.2:

- Clauses representing the computation abilities of the attacker: constructors, destructors, and name generation.
- Facts corresponding to the initial knowledge of the attacker. In general, there are facts giving the public keys of the participants and/or their names to the attacker.

– Clauses representing the messages of the protocol itself. There is one set of clauses for each message in the protocol. In the set corresponding to the ith message, sent by principal X, the clauses are of the form $\mathsf{attacker}(p_{j_1}) \wedge \ldots \wedge \mathsf{attacker}(p_{j_n}) \Rightarrow \mathsf{attacker}(p_i)$ where $p_{j_1}, \ldots, p_{j_n}$ are the patterns of the messages received by X before sending the ith message, and p_i is the pattern of the ith message.

Approximations. The reader can notice that the Horn clause representation of protocols is approximate. Specifically, the number of repetitions of each action is ignored, since Horn clauses can be applied any number of times. So a step of the protocol can be completed several times, as long as the previous steps have been completed at least once between the same principals (even when future steps have already been completed). For instance, consider the following protocol (communicated by Véronique Cortier)

> First step: A sends $\{(N_1, M)\}_k, \{(N_2, M)\}_k$
> Second step: If A receives $\{(x, M)\}_k$, he replies with x
> Third step: If A receives N_1, N_2, he replies with s

where N_1, N_2, and M are nonces. In an exact model, A never sends s, since $\{(N_1, M)\}_k$ or $\{(N_2, M)\}_k$ can be decrypted, but not both. In the Horn clause model, even though the first step is executed once, the second step may be executed twice for the same M (that is, the corresponding clause can be applied twice), so that both $\{(N_1, M)\}_k$ and $\{(N_2, M)\}_k$ can be decrypted, and A may send s. We have a false attack against the secrecy of s.

However, the important point is that the approximations are sound: if an attack exists in a more precise model, such as the applied pi calculus [5] or multiset rewriting [43], then it also exists in the Horn clause representation. This is shown for the applied pi calculus in [2] and for multiset rewriting in [24]. In particular, [24] shows formally that the only approximation with respect to the multiset rewriting model is that the number of repetitions of actions is ignored. Performing approximations enables us to build a much more efficient verifier, which will be able to handle larger and more complex protocols. Another advantage is that the verifier does not have to limit the number of runs of the protocol. The price to pay is that false attacks may be found by the verifier: sequences of clause applications that do not correspond to a protocol run, as illustrated above. False attacks appear in particular for protocols with temporary secrets: when some value first needs to be kept secret and is revealed later in the protocol, the Horn clause model considers that this value can be reused in the beginning of the protocol, thus breaking the protocol. When a false attack is found, we cannot know whether the protocol is secure or not: a real attack may also exist. A more precise analysis is required in this case. Fortunately, the Horn clause representation is precise enough so that false attacks are rare. (This is demonstrated by the experiments, see Sect. 6.)

Secrecy Criterion. A basic goal is to determine secrecy properties: for instance, can the attacker get the secret s? That is, can the fact attacker(s) be derived from the clauses? If attacker(s) can be derived, the sequence of clauses applied to derive attacker(s) will lead to the description of an attack. This is the notion of secrecy of Sect. 3.4.

In our running example, attacker(s) is derivable from the clauses. The derivation is as follows. The attacker generates a fresh name $a[\,]$ (considered as a secret key), it computes $\mathsf{pk}(a[\,])$ by the clause for pk, obtains $\mathsf{aenc}(\mathsf{sign}(k[\mathsf{pk}(a[\,])],$ $sk_A[\,]), \mathsf{pk}(a[\,]))$ by the clause for the first message. It decrypts this message using the clause for pdec and its knowledge of $a[\,]$, thus obtaining $\mathsf{sign}(k[\mathsf{pk}(a[\,])], sk_A[\,])$. It reencrypts the signature under $\mathsf{pk}(sk_B[\,])$ by the clause for aenc (using its initial knowledge of $\mathsf{pk}(sk_B[\,]))$, thus obtaining $\mathsf{aenc}(\mathsf{sign}(k[\mathsf{pk}(a[\,])], sk_A[\,]), \mathsf{pk}(sk_B[\,]))$. By the clause for the second message, it obtains $\mathsf{senc}(s, k[\mathsf{pk}(a[\,])])$. On the other hand, from $\mathsf{sign}(k[\mathsf{pk}(a[\,])], sk_A[\,])$, it obtains $k[\mathsf{pk}(a[\,])]$ by the clause for $\mathsf{getmess}$, so it can decrypt $\mathsf{senc}(s, k[\mathsf{pk}(a[\,])])$ by the clause for sdec, thus obtaining s. In other words, the attacker starts a session between A and a dishonest participant of secret key $a[\,]$. It gets the first message $\mathsf{aenc}(\mathsf{sign}(k, sk_A[\,]), \mathsf{pk}(a[\,]))$, decrypts it, reencrypts it under $\mathsf{pk}(sk_B[\,])$, and sends it to B. For B, this message looks like the first message of a session between A and B, so B replies with $\mathsf{senc}(s, k)$, which the attacker can decrypt since it obtains k from the first message. The obtained derivation corresponds to the known attack against this protocol. In contrast, if we fix the protocol by adding the public key of B in the first message $\{\{(pk_B, k)\}_{sk_A}\}_{pk_B}$, attacker(s) is not derivable from the clauses, so the fixed protocol preserves the secrecy of s.

Next, we formally define when a given fact can be derived from a given set of clauses. We shall see in the next section how we determine that. Technically, the hypotheses $F_1, \ldots, F_n$ of a clause are considered as a multiset. This means that the order of the hypotheses is irrelevant, but the number of times a hypothesis is repeated is important. (This is not related to multiset rewriting models of protocols: the semantics of a clause does not depend on the number of repetitions of its hypotheses, but considering multisets is necessary in the proof of the resolution algorithm.) We use R for clauses (logic programming *rules*), H for hypothesis, and C for conclusion.

Definition 4 (Subsumption). *We say that* $H_1 \Rightarrow C_1$ *subsumes* $H_2 \Rightarrow C_2$, *and we write* $(H_1 \Rightarrow C_1) \sqsupseteq (H_2 \Rightarrow C_2)$, *if and only if there exists a substitution* σ *such that* $\sigma C_1 = C_2$ *and* $\sigma H_1 \subseteq H_2$ *(multiset inclusion).*

We write $R_1 \sqsupseteq R_2$ when R_2 can be obtained by adding hypotheses to a particular instance of R_1. In this case, all facts that can be derived by R_2 can also be derived by R_1.

A derivation is defined as follows, as illustrated in Fig. 7.

Definition 5 (Derivability). *Let* F *be a closed fact, that is, a fact without variable. Let* $\mathcal{R}$ *be a set of clauses.* F *is derivable from* $\mathcal{R}$ *if and only if there exists a derivation of* F *from* $\mathcal{R}$, *that is, a finite tree defined as follows:*

1. *Its nodes (except the root) are labeled by clauses $R \in \mathcal{R}$;*
2. *Its edges are labeled by closed facts;*
3. *If the tree contains a node labeled by R with one incoming edge labeled by F_0 and n outgoing edges labeled by $F_1, \ldots, F_n$, then $R \sqsupseteq F_1 \land \ldots \land F_n \Rightarrow F_0$.*
4. *The root has one outgoing edge, labeled by F. The unique son of the root is named the* subroot.

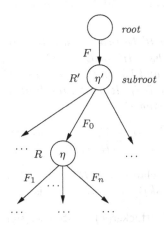

Fig. 7. Derivation of F

In a derivation, if there is a node labeled by R with one incoming edge labeled by F_0 and n outgoing edges labeled by $F_1, \ldots, F_n$, then F_0 can be derived from $F_1, \ldots, F_n$ by the clause R. Therefore, there exists a derivation of F from $\mathcal{R}$ if and only if F can be derived from clauses in $\mathcal{R}$ (in classical logic).

4.2   Resolution Algorithm

The internal protocol representation is a set of Horn clauses, and our goal is to determine whether a given fact can be derived from these clauses or not. This is exactly the problem solved by usual Prolog systems. However, we cannot use such systems here, because they would not terminate. For instance, the clause

$$\mathsf{attacker}(\mathsf{aenc}(m, \mathsf{pk}(sk))) \land \mathsf{attacker}(sk) \Rightarrow \mathsf{attacker}(m)$$

leads to considering more and more complex terms, with an unbounded number of encryptions. We could of course limit arbitrarily the depth of terms to solve the problem, but we can do much better than that.

As detailed below, the main idea is to combine pairs of clauses by resolution, and to guide this resolution process by a selection function: ProVerif's resolution algorithm is resolution with free selection [66,61,14]. This algorithm is similar to ordered resolution with selection, used by [71], but without the ordering constraints.

Notice that, since a term is secret when a fact is *not* derivable from the clauses, soundness in terms of security (if the verifier claims that there is no attack, then there is no attack) corresponds to the completeness of the resolution algorithm in terms of logic programming (if the algorithm claims that a fact is not derivable, then it is not). The resolution algorithm that we use must therefore be complete.

Let us first define resolution: when the conclusion of a clause R unifies with a hypothesis of another (or the same) clause R', resolution infers a new clause that corresponds to applying R and R' one after the other. Formally, resolution is defined as follows:

Definition 6. *Let R and R' be two clauses, $R = H \Rightarrow C$, and $R' = H' \Rightarrow C'$. Assume that there exists $F_0 \in H'$ such that C and F_0 are unifiable and σ is the most general unifier of C and F_0. In this case, we define $R \circ_{F_0} R' = \sigma(H \cup (H' \setminus \{F_0\})) \Rightarrow \sigma C'$. The clause $R \circ_{F_0} R'$ is the result of resolving R' with R upon F_0; it can be inferred from R and R':*

$$\frac{R = H \Rightarrow C \qquad R' = H' \Rightarrow C'}{R \circ_{F_0} R' = \sigma(H \cup (H' \setminus \{F_0\})) \Rightarrow \sigma C'}$$

For example, if R is the clause (2), R' is the clause (1), and the fact F_0 is $F_0 = \mathsf{attacker}(\mathsf{aenc}(m, \mathsf{pk}(sk)))$, then $R \circ_{F_0} R'$ is

$$\mathsf{attacker}(\mathsf{pk}(x)) \wedge \mathsf{attacker}(x) \Rightarrow \mathsf{attacker}(\mathsf{sign}(k[\mathsf{pk}(x)], sk_A[\,]))$$

with the substitution $\sigma = \{sk \mapsto x, m \mapsto \mathsf{sign}(k[\mathsf{pk}(x)], sk_A[\,])\}$.

We guide the resolution by a selection function:

Definition 7. *A* selection function *sel is a function from clauses to sets of facts, such that $sel(H \Rightarrow C) \subseteq H$. If $F \in sel(R)$, we say that F is selected in R. If $sel(R) = \emptyset$, we say that no hypothesis is selected in R, or that the conclusion of R is selected.*

The resolution algorithm is correct (sound and complete) with any selection function, as we show below. However, the choice of the selection function can change dramatically the behavior of the algorithm. The essential idea of the algorithm is to combine clauses by resolution only when the facts unified in the resolution are selected. We will therefore choose the selection function to reduce the number of possible unifications between selected facts. Having several selected facts slows down the algorithm, because it has more choices of resolutions to perform, therefore we will select at most one fact in each clause. In the case of protocols, facts of the form $\mathsf{attacker}(x)$, with x variable, can be unified will all facts of the form $\mathsf{attacker}(p)$. Therefore, we should avoid selecting them. So a basic selection function is a function sel_0 that satisfies the constraint

$$sel_0(H \Rightarrow C) = \begin{cases} \emptyset & \text{if } \forall F \in H, \exists x \text{ variable}, F = \mathsf{attacker}(x) \\ \{F_0\} & \text{where } F_0 \in H \text{ and } \forall x \text{ variable}, F_0 \neq \mathsf{attacker}(x) \end{cases} \tag{3}$$

The resolution algorithm is described in Fig. 8. It transforms the initial set of clauses into a new one that derives the same facts.

saturate($\mathcal{R}_0$) =
  1. $\mathcal{R} \leftarrow \emptyset$.
     For each $R \in \mathcal{R}_0$, $\mathcal{R} \leftarrow$ elim($\{R\} \cup \mathcal{R}$).
  2. Repeat until a fixpoint is reached
       for each $R \in \mathcal{R}$ such that $sel(R) = \emptyset$,
         for each $R' \in \mathcal{R}$, for each $F_0 \in sel(R')$ such that $R \circ_{F_0} R'$ is defined,
           $\mathcal{R} \leftarrow$ elim($\{R \circ_{F_0} R'\} \cup \mathcal{R}$).
  3. Return $\{R \in \mathcal{R} \mid sel(R) = \emptyset\}$.

Fig. 8. Resolution algorithm

The resolution algorithm, saturate($\mathcal{R}_0$), contains 3 steps.

- The first step inserts in $\mathcal{R}$ the initial clauses representing the protocol and the attacker (clauses that are in $\mathcal{R}_0$), after elimination of subsumed clauses by elim: if R' subsumes R, and R and R' are in $\mathcal{R}$, then R is removed by elim($\mathcal{R}$).
- The second step is a fixpoint iteration that adds clauses created by resolution. The resolution of clauses R and R' is added only if no hypothesis is selected in R and the hypothesis F_0 of R' that we unify is selected. When a clause is created by resolution, it is added to the set of clauses $\mathcal{R}$. Subsumed clauses are eliminated from $\mathcal{R}$.
- At last, the third step returns the set of clauses of $\mathcal{R}$ with no selected hypothesis.

Basically, saturate preserves derivability (it is both sound and complete):

Theorem 1 (Correctness of saturate). *Let F be a closed fact. F is derivable from $\mathcal{R}_0$ if and only if it is derivable from* saturate($\mathcal{R}_0$).

This result is proved by transforming a derivation of F from $\mathcal{R}_0$ into a derivation of F from saturate($\mathcal{R}_0$). Basically, when the derivation contains a clause R' with $sel(R') \neq \emptyset$, we replace in this derivation two clauses R, with $sel(R) = \emptyset$, and R' that have been combined by resolution during the execution of saturate with a single clause $R \circ_{F_0} R'$. This replacement decreases the number of clauses in the derivation, so it terminates, and, upon termination, all clauses of the obtained derivation satisfy $sel(R') = \emptyset$ so they are in saturate($\mathcal{R}_0$). A detailed proof is given in Sect. 4.3.

Usually, resolution with selection is used for proofs by refutation. That is, the negation of the goal F is added to the clauses, under the form of a clause without conclusion: $F \Rightarrow$. The goal F is derivable if and only if the empty clause "$\Rightarrow$" can be derived. Here, for non-closed goals, we also want to be able to know which instances of the goal can be derived. That is why we prove that the clauses in saturate($\mathcal{R}_0$) derive the same facts as the clauses in $\mathcal{R}_0$.

We can determine which instances of $pred(p_1, \ldots, p_n)$ are derivable, as follows:

Corollary 1. *Let* $\mathsf{solve}_{\mathcal{R}_0}(pred(p_1, \ldots, p_n)) = \{H \Rightarrow pred'(p_1', \ldots, p_n') \mid H \Rightarrow pred'(p_1', \ldots, p_n') \in \mathsf{saturate}(\mathcal{R}_0')\}$, *where* $pred'$ *is a new predicate and* $\mathcal{R}_0' = \mathcal{R}_0 \cup \{pred(p_1, \ldots, p_n) \Rightarrow pred'(p_1, \ldots, p_n)\}$.

The fact $\sigma pred(p_1, \ldots, p_n)$ *is derivable from* $\mathcal{R}_0$ *if and only if there exists a clause* $H \Rightarrow pred(p_1', \ldots, p_n')$ *in* $\mathsf{solve}_{\mathcal{R}_0}(pred(p_1, \ldots, p_n))$ *and a substitution* σ' *such that* $\sigma' pred(p_1', \ldots, p_n') = \sigma pred(p_1, \ldots, p_n)$ *and* $\sigma' H$ *is derivable from* $\mathcal{R}_0'$.

Proof. The fact $\sigma pred(p_1, \ldots, p_n)$ is derivable from $\mathcal{R}_0$ if and only if $\sigma pred'(p_1, \ldots, p_n)$ is derivable from $\mathcal{R}_0'$, so by Theorem 1, if and only if $\sigma pred'(p_1, \ldots, p_n)$ is derivable from $\mathsf{saturate}(\mathcal{R}_0')$, so if and only if there exists a clause $H \Rightarrow pred(p_1', \ldots, p_n')$ in $\mathsf{solve}_{\mathcal{R}_0}(pred(p_1, \ldots, p_n))$ and a substitution σ' such that $\sigma' pred(p_1', \ldots, p_n') = \sigma pred(p_1, \ldots, p_n)$ and $\sigma' H$ is derivable from $\mathsf{saturate}(\mathcal{R}_0')$, that is, from $\mathcal{R}_0'$. □

In particular, if $\mathsf{solve}_{\mathcal{R}_0}(\mathsf{attacker}(p)) = \emptyset$, then $\mathsf{attacker}(p)$ is not derivable from $\mathcal{R}_0$. Moreover, if $\mathsf{solve}_{\mathcal{R}_0}(\mathsf{attacker}(p))$ is not empty for the selection function sel_0, at least one instance of $\mathsf{attacker}(p)$ is derivable, since H will contain facts of the form $\mathsf{attacker}(x)$, an instance of which is derivable by $\mathsf{attacker}(a[])$.

4.3   Proofs

In this section, we detail the proof of Theorem 1. We first need to prove a few preliminary lemmas. The first one shows that two nodes in a derivation can be replaced by one when combining their clauses by resolution.

Lemma 1 (Resolution). *Consider a derivation containing a node* η', *labeled* R'. *Let* F_0 *be a hypothesis of* R'. *Then there exists a son* η *of* η', *labeled* R, *such that the edge* $\eta' \to \eta$ *is labeled by an instance of* F_0, $R \circ_{F_0} R'$ *is defined, and one obtains a derivation of the same fact by replacing the nodes* η *and* η' *with a node* η'' *labeled* $R'' = R \circ_{F_0} R'$.

Proof. This proof is illustrated in Fig. 9. Let $R' = H' \Rightarrow C'$, H_1' be the multiset of the labels of the outgoing edges of η', and C_1' the label of its incoming edge. We have $R' \sqsupseteq (H_1' \Rightarrow C_1')$, so there exists a substitution σ such that $\sigma H' \subseteq H_1'$ and $\sigma C' = C_1'$. Since $F_0 \in H'$, $\sigma F_0 \in H_1'$, so there is an outgoing edge of η' labeled σF_0. Let η be the node at the end of this edge, let $R = H \Rightarrow C$ be the label of η. We rename the variables of R so that they are distinct from the variables of R'. Let H_1 be the multiset of the labels of the outgoing edges of η. So $R \sqsupseteq (H_1 \Rightarrow \sigma F_0)$. By the above choice of distinct variables, we can then extend σ so that $\sigma H \subseteq H_1$ and $\sigma C = \sigma F_0$.

The edge $\eta' \to \eta$ is labeled σF_0, instance of F_0. Since $\sigma C = \sigma F_0$, the facts C and F_0 are unifiable, so $R \circ_{F_0} R'$ is defined. Let σ' be the most general unifier of C and F_0, and σ'' such that $\sigma = \sigma'' \sigma'$. We have $R \circ_{F_0} R' = \sigma'(H \cup (H' \setminus \{F_0\})) \Rightarrow \sigma' C'$. Moreover, $\sigma'' \sigma'(H \cup (H' \setminus \{F_0\})) \subseteq H_1 \cup (H_1' \setminus \{\sigma F_0\})$ and

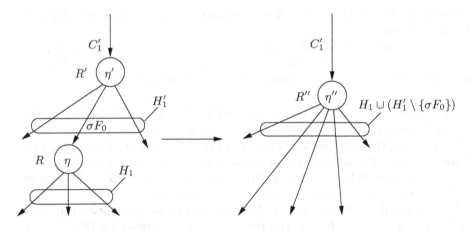

Fig. 9. Merging of nodes of Lemma 1

$\sigma''\sigma'C' = \sigma C' = C_1'$. Hence $R'' = R \circ_{F_0} R' \sqsupseteq (H_1 \cup (H_1' \setminus \{\sigma F_0\})) \Rightarrow C_1'$. The multiset of labels of outgoing edges of η'' is precisely $H_1 \cup (H_1' \setminus \{\sigma F_0\})$ and the label of its incoming edge is C_1', therefore we have obtained a correct derivation by replacing η and η' with η''. □

Lemma 2 (Subsumption). *If a node η of a derivation D is labeled by R, then one obtains a derivation D' of the same fact as D by relabeling η with a clause R' such that $R' \sqsupseteq R$.*

Proof. Let H be the multiset of labels of outgoing edges of the considered node η, and C be the label of its incoming edge. We have $R \sqsupseteq H \Rightarrow C$. By transitivity of $\sqsupseteq$, $R' \sqsupseteq H \Rightarrow C$. So we can relabel η with R'. □

Lemma 3 (Saturation). *At the end of* saturate, $\mathcal{R}$ *satisfies the following properties:*

1. *For all $R \in \mathcal{R}_0$, R is subsumed by a clause in $\mathcal{R}$;*
2. *Let $R \in \mathcal{R}$ and $R' \in \mathcal{R}$. Assume that $sel(R) = \emptyset$ and there exists $F_0 \in sel(R')$ such that $R \circ_{F_0} R'$ is defined. In this case, $R \circ_{F_0} R'$ is subsumed by a clause in $\mathcal{R}$.*

Proof. To prove the first property, let $R \in \mathcal{R}_0$. We show that, after the addition of R to $\mathcal{R}$, R is subsumed by a clause in $\mathcal{R}$.

In the first step of saturate, we execute the instruction $\mathcal{R} \leftarrow elim(\{R\} \cup \mathcal{R})$. After execution of this instruction, R is subsumed by a clause in $\mathcal{R}$.

Assume that we execute $\mathcal{R} \leftarrow elim(\{R''\} \cup \mathcal{R})$ for some clause R'' and that, before this execution, R is subsumed by a clause in $\mathcal{R}$, say R'. If R' is removed by this instruction, there exists a clause R_1' in $\mathcal{R}$ that subsumes R', so by transitivity of subsumption, R_1' subsumes R, hence R is subsumed by the clause $R_1' \in \mathcal{R}$ after this instruction. If R' is not removed by this instruction, then R is subsumed by the clause $R' \in \mathcal{R}$ after this instruction.

Hence, at the end of saturate, R is subsumed by a clause in $\mathcal{R}$, which proves the first property.

In order to prove the second property, we just need to notice that the fixpoint is reached at the end of saturate, so $\mathcal{R} = \mathsf{elim}(\{R \circ_{F_0} R'\} \cup \mathcal{R})$. Hence, $R \circ_{F_0} R'$ is eliminated by elim, so it is subsumed by some clause in $\mathcal{R}$. ☐

Proof of Theorem 1: Assume that F is derivable from $\mathcal{R}_0$ and consider a derivation of F from $\mathcal{R}_0$. We show that F is derivable from $\mathsf{saturate}(\mathcal{R}_0)$.

We consider the value of the set of clauses $\mathcal{R}$ at the end of saturate. For each clause R in $\mathcal{R}_0$, R is subsumed by a clause in $\mathcal{R}$ (Lemma 3, Property 1). So, by Lemma 2, we can replace all clauses R in the considered derivation with a clause in $\mathcal{R}$. Therefore, we obtain a derivation D of F from $\mathcal{R}$.

Next, we build a derivation of F from $\mathcal{R}_1$, where $\mathcal{R}_1 = \mathsf{saturate}(\mathcal{R}_0)$. If D contains a node labeled by a clause not in $\mathcal{R}_1$, we can transform D as follows. Let η' be a lowest node of D labeled by a clause not in $\mathcal{R}_1$. So all sons of η' are labeled by elements of $\mathcal{R}_1$. Let R' be the clause labeling η'. Since $R' \notin \mathcal{R}_1$, $sel(R') \neq \emptyset$. Take $F_0 \in sel(R')$. By Lemma 1, there exists a son of η of η' labeled by R, such that $R \circ_{F_0} R'$ is defined, and we can replace η and η' with a node η'' labeled by $R \circ_{F_0} R'$. Since all sons of η' are labeled by elements of $\mathcal{R}_1$, $R \in \mathcal{R}_1$. Hence $sel(R) = \emptyset$. So, by Lemma 3, Property 2, $R \circ_{F_0} R'$ is subsumed by a clause R'' in $\mathcal{R}$. By Lemma 2, we can relabel η'' with R''. The total number of nodes strictly decreases since η and η' are replaced with a single node η''.

So we obtain a derivation D' of F from $\mathcal{R}$, such that the total number of nodes strictly decreases. Hence, this replacement process terminates. Upon termination, all clauses are in $\mathcal{R}_1$. So we obtain a derivation of F from $\mathcal{R}_1$, which is the expected result.

For the converse implication, notice that, if a fact is derivable from $\mathcal{R}_1$, then it is derivable from $\mathcal{R}$, and that all clauses added to $\mathcal{R}$ do not create new derivable facts: if a fact is derivable by applying the clause $R \circ_{F_0} R'$, then it is also derivable by applying R and R'. ☐

4.4   Optimizations

The resolution algorithm uses several optimizations, in order to speed up resolution. The first two are standard, while the last three are specific to protocols.

Elimination of Duplicate Hypotheses. If a clause contains several times the same hypotheses, the duplicate hypotheses are removed, so that at most one occurrence of each hypothesis remains.

Elimination of Tautologies. If a clause has a conclusion that is already in the hypotheses, this clause is a tautology: it does not derive new facts. Such clauses are removed.

Elimination of Hypotheses attacker(x). If a clause $H \Rightarrow C$ contains in its hypotheses attacker(x), where x is a variable that does not appear elsewhere in the clause, then the hypothesis attacker(x) is removed. Indeed, the attacker always has at least one message, so attacker(x) is always satisfied for some value of x.

Decomposition of Data Constructors. A data constructor is a constructor f of arity n that comes with associated destructors g_i for $i \in \{1, \ldots, n\}$ defined by $g_i(f(x_1, \ldots, x_n)) \to x_i$. Data constructors are typically used for representing data structures. Tuples are examples of data constructors. For each data constructor f, the following clauses are generated:

$$\text{attacker}(x_1) \wedge \ldots \wedge \text{attacker}(x_n) \Rightarrow \text{attacker}(f(x_1, \ldots, x_n)) \qquad \text{(Rf)}$$

$$\text{attacker}(f(x_1, \ldots, x_n)) \Rightarrow \text{attacker}(x_i) \qquad \text{(Rg)}$$

Therefore, attacker($f(p_1, \ldots, p_n)$) is derivable if and only if $\forall i \in \{1, \ldots, n\}$, attacker($p_i$) is derivable. When a fact of the form attacker($f(p_1, \ldots, p_n)$) is met, it is replaced with attacker(p_1) $\wedge \ldots \wedge$ attacker(p_n). If this replacement is done in the conclusion of a clause $H \Rightarrow$ attacker($f(p_1, \ldots, p_n)$), n clauses are created: $H \Rightarrow$ attacker(p_i) for each $i \in \{1, \ldots, n\}$. This replacement is of course done recursively: if p_i itself is a data constructor application, it is replaced again. The clauses (Rf) and (Rg) for data constructors are left unchanged. (When attacker(x) cannot be selected, the clauses (Rf) and (Rg) for data constructors are in fact not necessary, because they generate only tautologies during resolution. However, when attacker(x) can be selected, which cannot be excluded with certain extensions, these clauses may become necessary for soundness.)

Secrecy Assumptions. When the user knows that a fact will not be derivable, he can tell it to the verifier. (When this fact is of the form attacker(p), the user tells that p remains secret.) The tool then removes all clauses which have this fact in their hypotheses. At the end of the computation, the tool checks that the fact is indeed underivable from the obtained clauses. If the user has given erroneous information, an error message is displayed. Even in this case, the verifier never wrongly claims that a protocol is secure.

Mentioning such underivable facts prunes the search space, by removing useless clauses. This speeds up the resolution algorithm. In most cases, the secret keys of the principals cannot be known by the attacker. So, examples of underivable facts are attacker($sk_A[\,]$), attacker($sk_B[\,]$), $\ldots$

For simplicity, the proofs given in Sect. 4.3 do not take into account these optimizations. For a full proof, we refer the reader to [25, Appendix C].

4.5 Termination

In general, the resolution algorithm may not terminate. (The derivability problem is undecidable.) In practice, however, it terminates in most examples.

Blanchet and Podelski have shown that it always terminates on a large and interesting class of protocols, the *tagged protocols* [31]. They consider protocols that use as cryptographic primitives only public-key encryption and signatures with atomic keys, shared-key encryption, message authentication codes, and hash functions. Basically, a protocol is tagged when each application of a cryptographic primitive is marked with a distinct constant tag. It is easy to transform a protocol into a tagged protocol by adding tags. For instance, our example of protocol can be transformed into a tagged protocol, by adding the tags c_0, c_1, c_2 to distinguish the encryptions and signature:

$$\text{Message 1. } A \rightarrow B : \{(c_1, \{(c_0, k)\}_{sk_A})\}_{pk_B}$$
$$\text{Message 2. } B \rightarrow A : \{(c_2, s)\}_k$$

Adding tags preserves the expected behavior of the protocol, that is, the attack-free executions are unchanged. In the presence of attacks, the tagged protocol may be more secure. Hence, tagging is a feature of good protocol design, as explained e.g. in [7]: the tags are checked when the messages are received; they facilitate the decoding of the received messages and prevent confusions between messages. More formally, tagging prevents type-flaw attacks [53], which occur when a message is taken for another message. However, the tagged protocol is potentially more secure than its untagged version, so, in other words, a proof of security for the tagged protocol does not imply the security of its untagged version.

To illustrate the effect of tagging, we consider the Needham-Schroeder shared-key protocol [65]. The algorithm does not terminate on its original version, which is untagged. It terminates after adding tags. In this protocol, we have two messages of the form:

$$\text{Message 4. } B \rightarrow A : \{N_B\}_K$$
$$\text{Message 5. } A \rightarrow B : \{N_B - 1\}_K$$

where N_B is a nonce. Representing $N_B - 1$ using a function $\mathsf{minusone}(x) = x - 1$, the algorithm does not terminate.

Indeed, message 5 is represented by a clause of the form:

$$H \wedge \mathsf{attacker}(\mathsf{senc}(n, k)) \Rightarrow \mathsf{attacker}(\mathsf{senc}(\mathsf{minusone}(n), k))$$

where the hypothesis H describes other messages previously received by A. After some resolution steps, we obtain a clause of the form

$$\mathsf{attacker}(\mathsf{senc}(n, K)) \Rightarrow \mathsf{attacker}(\mathsf{senc}(\mathsf{minusone}(n), K)) \qquad \text{(Loop)}$$

for some term K. The fact $\mathsf{attacker}(\mathsf{senc}(\mathsf{minusone}(N_B), K))$ is also derived, so a resolution step with (Loop) yields: $\mathsf{attacker}(\mathsf{senc}(\mathsf{minusone}(\mathsf{minusone}(N_B)), K))$. This fact can again be resolved with (Loop), so that we finally have a cycle that derives $\mathsf{attacker}(\mathsf{senc}(\mathsf{minusone}^n(N_B), K))$ for all n.

When tags are added, the rule (Loop) becomes:

$$\mathsf{attacker}(\mathsf{senc}((c_1, n), K)) \Rightarrow \mathsf{attacker}(\mathsf{senc}((c_2, \mathsf{minusone}(n)), K)) \qquad \text{(NoLoop)}$$

and the previous loop is removed because c_2 does not unify with c_1. The fact attacker(senc((c_2, minusone(N_B)), K)) is derived, but this does not yield a loop.

Other authors have proved related results: Ramanujan and Suresh [68] have shown that secrecy is decidable for tagged protocols. However, their tagging scheme is stronger since it forbids blind copies. A blind copy happens when a protocol participant sends back part of a message he received without looking at what is contained inside this part. On the other hand, they obtain a decidability result, while [31] obtains a termination result for an algorithm which is sound, efficient in practice, but approximate. Arapinis and Duflot [11] extend this result but still forbid blind copies. Comon-Lundh and Cortier [39] show that an algorithm using ordered binary resolution, ordered factorization and splitting terminates on protocols that blindly copy at most one term in each message. In contrast, the result of [31] puts no limit on the number of blind copies, but requires tagging.

For protocols that are not tagged, heuristics have been designed to adapt the selection function in order to obtain termination more often. We refer the reader to [26, Sect. 8.2] for more details.

It is also possible to obtain termination in all cases at the cost of additional abstractions. For instance, Goubault-Larrecq shows that one can abstract the clauses into clauses in the decidable class $\mathcal{H}_1$ [51], by losing some relational information on the messages.

5 Translation from the Pi Calculus

Given a closed process P_0 in the language of Sect. 3 and a set of names S, ProVerif builds a set of Horn clauses, representing the protocol P_0 in parallel with any S-adversary, in the same style as the clauses presented in the previous section. This translation was originally given in [2]. The clauses use *facts* defined by the following grammar:

$F ::=$	facts
attacker(p)	attacker knowledge
mess(p, p')	message on a channel

The fact attacker(p) means that the attacker may have p, and the fact mess(p, p') means that the message p' may appear on channel p. The clauses are of the form $F_1 \wedge \ldots \wedge F_n \Rightarrow F$, where $F_1, \ldots, F_n, F$ are facts. They comprise clauses for the attacker and clauses for the protocol, defined below. These clauses form the set $\mathcal{R}_{P_0, S}$.

5.1 Clauses for the Attacker

The abilities of the attacker are represented by the following clauses:

For each $a \in S$, attacker($a[\,]$) (Init)

attacker($b_0[\,]$) (Rn)

For each constructor f of arity n,

$$\text{attacker}(x_1) \wedge \ldots \wedge \text{attacker}(x_n) \Rightarrow \text{attacker}(f(x_1, \ldots, x_n)) \qquad \text{(Rf)}$$

For each destructor g,

for each rewrite rule $g(M_1, \ldots, M_n) \to M$ in $\text{def}(g)$, $\qquad$ (Rg)

$$\text{attacker}(M_1) \wedge \ldots \wedge \text{attacker}(M_n) \Rightarrow \text{attacker}(M)$$

$$\text{mess}(x, y) \wedge \text{attacker}(x) \Rightarrow \text{attacker}(y) \qquad \text{(Rl)}$$

$$\text{attacker}(x) \wedge \text{attacker}(y) \Rightarrow \text{mess}(x, y) \qquad \text{(Rs)}$$

The clause (Init) represents the initial knowledge of the attacker. The clause (Rn) means that the attacker can generate new names. The clauses (Rf) and (Rg) mean that the attacker can apply all operations to all terms it has, (Rf) for constructors, (Rg) for destructors. For (Rg), notice that the rewrite rules in $\text{def}(g)$ do not contain names and that terms without names are also patterns, so the clauses have the required format. Clause (Rl) means that the attacker can listen on all channels it has, and (Rs) that it can send all messages it has on all channels it has.

If $c \in S$, we can replace all occurrences of $\text{mess}(c[], p)$ with $\text{attacker}(p)$ in the clauses. Indeed, these facts are equivalent by the clauses (Rl) and (Rs).

5.2   Clauses for the Protocol

When a function ρ associates a pattern with each name and variable, and f is a constructor, we extend ρ as a substitution by $\rho(f(M_1, \ldots, M_n)) = f(\rho(M_1), \ldots, \rho(M_n))$.

The translation $[\![P]\!]\rho H$ of a process P is a set of clauses, where ρ is a function that associates a pattern with each name and variable, and H is a sequence of facts of the form $\text{mess}(p, p')$. The environment ρ maps each variable and name to its associated pattern representation. The sequence H keeps track of messages received by the process, since these may trigger other messages. The empty sequence is denoted by $\emptyset$; the concatenation of a fact F to the sequence H is denoted by $H \wedge F$.

$[\![0]\!]\rho H = \emptyset$

$[\![P \mid Q]\!]\rho H = [\![P]\!]\rho H \cup [\![Q]\!]\rho H$

$[\![!P]\!]\rho H = [\![P]\!]\rho H$

$[\![(\nu a)P]\!]\rho H = [\![P]\!](\rho[a \mapsto a[p_1', \ldots, p_n']])H$

$\quad$ where $H = \text{mess}(p_1, p_1') \wedge \ldots \wedge \text{mess}(p_n, p_n')$

$[\![M(x).P]\!]\rho H = [\![P]\!](\rho[x \mapsto x])(H \wedge \text{mess}(\rho(M), x))$

$[\![\overline{M}\langle N\rangle.P]\!]\rho H = [\![P]\!]\rho H \cup \{H \Rightarrow \text{mess}(\rho(M), \rho(N))\}$

$[\![\text{let } x = g(M_1, \ldots, M_n) \text{ in } P \text{ else } Q]\!]\rho H = \bigcup\{[\![P]\!]((\sigma\rho)[x \mapsto \sigma'p'])(\sigma H)$

$\quad \mid g(p_1', \ldots, p_n') \to p'$ is in $\text{def}(g)$ and (σ, σ') is a most general pair of

$\quad$ substitutions such that $\sigma\rho(M_1) = \sigma'p_1', \ldots, \sigma\rho(M_n) = \sigma'p_n'\} \cup [\![Q]\!]\rho H$

$\llbracket$let $x = M$ in $P\rrbracket\rho H = \llbracket P\rrbracket(\rho[x \mapsto \rho(M)])H$

$\llbracket$if $M = N$ then P else $Q\rrbracket\rho H =$

$$\begin{cases} \llbracket P\rrbracket(\sigma\rho)(\sigma H) \cup \llbracket Q\rrbracket\rho H \\ \quad \text{when } \rho(M) \text{ and } \rho(N) \text{ unify and } \sigma \text{ is their most general unifier} \\ \llbracket Q\rrbracket\rho H \text{ when } \rho(M) \text{ and } \rho(N) \text{ do not unify} \end{cases}$$

The translation of a process is a set of Horn clauses that express that it may send certain messages.

- The nil process does nothing, so its translation is empty.
- The clauses for the parallel composition of processes P and Q are the union of clauses for P and Q.
- The replication is ignored, because all Horn clauses are applicable arbitrarily many times.
- For the restriction, we replace the restricted name a in question with the pattern $a[p'_1, \ldots, p'_n]$, where $p'_1, \ldots, p'_n$ are the previous inputs.
- The sequence H is extended in the translation of an input, with the input in question.
- The translation of an output adds a clause, meaning that the output is triggered when all conditions in H are true.
- The translation of a destructor application is the union of the clauses for the cases where the destructor succeeds (with an appropriate substitution) and where the destructor fails. For simplicity, we assume that the else branch of destructors may always be executed; this is sufficient in most cases, since the else branch is often empty or just sends an error message. For a more precise treatment, see [26, Sect. 9.2].
- The local definition let $x = M$ in P is in fact equivalent to let $x = id(M)$ in P else 0, where the destructor id is defined by $id(x) \to x$. The conditional if $M = N$ then P else Q is in fact equivalent to let $x = \text{equal}(M, N)$ in P else Q, where the destructor equal is defined by $\text{equal}(x, x) \to x$. So the translations of these constructs is a particular case of the destructor application. We give them explicitly since they are particularly simple.

This translation of the protocol into Horn clauses introduces approximations. The actions are considered as implicitly replicated, since the clauses can be applied any number of times. This approximation implies that the tool fails to prove protocols that first need to keep some value secret and later reveal it. For instance, consider the process $(\nu d)(\overline{d}\langle s\rangle.\overline{c}\langle d\rangle \mid d(x))$. This process preserves the secrecy of s, because s is output on the private channel d and received by the input on d, before the adversary gets to know d by the output of d on the public channel c. However, the Horn clause method cannot prove this property, because it treats this process like a variant with additional replications $(\nu d)(!\overline{d}\langle s\rangle.\overline{c}\langle d\rangle \mid !d(x))$, which does not preserve the secrecy of s.

5.3   Summary and Correctness

Let $\rho = \{a \mapsto a[] \mid a \in fn(P_0)\}$. We define the clauses corresponding to the process P_0 as:

$$\mathcal{R}_{P_0,S} = [\![P_0]\!]\rho\emptyset \cup \{\mathsf{attacker}(a[]) \mid a \in S\} \cup \{(\mathrm{Rn}), (\mathrm{Rf}), (\mathrm{Rg}), (\mathrm{Rl}), (\mathrm{Rs})\}$$

Theorem 2 (Correctness of the clauses). *Let P_0 be a closed process. Let M be a closed term and p be the pattern obtained from the term M by replacing all names a with $a[]$. If $\mathsf{attacker}(p)$ is not derivable from $\mathcal{R}_{P_0,S}$, then P_0 preserves the secrecy of M from S.*

The proof of this result relies on a type system to express the soundness of the clauses on P_0, and on the subject reduction of this type system to show that soundness of the clauses is preserved during all executions of the process. This technique was introduced in [2] where a similar result is proved. [2] also shows an equivalence between an instance of a generic type system for proving secrecy properties of protocols and the Horn clause verification method. This instance is the most precise instance of this generic type system.

By combining Theorem 2 with Corollary 1, we obtain:

Corollary 2. *Let P_0 be a closed process. Let M be a closed term and p be the pattern obtained from the term M by replacing all names a with $a[]$. If $\mathsf{solve}_{\mathcal{R}_{P_0,S}}(\mathsf{attacker}(p)) = \emptyset$, then P_0 preserves the secrecy of M from S.*

5.4   Extension to Equational Theories

ProVerif has been extended to handle primitives defined by equational theories [29]. The term algebra consists of constructors equipped with an equational theory, defined by a finite set of equations. For example, we can model a symmetric encryption scheme in which decryption always succeeds (but may return a meaningless message) by the equations

$$\begin{aligned}
\mathsf{sdec}(\mathsf{senc}(x,y),y) &= x \\
\mathsf{senc}(\mathsf{sdec}(x,y),y) &= x
\end{aligned} \tag{4}$$

where senc and sdec are constructors. The first equation is standard; the second one avoids that the equality test $\mathsf{senc}(\mathsf{sdec}(M,N),N) = M$ reveals that M is a ciphertext under N: in the presence of the second equation, this equality always holds, even when M is not a ciphertext under N. These equations are satisfied by block ciphers, which are bijective.

We can also model the Diffie-Hellman key agreement [45] using equations. The Diffie-Hellman key agreement relies on the following property of modular exponentiation: $(g^a)^b = (g^b)^a = g^{ab}$ in a cyclic multiplicative subgroup G of $\mathbb{Z}_p^*$, where p is a large prime number and g is a generator of G, and on the assumption that it is difficult to compute g^{ab} from g^a and g^b, without knowing the random numbers a and b (computational Diffie-Hellman assumption), or on the stronger assumption that it is difficult to distinguish g^a, g^b, g^{ab} from g^a, g^b, g^c without knowing the random numbers a, b, and c (decisional Diffie-Hellman assumption). These properties are exploited to establish a shared key between two participants A and B of a protocol: A chooses randomly a and sends g^a to B; symmetrically, B chooses randomly b and sends g^b to A. A can then compute $(g^b)^a$, since it has a and receives g^b, while B computes $(g^a)^b$. These two values being equal, they can be used to compute the shared key. The adversary, on the other hand, has g^a and g^b but not a and b so by the computational Diffie-Hellman assumption, it cannot compute the key. (This exchange resists passive attacks only; to resist active attacks, we need additional ingredients, for instance signatures.) We can model the Diffie-Hellman key agreement by the equation [5,4]

$$\exp(\exp(\mathsf{g}, x), y) = \exp(\exp(\mathsf{g}, y), x) \tag{5}$$

where g is a constant and $\exp$ is modular exponentiation. Obviously, this is a basic model: it models the main functional equation but misses many algebraic relations that exist in the group G.

The main idea of our extension to equations is to translate these equations into a set of rewrite rules associated to constructors. For instance, the equations (4) are translated into the rewrite rules

$$\begin{aligned} \mathsf{senc}(x,y) &\to \mathsf{senc}(x,y) & \mathsf{sdec}(x,y) &\to \mathsf{sdec}(x,y) \\ \mathsf{senc}(\mathsf{sdec}(x,y),y) &\to x & \mathsf{sdec}(\mathsf{senc}(x,y),y) &\to x \end{aligned} \tag{6}$$

while the equation (5) is translated into

$$\exp(x,y) \to \exp(x,y) \qquad \exp(\exp(\mathsf{g}, x), y) \to \exp(\exp(\mathsf{g}, y), x) \tag{7}$$

Intuitively, these rewrite rules allow one, by applying them *exactly once* for each constructor, to obtain the various forms of the terms modulo the considered equational theory.[1] The constructors are then simply evaluated like destructors in the calculus above. With Abadi and Fournet, we have formally defined when a set of rewrite rules models an equational theory, and designed algorithms that compute translate equations into rewrite rules that model them [29, Sect. 5]. Then, each trace in the calculus with equational theory corresponds to a trace in the calculus with rewrite rules, and conversely [29, Lemma 1].[2] We are then reduced to the simpler case in which there are no equations. The main advantage of this technique is that resolution can still use ordinary syntactic unification (instead of having to use unification modulo the equational theory), and therefore remains efficient.

---

[1] The rewrite rules like $\mathsf{sdec}(x,y) \to \mathsf{sdec}(x,y)$ are necessary so that sdec always succeeds. Thanks to this rule, the evaluation of $\mathsf{sdec}(M, N)$ succeeds and leaves this term unchanged when M is not of the form $\mathsf{senc}(M', N)$.

[2] More precisely, the inequality tests of (Red Destr 2) must still be performed modulo the equational theory, even in the calculus with rewrite rules.

This extension to equations still has limitations: it does not allow us to model associative operations, such as exclusive or, since this would require an infinite number of rewrite rules. It may be possible to handle these symbols using unification modulo the equational theory instead of syntactic unification, at the cost of a larger complexity. In the case of a bounded number of sessions, exclusive or is handled in [41,37] and a more complete theory of modular exponentiation is handled in [36]. A unification algorithm for modular exponentiation is presented in [63]. For an unbounded number of sessions, extensions of the Horn clause approach that can handle XOR and Diffie-Hellman key agreements with more detailed algebraic relations (including equations of the multiplicative group modulo p) have been proposed by Küsters and Truderung: they handle XOR provided one of its two arguments is a constant in the clauses that model the protocol [57] and Diffie-Hellman key agreements provided the exponents are constants in the clauses that model the protocol [58]; they proceed by transforming the initial clauses into richer clauses on which the standard resolution algorithm is applied.

6   Applications

The automatic protocol verifier ProVerif is available at `http://proverif.inria.fr/`. Even though we focused only on secrecy in this chapter, ProVerif can also verify authentication [26] and some observational equivalence properties [29]. It can also reconstruct attacks against protocols [10] from the Horn clause derivation, when the desired property does not hold. It was successfully applied to many protocols of the literature, to prove secrecy and authentication properties [26]: no false attack was found in the 19 protocols tested in [26]. It was also used in more substantial case studies:

- With Abadi [3], we applied it to the verification of a certified email protocol [6]. We used correspondence properties to prove that the receiver receives the message if and only if the sender has a receipt for the message. (We used simple manual arguments to take into account that the reception of sent messages is guaranteed.) One of the tested versions includes the SSH transport layer in order to establish a secure channel.
- With Abadi and Fournet [4], we studied the JFK protocol (*Just Fast Keying*) [8], which was one of the candidates to the replacement of IKE as key exchange protocol in IPSec. We combined manual proofs and ProVerif to prove correspondences and equivalences.
- With Chaudhuri [30], we studied the secure filesystem Plutus [54] with ProVerif, which allowed us to discover and fix weaknesses of the initial system.
- ProVerif was also used for verifying a certified email web service [60], a certified mailing-list protocol [55], e-voting protocols [56,15], the ad-hoc routing protocol ARAN (*Authenticated Routing for Adhoc Networks*) [49], and zero-knowledge protocols [16], for instance.

It was also used as a back-end for building other verification tools:

- Bhargavan et al. [21] use it to build the Web services verification tool Tu-laFale: Web services are protocols that send XML messages; TulaFale trans-lates them into the input format of ProVerif and uses ProVerif to prove the desired security properties.
- Bhargavan et al. [22] use ProVerif for verifying implementations of protocols in F# (a functional language of the Microsoft .NET environment): a subset of F# large enough for expressing security protocols is translated into the input format of ProVerif. The TLS protocol, in particular, was studied using this technique [20].
- Aizatulin et al. [9] use symbolic execution in order to extract ProVerif models from pre-existing protocol implementations in C. This technique currently analyzes a single execution path of the protocol, so it is limited to protocols without branching. An earlier related approach is that of Goubault-Larrecq and Parrennes [52]: they also use the Horn clause method for analyzing implementations of protocols written in C. However, they translate protocols into clauses of the $\mathcal{H}_1$ class and use the $\mathcal{H}_1$ prover by Goubault-Larrecq [51] rather than ProVerif to prove secrecy properties of the protocol.
- Bansal et al. [17] built the Web-spi library which allows one to model web security mechanisms and protocols and verify them using ProVerif.

Canetti and Herzog [34] use ProVerif for verifying protocols in the computational model: they show that, for a restricted class of protocols that use only public-key encryption, a proof in the Dolev-Yao model implies security in the computational model, in the universal composability framework.

7 Conclusion

ProVerif is an automatic protocol verifier that relies on the symbolic model of cryptography. Its main strengths are that it supports a wide range of crypto-graphic primitives, defined by rewrite rules and equations, that it can prove various security properties, including secrecy, authentication, and some obser-vational equivalences, and that it handles an unbounded number of protocol executions. This is possible thanks to an abstract representation of the protocol by Horn clauses. Its main limitations are that it may fail to prove some secu-rity properties that actually hold, and that it may not terminate. However, it is precise and efficient on many practical examples. Other limitations concern the treatment of equations and the class of observational equivalences that it can prove.

ProVerif verifies specifications of protocols in the symbolic model, which can also be seen as a limitation, since the symbolic model abstracts away the details of cryptographic operations, and specifications do not take into account all im-plementation details. Going further is a topic of active research. Some tools, such as EasyCrypt [18] and CryptoVerif [27], already tackle the more difficult problem of verifying protocols in the computational model. Other tools verify implementations of protocols rather than specifications, some of them by translating the implementation into a ProVerif model, as mentioned in Section 6.

References

1. Abadi, M., Blanchet, B.: Secrecy types for asymmetric communication. Theoretical Computer Science 298(3), 387–415 (2003), special issue FoSSaCS 2001
2. Abadi, M., Blanchet, B.: Analyzing security protocols with secrecy types and logic programs. Journal of the ACM 52(1), 102–146 (2005)
3. Abadi, M., Blanchet, B.: Computer-assisted verification of a protocol for certified email. Science of Computer Programming 58(1-2), 3–27 (2005), special issue SAS 2003
4. Abadi, M., Blanchet, B., Fournet, C.: Just Fast Keying in the pi calculus. ACM TISSEC 10(3), 1–59 (2007)
5. Abadi, M., Fournet, C.: Mobile values, new names, and secure communication. In: POPL 2001, pp. 104–115. ACM Press, New York (2001)
6. Abadi, M., Glew, N., Horne, B., Pinkas, B.: Certified email with a light on-line trusted third party: Design and implementation. In: 11th International World Wide Web Conference, pp. 387–395. ACM, New York (2002)
7. Abadi, M., Needham, R.: Prudent engineering practice for cryptographic protocols. IEEE Transactions on Software Engineering 22(1), 6–15 (1996)
8. Aiello, W., Bellovin, S.M., Blaze, M., Canetti, R., Ioannidis, J., Keromytis, K., Reingold, O.: Just Fast Keying: Key agreement in a hostile Internet. ACM TISSEC 7(2), 242–273 (2004)
9. Aizatulin, M., Gordon, A.D., Jürjens, J.: Extracting and verifying cryptographic models from C protocol code by symbolic execution. In: CCS 2011, pp. 331–340. ACM, New York (2011)
10. Allamigeon, X., Blanchet, B.: Reconstruction of attacks against cryptographic protocols. In: CSFW 2005, pp. 140–154. IEEE, Los Alamitos (2005)
11. Arapinis, M., Duflot, M.: Bounding messages for free in security protocols. In: Arvind, V., Prasad, S. (eds.) FSTTCS 2007. LNCS, vol. 4855, pp. 376–387. Springer, Heidelberg (2007)
12. Armando, A., et al.: The AVISPA tool for the automated validation of internet security protocols and applications. In: Etessami, K., Rajamani, S.K. (eds.) CAV 2005. LNCS, vol. 3576, pp. 281–285. Springer, Heidelberg (2005)
13. Armando, A., Compagna, L., Ganty, P.: SAT-based model-checking of security protocols using planning graph analysis. In: Araki, K., Gnesi, S., Mandrioli, D. (eds.) FME 2003. LNCS, vol. 2805, pp. 875–893. Springer, Heidelberg (2003)
14. Bachmair, L., Ganzinger, H.: Resolution theorem proving. In: Robinson, A., Voronkov, A. (eds.) Handbook of Automated Reasoning, vol. 1, ch. 2, pp. 19–100. North Holland (2001)
15. Backes, M., Hritcu, C., Maffei, M.: Automated verification of remote electronic voting protocols in the applied pi-calculus. In: CSF 2008, pp. 195–209. IEEE, Los Alamitos (2008)
16. Backes, M., Maffei, M., Unruh, D.: Zero-knowledge in the applied pi-calculus and automated verification of the direct anonymous attestation protocol. In: S& P 2008, pp. 202–215. IEEE, Los Alamitos (2008), technical report version available at http://eprint.iacr.org/2007/289

17. Bansal, C., Bhargavan, K., Maffeis, S.: Discovering concrete attacks on website authorization by formal analysis. In: CSF 2012, pp. 247–262. IEEE, Los Alamitos (2012)
18. Barthe, G., Grégoire, B., Heraud, S., Béguelin, S.Z.: Computer-aided security proofs for the working cryptographer. In: Rogaway, P. (ed.) CRYPTO 2011. LNCS, vol. 6841, pp. 71–90. Springer, Heidelberg (2011)
19. Basin, D., Mödersheim, S., Viganò, L.: An on-the-fly model-checker for security protocol analysis. In: Snekkenes, E., Gollmann, D. (eds.) ESORICS 2003. LNCS, vol. 2808, pp. 253–270. Springer, Heidelberg (2003)
20. Bhargavan, K., Corin, R., Fournet, C., Zălinescu, E.: Cryptographically verified implementations for TLS. In: CCS 2008, pp. 459–468. ACM, New York (2008)
21. Bhargavan, K., Fournet, C., Gordon, A.: Verifying policy-based security for web services. In: CCS 2004, pp. 268–277. ACM, New York (2004)
22. Bhargavan, K., Fournet, C., Gordon, A., Tse, S.: Verified interoperable implementations of security protocols. In: CSFW 2006, pp. 139–152. IEEE, Los Alamitos (2006)
23. Blanchet, B.: An efficient cryptographic protocol verifier based on Prolog rules. In: CSFW-14, pp. 82–96. IEEE, Los Alamitos (June 2001)
24. Blanchet, B.: Security protocols: From linear to classical logic by abstract interpretation. Information Processing Letters 95(5), 473–479 (2005)
25. Blanchet, B.: Automatic verification of correspondences for security protocols. Report arXiv:0802.3444v1 (2008), http://arxiv.org/abs/0802.3444v1
26. Blanchet, B.: Automatic verification of correspondences for security protocols. Journal of Computer Security 17(4), 363–434 (2009)
27. Blanchet, B.: Mechanizing game-based proofs of security protocols. In: Nipkow, T., Grumberg, O., Hauptmann, B. (eds.) Software Safety and Security - Tools for Analysis and Verification. NATO Science for Peace and Security Series – D: Information and Communication Security, vol. 33, pp. 1–25. IOS Press (May 2012), Proceedings of the 2011 MOD Summer School
28. Blanchet, B.: Security protocol verification: Symbolic and computational models. In: Degano, P., Guttman, J.D. (eds.) POST 2012. LNCS, vol. 7215, pp. 3–29. Springer, Heidelberg (2012)
29. Blanchet, B., Abadi, M., Fournet, C.: Automated verification of selected equivalences for security protocols. Journal of Logic and Algebraic Programming 75(1), 3–51 (2008)
30. Blanchet, B., Chaudhuri, A.: Automated formal analysis of a protocol for secure file sharing on untrusted storage. In: S&P 2008, pp. 417–431. IEEE, Los Alamitos (2008)
31. Blanchet, B., Podelski, A.: Verification of cryptographic protocols: Tagging enforces termination. Theoretical Computer Science 333(1-2), 67–90 (2005), special issue FoSSaCS 2003
32. Bodei, C.: Security Issues in Process Calculi. Ph.D. thesis, Università di Pisa (January 2000)
33. Boichut, Y., Kosmatov, N., Vigneron, L.: Validation of Prouvé protocols using the automatic tool TA4SP. In: Proceedings of the Third Taiwanese-French Conference on Information Technology (TFIT 2006), Nancy, France, pp. 467–480 (March 2006)
34. Canetti, R., Herzog, J.: Universally composable symbolic analysis of mutual authentication and key-exchange protocols. In: Halevi, S., Rabin, T. (eds.) TCC 2006. LNCS, vol. 3876, pp. 380–403. Springer, Heidelberg (2006), extended version available at http://eprint.iacr.org/2004/334

35. Cardelli, L., Ghelli, G., Gordon, A.D.: Secrecy and group creation. In: Palamidessi, C. (ed.) CONCUR 2000. LNCS, vol. 1877, pp. 365–379. Springer, Heidelberg (2000)
36. Chevalier, Y., Küsters, R., Rusinowitch, M., Turuani, M.: Deciding the security of protocols with Diffie-Hellman exponentiation and products in exponents. In: Pandya, P.K., Radhakrishnan, J. (eds.) FSTTCS 2003. LNCS, vol. 2914, pp. 124–135. Springer, Heidelberg (2003)
37. Chevalier, Y., Küsters, R., Rusinowitch, M., Turuani, M.: An NP decision procedure for protocol insecurity with XOR. Theoretical Computer Science 338(1-3), 247–274 (2005)
38. Chevalier, Y., Vigneron, L.: A tool for lazy verification of security protocols. In: ASE 2001, pp. 373–376. IEEE, Los Alamitos (2001)
39. Comon-Lundh, H., Cortier, V.: New decidability results for fragments of first-order logic and application to cryptographic protocols. In: Nieuwenhuis, R. (ed.) RTA 2003. LNCS, vol. 2706, pp. 148–164. Springer, Heidelberg (2003)
40. Comon-Lundh, H., Cortier, V.: Security properties: two agents are sufficient. Science of Computer Programming 50(1-3), 51–71 (2004)
41. Comon-Lundh, H., Shmatikov, V.: Intruder deductions, constraint solving and insecurity decision in presence of exclusive or. In: LICS 2003, pp. 271–280. IEEE, Los Alamitos (2003)
42. Cremers, C.J.F.: Scyther - Semantics and Verification of Security Protocols. Ph.D. dissertation, Eindhoven University of Technology (2006)
43. Denker, G., Meseguer, J., Talcott, C.: Protocol specification and analysis in Maude. In: FMSP 1998 (June 1998)
44. Denning, D.E., Sacco, G.M.: Timestamps in key distribution protocols. Commun. ACM 24(8), 533–536 (1981)
45. Diffie, W., Hellman, M.: New directions in cryptography. IEEE Transactions on Information Theory IT-22(6), 644–654 (1976)
46. Dolev, D., Yao, A.C.: On the security of public key protocols. IEEE Transactions on Information Theory IT-29(12), 198–208 (1983)
47. Durgin, N., Lincoln, P., Mitchell, J.C., Scedrov, A.: Multiset rewriting and the complexity of bounded security protocols. Journal of Computer Security 12(2), 247–311 (2004)
48. Escobar, S., Meadows, C., Meseguer, J.: A rewriting-based inference system for the NRL protocol analyzer and its meta-logical properties. Theoretical Computer Science 367(1-2), 162–202 (2006)
49. Godskesen, J.C.: Formal verification of the ARAN protocol using the applied pi-calculus. In: WITS 2006, pp. 99–113 (March 2006)
50. Gordon, A., Jeffrey, A.: Types and effects for asymmetric cryptographic protocols. Journal of Computer Security 12(3/4), 435–484 (2004)
51. Goubault-Larrecq, J.: Deciding $\mathcal{H}_1$ by resolution. Information Processing Letters 95(3), 401–408 (2005)
52. Goubault-Larrecq, J., Parrennes, F.: Cryptographic protocol analysis on real C code. In: Cousot, R. (ed.) VMCAI 2005. LNCS, vol. 3385, pp. 363–379. Springer, Heidelberg (2005)
53. Heather, J., Lowe, G., Schneider, S.: How to prevent type flaw attacks on security protocols. In: CSFW 2000, pp. 255–268. IEEE, Los Alamitos (2000)
54. Kallahalla, M., Riedel, E., Swaminathan, R., Wang, Q., Fu, K.: Plutus: Scalable secure file sharing on untrusted storage. In: FAST 2003, pp. 29–42. Usenix, Berkeley (2003)
55. Khurana, H., Hahm, H.S.: Certified mailing lists. In: ASIACCS 2006, pp. 46–58. ACM, New York (2006)

56. Kremer, S., Ryan, M.D.: Analysis of an electronic voting protocol in the applied pi calculus. In: Sagiv, M. (ed.) ESOP 2005. LNCS, vol. 3444, pp. 186–200. Springer, Heidelberg (2005)

57. Küsters, R., Truderung, T.: Reducing protocol analysis with XOR to the XOR-free case in the Horn theory based approach. In: CCS 2008, pp. 129–138. ACM, New York (2008)

58. Küsters, R., Truderung, T.: Using ProVerif to analyze protocols with Diffie-Hellman exponentiation. In: CSF 2009, pp. 157–171. IEEE, Los Alamitos (2009)

59. Lowe, G.: Breaking and fixing the Needham-Schroeder public-key protocol using FDR. In: Margaria, T., Steffen, B. (eds.) TACAS 1996. LNCS, vol. 1055, pp. 147–166. Springer, Heidelberg (1996)

60. Lux, K.D., May, M.J., Bhattad, N.L., Gunter, C.A.: WSEmail: Secure internet messaging based on web services. In: ICWS 2005, pp. 75–82. IEEE, Los Alamitos (2005)

61. Lynch, C.: Oriented equational logic programming is complete. Journal of Symbolic Computation 21(1), 23–45 (1997)

62. Meadows, C.A.: The NRL protocol analyzer: An overview. Journal of Logic Programming 26(2), 113–131 (1996)

63. Meadows, C., Narendran, P.: A unification algorithm for the group Diffie-Hellman protocol. In: WITS 2002 (January 2002)

64. Monniaux, D.: Abstracting cryptographic protocols with tree automata. Science of Computer Programming 47(2-3), 177–202 (2003)

65. Needham, R.M., Schroeder, M.D.: Using encryption for authentication in large networks of computers. Commun. ACM 21(12), 993–999 (1978)

66. de Nivelle, H.: Ordering Refinements of Resolution. Ph.D. thesis, Technische Universiteit Delft (October 1995)

67. Paulson, L.C.: The inductive approach to verifying cryptographic protocols. Journal of Computer Security 6(1-2), 85–128 (1998)

68. Ramanujam, R., Suresh, S.P.: Tagging makes secrecy decidable with unbounded nonces as well. In: Pandya, P.K., Radhakrishnan, J. (eds.) FSTTCS 2003. LNCS, vol. 2914, pp. 363–374. Springer, Heidelberg (2003)

69. Rusinowitch, M., Turuani, M.: Protocol insecurity with finite number of sessions is NP-complete. Theoretical Computer Science 299(1-3), 451–475 (2003)

70. Schmidt, B., Meier, S., Cremers, C., Basin, D.: Automated analysis of Diffie-Hellman protocols and advanced security properties. In: CSF 2012, pp. 78–94. IEEE, Los Alamitos (2012)

71. Weidenbach, C.: Towards an automatic analysis of security protocols in first-order logic. In: Ganzinger, H. (ed.) CADE-16. LNCS (LNAI), vol. 1632, pp. 314–328. Springer, Heidelberg (1999)

Defensive JavaScript
Building and Verifying Secure Web Components

Karthikeyan Bhargavan[1], Antoine Delignat-Lavaud[1], and Sergio Maffeis[2]

[1] INRIA Paris-Rocquencourt, France
[2] Imperial College London, UK

Abstract. Defensive JavaScript (DJS) is a typed subset of JavaScript that guarantees that the functional behavior of a program cannot be tampered with even if it is loaded by and executed within a malicious environment under the control of the attacker. As such, DJS is ideal for writing JavaScript security components, such as bookmarklets, single sign-on widgets, and cryptographic libraries, that may be loaded within untrusted web pages alongside unknown scripts from arbitrary third parties. We present a tutorial of the DJS language along with motivations for its design. We show how to program security components in DJS, how to verify their defensiveness using the DJS typechecker, and how to analyze their security properties automatically using ProVerif.

1 Introduction

Since the advent of asynchronous web applications, popularly called AJAX or Web 2.0, JavaScript has become the predominant programming language for client-side web applications. JavaScript programs are widely deployed as scripts in web pages, but also as small storable snippets called bookmarklets, as downloadable web apps,[1] and as plugins or extensions to popular browsers.[2] Mainstream browsers compete with each other in providing convenient APIs and fast JavaScript execution engines. More recently, Javascript is being used to program smartphone and desktop applications[3], and also cloud-based server applications,[4] so that now programmers can use the same idioms and libraries to write and deploy a variety of client- and server-side programs.

As more and more sensitive user data passes though JavaScript applications, its confidentiality and integrity becomes an important security goal. Consequently, JavaScript applications rely on a number of security libraries for cryptography and access control. However, neither the JavaScript language nor its execution environment (e.g. the web browser) are particularly well suited for security programming. For example, to aid uniform deployment across different

---

[1] https://chrome.google.com/webstore/category/apps
[2] https://addons.mozilla.org/
[3] http://dev.windowsphone.com/develop
[4] http://node.js

A. Aldini et al. (Eds.): FOSAD VII, LNCS 8604, pp. 88–123, 2014.

browsers, JavaScript allows a number of core language primitives to be redefined and customized. This means that a JavaScript security library that may
run alongside other partially-trusted libraries must take extra care so that its
functionality is not subverted and its secrets are not leaked.

In this tutorial, we investigate approaches to build and verify JavaScript programs that implement security-criticial tasks, such as cryptographic protocols.
Our programs must contend not just with the traditional network attacker, but
also with a variety of web-specific attacks, such as malicious hosting websites and
Cross-Site Scripting (XSS). In other words, not just the communication channel
but even parts of the execution environment may be under the control of the
adversary. We propose a typed subset of JavaScript, called Defensive JavaScript,
that enables formal security guarantees for programs even in this threat model.
Our language and verification results previously appeared in [12].

Many existing works investigate the security of formal models of web application protocols [3,17,8], but none of them can provide concrete security guarantees
for JavaScript code. Still, we build upon these prior results (especially [8]) to develop our threat model and verification techniques. Another closely related line
of work investigates the use of type-preserving compilers to generate JavaScript
programs that are secure-by-construction [18,25]. We will focus only on language-
based protections in JavaScript, but note that HTML-level isolation techniques
may also be effectively used to separate trusted web security components from
untrusted JavaScript [4].

In the rest of this section, we will seek to better understand the threat model
and security goals of JavaScript security components through three examples.

1.1 Encrypted Cloud Storage Websites

Storage services (e.g. Dropbox) allow users to store their personal files on servers
hosted within some cloud infrastructure. Since users often rely on these services
to back up important files and share them across devices, the integrity and confidentiality of this data is an important security requirement, especially since
the cloud servers may be under the control of a third party. Consequently, mainstream storage services typically encrypt user files before storing them in the
cloud. A hacker who breaks into the cloud server to obtain the encrypted files
would also need to steal the file encryption key from the storage service.

Some services, such as SpiderOak and Mega, seek to provide a stronger privacy
guarantee to their users, sometimes called *host-proof* hosting — even if the
storage service and its cloud servers are both hacked, the user's files should
remain confidential. The key mechanism to achieve this goal is that a user's file
encryption keys are generated and stored on the client-side; even the storage
service does not get to see it, and so cannot accidentally leak it.

For example, to access their files stored on Mega, users visit the Mega website,
which downloads and runs a JavaScript program in the browser. The program
asks the user for a master passphrase, derives an authentication token and an
encryption key from the passphrase, and sends the username and authentication
token to the website. If the token matches the username, the web page allows the

user to download or upload encrypted files from a cloud server. The JavaScript program encrypts and decrypts user files upon request, using the encryption key derived from the master passphrase, but the key and the passphrase never leave the browser.

Hence, the storage service implements an application-level cryptographic protocol in JavaScript. This programming pattern is also popular with other security web applications such as password managers (more below) and with privacy-preserving websites like ConfiChair [5] and Helios [1].

The main threat to this design is that if the attacker manages to inject a malicious script into the website, that script will be able to steal the master passphrase (and hence the user's files). This script injection may be achieved by hacking the web server, or by tampering with externally loaded scripts on the network, or by exploiting a cross-site scripting (XSS) attack. Many such attacks have been found in previous work [10,7,12] and reports from the MEGA bug bounty program indicate that such attacks are a common concern. Cloud storage websites employ many techniques to block these attack vectors, such as Strict Transport Layer Security [20] and Content Security Policy [24], but the increasing incidence of server-side compromises, man-in-the-middle attacks on TLS, and XSS vulnerabilities on websites, indicates that it would be prudent to try to protect user data even if the website had a malicious script.

Even ignoring malicious scripts, to provide any formal security guarantee for a website security component that runs alongside unknown third party scripts, the component would need to be robust against bugs in these scripts. To give a concrete example, the MEGA website relies on about 70 scripts, and less than 10% of their code is related to cryptography; most of the rest implements the user interface. So the correctness of the cryptographic library and the secrecy of its keys relies on the good behavior of these UI scripts, which are not written by security experts and may be difficult to formally review.

1.2   Password Manager Bookmarklets and Browser Extensions

Password managers (e.g. LastPass) help users manage and remember their passwords (and other sensitive data such as credit card numbers) on various websites. They are often implemented in JavaScript and deployed as a browser extension or bookmarklet that detects the login page of a website, looks up a password database for a matching username and password, and offers to fill it in automatically. If there is no matching password, it may offer to generate a difficult-to-guess password and store it in the database. To synchronize and backup the password database across a user's devices, many password managers implement the host-proof encrypted cloud storage pattern described above.

For example, LastPass users can generate a "Login" bookmarklet and add it to their browser's bookmarks. The bookmarklet contains a JavaScript program embedded with an encryption key for the user's password database. When a user next visits the login page at some website, she may click on the bookmarklet to automatically log in. Clicking on the bookmarklet executes its JavaScript program in the scope of the current page. The program contacts the LastPass website and retrieves the currently logged-in LastPass user's encrypted password data from the cloud server. It then uses the encryption key embedded in the bookmarklet code to decrypt the password for the current page and fills in the login form. If the browser does not have an active login session with LastPass, the bookmarklet has no effect.

The main threat to the bookmarklet design is that it may be clicked on a malicious website that may then tamper with the JavaScript environment to subvert the bookmarklet's functionality. A typical case is if the user accidentally clicks the bookmarklet on a website that looks like a known trusted site. Or the user has passwords for two different sites stored in her database, and one of them may have been compromised. In these situations, the main goal of the malicious website is to steal the user's password at a different honest website. The bookmarklet tries to prevent such attacks by identifying the website the bookmarklet has been clicked on and only using its embedded secret on trusted websites. However, identifying the host website and protecting the bookmarklet secret are difficult in a tampered JavaScript environment, leading to many attacks [2,10,7,12]. We propose a programming discipline that enables secret-keeping bookmarklets that are robust against tampered environments.

As an alternative to bookmarklets, many password managers also provide a downloadable browser extension that executes a similar JavaScript program, but in a safer, more isolated JavaScript context. Password manager browser extensions are subject to their own threat model [9], not detailed here. In particular, even extensions must protect their secrets from being leaked by bugs in other included JavaScript programs. To give a concrete example, the LastPass extension for the Google Chrome browser has 119 JavaScript files, of which only 5 contain any cryptography, but their security guarantees still must rely on the correctness of these other scripts.

1.3   Single Sign-On and Social Sharing Buttons

Single Sign-On protocols (e.g Facebook's Login button) are widely used by websites that wish to implement authenticated sessions without the hassle of user registration and password management. Another advantage is that the website can leverage their users' social networks to provide a richer experience (e.g. Facebook's Like button). From the user's viewpoint, single sign-on and social sharing buttons offer her a convenient and secure way of accessing and sharing data across different websites, without needing to remember different passwords.

For example, to include the Facebook Login button on a web page, a website W loads a JavaScript library provided by Facebook that displays the button. When a user clicks on the button, the program asks Facebook for the currently logged-in user's access token for the current website W. If the user is logged in and has previously authorized Facebook to provide an access token to W, Facebook returns the access token in a URL. Otherwise, the user is forwarded to a page where she may login and authorize W (or not). The program then gives the access token to the website and also provides functions to access the Facebook API and read or write (authorized elements of) the current user's social profile.

The protocol implemented by Facebook is OAuth 2.0 [19], which also prescribes other message flows for server-side tokens and smartphones. Other popular single sign-on protocols, such as OpenID, SAML, and BrowserID, provide similar message flows that websites may use to obtain access tokens as user-specific credentials.

The main threat to the single sign-on interaction above is that the access token may be stolen by a malicious website and then used to impersonate the user at an honest website, or to read or write the user's profile information on her social network. The OAuth 2.0 flow is particularly vulnerable since access tokens are sent in URLs which may be leaked by Referer headers, or by HTTP redirection, or by various browser and application bugs [8,26,12]. Since the access token is used as a bearer token, and is often not specific to a website, it can be immediately used by the adversary on any website to impersonate the user.

The BrowserID single sign-on protocol seeks to mitigate the effects of token theft by using public key cryptography to authenticate the client[5]. Mozilla's implementation of BrowserID is written fully in JavaScript. The client includes a JavaScript cryptography library that may be included by any site to retrieve and sign tokens on behalf of the user. Even the single sign-on server is written in JavaScript and deployed over `node.js`. The design of BrowserID has been carefully evaluated by formal analysis [17], but to prove the code correct, one must show that all the scripts loaded alongise behave safely. In Mozilla's implementation, the server-side protocol moduls is loaded among 158 other `node.js` modules, and a bug or malicious function in any of these modules could compromise both ther server's and user's private keys.

1.4   Towards Verifiably Secure Web Components

We have discussed three popular categories of JavaScript security components that seek to protect sensitive user data such as files, passwords, and access tokens from malicious websites using various combinations of authentication protocols and cryptography. Each of these components is used in conjunction with a number of other scripts that may modify the JavaScript environment.

Our goal is to write JavaScript security components in a style that their security can be formally proved even if the context is malicious. In particular, we aim for a language-level isolation guarantee for our programs — that their input-output functional behavior cannot be tampered with by the environment. As a corollary, any secrets that are correctly protected by cryptography in our programs cannot be stolen or modified by the adversary. This simple-sounding isolation guarantee would be trivial to obtain in traditional programming langugages with sound type systems, such as OCaml and Java. However, the flexibility of JavaScript breaks many guarantees presumed by the programmer and the language must be reined in before we can achieve our goal.

In Section 2, we discuss the peculiarities of JavaScript and the browser environment that make it difficult to isolate security components. In Section 3, we

---

[5] http://login.persona.org

present Defensive JavaScript (DJS), a typed subset of JavaScript that guarantees isolation from the environment. In Section 4, we present a large cryptographic library written in DJS and use it to write and verify simple cryptographic web applications. Section 5 concludes.

2   Secure Messaging in an Untrusted Environment

As a motivating example, we consider how to implement a JavaScript program that sends an authenticated message to a server. Our target web page is hosted on a website W at URL http://W.com and it loads three scripts:

```
1 <html>
2  <body>
3  <script src="attacker1.js"></script>
4  <script src="messaging.js"></script>
5  <script src="attacker2.js"></script>
6  </body>
7 </html>
```

The first and third scripts are arbitrary malicious scripts chosen by the attacker. The second script is our program that provides an API to send messages to a server S at the URL http://S.com, via the XMLHttpRequest asynchronous messaging API provided by the browser. (In some cases, W may be the same site as S.) We assume that the program and S share a secret MACing key k. The program uses this key to attach a MAC to each message sent to S.

The security goal is message authentication: every message received and verified by S must have been sent by our program running at W. In particular, it should not be possible for the attacker scripts to steal the MAC key k and forge messages to S. The above web page scenario may seem too paranoid, but more generally, we want to guarnatee that that even if the surrounding scripts are just buggy, not malicious, they still cannot accidentally leak the key.

2.1   Secure Delivery of the Secret Key

The first challenge is to deliver the MAC key to messaging.js in a way that cannot be read by the other two attacker scripts.

Injecting the key as a token into the HTML document, or an HTTP cookie, or in browser local storage would not work; if the messaging script can read it, so can the attacker's script. The only safe place for the key is to embed it into the messaging program. But even in this case, there are many pitfalls. Consider the following messaging script messaging.js with a key included on top:

```
1 var key = k;
2 var api = function(msg){ .../*send authenticated message*/}
```

Unfortunately, the attacker script attacker2.js can simply read the variable key from the environment and obtain the key. A better solution would be to protect the key within the function:

```
1 var api = function(msg){
2   var key = k;
3   .../*send authenticated message*/
4 }
```

Now the script `attacker2.js` can no longer read the local variable `key`. However, it can retrieve the source code of the function `api` as a string by calling `api.toSource()`. It can then extract the embedded key k from the string. To protect the source code of the function, we need to rewrite the function by wrapping it within an anonymous function closure:

```
1 var api = (function (){
2             var _api = function(msg){
3                     var key = k;
4                     .../*send authenticated message*/}
5             return function(msg){return _api(msg);}
6           )();
```

Now, calling `api.toSource()` only reveals the code of the wrapper function, and the code of the real `_api` function (which embeds the key k) remains private.

There remains another way for the attacker scripts to obtain the source code of `_api`. If the script `messaging.js` is served from the current website's origin `http://W.com`, the source code of the whole script can be retrieved by either attacker script by making an `XMLHttpRequest` to the script's URL:

```
1 var xhr = new XMLHttpRequest();
2 xhr.open("GET","http://W.com/messaging.js",false);
3 xhr.send();
4 var program = xhr.responseText;
```

To prevent this, the messaging script must be served from a separate origin. For example, the website W could set aside a separate origin for serving only scripts, and place the messaging script at say `http://scripts.W.com/messaging.js`. in our example, it would also be suitable to source it from S's origin, say at `http://S.com/messaging.js`, so S can inject the shared key into the script. In both cases, the attacker scripts on `http://W.com` would be unable to make an `XMLHttpRequest` to read the code, due to the Same Origin Policy.

2.2   Calling External Functions

To construct and send a message, our messaging program will rely on several external functions either builtin to the JavaScript language or provided by the browser as part of the DOM library. For example, commonly used string functions such as concatenation (`s.concat(t)`) or search (`s.indexOf(t)`) are defined as methods in the `String` prototype. Other useful functions on arrays and objects are provided by the `Array` and `Object` prototypes. The `window.Math` object provides implementations of many mathematical functions. The `XMLHttpRequest` object allows asynchronous messaging with remote servers, and the `postMessage` API implements client-side messaging between windows. Finally, the `document` object (or DOM) provides functions for reading and writing the HTML document (e.g. `document.getElementById(''body'')`).

These external library functions are widely used by JavaScript programs. However, in our threat scenario, the attacker script `attacker1.js` may have redefined every one of these functions by modifying the `String`, `Array`, and `Object` prototypes, or by redefining these functions and objects in the `window` and `document` objects. For example, the following code redefines the `XMLHttpRequest` object, so that all messages send by the messaging script can be intercepted:

```
1 window.XMLHttpRequest =
2   function(){
3     return {open: function(){/*do whatever*/},
4             send: function(){/*do whatever*/}}}
```

Suppose our messaging program is written as follows; in addition to the `XMLHttpRequest` object (and its methods), the code calls `Crypto.HMAC`:

```
1 var api = (function (){
2           var _api = function(msg){
3                   var key = k;
4                   var xhr = new XMLHttpRequest();
5                   xhr.open("GET","http://S.com",false);
6                   xhr.send(Crypto.HMAC(key,msg) + "," + msg);
7                   }
8           return function(msg){return _api(msg);}}
9           )();
```

This code exemplifies three dangers of calling an external function.

First, the call to `Crypto.HMAC` leaks the key, since the attacker may have redefined the function. Consequently, the only safe choice here is to inline the code of the `HMAC` function into the messaging program. The `HMAC` function in turn relies on a hashing function (say `SHA-256`) which would also need to be included within the program. (To see what these functions look like in JavaScript, see our implementation in Appendix A.)

Second, the call to any external function exposes `_api` function to a stack-walking attack. For example, the attacker can redefine `XMLHttpRequest.send` so that when it is called, it reads the source code of its calling function using the `caller` method in the `Function` prototype:

```
1 stackwalk = function(){var program = stackwalk.caller.toSource();...}
2 window.XMLHttpRequest =
3   function(){
4     return {open: stackwalk,
5             send: stackwalk}}
```

Adding the above code in `attacker1.js` will set up the environment such that when `_api` calls `xhr.open`, the attacker obtains the source code of `_api` and hence its embedded key. The attack relies on the implementation of the `caller` method, and it it works at least in Firefox at the time of writing. More generally, this kind of stack-walking is a powerful attack vector. Whenever a function `f` is called, it can access its caller by accessing `f.caller`, and the next level on the call stack by accessing `f.caller.caller`. At each level, it may examine (and even overwrite) the arguments of the function.

Third, if our messaging script ever calls an external function, the attacker may redefine its behavior so that the result of the function is not as expected. For example, `s.concat(t)` may always return a constant string or `Math.pow` may always return 0. In such cases, the functional integrity of our script has been compromised, and if the results of these functions are used in the `MAC` function, the authentication protocol may be broken even without leaking the secret key.

In summary, any external function calls from a the messaging script may lead to a full compromise of its secrets and its functionality. To be safe, the script must never call functions from within security sensitive functions whose source code or arguments may be secret. Instead, all external function calls should be factored out into a top-level wrapper function that calls a self-contained API:

```
1 var api = (function (){
2              var hmac = function(key,msg){/* inlined HMAC code */}
3              var _api = function(msg){
4                           var key = k;
5                           return (hmac(key,msg) + "," + msg);
6                    }
7              return function(msg){return _api(msg);}
8           )();
9 var msg_api = function (msg) {
10             var mac = api(msg);
11             var xhr = new XMLHttpRequest();
12             xhr.open("GET","http://S.com",false);
13             xhr.send(mac);
14           }
```

Here, the external function call to `XMLHttpRequest` is performed outside the sensitive API by a function `msg_api` that has no access to the secret MACing key. Walking the stack to get to `msg_api` does not allow the attacker to steal any secrets or to tamper with the `_api` function.

2.3 Implicit Calls to External Functions

In addition to explicit function calls, many JavaScript constructs implicitly trigger methods defined in various prototypes. Since these prototypes may be modified by the adversary, we must also avoid such implicit calls in defensive code.

The first category of implicit function calls are *coercions*. For example, in the expression `e == e'`, if `e` is an object and `e'` is a number, then the equality will trigger an implicit coercion `e.valueOf` e was an object; rest of paragraph assumes string. This method `valueOf` is defined in the `String` prototype. More generally, comparison between any object and a string or a number may trigger the `valueOf` or `toString` methods in that object's prototype. Hence, by redefining these methods in the `Object` prototype, the attacker can intercept any function that triggers an implicit coercion and mount the attacks described in the previous subsection.

The second category of implicit function calls are *getters* and *setters*. Whenever an object is accessed at an undefined property (e.g. o.x), the JavaSript interpreter traverses the prototype hierarchy to see if the property x is defined in one of the prototypes that the object is derived from. If, say, none of the prototypes has defined x, but the Object prototype defines a getter function for x, then reading the property o.x will trigger this function. Similarly, if the Object prototype has a setter function for x, writing to o.x will call the setter.

By defining getters and setters for specific properties, an attacker script can cause trusted code to trigger an external function if it ever accesses an undefined property. Similarly, if an array or string is every indexed out of bounds, it may trigger a getter or setter in the Array prototype. Consequently, in our setting, the messaging program should never access arrays, strings, or objects outside their declared ranges. In particular, the popular JavaScript idiom of first declaring an empty object and then extending it is vulnerable to attack:

```
1 Object.defineProperty(Object.prototype,"a",{set:function(){...}});
2 var x = {};
3 x.a = 1; // triggers malicious setter
4 Object.defineProperty(Array.prototype,"0",{set:function(){...}});
5 var y = [];
6 y[0] = 1; // triggers malicious setter
7 Object.defineProperty(Array.prototype,"1",{get:function(){...}});
8 y[0] = y[1]; // should be undefined, but triggers malicious getter
```

A particular subcase of prototype poisoning is worth mentioning. JavaScript offers a for...in loop construct that goes through all the properties of an object. For example for (i in {x:1})print(i) is expected to print ``x'' and for (i in [1])print(i) is expected to print the single array index 0. However, if the attacker modifies Object and Array prototypes to add more properties, those properties will also be printed here. Even checking that each property was defined locally within the object using the Object.hasOwnProperty function does not help, since this function could also be modified by the adversary.

2.4   Defensive Programming Idioms

We have discussed many potential attack vectors that a malicious script may employ when trying to subvert an honest JavaScript program running in the same environment. To prevent these attacks, we advocate a defensive programming discipline where programs aim to isolate their security-critical code from the environment by using function closures, by being loaded from a different origin, by refusing to explicitly call external functions, and by carefully preventing the triggering of coercions and prototype lookups. To systematically check our programs for all these isolation conditions, we propose a static type system. Defensiveness is a first step towards formal security guarantees. Once scripts like our messaging program are correctly isolated, we may rely on their context-independent semantics and on the functional integrity of their cryptographic libraries to build automated security verification tools.

Alternative Mitigations. The injunction that the core messaging API must be fully self-contained may seem draconian and one may wonder if there are some cases in which calling external functions is safe. If the goal is only to prevent stack-walking, one may hide the stack by calling all external functions through a recursive wrapper function [25]. However, this requires a source-to-source translation to implement effectively, especially for object methods like xhr.send.

Recent versions of JavaScript give programs the ability to freeze objects and mark various properties as unmodifiable and/or unconfigurable (cannot be deleted). It is tempting to suggest that the website W should freeze some objects or that the browser should guarantee that some DOM properties are unforgeable. These objects and properties would then be safe to access. However, the problem with both Object.freeze and Object.defineProperty is that they need to apply to the top object in the object hierarchy, otherwise it is ineffective. For example, the properties document.location.href and window.location.href are commonly considered unforgeable since modifying them would take the webpage to a new location. Indeed, most browsers prevent JavaScript from redefining these properties. However, the attacker may directly redefine the window.document object (FireFox) or the window.location object (Internet Explorer).

Another option is for the website W to run a script first that makes copies of all relevant objects before they have been tampered by the attacker [18]. However, ensuring that a script runs first on a web page is surprisingly tricky [25]. Moreover, this solution does not work in scenarios where the website W itself may be malicious or compromised.

One may also use isolation mechanisms outside JavaScript, such as HTML iframes to effectively separate trusted and untrusted code [4]. In this paper, we do not investigate such mechanisms and instead focus only on language-based isolation. We note that the use of iframes relies on the semantics of the Same Origin Policy which remains to be fully standardized, let alone formalized [28]. Furthermore, iframes may not be available in some JavaScript runtime environments, such as smartphones and server applications. In these environments, defensive programming becomes necessary.

3   Defensive JavaScript

We present a subset of JavaScript that enforces a strong defensive programming discipline. Our language, Defensive JavaScript (DJS), imposes restrictions on JavaScript code both at the syntactic level and through a static type system. The main elements guiding the design of DJS are as follows:

Static Scopes. The variable scoping rules of JavaScript are notoriously difficult to understand. For example, functions may use local variables before they are declared. More worryingly, if a JavaScript program ever accesses a variable that is not in its local scope, this access may trigger a getter or setter in some prototype object. Consequently, we require that all variables in DJS programs be strictly statically scoped. We impose this by restricting the occurance of variable declarations (`var`) and by enforcing a strong scoping restriction on the bodies of `with` statements.

Static Types for Functions, Objects, and Arrays. To prevent out-of-bound accesses to object properties, function arguments, and array indices, we require that all these objects be statically types. Notably, this means that the objects and arrays are not extensible and the types of variables cannot be changed. Furthermore, dynamic accesses to arrays and strings are only allowed when the index can be guaranteed to fall within bounds.

Coercion-Free Operations. To avoid triggering coercions, we enforce strict types for all unary and binary operators. Comparisons, for example, can only be performed between expressions of the same types.

Disjoint Heaps. To provide full isolation for our programs, we require that no heap references are imported or exported by DJS code. Importing an external object (array, function) is forbidden since accessing any of its properties may trigger malicious code. Exporting an internal object is forbidden because it may expose internal program state (and secrets) to the attacker. Hence, we require that DJS programs can only export scalar (`string -> string`) APIs.

3.1 Syntax

The syntax of DJS depicted in Figure 1 reflects these design constraints. Since DJS is a subset of JavaScript, much of the syntax is standard JavaScript and we refer the reader to the full language specification for more syntactic details [16].

DJS includes the standard JavaScript literals: booleans, numbers, strings, objects, and arrays. In fact, literals are the only way one may construct an object or an array. DJS does not allow object constructors, and extending an existing object or an array is forbidden.

DJS supports several unary ($\triangleright$) and binary ($\diamond$) operators over numbers, strings, and booleans. Since these operators are built into the language and cannot be modified we can use them freely, except that the type system ensures that we do not trigger coercions.

Left-hand-side expressions denote the various ways that objects, strings, and arrays may be accessed in DJS code. Notably, dynamic accessors are severely limited. For example, properties cannot be accessed via the `e[i]` syntax (where `i` may have been dynamically computed). Instead, they must use the static accessor `e.x`. This helps the typechecker ensure (statically) that only explicitly defined properties are accessed (at runtime).

Arrays (and strings) can be accessed only at indexes that can be statically shown to fall within the array (and string) bounds. We allow three kinds of array indexes. The constant index $e[\eta]$ is allowed when η is known to be within the bounds of the array. The integer index $e[e' \& \eta]$ is allowed when η is an integer ($0 \le \eta < 2^{30}$) and is within the array bounds. The bounded access $x[(e{>}{>}{>}0)\% x.length]$ is always allowed.

Strings can be accessed with the three array access forms as well as a conditional form that checks that the index is within the length of the string before

$$
\begin{aligned}
a, b, c ::= & \qquad\qquad\qquad\qquad\qquad && \text{literals} \\
\quad \eta && \text{numbers } (0, 1, ...)\text{xo} \\
\quad \sigma && \text{strings } (``...\,'') \\
\quad \mathbf{true}, \mathbf{false} && \text{booleans} \\
\quad [e_1, \ldots, e_n] && \text{array literals } (n \geq 0) \\
\quad \{x_1 : e_1, \ldots, x_n : e_n\} && \text{object literals } (n \geq 0) \\
\triangleright ::= +, -, !, \sim && \text{unary operators} \\
\diamond ::= && \text{binary operators} \\
\quad +, -, *, /, \% && \text{arithmetic operators} \\
\quad \&, |, \hat{}\,, \mathtt{<<}, \mathtt{>>}, \mathtt{>>>}, \mathtt{>>>=} && \text{bitwise operators} \\
\quad \mathtt{\&\&}, \mathtt{||} && \text{boolean operators} \\
\quad \mathtt{==}, \mathtt{!=}, \mathtt{>}, \mathtt{<}, \mathtt{>=}, \mathtt{<=} && \text{comparison operators} \\
l, m, n ::= && \text{left-hand-side expressions} \\
\quad x, \mathtt{this}.x && \text{variables} \\
\quad e.x && \text{object property} \\
\quad e[\eta] && \text{constant array index} \\
\quad e[e' \& \eta] && \text{integer index } (0 \leq \eta < 2^{30}) \\
\quad x[(e\mathtt{>>>}0)\%x.\mathtt{length}] && \text{bounded array index} \\
\quad (e\mathtt{>>>=}0) < x.\mathtt{length}?x[e] : \sigma && \text{conditional string index} \\
e ::= && \text{expressions} \\
\quad a && \text{literals} \\
\quad l && \text{left-hand-side expressions} \\
\quad l = e && \text{assignment} \\
\quad \triangleright e && \text{unary operation} \\
\quad e \diamond e' && \text{binary operation} \\
\quad e_f(e_1, \ldots, e_n) && \text{function application } (n \geq 0) \\
s ::= && \text{statement} \\
\quad e && \text{expression} \\
\quad \mathbf{with}\ (e)\ s && \text{scope} \\
\quad \mathbf{if}\ (e)\ s_1\ \mathbf{else}\ s_2 && \text{conditional } (\mathbf{else}\ \text{optional}) \\
\quad \mathbf{while}\ (e)s && \text{while loop} \\
\quad \{s_1; \ldots s_n; \} && \text{sequential composition } (n \geq 0) \\
f ::= && \text{function expression} \\
\quad \mathbf{function}\ (x_1, \ldots, x_n)\{ && (n, m, k \geq 0) \\
\qquad\quad \mathbf{var}\ y_1 = d_1, \ldots, y_m = d_m; \\
\qquad\quad s_1; \ldots s_k;\ \mathbf{return}\ e; \} \\
d ::= e \mid f && \text{defined expression} \\
p_f ::= && \text{program (wrapping function } f) \\
\quad (\mathbf{function}\ ()\ \{ \\
\qquad \mathbf{var}\ \_ = f; \\
\qquad \mathbf{return\ function}\ (x)\ \{\mathbf{if}\ (\mathtt{typeof}\ x\ \mathtt{==}\ ``\mathtt{string}\,''\,)\ \mathbf{return}\ \_(x); \}\})();
\end{aligned}
$$

Fig. 1. Defensive JavaScript: Syntax

accessing it, otherwise it returns a new string constant. The restrictions on dynamic accesses to objects, strings, and arrays are governed by the limits of our type system and type inference algorithm. With a more expressive type system, one may be able to allow other safe dynamic accessors.

Expressions include assignments, unary and binary operations, and function and method applications. Functions and methods must be fully applied; we do not allow optional arguments that may be left undefined.

Statements include if-then-else conditionals, while loops, and sequencing. Notably, variable declarations `var x` cannot appear in statements and property enumeration via `for-in` is forbidden. General `for` loops are allowed by the type-checker, even though they are not part of the formal syntax.

There are two mechanisms of introducing scope frames in DJS; functions (and methods) and `with`. The statement `with` (e) s takes an object expression e and makes its properties available as local variables to the statement s. To enforce static scoping, we require that all the free unqualified variables of s be properties in e. That is, looking up a free variable in the body of a `with` statement should never require looking beyond the current `with` context.

The syntax of functions is restricted to make it easier to infer their scope frames and return types. The function body begins with a series of variable declarations; in fact, this is the only place where `var` statements appear in DJS programs. The body continues with a series of statements and ends with a single `return` statement. The function is not allowed to invoke `return` anywhere else.

The top-level program p_f is a wrapper around a single function f; it ensures that the argument to the function is a string, calls the function, and returns the result. The wrapping ensures that the source code of the internal function is not leaked to the environment, and the argument typecheck ensures that the program does not accidentally import an external heap reference.

3.2 Typing

The type rules depicted in Figures 2 and 3 enforce the language restrictions described informally above. We write types and typing environments as follows:

Types and Environments

$\tau ::=$	Types
number | boolean | string | undefined	Base Types
ρ	Object
$[\tau]_n$	Array of length $n \geq 0$
$(\tau_1, \ldots, \tau_n) \rightarrow \tau_e$	Function $n \geq 0$
$(\tau_1, \ldots, \tau_n)[\rho] \rightarrow \tau_r$	Method on object of type ρ $(n \geq 0)$
$\rho ::= \{x_1 : \tau_1, \ldots, x_n : \tau_n\}$	Object Type $(n \geq 0)$
$\kappa ::= \mathsf{f} \mid \mathsf{w}$	Scope frame kind: `function` or `with`
$\Gamma ::= \varepsilon \mid \Gamma, [\rho]_\kappa$	Typing Environment

Types τ include the primitive base types of JavaScript, plus static types for objects, arrays, functions, and methods. Object types ρ look like records; they declare a fixed set of properties and assign a static type to each property. Unlike JavaScript, DJS array types $[\tau]_n$ require that all elements of the array must have the same type τ and that the array length (n) must be fixed at initialization.

Each function is given a type $(\tau_1, \ldots, \tau_n) \to \tau_r$, which says that the function expects n arguments with the indicated types $\tau_1, \ldots, \tau_n$ and returns a result of type τ_r. Method types look like function types, except that they have an additional implicit argument — the object within which the method resides, denoted by its type ρ. In DJS, methods may only be invoked with the syntax $e.m(x_1, \ldots, x_n)$; it is, for example, forbidden to copy a method into a variable and invoke it without the object prefix.

Typing environments consist of a sequence of scope frames, where each frame looks like an object type ρ: it declares the types for a set of variables local to the frame. Each frame also has a kind annotation that denotes whether the frame was generated by a `with` statement or by a `function` (or `method`).

Most of the typing rules of DJS (Figures 2 and 3) are straightforwars. We give a brief overview, focusing on the more unusual rules:

- The rules for typing literals (Num, String, BoolTrue, BoolFalse, Object, Array) are standard.
- The casting rules (BoolCast, NumCast, StrCast) allow specific conversions between primitive types that do not trigger coercions.
- The type rules for operators (Concat, UnaryOp, ArithmeticOp, ComparisonOp, BooleanOp) ensure that their arguments are already of the required type, so that no coercions will be triggered during their execution.
- The object access rule (Property) ensures that the property is declared within the object's type.
- The three array access rules (ConstantIndex, IntegerIndex, BoundedIndex) ensure that the index is an unsigned integer between 0 (inclusive) and the array length (exclusive). The additional string indexing rule (ConditionalStringIndex) also ensures that the string is accessed at an unsigned integer index within the string.
- Assignment requires the left and right hand sides to have the same type. Formally, there is no subtyping in DJS, even though the DJS typechecker internally infers subtyping constraints.
- The rules for control-flow statements (Sequence, If, While) are standard.
- The rule for `with` e s (With) introduces a new frame of kind w into the typing environment and uses this frame to typecheck the statement s. The frame consists of the properties in the object type of the expression e.
- The variable scoping rules (VarLocal, VarFunctionScope) prescribe how to lookup a variable in the typing environment. We first look for a local variable in the current scope frame (VarLocal); if we fail, and if the current scope frame was introduced by a function definition, we look further back into the environment. If the current scope frame was introduced by a `with` statement, we never look further. Hence, a well-typed `with` context in DJS must define all the variables that may be used in its body, it cannot let any variable lookup escape to the surrounding context.

$$\text{Num} \frac{}{\vdash \eta : \text{number}} \qquad \text{String} \frac{}{\vdash \sigma : \text{string}}$$

$$\text{BoolTrue} \frac{}{\vdash \text{true} : \text{boolean}} \qquad \text{BoolFalse} \frac{}{\vdash \text{false} : \text{boolean}}$$

$$\text{BoolCast} \frac{\Gamma \vdash e : \tau}{\Gamma \vdash !e : \text{boolean}} \qquad \text{NumCast} \frac{\Gamma \vdash e : \text{string}}{\Gamma \vdash +e : \text{number}}$$

$$\text{StrCast} \frac{\Gamma \vdash e : \text{number}}{\Gamma \vdash e + \text{""} : \text{string}} \qquad \text{Concat} \frac{\Gamma \vdash e_1 : \text{string} \quad \Gamma \vdash e_2 : \text{string}}{\Gamma \vdash e_1 + e_2 : \text{string}}$$

$$\text{UnaryOp} \frac{\Gamma \vdash e : \text{number} \quad \triangleright \in \{-, \sim\}}{\Gamma \vdash \triangleright e : \text{number}}$$

$$\text{ArithmeticOp} \frac{\Gamma \vdash e_1 : \text{number} \qquad \Gamma \vdash e_2 : \text{number} \quad \diamond \in \{+, -, *, /, \%, \&, |, \char`^, \texttt{<<}, \texttt{>>}, \texttt{>>>}, \texttt{>>>=}\}}{\Gamma \vdash e_1 \diamond e_2 : \text{number}}$$

$$\text{ComparisonOp} \frac{\Gamma \vdash e_1 : \tau \qquad \Gamma \vdash e_2 : \tau \quad \tau \in \{\text{number}, \text{string}\} \quad \diamond \in \{\texttt{==}, \texttt{!=}, \texttt{<}, \texttt{>}, \texttt{>=}, \texttt{<=}\}}{\Gamma \vdash e_1 \diamond e_2 : \text{boolean}}$$

$$\text{BooleanOp} \frac{\Gamma \vdash e : \text{boolean} \quad \Gamma \vdash f : \text{boolean} \quad \diamond \in \{\texttt{\&\&}, \texttt{||}\}}{\Gamma \vdash e \diamond f : \text{boolean}}$$

$$\text{Object} \frac{\vdash e_i : \tau_i \quad i \in [1..n]}{\vdash \{x_1 : e_1, \ldots, x_n : e_n\} : \{x_1 : \tau_1, \ldots, x_n : \tau_n\}} \qquad \text{Array} \frac{\vdash e_i : \tau \quad i \in [1..n]}{\vdash [e_1, \ldots, e_n] : [\tau]_n}$$

$$\text{Property} \frac{\Gamma \vdash e : \{x_1 : \tau_1, \ldots, x_n : \tau_n\}}{\Gamma \vdash e.x_i : \tau_i} \qquad \text{ConstantIndex} \frac{\Gamma \vdash e : [\tau]_m \quad m > \eta \geq 0}{\Gamma \vdash e[\eta] : \tau}$$

$$\text{IntegerIndex} \frac{\Gamma \vdash e : [\tau]_m \quad \Gamma \vdash e' : \text{number} \quad 2^{30} \geq m > \eta \geq 0}{\Gamma \vdash e[e'\&\eta] : \tau}$$

$$\text{BoundedArrayIndex} \frac{\Gamma \vdash x : [\tau]_n \quad \Gamma \vdash e : \text{number} \quad n > 0}{\Gamma \vdash x[(e\texttt{>>>}0)\%x.\texttt{length}] : \tau}$$

$$\text{ConditionalStringIndex} \frac{\Gamma \vdash x : \text{string} \quad \Gamma \vdash y : \text{number}}{\Gamma \vdash ((y\texttt{>>>}0) < x.\texttt{length}?x[y] : \sigma) : \text{string}}$$

Fig. 2. Defensive JavaScript: Typing Rules (Literals and Expressions)

Assign $\dfrac{\Gamma \vdash l : \tau \quad \Gamma \vdash e : \tau}{\Gamma \vdash l = e : \tau}$ Sequence $\dfrac{\Gamma \vdash s_i : \mathsf{undefined} \quad i \in [1..n]}{\Gamma \vdash \{s_1; \ldots ; s_n; \} : \mathsf{undefined}}$

If $\dfrac{\Gamma \vdash e : \mathsf{boolean} \quad \Gamma \vdash s, t : \mathsf{undefined}}{\Gamma \vdash \mathtt{if}(e) \ s \ \mathtt{else} \ t : \mathsf{undefined}}$

While $\dfrac{\Gamma \vdash e : \mathsf{boolean} \quad \Gamma \vdash s : \mathsf{undefined}}{\Gamma \vdash \mathtt{while}(e) \ s : \mathsf{undefined}}$

With $\dfrac{\Gamma \vdash e : \rho \quad \Gamma, [\rho]_\mathsf{w} \vdash s : \mathsf{undefined}}{\Gamma \vdash \mathtt{with}(e) \ s : \mathsf{undefined}}$

VarLocal $\dfrac{\Phi(x) = \tau}{\Gamma, [\Phi]_\kappa \vdash x : \tau}$ VarFunctionScope $\dfrac{x \notin dom(\Phi) \quad \Gamma \vdash x : \tau}{\Gamma, [\Phi]_\mathsf{f} \vdash x : \tau}$

FunctionCall $\dfrac{\Gamma \vdash f : (\tau_1, \ldots, \tau_n) \to \tau_r \quad \Gamma \vdash e_i : \tau_i \quad i \in [1..n]}{\Gamma \vdash f(e_1, \ldots, e_n) : \tau_r}$

MethodCall $\dfrac{\Gamma \vdash e : \rho = \{x_1 : \tau_1, \ldots, x_n : \tau_n\} \quad \tau_i = (\tau_1', \ldots, \tau_m')[\rho] \to \tau_r}{\dfrac{\Gamma \vdash e_i : \tau_i' \quad i \in [1..m]}{\Gamma \vdash e.x_i(e_1, \ldots, e_m) : \tau_r}}$

FunctionDef $\dfrac{\begin{array}{c} \rho_k = \{(x_i : \tau_i)_{i \in [1..n]}, (y_j : \mu_j)_{j \in [1..k]}\} \\ \Gamma, [\rho_{k-1}]_\mathsf{f} \vdash d_k : \mu_k \quad k \in [1..m] \\ \Gamma, [\rho_m]_\mathsf{f} \vdash s : \mathsf{undefined} \quad \Gamma, [\rho_m]_\mathsf{f} \vdash e_r : \tau_r \end{array}}{\Gamma \vdash \mathtt{function}(\tilde{x})\{\mathtt{var} \ y_1\mathtt{=}d_1, \ldots, y_m\mathtt{=}d_m; \ s \ ; \ \mathtt{return} \ e_r\} : \tilde{\tau} \to \tau_r}$

MethodDef $\dfrac{\Gamma \vdash \mathtt{function} \ (\mathtt{this}, \tilde{x})\{\mathtt{body}\} : (\rho, \tilde{\tau}) \to \tau_r}{\Gamma \vdash \mathtt{function} \ (\tilde{x})\{\mathtt{body}\} : \tilde{\tau}[\rho] \to \tau_r}$

Program $\dfrac{\Gamma \vdash f : \mathsf{string} \to \mathsf{string}}{\Gamma \vdash p_f : \mathsf{string} \to \mathsf{string}}$

Fig. 3. Defensive JavaScript: Typing Rules (Statements and Programs)

- Function and method calls must be fully applied with arguments of the right types. Additionally, a method may only be called with an object of the expected object type ρ.
- Function definitions introduce a sequence of scope frames. The first frame consists of only the argument variables, and is used to typecheck the first variable declaration. Each successive frame adds one local variable and is used to typecheck the next variable definition. After all local variables have been declared, the rest of the function body is typechecked with a frame that consists of all arguments and all local variables.
- The rule for method definitions is similar to function definitions, except that the body is typechecked in a frame that includes an implicit `this` argument that has the object type ρ declared in the method type.
- Programs have the scalar API type `string -> string`. In practice, the DJS typechecker is more general; it allows programs to export an object containing multiple scalar functions.

These typing rules are implemented by the DJS typechecker, which infers types automatically without any annotations. The source code and an online demo of the typechecker is available at `http://defensivejs.com`.

The DJS language and its type system imposes many restrictions on JavaScript programs. In exchange, well-typed DJS programs enjoy strong isolation guarantees. The key functional integrity property is called *independence* [12]:

Definition 1 (Independence). *A program p_f preserves the* independence *of f if any two sequences of calls to the result of p_f with the same sequence of arguments, interleaved with arbitrary JavaScript code, return the same sequence of return values, as long as no call triggered an exception.*

The other key property, called *encapsulation* [12], guarantees that the DJS program's internal heap is isolated from the environment and that any internal secrets can only be leaked though the exported API.

Definition 2 (Encapsulation). *A program p_f encapsulates f over domain $\mathcal{D}$ if no JavaScript program that runs p_f can distinguish between running p_f and running p'_f for an arbitrary function f' without calling the wrapped function returned by p_f. Moreover, for any tuple of values $\tilde{v} \in \mathcal{D}$, the heap resulting from calling $p_f(\tilde{v})$ is equivalent to the heap resulting from calling $f(\tilde{v})$.*

Well-typed DJS programs are guaranteed both these properties [12].

Theorem 1 (Defensiveness). *If $\vdash f : \text{string} \to \text{string}$ then the DJS program p_f encapsulates f over strings and preserves its independence.*

4   Writing Defensive Cryptographic Applications

We present several case studies illustrating the use of DJS for building secure web components. We begin by describing three libraries, and then describing applications built with these libraries. Code sizes and verification details for these programs are listed in Table 1. All our libraries, applications, and verification tools are available from `http://defensivejs.com`.

Table 1. Defensive JavaScript Libraries and Verified Applications

Program	LOC	Typechecking	ProVerif LOC	ProVerif
Encodings	339	24ms	-	-
DJCL	1425	300ms	-	-
DJSON and JOSE	433	36ms	-	-
Secure RPC	61	7ms	243	12s
Password Manager Bookmarklet	43	42ms	164	21s
Single Sign-On Library	135	42ms	356	43s
Encrypted Storage API	80	31ms	203	25s

4.1   Encoding and Decoding Strings

JavaScript applications often have to convert between different data encodings. Unicode strings are typically encoded in UTF-8. Byte arrays can be stored in integer arrays and converted either to ASCII strings, where each character represents a byte, or encoded in Base64, say for use in URLs.

Typical website JavaScript relies on a variety of libraries to implicitly and explicitly interconvert between strings and byte arrays in various formats (e.g. window.atob, s.charCodeAt(i)). Since defensive code cannot rely on these libraries, we built our own encoding library that performs these conversions. The library currently supports byte arrays encoded in Hexadecimal, UTF-8, Base64, and ASCII and conversions between these formats.

The main limitation to using our DJS encoding library is performance, since it has no access to native objects and libraries. Since we cannot trust that the attacker has not tampered with efficient library objects like Int32Array, we encode all byte arrays as ASCII strings. Instead of relying on the String methods fromCharCode and charCodeAt, which may be modified by the adversary, we use large tables that map UTF-8 codes to their byte representations. The resulting performance penalty depends on the amount of data being encoded, and on the browser and hardware being used. We measured its impact on several applications (listed below), and surprisingly, even with the cost of encoding and decoding, DJS applications run as fast or faster than comparable JavaScript code. Of course, encoding performance could be vastly improved if the browser could provide access to an untamperable native library, such as the String prototype.

4.2   DJCL: Defensive JavaScript Crypto Library

We built a fully-featured JavaScript cryptography library in DJS, by adapting and rewriting well-reputed libraries like SJCL [23] (for symmetric cryptography) and JSBN (for public-key cryptography). Our implementation covers the following primitives: AES on 256 bit keys in CBC and CCM or GCM modes, SHA-1 and SHA-256, HMAC, RSA encryption and signature on keys up to 2048 bits with OAEP, PKCS1, or PSS padding. All our functions operate on byte arrays encoded as ASCII strings. Appendix A presents a detailed listing of the full code for our HMAC and SHA-256 functions.

Typing guarantees that the input-output behavior of the cryptographic functions cannot be tampered with by a malicious environment. However, this does not mean that our code correctly implements the cryptographic algorithm, or that it does not accidentally leak its secrets either explicitly in a return value or implicitly via a side-channel. Proving the functional correctness of our cryptographic library or its robustness against side-channels remains an open problem.

We evaluated the performance of various DJCL functions using the `jsperf` benchmark engine[6] on Chrome 24, Firefox 18, Safari 6.0 and IE 9. We found that our AES block function, SHA compression functions and RSA exponentiation performed at least as fast as their SJCL and JSBN counterparts, and sometimes even faster. We conclude that defensive coding is well suited for bit-level, self-contained crypto computations, and JavaScript engines find it easy to optimize our non-extensible arrays and objects.

On the other hand, when implementing high-level constructions such as HMAC or CCM encryption that operate on variable-length inputs, we must pay the cost of encoding and decoding data as ASCII strings. Despite this performance penalty, even on mobile devices, DJCL achieves encryption and hashing rates upwards of 150KB/s, which is sufficient for most applications.

To further exercise our cryptographic library, we built an implementation of the upcoming W3C Web Cryptography API standard [15], which is currently being implemented by various browsers and JavaScript libraries as an extension to the `window` object. We implement this API as a set of non-defensive functions that wrap DJCL. We compared the performance of our implementation on benchmarks provided by Chrome and Microsoft; our code is as fast as both native and JavaScript implementations provided by mainstream browsers.

4.3 JSON Serialization

Messaging applications in JavaScript widely use the JSON format, which is considered more compact and easier to use programmatically than XML. JSON defines a JavaScript-like syntax for serializing scalar objects and arrays. For example, the object `{a:"s",b:[0,1]}` is written in JSON notation as the string '`{"a":"s","b":[0,1]}`'.

All modern browsers provide libraries for serializing and deserializing JSON objects. The function `JSON.stringify` takes any JavaScript object and serializes it as a string, typically by ignoring any functions it finds in the object's structure. Conversely, the function `JSON.parse` takes a string and attempts to reconstruct a scalar JavaScript object from the string. DJS programs cannot use the browser's JSON library, since it may have been tampered by the adversary. So we build a defensive JSON library (DJSON) to provide this functionality.

`DJSON.stringify` is conceptually a simple function; it takes an object, enumerates its properties, and writes them out to a string. However, since the attacker

---

[6] http://jsperf.org

may tamper the `Object` and `Array` prototypes, neither the `for...in` loop nor new APIs like `Object.keys` can be trusted to correctly enumerate properties. Consequently, `DJSON.stringify` takes an additional parameter — an object "schema" that describes the type of the JSON object. For example, to serialize the JSON example above, an application would call `DJSON.stringify` as follows:

```
1 DJSON.stringify({a:"s",b:[0,1]}, // JSON object
2              {type:"object", // Schema object
3               props: [
4                 {name:"a",value:"string"},
5                 {name:"b",value:{
6                       type:"array",
7                       props:[{name:"0",value:"number"},
8                              {name:"1",value:"number"}]}}]})
```

Given such a schema, `DJSON.stringify` ensures that the given object has all the fields and array indices declared in the schema before returning the serialized string; if the object does not match the schema it returns an error.

Implementing `DJSON.parse` is a bit more challenging, since the function needs to create a new object with an arbitrary number of properties. Creating an empty object and adding properties to it would not work, since the attacker may have set up malicious setter functions on the Object prototype. We define a defensive `DJSON.parse` function that requires three parameters — the string to parse, the schema for the expected JSON object, and a pre-allocated object that matches this expected schema. `DJSON.parse` does not create a new object; instead, it fills in this pre-allocated object. To return to our example, to parse the serialized JSON string, the application would first create an object `result` and then call `DJSON.parse` as follows:

```
1 var result = {a:"",b:[-1,-1]}; // Pre-allocated JSON object
2 DJSON.parse('{"a":"s","b":[0,1]}', // Serialized JSON string
3              {type:"object", // Schema object
4               props: [
5                 {name:"a",value:"string"},
6                 {name:"b",value:{
7                       type:"array",
8                       props:[{name:"0",value:"number"},
9                              {name:"1",value:"number"}]}}]},
10             result)
```

The schemas used for these two functions are closely related to the expected object types of the JSON objects. Indeed, our typechecker processes these schemas as type annotations and uses them to infer types for code that uses these functions.

Using explicit schemas with fixed object and array lengths imposes an important restriction; our JSON library only works with objects whose sizes are known in advance to the programmer. We have implemented extensions of DJS that use ML-style algebraic constructors (e.g. `cons`, `nil`) to allow extensible objects and arrays. The resulting encoded objects are less efficient than object literals but more flexible since they can represent dynamically-sized objects.

By combining our cryptographic library DJCL with DJSON, we implemented a family of IETF standards collectively called Javascript Object Signing and Encryption (JOSE) [21]. These standards include JSON Web Tokens (JWT), which specifies authenticated JSON messages, and JSON Web Encryption, which specifies encrypted JSON messages. Our defensive JOSE library interoperates with other implementations of these specfications, and we use it to implement various cryptographic messaging protocols, such as Secure RPC (see below).

4.4   Applications

We briefly describe four DJS applications that we built using our libraries. We ran the DJS typechecker to verify their defensiveness. Furthermore, as we shall see in the next subsection, we also verifed their cryptographic security against both network and web attackers by translation to the applied pi calculus.

Secure RPC. Using the JOSE libraries, we programmed a variation of the secure messaging program of Section 2 in DJS. The program consists of a core typechecked API object that embeds a secret shared between the program and a trusted server S.

The API provides two functions: makeRequest takes a string and returns a serialized JWT object containing the argument and its HMAC; processResponse takes a string, parses it as a JWT object, verifies the HMAC and returns the payload (or an error). A non-defensive function then wraps this API to implement a secure RPC: it calls makeRequest to create the request, sends this request via XMLHttpRequest (or postMessage) to a recipient, waits for a response, calls processResponse and returns the result.

The security goal of this RPC application is authentication and correlation for the request and response. The goal relies on the secrecy of the HMAC key and the correct use of the HMAC function. Defensiveness guarantees that the key is not accidentally leaked, but the authentication protocol implemented by the application may still fail to achieve its goals. For example, the application may leak the key in its outgoing message or serialize the message incorrectly before MACing. We will see how to analyze the cryptographic security of the application using the protocol analyzer ProVerif [13].

Password Manager Bookmarklet. We implemented a version of the LastPass password manager bookmarklet in DJS. The bookmarklet embeds a secret HMAC key, and when it is clicked on a website W, it performs a secure RPC with the LastPass website using this key to retrieve the currently logged in LastPass user's username and password for the website W and fill it in.

The security goal of the bookmarklet is to enable LastPass to authenticate that the user clicked the bookmarklet on the hosting website W. In particular, a malicious website W should not be able to steal the secret HMAC key or impersonate another website S, even if the user clicks the bookmarklet at W. At LastPass, the bookmarklet is authenticated by the secret key, whereas the website W is authenticated by the Origin header that the browser sends along with the `XMLHttpRequest` message. While many previous attacks have been found on password manager bookmarklets [2,10], our DJS-based solution is the first that can verifiably protect the bookmarklet and its secrets in this scenario.

Protecting Single Sign-On Tokens. We implemented a version of the Facebook JavaScript library that uses a DJS component to protect the user's Facebook access token from other scripts on the page. The DJS component embeds the access token and provides an API though which scripts on the page can access an authorized subset of the user's Facebook profile. The DJS script uses the access token as a MAC key to avoid leaking it to the environment.

In this design, malicious scripts on the page can access (parts of) the user's Facebook profile as long as the page is open, but do not get direct (long-term, offline) access to the access token, and they lose all access when the page is closed and the DJS script stops executing. In particular, the malicious script can never use the token to impersonate the user at another website.

An Encrypted Storage API. Our final DJS application implements an API for encrypted cloud storage. User files are encrypted at the client (via DJCL) and uploaded to a cloud server. The file encryption keys themselves are stored encrypted in local storage, using a master encryption key derived from a passphrase that is known only to the user. The user enters the passphrase on a protected login page (served from a distinct origin), and the derived key is subsequently embedded into a DJS script on the main storage service website.

By using DJS, we isolate the application code that implements cryptography from the rest of the page. Hence, an XSS attack on the main website cannot steal the file encryption key or the master encryption key. However, it can still read and modify user files as long as the page is open. As such, our proposed DJS API is the first to protect long term secrets on encrypted cloud storage websites from XSS attacks, unlike many previous designs [7].

4.5   Verifying Applications with ProVerif

Well-typed programs in DJS enjoy functional integrity and heap isolation, so the environment can only interact with them through their exported scalar (`string -> string`) APIs. Even if the environment is malicious, it cannot access or interfere with the internal state of the program. This isolation guarantee makes it possible to analyze a DJS program independently of its environment, an immense advantage over traditional JavaScript.

DJS prevents some kinds of accidental leakage of secrets, but it cannot protect a program that leaks secrets through its exported interface. For example, even a well-typed DJS program may foolishly return a secret in the result of a public function. Furthermore, even though the DJCL cryptographic library is defensive, it cannot ensure that the application uses it correctly to achieve its security goals.

Designing application-layer cryptographic protocols is an error prone task (e.g. see the attacks in [10]). We advocate the use of formal protocol analysis tools that can verify that DJS applications meet their goals.

We define a translation from DJS programs to processes in the applied pi calculus. The translation mimics previous formal translations to the applied pi calculus from F# [11] and Java [6]. These previous works prove translation soundness — every attack on the source program is present in its translation. However, we do not prove any soundness result for our translation.

Appendix B provides a detailed listing of the applied pi calculus translation for a simple DJS program that can send and receive authenticated messages.

Each DJS function is translated to a process following Milner's famous "functions as processes" encoding of the lambda calculus into the pi calculus [22]. The translated process waits for arguments on an input channel, computes the function result and sends it back on an output channel.

The DJS programmer may selectively prefix any function name by _lib. (thus placing it in the _lib object) to indicate that the code of the function should not be translated; instead the function should be treated as a trusted primitive. For example, we label all cryptographic primitives and encoding functions as trusted. Their code is not verified; instead, calls to these functions are translated to calls to symbolic constructors and destructors in the applied pi calculus.

The JavaScript heap and stack frames are modeled by a global private table heap that is indexed by unique references (fresh pi calculus names). Each object, array, function, and local variable corresponds to an entry in the table. A function can read and write an entry as long as it knows its reference.

Programs may contain two kinds of security annotations that will be treated specially in the translation. A function may log a security event by calling _lib. event. For example, _lib.event(Send(a,b,x)) may indicate that a is going to use a secret key to authenticate a message x to b. These are translated to events in the applied pi calculus and are then used to specify authentication goals. A function may also label a certain value as secret (_lib.secret(x)). This expression is translated as the application of a private constructor, and is used to specify secrecy goals for an application.

The translated applied pi calculus process is composed with the WebSpi library and analyzed for violations of its security goals using the cryptographic protocol analyzer ProVerif. The WebSpi library models web browsers, web servers, and enables a variety of well-known web and network attacks. To model the malicious JavaScript environment, we give the attacker read and write access to the global heap table, but only for the entries for which he knows the references. The attacker cannot forge pointers. In addition, the attacker is given control over all public channels and access to the function input and output channels for the API exported by the DJS program. The attacker cannot directly access the processes corresponding to internal functions.

Table 1 reports the ProVerif verification time for a few DJS applications. As depicted in Appendix B, ProVerif may find a counterexample to the security goals, which probably indicates an attack on the source DJS program. If ProVerif verifies the security goals, one gain some confidence in the application, but we caution that there may be other attacks not captured by our WebSpi model. Occasionally, ProVerif may not terminate, typically when the source program uses loops or recursive functions. In this case, the programmer may need to edit the source program or its translation to help ProVerif reach a conclusion.

5 Conclusions

We presented the design of DJS, a defensive subset of JavaScript that is particularly suited for programming web security components that may execute in malicious environments. DJS is not meant for programming whole websites. It does not allow access to any external libraries and imposes many language restrictions that may feel awkward to a typical JavaScript programmer, but are necessary for security on malicious websites. We have shown that large libraries such as DJCL and various applications can be programmed in DJS, at little cost to performance but great gains in security. We showed how DJS applications can be automatically verified for security using the cryptographic protocol analyzer ProVerif. As future work, we plan to relax some of the restrictions of DJS by relying on frozen and unforgeable objects in the environment, as well as by using more expressive types to capture more safe programs. We also plan to prove a formal soundness result for our translation from DJS to the applied pi calculus.

References

1. Adida, B.: Helios: Web-based open-audit voting. In: USENIX Security Symposium, pp. 335–348 (2008)
2. Adida, B., Barth, A., Jackson, C.: Rootkits for JavaScript environments. In: WOOT (2009)
3. Akhawe, D., Barth, A., Lam, P., Mitchell, J., Song, D.: Towards a formal foundation of web security. In: IEEE CSF 2010, pp. 290–304 (2010)
4. Akhawe, D., Saxena, P., Song, D.: Privilege separation in HTML5 applications. In: USENIX Security (2012)
5. Arapinis, M., Bursuc, S., Ryan, M.: Privacy supporting cloud computing: ConfiChair, a case study. In: Degano, P., Guttman, J.D. (eds.) POST 2012. LNCS, vol. 7215, pp. 89–108. Springer, Heidelberg (2012)
6. Avalle, M., Pironti, A., Pozza, D., Sisto, R.: JavaSPI: A framework for security protocol implementation. International Journal of Secure Software Engineering 2, 34–48 (2011)
7. Bansal, C., Bhargavan, K., Delignat-Lavaud, A., Maffeis, S.: Keys to the cloud: Formal analysis and concrete attacks on encrypted web storage. In: Basin, D., Mitchell, J.C. (eds.) POST 2013. LNCS, vol. 7796, pp. 126–146. Springer, Heidelberg (2013)
8. Bansal, C., Bhargavan, K., Maffeis, S.: Discovering concrete attacks on website authorization by formal analysis. In: CSF, pp. 247–262 (2012)
9. Barth, A., Felt, A.P., Saxena, P., Boodman, A.: Protecting browsers from extension vulnerabilities. In: Network and Distributed System Security Symposium, NDSS (2010)
10. Bhargavan, K., Delignat-Lavaud, A.: Web-based attacks on host-proof encrypted storage. In: WOOT (2012)
11. Bhargavan, K., Fournet, C., Gordon, A.D., Tse, S.: Verified interoperable implementations of security protocols. In: CSFW, pp. 139–152 (2006)
12. Bhargavan, K., Delignat-Lavaud, A., Maffeis, S.: Language-based defenses against untrusted browser origins. In: 22nd USENIX Security Symposium (2013)

13. Blanchet, B.: Automatic verification of correspondences for security protocols. Journal of Computer Security 17(4), 363–434 (2009)
14. Blanchet, B., Smyth, B.: ProVerif: Automatic Cryptographic Protocol Verifier, User Manual and Tutorial, http://www.proverif.inria.fr/manual.pdf
15. Dahl, D., Sleevi, R.: Web Cryptography API. W3C Working Draft (2013)
16. ECMA International: ECMAScript language specification. Stardard ECMA-262, 3rd edn. (1999)
17. Fett, D., Küsters, R., Schmitz, G.: An Expressive Model for the Web Infrastructure: Definition and Application to the BrowserID SSO System. In: 35th IEEE Symposium on Security and Privacy (S&P 2014). IEEE Computer Society (2014)
18. Fournet, C., Swamy, N., Chen, J., Dagand, P., Strub, P., Livshits, B.: Fully abstract compilation to JavaScript. In: POPL 2013 (2013)
19. Hardt, D.: The OAuth 2.0 authorization framework. IETF RFC 6749 (2012)
20. Hodges, J., Jackson, C., Barth, A.: HTTP Strict Transport Security (HSTS). IETF RFC 6797 (2012)
21. IETF: JavaScript Object Signing and Encryption, JOSE (2012), http://tools.ietf.org/wg/jose/
22. Milner, R.: Functions as processes. In: Paterson, M. (ed.) ICALP 1990. LNCS, vol. 443, pp. 167–180. Springer, Heidelberg (1990)
23. Stark, E., Hamburg, M., Boneh, D.: Symmetric cryptography in JavaScript. In: ACSAC, pp. 373–381 (2009)
24. Sterne, B., Barth, A.: Content Security Policy 1.0. W3C Candidate Recommendation (2012)
25. Swamy, N., Fournet, C., Rastogi, A., Bhargavan, K., Chen, J., Strub, P.Y., Bierman, G.M.: Gradual typing embedded securely in javascript. In: ACM Symposium on Principles of Programming Languages (POPL), pp. 425–438 (2014)
26. Wang, R., Chen, S., Wang, X.: Signing me onto your accounts through facebook and google: A traffic-guided security study of commercially deployed single-sign-on web services. In: IEEE S&P, pp. 365–379. IEEE Computer Society (2012)
27. Woo, T., Lam, S.: A semantic model for authentication protocols. In: IEEE Symposium on Security and Privacy, pp. 178–194 (1993)
28. Zalewski, M.: Browser Security Handbook

A   Defensive HMAC-SHA-256 Code

To illustrate the DJS programming style as it is used in cryptographic libraries, we present below the full code for the HMAC and SHA-256 functions implemented in DJCL. The code shown here is accepted by the DJS typechecker and hence does not rely on any external functions. To see the code for other defensive cryptographic functions and applications and to try out variations of these programs against the DJS tpechecker, visit http://defesnsivejs.com.

```
1 /**
2  * A hashing library to include with Defensive Applications
3  */
4 var hashing = (function()
5 {
6
7   return {
```

```
 8  /** SHA-256 hash function.
 9   * @param {string} msg message to hash, as a hex string
10   * @returns {string} hash, as an hex string.
11   * @alias hashing.sha256
12   */
13    sha256: {
14      name: 'sha-256',
15      identifier: '608648016503040201',
16      size: 32,
17      block: 64,
18
19      key: [0x428a2f98, 0x71374491, 0xb5c0fbcf, 0xe9b5dba5,
20            0x3956c25b, 0x59f111f1, 0x923f82a4, 0xab1c5ed5,
21            0xd807aa98, 0x12835b01, 0x243185be, 0x550c7dc3,
22            0x72be5d74, 0x80deb1fe, 0x9bdc06a7, 0xc19bf174,
23            0xe49b69c1, 0xefbe4786, 0x0fc19dc6, 0x240ca1cc,
24            0x2de92c6f, 0x4a7484aa, 0x5cb0a9dc, 0x76f988da,
25            0x983e5152, 0xa831c66d, 0xb00327c8, 0xbf597fc7,
26            0xc6e00bf3, 0xd5a79147, 0x06ca6351, 0x14292967,
27            0x27b70a85, 0x2e1b2138, 0x4d2c6dfc, 0x53380d13,
28            0x650a7354, 0x766a0abb, 0x81c2c92e, 0x92722c85,
29            0xa2bfe8a1, 0xa81a664b, 0xc24b8b70, 0xc76c51a3,
30            0xd192e819, 0xd6990624, 0xf40e3585, 0x106aa070,
31            0x19a4c116, 0x1e376c08, 0x2748774c, 0x34b0bcb5,
32            0x391c0cb3, 0x4ed8aa4a, 0x5b9cca4f, 0x682e6ff3,
33            0x748f82ee, 0x78a5636f, 0x84c87814, 0x8cc70208,
34            0x90befffa, 0xa4506ceb, 0xbef9a3f7, 0xc67178f2],
35
36      hash: function(s)
37      {
38      var s = s + '\x80', len = s.length, blocks = len >> 6,
39          chunk = len & 63, res = '', p = '',
40          i = 0, j = 0, k = 0, l = 0,
41          H = [0x6a09e667, 0xbb67ae85, 0x3c6ef372, 0xa54ff53a,
42               0x510e527f, 0x9b05688c, 0x1f83d9ab, 0x5be0cd19],
43          w = [0,0,0,0,0,0,0,0,0,0,0,0,0,0,0,0];

45      while(chunk++ != 56)
46      {
47       s+="\x00";
48       if(chunk == 64){ blocks++; chunk = 0; }
49      }

51      for(s+="\x00\x00\x00\x00", chunk=3, len=8*(len-1);
52          chunk >= 0; chunk--)
53       s += encoding.b2a(len >> (8*chunk) &255);

55      for(i=0; i < s.length; i++)
56      {
57       j = (j<<8) + encoding.a2b(s[i]);
```

```
58        if((i&3)==3){ w[(i>>2)&15] = j; j = 0; }
59        if((i&63)==63) this._round(H,w);
60      }
61
62      for(i=0; i < H.length; i++)
63       for(j=3; j >= 0; j--)
64        res += encoding.b2a(H[i] >> (8*j) & 255);
65
66      return res;
67      },
68
69      _round: function(H,w)
70      {
71      var a = H[0], b = H[1], c = H[2], d = H[3], e = H[4],
72         f = H[5], g = H[6], h = H[7], t = 0, u = 0, v = 0, tmp = 0;
73
74      for(t=0; t < 64; t++)
75      {
76       if(t < 16) tmp = w[t&15];
77       else
78       {
79        u = w[(t+1)&15]; v = w[(t+14)&15];
80        tmp = w[t&15] = ((u>>>7 ^ u>>>18 ^ u>>>3 ^ u<<25 ^ u<<14) +
81                        (v>>>17 ^ v>>>19 ^ v>>>10 ^ v<<15 ^ v<<13) +
82                        w[t&15] + w[(t+9)&15]) | 0;
83       }
84
85       tmp = (tmp + h + (e>>>6 ^ e>>>11 ^ e>>>25 ^ e<<26 ^ e<<21 ^ e<<7)
86           + (g ^ e & (f^g)) + this.key[t&63]);
87       h = g; g = f; f = e; e = d + tmp | 0; d = c; c = b; b = a;
88       a = (tmp + ((b&c) ^ (d&(b^c))) + (b>>>2 ^ b>>>13 ^ b>>>22 ^ b<<30
89           ^ b<<19 ^ b<<10)) | 0;
89      }
90
91      H[0]=H[0]+a|0; H[1]=H[1]+b|0; H[2]=H[2]+c|0; H[3]=H[3]+d|0;
92      H[4]=H[4]+e|0; H[5]=H[5]+f|0; H[6]=H[6]+g|0; H[7]=H[7]+h|0;
93      }
94    },
95
96 /** The hash function to use for HMAC, hashing.sha256 by default
97  * @alias hashing.hmac_hash
98  */
99  hmac_hash: sha256,
100
101 /** HMAC: Hash-based message authentication code
102  * @param {string} key key of the authentication
103  * @param {string} msg message to authenticate
104  * @returns {string} authentication code, as an hex string.
105  * @alias hashing.HMAC
106  */
```

```
107   HMAC: function(key, msg)
108   {
109     var key = key+'', msg = msg+'', i = 0, h = this.hmac_hash,
110         c = 0, p = '', inner = "", outer = "";
111
112     if(key.length > h.block) key = h.hash(key);
113     while(key.length < h.block) key += "\x00";
114
115     for(i=0; i < key.length; i++)
116     {
117       c = encoding.a2b(key[i]);
118       inner += encoding.b2a(c ^ 0x36);
119       outer += encoding.b2a(c ^ 0x5C);
120     }
121
122     return encoding.astr2hstr(h.hash(outer + h.hash(inner + msg)));
123   }
124   };
125 })();
```

B   Verification Example

Source Program. We begin with the following DJS program that uses a cryptographic hash function _lib.hmac (as defined above) to authenticated messages between two scripts that are running on the same malicious page and which share a symmetric HMAC key.

Both scripts run the same core DJS program that embeds the key mac_key and provides an API with three functions:

- mac takes a string message x, logs a security event Send(x), and returns the HMAC of x using the key mac_key.
- verify takes a string message x and a string t and verifies that t is the HMAC of x using mac_key. It then logs the event Accept(x,t,res) with the boolean result of the verification and returns the boolean.
- guess is used to specify syntactic secrecy. It takes a string argument k and logs the event Leaked(k,**true**) if k is the same as the secret key mac_key.

These core functions may be used by untrusted wrapper functions to create messages that are then sent from one script to other via any communication mechanism, such as window.postMessage. We assume that this external wrapper code is under the control of the adversary, who may subvert it by tampering with the window object. Hence, for verification, we assume that the attacker can directly call our core API and state our goals using security events in this API.

The intuition for the security events is that whenever Accept(x,t,**true**) is logged for a message x, that is the recipient program accepts x, it must be the case that Send(x) has been logged before, that is the sender program must have intended to send x. This is called a correspondence assertion [27] and is a common way of formalizing authentication goals in cryptographic protocols. Conversely, we expect that the event Leaked(k,true) is never logged, that is the HMAC key remains unknown to the adversary.

These authentication and secrecy queries are embedded on the top of the script using the _lib.spec function, which tells the ProVerif translator to directly embed its argument into the generated scripts. We run the ProVerif translator on this simple DJS library and verify that the API satisfies these queries.

```
1  /* Declaring Events */
2  _lib.spec("event Send(String)");
3  _lib.spec("event Accept(String,String,Boolean)");
4  _lib.spec("event Leaked(String,Boolean)");
5
6  /* Sanity Check: Are the Events Reachable? */
7  _lib.spec("query x:String; event(Send(x))");
8  _lib.spec("query x:String,t:String; event(Accept(x,t,bool_true()))");
9
10 /* Authentication Query */
11 _lib.spec("query x:String,t:String; event(Accept(x,t,bool_true())) ==>
       event(Send(x))");
12
13 /* Secrecy Query */
14 _lib.spec("query x:String; event(Leaked(x,bool_true()))");
15
16 x = (function()
17 {
18   var mac_key = _lib.secret("xxx");
19
20   var mac = function (x) {
21     _lib.event(_lib.Send(x));
22     return _lib.hmac(x, mac_key);
23   }
24
25   var verify = function (x,t) {
26     var res = _lib.hmac(x, mac_key) === t;
27     _lib.event(_lib.Accept(x,t,res));
28     return res ? "yes" : "no";
29   }
30
31   var guess = function (k) {
32     var res = k == mac_key;
33     _lib.event(_lib.Leaked(k,res));
34     return res ? "yes" : "no";
35   }
36
37   var _ = function(s)
38   {
39     var o = _lib.DJSON_parse(s, {t: "", h: ""});
40     var h = o.h;
41
```

```
42 // oops = mac_key;
43    return (o.t == "" ? guess(h) :
44          (h == "" ? mac(o.t) :
45          verify(o.t, h)));
46  }
47
48    return function(s){if(typeof s=="string") return _(s)};
49 })();
```

Generated Model. The ProVerif script generated by our model extraction tool (DJS2PV) is presented below to illustrate the translation. The script uses the typed applied pi calculus syntax described in [14]. It shows how the various DJS objects and variables are stored in the `heap` table, how the functions are encoded as processes, how the call to the `_lib.hmac` function is turned into a function call, and how all constant strings are extracted as top-level declarations.

The generated script relies on an external WebSpi library that defines all the types (`String`, `Boolean`, `MemLoc`, `Function`), the cryptographic functions (`hmac`, `secret`), and a table representing the JavaScript heap (`heap`). The WebSpi library encodes a rich attacker model that includes both web and network attacks. To verify DJS, we extend WebSpi to allow the attacker direct access to the JavaScript heap: the attacker can insert any object into the heap and read any object for which he knows the table index (representing the heap reference). More details on the original WebSpi library can be obtained from `http://prosecco.inria.fr/webspi`. Other verification examples that rely on WebSpi have appeared in [8,7].

```
 1 free var_x:Memloc.
 2
 3 free str_1:String.
 4 free str_2:String.
 5 free str_3:String.
 6 free str_4:String.
 7 free str_5:String.
 8
 9 event Send(String).
10 event Accept(String,String,Boolean).
11 event Leaked(String,Boolean).
12 query x:String; event(Leaked(x,bool_true())).
13 query x:String; event(Send(x)).
14 query x:String,y:String; event(Accept(x,y,bool_true())).
15 query x:String,y:String; event(Accept(x,y,bool_true())) => event(Send(x))
16
17 process
18 (new fun_1:channel;
19 (!in(fun_1, (ret_1:channel));
20 new var_mac_key:Memloc;
21 insert heap(var_mac_key,mem_string(secret(str_1)));
22 new var_mac:Memloc;
```

```
23 new fun_2:channel;
24 (!in(fun_2, (ret_2:channel,arg_x:String));
25 new var_x:Memloc;
26 insert heap(var_x,mem_string(arg_x));
27 get heap(=var_x, mem_string(val_1)) in
28 event Send(val_1);
29 get heap(=var_x, mem_string(val_2)) in
30 get heap(=var_mac_key, mem_string(val_3)) in
31 out(ret_2,hmac(val_2,val_3));
32 0)|
33 insert heap(var_mac,
34   mem_function(function(fun_2)));
35 new var_verify:Memloc;
36 new fun_3:channel;
37 (!in(fun_3, (ret_3:channel,arg_x:String,arg_t:String));
38 new var_x:Memloc;
39 insert heap(var_x,mem_string(arg_x));
40 new var_t:Memloc;
41 insert heap(var_t,mem_string(arg_t));
42 new var_res:Memloc;
43 get heap(=var_x, mem_string(val_4)) in
44 get heap(=var_mac_key, mem_string(val_5)) in
45 get heap(=var_t, mem_string(val_6)) in
46 insert heap(var_res,mem_boolean(equal(mem_string(hmac(val_4,val_5)),
        mem_string(val_6))));
47 get heap(=var_x, mem_string(val_7)) in
48 get heap(=var_t, mem_string(val_8)) in
49 get heap(=var_res, mem_boolean(val_9)) in
50 event Accept(val_7,val_8,val_9);
51 get heap(=var_res, mem_boolean(val_10)) in
52 let val_11=(if val_10=bool_true() then str_2 else str_3) in
53 out(ret_3,val_11);
54 0)|
55 insert heap(var_verify,
56   mem_function(function(fun_3)));
57 new var_guess:Memloc;
58 new fun_4:channel;
59 (!in(fun_4, (ret_4:channel,arg_k:String));
60 new var_k:Memloc;
61 insert heap(var_k,mem_string(arg_k));
62 new var_res:Memloc;
63 get heap(=var_k, mem_string(val_12)) in
64 get heap(=var_mac_key, mem_string(val_13)) in
65 insert heap(var_res,mem_boolean(equal(mem_string(val_12),mem_string(
        val_13))));
66 get heap(=var_k, mem_string(val_14)) in
67 get heap(=var_res, mem_boolean(val_15)) in
68 event Leaked(val_14,val_15);
69 get heap(=var_res, mem_boolean(val_16)) in
70 let val_17=(if val_16=bool_true() then str_2 else str_3) in
```

```
71 out(ret_4,val_17);
72 0)|
73 insert heap(var_guess,
74   mem_function(function(fun_4)));
75 new var__:Memloc;
76 new fun_5:channel;
77 (!in(fun_5, (ret_5:channel,arg_s:String));
78 new var_s:Memloc;
79 insert heap(var_s,mem_string(arg_s));
80 new var_o:Memloc;
81 get heap(=var_s, mem_string(val_18)) in
82 insert heap(var_o,mem_object(DJSON_parse(val_18,obj_add(obj_add(obj_empty
       (), obj_prop(str_4, mem_string(string_empty))), obj_prop(str_5,
       mem_string(string_empty))))));
83 new var_h:Memloc;
84 get heap(=var_o, mem_object(val_19)) in
85 insert heap(var_h,mem_string(obj_property_string(val_19,str_4)));
86 get heap(=var_o, mem_object(val_32)) in
87 get heap(=var_guess, mem_function(val_20)) in
88 get heap(=var_h, mem_string(val_21)) in
89 let function(fun_6)=val_20 in
90 new ret_6:channel;
91 out(fun_6, (ret_6,val_21));
92 in(ret_6, val_22:String);
93 get heap(=var_h, mem_string(val_30)) in
94 get heap(=var_mac, mem_function(val_23)) in
95 get heap(=var_o, mem_object(val_24)) in
96 let function(fun_7)=val_23 in
97 new ret_7:channel;
98 out(fun_7, (ret_7,obj_property_string(val_24,str_5)));
99 in(ret_7, val_25:String);
100 get heap(=var_verify, mem_function(val_26)) in
101 get heap(=var_o, mem_object(val_27)) in
102 get heap(=var_h, mem_string(val_28)) in
103 let function(fun_8)=val_26 in
104 new ret_8:channel;
105 out(fun_8, (ret_8,obj_property_string(val_27,str_5),val_28));
106 in(ret_8, val_29:String);let val_31=(if equal(mem_string(val_30),
       mem_string(string_empty))=bool_true() then val_25 else val_29) in
107 let val_33=(if equal(mem_string(obj_property_string(val_32,str_5)),
       mem_string(string_empty))=bool_true() then val_22 else val_31) in
108 out(ret_5,val_33);
109 0)|
110 insert heap(var__,
111   mem_function(function(fun_5)));
112 new fun_9:channel;(!in(fun_9, (ret_9:channel, arg_s:Memval));let
       mem_string(s)=arg_s in (new var_s:Memloc;insert heap(var_s,arg_s);
       get heap(=var__, mem_function(val_34)) in
113 get heap(=var_s, mem_string(val_35)) in
114 let function(fun_10)=val_34 in
```

```
115 new ret_10:channel;
116 out(fun_10, (ret_10,val_35));
117 in(ret_10, val_36:String);
118 out(ret_9,val_36);
119 0) else out(ret_9, undefined()))|
120 out(ret_1,function(fun_9));
121 0)| let function(fun_11)=function(fun_1) in
122 new ret_11:channel;
123 out(fun_11, (ret_11));
124 in(ret_11, val_37:Function);
125 insert heap(var_x, mem_function(val_37));
126 0) |
127 attackerHeap()
```

Example Attack. If line 42 is uncommented in the source DJS program (causing the key to be accidentally written to a global variable oops, ProVerif is able to show that the Leaked event is triggered, and produces the following trace. (Note: this bug is also caught by the DJS typechecker as a defensiveness violation.)

```
1 new fun_8 creating fun_398886 at {1}
2 new ret_260 creating ret_398877 at {419}
3 out(fun_398886, ret_398877) at {420} received at {3} in copy a_398865
4 new var_mac_key creating var_mac_key_398884 at {4} in copy a_398865
5 new k_11 creating k_398878 at {6} in copy a_398865
6 insert heap(var_mac_key_398884,mem_string(k_398878)) at {7} in copy
       a_398865
7 new var_mac creating var_mac_399613 at {8} in copy a_398865
8 new fun_12 creating fun_399614 at {9} in copy a_398865
9 insert heap(var_mac_399613,mem_function(function(fun_399614))) at {19} in
       copy a_398865
10 new var_verify creating var_verify_399615 at {20} in copy a_398865
11 new fun_18 creating fun_399616 at {21} in copy a_398865
12 insert heap(var_verify_399615,mem_function(function(fun_399616))) at {43}
       in copy a_398865
13 new var_guess creating var_guess_398890 at {44} in copy a_398865
14 new fun_31 creating fun_398879 at {45} in copy a_398865
15 insert heap(var_guess_398890,mem_function(function(fun_398879))) at {63}
       in copy a_398865
16 new var__ creating var___398897 at {64} in copy a_398865
17 new fun_41 creating fun_398880 at {65} in copy a_398865
18 insert heap(var___398897,mem_function(function(fun_398880))) at {402} in
       copy a_398865
19 new fun_249 creating fun_398892 at {403} in copy a_398865
20 out(ret_398877, function(fun_398892)) at {417} in copy a_398865 received
       at {421}
21 insert heap(var_x,mem_function(function(fun_398892))) at {422}
22 in(pub, var_x) at {424} in copy a_398875
23 get heap(var_x,mem_function(function(fun_398892))) at {425} in copy
       a_398875
24 out(pub, mem_function(function(fun_398892))) at {426} in copy a_398875
```

```
25 in(fun_398892, (a_398872,mem_string(DJSON_stringify(a_398871)))) at {405}
      in copy a_398865, a_398873
26 new var_s_253 creating var_s_398896 at {407} in copy a_398865, a_398873
27 insert heap(var_s_398896,mem_string(DJSON_stringify(a_398871))) at {408}
      in copy a_398865, a_398873
28 get heap(var___398897,mem_function(function(fun_398880))) at {409} in
      copy a_398865, a_398873
29 get heap(var_s_398896,mem_string(DJSON_stringify(a_398871))) at {410} in
      copy a_398865, a_398873
30 new ret_257 creating ret_398893 at {412} in copy a_398865, a_398873
31 out(fun_398880, (ret_398893,DJSON_stringify(a_398871))) at {413} in copy
      a_398865, a_398873 received at {67} in copy a_398865, a_398874
32 new var_s creating var_s_398895 at {68} in copy a_398865, a_398874
33 insert heap(var_s_398895,mem_string(DJSON_stringify(a_398871))) at {69}
      in copy a_398865, a_398874
34 new var_o creating var_o_398894 at {70} in copy a_398865, a_398874
35 get heap(var_s_398895,mem_string(DJSON_stringify(a_398871))) at {71} in
      copy a_398865, a_398874
36 insert heap(var_o_398894,mem_object(DJSON_parse(DJSON_stringify(a_398871)
      ,obj_add(obj_add(obj_empty,obj_prop(str_4,mem_string(string_empty)))
      ,obj_prop(str_5,mem_string(string_empty)))))) at {72} in copy
      a_398865, a_398874
37 new var_h creating var_h_400490 at {73} in copy a_398865, a_398874
38 get heap(var_o_398894,mem_object(a_398871)) at {74} in copy a_398865,
      a_398874
39 insert heap(var_h_400490,mem_string(undefined_string)) at {240} in copy
      a_398865, a_398874
40 get heap(var_mac_key_398884,mem_string(k_398878)) at {241} in copy
      a_398865, a_398874
41 insert heap(var_oops,mem_string(k_398878)) at {242} in copy a_398865,
      a_398874
42 in(pub, var_oops) at {424} in copy a_398876
43 get heap(var_oops,mem_string(k_398878)) at {425} in copy a_398876
44 out(pub, mem_string(k_398878)) at {426} in copy a_398876
45 in(fun_398892, (a_398867,mem_string(DJSON_stringify(obj_add(a_398866,
      obj_prop(str_4,mem_string(k_398878))))))) at {405} in copy a_398865,
      a_398868
46 new var_s_253 creating var_s_398891 at {407} in copy a_398865, a_398868
47 insert heap(var_s_398891,mem_string(DJSON_stringify(obj_add(a_398866,
      obj_prop(str_4,mem_string(k_398878)))))) at {408} in copy a_398865,
      a_398868
48 get heap(var___398897,mem_function(function(fun_398880))) at {409} in
      copy a_398865, a_398868
49 get heap(var_s_398891,mem_string(DJSON_stringify(obj_add(a_398866,
      obj_prop(str_4,mem_string(k_398878)))))) at {410} in copy a_398865,
      a_398868
50 new ret_257 creating ret_398881 at {412} in copy a_398865, a_398868
51 out(fun_398880, (ret_398881,DJSON_stringify(obj_add(a_398866,obj_prop(
      str_4,mem_string(k_398878)))))) at {413} in copy a_398865, a_398868
      received at {67} in copy a_398865, a_398869
```

```
52 new var_s creating var_s_398889 at {68} in copy a_398865, a_398869
53 insert heap(var_s_398889,mem_string(DJSON_stringify(obj_add(a_398866,
       obj_prop(str_4,mem_string(k_398878)))))) at {69} in copy a_398865,
       a_398869
54 new var_o creating var_o_398888 at {70} in copy a_398865, a_398869
55 get heap(var_s_398889,mem_string(DJSON_stringify(obj_add(a_398866,
       obj_prop(str_4,mem_string(k_398878)))))) at {71} in copy a_398865,
       a_398869
56 insert heap(var_o_398888,mem_object(DJSON_parse(DJSON_stringify(obj_add(
       a_398866,obj_prop(str_4,mem_string(k_398878)))),obj_add(obj_add(
       obj_empty,obj_prop(str_4,mem_string(string_empty))),obj_prop(str_5,
       mem_string(string_empty)))))) at {72} in copy a_398865, a_398869
57 new var_h creating var_h_398887 at {73} in copy a_398865, a_398869
58 get heap(var_o_398888,mem_object(obj_add(a_398866,obj_prop(str_4,
       mem_string(k_398878))))) at {74} in copy a_398865, a_398869
59 insert heap(var_h_398887,mem_string(k_398878)) at {78} in copy a_398865,
       a_398869
60 get heap(var_mac_key_398884,mem_string(k_398878)) at {79} in copy
       a_398865, a_398869
61 insert heap(var_oops,mem_string(k_398878)) at {80} in copy a_398865,
       a_398869
62 get heap(var_o_398888,mem_object(obj_add(a_398866,obj_prop(str_4,
       mem_string(k_398878))))) at {81} in copy a_398865, a_398869
63 get heap(var_guess_398890,mem_function(function(fun_398879))) at {82} in
       copy a_398865, a_398869
64 get heap(var_h_398887,mem_string(k_398878)) at {83} in copy a_398865,
       a_398869
65 new ret_52 creating ret_398882 at {85} in copy a_398865, a_398869
66 out(fun_398879, (ret_398882,k_398878)) at {86} in copy a_398865, a_398869
       received at {47} in copy a_398865, a_398870
67 new var_k creating var_k_398885 at {48} in copy a_398865, a_398870
68 insert heap(var_k_398885,mem_string(k_398878)) at {49} in copy a_398865,
       a_398870
69 new var_res_33 creating var_res_398883 at {50} in copy a_398865, a_398870
70 get heap(var_k_398885,mem_string(k_398878)) at {51} in copy a_398865,
       a_398870
71 get heap(var_mac_key_398884,mem_string(k_398878)) at {52} in copy
       a_398865, a_398870
72 insert heap(var_res_398883,mem_boolean(equal(mem_string(k_398878),
       mem_string(k_398878)))) at {53} in copy a_398865, a_398870
73 get heap(var_k_398885,mem_string(k_398878)) at {54} in copy a_398865,
       a_398870
74 get heap(var_res_398883,mem_boolean(bool_true)) at {55} in copy a_398865,
       a_398870
75 event(Leaked(k_398878,bool_true)) at {56} in copy a_398865, a_398870
76 (*
77 The event Leaked(k_398878,bool_true) is executed.
78 A trace has been found.
79 RESULT not event(Leaked(x_338058,bool_true)) is false.
80 *)
```

Information Flow Control for Web Scripts

Willem De Groef, Dominique Devriese, Mathy Vanhoef, and Frank Piessens

iMinds-DistriNet,
KU Leuven,
3001 Leuven, Belgium
`firstname.lastname@cs.kuleuven.be`

Abstract. Modern web applications heavily rely on JavaScript code executing in the browser. These web scripts are useful for instance for improving the interactivity and responsiveness of web applications, and for gathering web analytics data. However, the execution of server-provided code in the browser also brings substantial security and privacy risks. Web scripts can access a fair amount of sensitive information, and can leak this information to anyone on the Internet. This tutorial paper discusses information flow control mechanisms for countering these threats. We formalize both a static, type-system based and a dynamic, multi-execution based enforcement mechanism, and show by means of examples how these mechanisms can enforce the security of information flows in web scripts.

Keywords: web scripts, JavaScript, security, information flow control.

1 Introduction

Modern interactive web applications heavily rely on browser-side scripts in languages such as JavaScript, for instance to propose completions while a user is typing into a text field. These scripts are usually event-driven programs that can react to user interface events such as key presses or mouse clicks, or to network events such as the arrival of HTTP responses. While handling events, scripts can display output to the user or send output on the network in the form of HTTP requests.

Listing 1.1 shows a simplified example of such a program that interactively proposes possible completions for a string that the user is typing into a textfield.

The first three lines declare an event handler for the *key up* event. That handler takes the current contents of the textfield with ID *field1*, and invokes a helper function that computes the possible completions (for instance by contacting a remote server). These possible completions are finally displayed in the text area with ID *suggestions*.

While browser-side scripts are very useful for building responsive interactive web applications, they also come with substantial security and privacy risks. Scripts have, and *need*, access to both user information and to remote HTTP servers. The completion example above can only perform its function if it can

A. Aldini et al. (Eds.): FOSAD VII, LNCS 8604, pp. 124–145, 2014.

Listing 1.1. Suggesting completions

```
1 window.onkeyup = function(e) {
2     suggestions.value = completions(field1.value);
3 }
4
5 function completions(s) {
6 // return possible completions of s
7 }
```

read what the user is typing, and if it can contact the remote server to retrieve possible completions. Unfortunately, a consequence of these capabilities of scripts is that they are commonly used to leak private information to untrusted network servers [18,26]. To illustrate these risks, Listing 1.2 shows an example of a script that implements a simple key logger in JavaScript. It installs an event handler to monitor key presses, and leaks every keystroke to `hacker.com`, using the jQuery ajax() function that sends an HTTP request to the URL provided as a parameter. The similarity of this example with the earlier completion example shows that it is a thin line between useful and dangerous scripts. The fact that many web sites include scripts from third parties [25] further amplifies the need for protective countermeasures.

Listing 1.2. Keylogger

```
1 var u = 'http://hacker.com/?=';
2 window.onkeypress = function(e) {
3     var leak = e.charCode;
4     $.ajax(u + leak);
5 }
```

Researchers have realized that mechanisms for information flow security are a promising countermeasure for web script-related threats, since such mechanisms allow the scripts to have access to private information but at the same time prevent it from leaking that information to untrusted servers.

Information flow security can be enforced *statically* or *dynamically*. The purpose of this tutorial article is to explain the essence of two techniques for enforcing information flow security for event-driven programs: a static technique based on typing, and a dynamic technique based on secure multi-execution.

The remainder of this tutorial paper is structured as follows. First, in Section 2, we define a formal scripting language that is a simple model of JavaScript. Then, in Section 3, we define information flow control and give both examples of scripts that are information flow secure and scripts that are insecure. Sections 4 and 5 define a static, respectively dynamic enforcement mechanism for information flow security and illustrate the mechanisms by means of examples. Section 6 provides a brief overview of the existing research in this area, and Section 7 concludes.

2   Formal Model of Web Scripts

2.1   Syntax

For the purpose of this tutorial paper, we use a very simple model of a web scripting language, strongly inspired by the model language introduced by Bohannon et al. [8]. The syntax is specified in Figure 1. We assume certain given disjoint sets of identifiers: $GVars$ is the set of identifiers for mutable global variables, $Chan$ is the set of identifiers for communication channel names, and Var is the set of identifiers for bound variables.

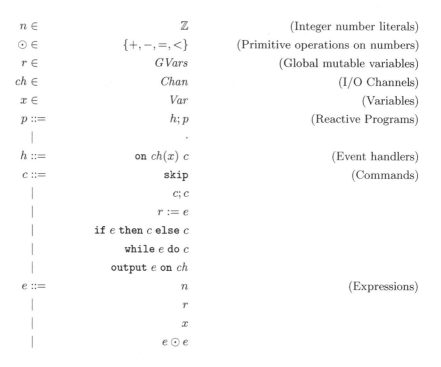

$n \in$	$\mathbb{Z}$	(Integer number literals)
$\odot \in$	$\{+,-,=,<\}$	(Primitive operations on numbers)
$r \in$	$GVars$	(Global mutable variables)
$ch \in$	$Chan$	(I/O Channels)
$x \in$	Var	(Variables)
$p ::=$	$h; p$	(Reactive Programs)
$\|$	$.$	
$h ::=$	$\textbf{on } ch(x)\ c$	(Event handlers)
$c ::=$	$\textbf{skip}$	(Commands)
$\|$	$c; c$	
$\|$	$r := e$	
$\|$	$\textbf{if } e \textbf{ then } c \textbf{ else } c$	
$\|$	$\textbf{while } e \textbf{ do } c$	
$\|$	$\textbf{output } e \textbf{ on } ch$	
$e ::=$	n	(Expressions)
$\|$	r	
$\|$	x	
$\|$	$e \odot e$	

Fig. 1. Formal syntax of our web scripting language

A program p is essentially a list of handlers, where each handler h specifies a command c to be executed on occurrence of an input event on channel ch. An input event always carries a single integer value, and that integer value is bound to the formal parameter x before the command c is executed. The syntax of commands is standard, with syntactic forms for the empty command (*skip*), sequential composition, assignment to global variables, conditional and looping constructs, and performing output on a channel. Expressions e are standard integer arithmetic expressions that can refer to formal parameters x declared in a handler definition, or to global variables r.

In examples we will assume the existence of I/O channels such as *KeyPress*, *Network*, *Display*, *MouseClick*, ... Scripts can output integers on these channels with the **output** command. For instance, **output** 10 **on** *Network* will output the integer 10 on the *Network* channel. They can react to inputs arriving on these channels by declaring event handlers. For instance, key presses are modeled as input events on the *KeyPress* channel carrying a single integer value that represents the scan code of the key that was pressed. For simplicity, we assume that all input events carry a single integer value, and that all output events are outputs of a single integer value.

As an example, the JavaScript key logger program from Listing 1.2 is rendered in our model language as:

$$\textbf{on } KeyPress(x) \textbf{ output } x \textbf{ on } Network$$

This script declares an event handler that upon each key press sends the key scan code on the network.

If we want to distinguish different network destinations (for instance communication to the same network origin the web page was loaded from and other network origins) we can use two separate channel identifiers *Network* and *SameOriginNetwork*. The completions example from Listing 1.1 could then be rendered as:

$$\textbf{on } KeyPress(x) \textbf{ output } x \textbf{ on } SameOriginNetwork$$

We could even use parameterized channel names such as *Network*(o) with o an *origin* of the form `http://www.kuleuven.be` for instance.

2.2 Semantics

To define the semantics of the model language, we define stores μ (assigning a current (integer) value to all global variable names) and outputs o (either the special "no output" constant • or an output of a number n on channel ch ($\text{out}_{ch(n)}$) (Figure 2). For updating of the store, we use the notation $\mu[r \mapsto n]$: it denotes the store equal to μ except that the global variable r now maps to the value n.

Using stores, we define a big-step operational semantics judgement for expressions $\mu \vdash e \downarrow n$ (in store μ, expression e evaluates to value n). This definition is completely standard (Figure 3).

Programs are event-driven. The judgement $(p)(i) \Downarrow c$ defines formally what command c program p will execute to handle the input event i. It is defined by the rules in Figure 4. Essentially, this looks up the handler for handling the input event, and substitutes the integer n received on the input channel for the

$$\mu \in \qquad\qquad Ref \to \mathbb{Z} \qquad\qquad \text{(Stores)}$$

$$o ::= \qquad\qquad \bullet \qquad\qquad \text{(Outputs)}$$

$$| \qquad\qquad \textbf{out}_{ch(n)}$$

$$i ::= \qquad\qquad \textbf{in}_{ch(n)} \qquad\qquad \text{(Input Events)}$$

$$ev ::= \qquad\qquad i \mid o \qquad\qquad \text{(Reactive Events)}$$

Fig. 2. Semantic structures

$$\frac{}{\mu \vdash n \downarrow n}\ (\text{E-Expr-Lit}) \qquad \frac{}{\mu \vdash r \downarrow \mu(r)}\ (\text{E-Expr-Ref})$$

$$\frac{\mu \vdash e_1 \downarrow n_1 \quad \mu \vdash e_2 \downarrow n_2}{\mu \vdash e_1 + e_2 \downarrow n_1 + n_2}\ (\text{E-Expr-Plus}) \qquad \frac{\mu \vdash e_1 \downarrow n_1 \quad \mu \vdash e_2 \downarrow n_2}{\mu \vdash e_1 - e_2 \downarrow n_1 - n_2}\ (\text{E-Expr-Minus})$$

$$\frac{\mu \vdash e_1 \downarrow n_1 \quad \mu \vdash e_2 \downarrow n_2 \quad n_1 \neq n_2}{\mu \vdash e_1 = e_2 \downarrow 0}\ (\text{E-Expr-Eq1})$$

$$\frac{\mu \vdash e_1 \downarrow n_1 \quad \mu \vdash e_2 \downarrow n_2 \quad n_1 = n_2}{\mu \vdash e_1 = e_2 \downarrow 1}\ (\text{E-Expr-Eq2})$$

$$\frac{\mu \vdash e_1 \downarrow n_1 \quad \mu \vdash e_2 \downarrow n_2 \quad n_1 \not< n_2}{\mu \vdash e_1 < e_2 \downarrow 0}\ (\text{E-Expr-Lt1})$$

$$\frac{\mu \vdash e_1 \downarrow n_1 \quad \mu \vdash e_2 \downarrow n_2 \quad n_1 < n_2}{\mu \vdash e_1 < e_2 \downarrow 1}\ (\text{E-Expr-Lt2})$$

Fig. 3. Semantics of expressions

formal parameter x in that handler. If no handler is defined in the program p for input i on this channel, we have $(p)(i) \Downarrow \texttt{skip}$.

$$\frac{}{(\textbf{on } ch(x) \textbf{ do } c; p)(\textbf{in}_{ch(n)}) \Downarrow [x \mapsto n]c}$$

$$\frac{(p)(\textbf{in}_{ch(n)}) \Downarrow c \quad ch \neq ch'}{(\textbf{on } ch'(x) \textbf{ do } c'; p)(\textbf{in}_{ch(n)}) \Downarrow c}$$

$$\frac{}{(\cdot)(\textbf{in}_{ch(n)}) \Downarrow \texttt{skip}}$$

Fig. 4. Determining the event handling command

Finally, the semantics of commands is given as a small-step operational semantics judgement $(\mu, c) \xrightarrow{o} (\mu', c')$ (executing command c in store μ produces an updated store μ' and new command c' producing output o). They are defined by the rules in Figure 5.

The *initial program state* is $(\mu_0, \texttt{skip})$ where μ_0 maps all global variables on 0. A program state is *passive* if it has the form $(\mu, \texttt{skip})$. We say a program is *well-formed* if it has no unbound variables (i.e. the only variable $x \in Var$ occurring

$$\frac{\rule{4cm}{0pt}}{(\mu, (\mathbf{skip}; c)) \overset{\cdot}{\to} (\mu, c)} \text{(E-STMT-SEQSKIP)}$$

$$\frac{(\mu, c_1) \overset{o}{\to} (\mu', c_1')}{(\mu, (c_1; c_2)) \overset{o}{\to} (\mu', (c_1'; c_2))} \text{(E-STMT-SEQ)}$$

$$\frac{\mu \vdash e \downarrow n}{(\mu, (r := e)) \overset{\cdot}{\to} (\mu[r \mapsto n], \mathbf{skip})} \text{(E-STMT-ASSIGN)}$$

$$\frac{\mu \vdash e \downarrow n \quad n \neq 0}{(\mu, \mathbf{if}\ e\ \mathbf{then}\ c_1\ \mathbf{else}\ c_2) \overset{\cdot}{\to} (\mu, c_1)} \text{(E-STMT-IF1)}$$

$$\frac{\mu \vdash e \downarrow n \quad n = 0}{(\mu, \mathbf{if}\ e\ \mathbf{then}\ c_1\ \mathbf{else}\ c_2) \overset{\cdot}{\to} (\mu, c_2)} \text{(E-STMT-IF2)}$$

$$\frac{\mu \vdash e \downarrow n \quad n \neq 0}{(\mu, \mathbf{while}\ e\ \mathbf{do}\ c) \overset{\cdot}{\to} (\mu, (c; \mathbf{while}\ e\ \mathbf{do}\ c))} \text{(E-STMT-WHILE1)}$$

$$\frac{\mu \vdash e \downarrow n \quad n = 0}{(\mu, \mathbf{while}\ e\ \mathbf{do}\ c) \overset{\cdot}{\to} (\mu, \mathbf{skip})} \text{(E-STMT-WHILE2)}$$

$$\frac{\mu \vdash e \downarrow n}{(\mu, \mathbf{output}\ e\ \mathbf{to}\ ch) \xrightarrow{\text{out}_{ch(n)}} (\mu, \mathbf{skip})} \text{(E-STMT-OUT)}$$

$$\frac{(p)(\mathbf{in}_{ch(n)}) \Downarrow c}{(\mu, \mathbf{skip}) \xrightarrow{\text{in}_{ch(n)}} (\mu, c)} \text{(E-INPUT)}$$

Fig. 5. Semantics of commands

in the body of a handler is the formal parameter of the handler – of course, the handler can also use global variables $r \in GVars$) . It is straightforward to prove that well-formed programs that are not in a passive state can always make a deterministic step. The only non-deterministic transitions are transitions that consume a new input, and these are only possible from a passive state.

An *execution* of a script is a finite or infinite sequence of events $\overline{ev}$:

$$\overline{ev} = (\mu_0, \mathbf{skip}) \xrightarrow{ev_0} (\mu_1, c_1) \xrightarrow{ev_1} (\mu_2, c_2) \xrightarrow{ev_2} \ldots$$

We say an execution is *event-complete* if it ends in a passive state: this means that all the input events the program has received have been fully handled, and that the only way to further extend the execution is by giving it a new input event.

2.3   Examples

Consider the following script:

on *KeyPress*(x) *total* := *total* + x;
on *MouseClick*(x) **output** *total* **on** *Display*

The script keeps a running total of the key scan codes of all key presses it has seen, and on a *MouseClick* input event, it displays the total on the *Display* channel. This models a simple JavaScript calculator.

The following is an example execution of the script. We denote a memory μ as the set that has an element $r \mapsto \mu(r)$ for every global variable r that has a non-zero value in μ. Hence, μ_0 is denoted as the empty set $\{\}$.

$$(\{\}, \texttt{skip}) \xrightarrow{\texttt{in}_{KeyPress(10)}} (\{\}, total := total + 10)$$

$$\xrightarrow{\bullet} (\{total \mapsto 10\}, \texttt{skip})$$

$$\xrightarrow{\texttt{in}_{KeyPress(20)}} (\{total \mapsto 10\}, total := total + 20)$$

$$\xrightarrow{\bullet} (\{total \mapsto 30\}, \texttt{skip})$$

$$\xrightarrow{\texttt{in}_{MouseClick(0)}} (\{total \mapsto 30\}, \texttt{output } total \texttt{ on } Display)$$

$$\xrightarrow{\texttt{out}_{Display(30)}} (\{total \mapsto 30\}, \texttt{skip})$$

For the remainder of this paper, we will usually not show the silent actions ($\bullet$) in example executions.

As a second example, consider again the key logger script:

$$\texttt{on } KeyPress(x) \texttt{ output } x \texttt{ on } Network$$

The following is an example execution of the script.

$$(\{\}, \texttt{skip}) \xrightarrow{\texttt{in}_{KeyPress(10)}} (\{\}, \texttt{output } 10 \texttt{ on } Network)$$

$$\xrightarrow{\texttt{out}_{Network(10)}} (\{\}, \texttt{skip})$$

$$\xrightarrow{\texttt{in}_{KeyPress(20)}} (\{\}, \texttt{output } 20 \texttt{ on } Network)$$

$$\xrightarrow{\texttt{out}_{Network(20)}} (\{\}, \texttt{skip})$$

$$\xrightarrow{\texttt{in}_{MouseClick(0)}} (\{\}, \texttt{skip})$$

Key press events get echoed on the network, while a mouse click event is just silently absorbed (there is no handler for these events).

3   Information Flow Control

3.1   Introduction

Web scripts can receive and send information on a variety of channels.

They need to *receive* information from both sensitive and less sensitive channels. For instance, a script may need to read a password from the user in order to estimate the strength of the password (clearly a sensitive piece of information). Scripts may also need to receive advertisements to be displayed from the network (an example of a script reading less sensitive information).

Scripts also need to *send* information both to trustworthy output channels as well as to less trustworthy output channels. For instance, in a web based document processor, scripts will send document content to the site hosting the document processing application (an output to a trustworthy channel). But scripts may also collect user interaction data to be sent to a web analytics site (outputs to a less trustworthy channel).

The key idea of information flow control is to allow scripts to perform all these inputs and outputs, as long as *no information received from a sensitive input channel leaks to a non-trustworthy output channel*. Let us assume for the sake of the following examples that:

- *Display* is a trustworthy output channel: the outputs on that channel can only be seen by a trusted observer – the user of the web application.
- *Network* is a non-trustworthy output channel: the outputs can possibly be seen by untrusted obervers, for instance attackers.
- *KeyPress* is a sensitive input channel: we do not want untrusted observers to know anything about what keys we press.
- *MouseClick* is a non-sensitive input channel: we do not care that information leaks about when and where we click the mouse.

To enforce information flow control, these assumptions are formalized in a *policy* that assigns a *security label* to each of the channels. These security labels should be thought of as *confidentiality levels*. For the purpose of this paper, we use only two such levels: H for high confidentiality and L for low confidentiality. The set of security labels is an ordered set: for our two element set, $H > L$.

For input channels, the label defines the level of confidentiality of information received on that channel. Hence, in our examples the label of *KeyPress* will be H and the label of *MouseClick* will be L.

For output channels, the label defines the trustworthiness of the observers of the output channel. A H observer is trusted and it is OK if that observer sees information of confidentiality levels H or L. A L observer is untrusted and should only ever see information of level L.

With these intuitions in mind, we can discuss some examples of secure and insecure scripts.

Consider again the JavaScript calculator:

$$\text{on } KeyPress(x) \; total := total + x;$$
$$\text{on } MouseClick(x) \; \texttt{output } total \text{ on } Display$$

This script is secure: it reads sensitive information from *KeyPress* but only discloses it to the trustworthy *Display* channel.

On the other hand, the key logger script:

$$\text{on } KeyPress(x) \; \texttt{output } x \text{ on } Network$$

is an example of an insecure script. It discloses information read from a H input channel (*KeyPress*) to a L output channel (*Network*). The variant of the script that outputs these key presses to a trustworthy network channel *SameOriginNetwork* would be secure.

The key logger script above has a blatant leak: it just copies information from a H channel to a L channel and hence is obviously insecure. But it is important to note that scripts can also leak information in more subtle ways. Consider for instance the following script:

> on *KeyPress*(x) r := x;
>
> on *MouseClick*(x) output r on *Network*

This script leaks information from *KeyPress* to *Network* by first storing the information in memory, and sending it out at a later moment in time. Hence this script is also insecure, but in a somewhat less obvious way.

Leaks can be even more indirect. Consider for instance:

> on *KeyPress*(x) if x = 100 then r := 1 else skip;
>
> on *MouseClick*(x) output r on *Network*

This script leaks whether the user ever pressed a key with scan code 100: it outputs 1 on the *Network* in case it has ever seen a *KeyPress*(100) event. Hence, it is also insecure but in an even more indirect way. Flows of information that, as in the example above, leak information by using the control flow of the program are often called *implicit* flows.

The objective of information flow security is to formalize the distinction between secure and insecure programs that we informally discussed in this section, and to develop enforcement mechanisms that prevent such insecure information leaks. We want to prevent both explicit and implicit flows.

3.2   Formal Definitions

The notion of information flow security discussed above can be formalized as *noninterference*, which roughly says that there should not be two executions of the program that (1) receive the same L inputs, but (2) produce different L outputs. The intuition is that if L outputs are always the same given the same L inputs, then the L outputs could not have been influenced in any way by the H inputs, and hence do not leak any information about the H inputs.

To make this formal for web scripts, we need a few definitions. We assume as given a *policy* that assigns security labels to channels in the form of a function lbl from $Chan$ to $\{L, H\}$.

For a sequence of events $\overline{ev} = ev_1 \cdots ev_n$, we define

- $\lfloor \overline{ev} \rfloor_I$ the subsequence of all input events.
- $\lfloor \overline{ev} \rfloor_O$ the subsequence of all output events.
- $\lfloor \overline{ev} \rfloor_{I,L}$ the subsequence of all input events $\mathtt{in}_{ch(n)}$ such that $lbl(ch) = L$.

– $\lfloor \overline{ev} \rfloor_{O,L}$ the subsequence of all output events $\mathbf{out}_{ch(n)}$ such that $lbl(ch) = L$.

Definition 1. *A program p is* noninterferent *iff for any two event-complete executions $\overline{ev_1}$ and $\overline{ev_2}$ it holds that:*

$$\lfloor \overline{ev_1} \rfloor_{I,L} = \lfloor \overline{ev_2} \rfloor_{I,L} \implies \lfloor \overline{ev_1} \rfloor_{O,L} = \lfloor \overline{ev_2} \rfloor_{O,L}$$

I.e. any two event-complete executions that receive the same L inputs will produce the same L outputs.

Example 1. The key logger script:

$$\text{on } KeyPress(x) \text{ output } x \text{ on } Network$$

is insecure according to this definition, because of the following two event-complete executions.

$$\overline{ev_1} = \quad (\{\}, \mathsf{skip}) \xrightarrow{\mathbf{in}_{KeyPress(10)}} (\{\}, \mathbf{output}\ 10\ \mathbf{on}\ Network) \xrightarrow{\mathbf{out}_{Network(10)}} (\{\}, \mathsf{skip})$$

$$\overline{ev_2} = \quad (\{\}, \mathsf{skip}) \xrightarrow{\mathbf{in}_{KeyPress(20)}} (\{\}, \mathbf{output}\ 20\ \mathbf{on}\ Network) \xrightarrow{\mathbf{out}_{Network(20)}} (\{\}, \mathsf{skip})$$

For these two executions, $\lfloor \overline{ev_1} \rfloor_{I,L} = \lfloor \overline{ev_2} \rfloor_{I,L}$ (both executions have no L input events), but $\lfloor \overline{ev_1} \rfloor_{O,L} \neq \lfloor \overline{ev_2} \rfloor_{O,L}$ (both executions have different L outputs on *Network*).

Example 2. Also the script with the more subtle leaks:

$$\text{on } KeyPress(x) \text{ if } x = 100 \text{ then } r := 1 \text{ else skip};$$
$$\text{on } MouseClick(x) \text{ output } r \text{ on } Network$$

can be seen to be insecure by considering the following two event-complete executions (we do not show the silent output events):

$$\overline{ev_1} = (\{\}, \mathsf{skip}) \xrightarrow{\mathbf{in}_{KeyPress(10)}} (\{\}, \mathsf{skip})$$
$$\xrightarrow{\mathbf{in}_{MouseClick(10)}} (\{\}, \mathbf{output}\ 0\ \mathbf{on}\ Network)$$
$$\xrightarrow{\mathbf{out}_{Network(0)}} (\{\}, \mathsf{skip})$$

$$\overline{ev_2} = (\{\}, \mathsf{skip}) \xrightarrow{\mathbf{in}_{KeyPress(100)}} (\{r \mapsto 1\}, \mathsf{skip})$$
$$\xrightarrow{\mathbf{in}_{MouseClick(10)}} (\{\}, \mathbf{output}\ 1\ \mathbf{on}\ Network)$$
$$\xrightarrow{\mathbf{out}_{Network(1)}} (\{\}, \mathsf{skip})$$

It is easy to check that $\lfloor \overline{ev_1} \rfloor_{I,L} = \lfloor \overline{ev_2} \rfloor_{I,L}$ but $\lfloor \overline{ev_1} \rfloor_{O,L} \neq \lfloor \overline{ev_2} \rfloor_{O,L}$.

3.3 Enforcement

Roughly speaking, there are two classes of approaches to enforce noninterference. We can *statically* check that a program is secure, by using techniques such as type systems or program verification. Or we can *dynamically* enforce that no information leaks by using techniques such as monitoring or multi-execution.

In the following two sections, we focus on one static enforcement technique (based on typing) and on one dynamic technique (based on multi-execution).

4 Static Enforcement

The idea of using static techniques to check noninterference was pioneered in the seventies by Denning and Denning [14]. There is a huge body of literature on static enforcement of information flow security. The survey by Sabelfeld and Myers [30] provides an excellent overview. We illustrate static enforcement by means of typing by showing a type system that is very similar to a type system proposed by Bohannon et al. [8].

Types are just security labels (hence, in our case, there are only two types: H and L). Programmers have to declare a type for every global variable and the type checker will enforce that the information stored in global variables of type L will only depend on L information.

We first define a typing judgment for expressions (Figure 6). The intuition is that the type l of an expression e is an upper bound for the level of the information that could have influenced e. The judgement $(x : l_c) \vdash e : l$ defines the type l of expression e in context $(x : l_c)$. The context $(x : l_c)$ defines the level of the bound variable x; for an expression that is part of a handler definition on a channel ch, the variable bound by the handler will get as type the level of the channel ch.

$$\frac{l_c \leq l}{(x : l_c) \vdash x : l} \text{ (T-EXPR-VAR)} \qquad \frac{}{(x : l_c) \vdash n : l} \text{ (T-EXPR-LIT)}$$

$$\frac{lbl(r) \leq l}{(x : l_c) \vdash r : l} \text{ (T-EXPR-REF)}$$

$$\frac{(x : l_c) \vdash e_1 : l_1 \qquad (x : l_c) \vdash e_2 : l_2 \qquad l_1 \leq l \qquad l_2 \leq l}{(x : l_c) \vdash e_1 \odot e_2 : l} \text{ (T-EXPR-OP)}$$

Fig. 6. Typing of expressions

The type system is polymorphic: an expression can have multiple types. Any type that is an upper bound for the level of the information that could have influenced e is a valid type. With our restriction to two security levels H and L, expressions can either have the H type, or both the L and H type. This simple form of polymorphism in the type system will make some of the typing rules for commands simpler.

The rule (T-Expr-Var) says that a variable assumed to have level l_c in the context can be given as type any level above or equal to l_c, and rule (T-Expr-Ref) says that global variables can be given as type any level above or equal to the level assigned to them by the programmer. Literals can have any level (T-Expr-Lit), and in a binary expression, the level of the result can be any level that is above or equal to the levels of the two operands (T-Expr-Op).

Next we turn to typing of commands (Figure 7). We define a typing judgement $(x : l_c) \vdash c : l$, expressing that command c is well-typed with type l in context $(x : l_c)$. The intuition is that the type of a command is a *lower* bound for the level of the side-effects (either assignments to global variables or outputs on channels) that a command can have. Hence typing is again polymorphic. In our system, a well-typed command can have both type H and L, meaning it definitely only performs H side effects, or a well-typed command can have type L only, if the command possibly performs some L side effect.

$$\frac{}{(x : l_c) \vdash \text{skip}: l} \ (\text{T-Cmd-Skip})$$

$$\frac{(x : l_c) \vdash c_1 : l_1 \quad (x : l_c) \vdash c_2 : l_2 \quad l \leq l_1 \quad l \leq l_2}{(x : l_c) \vdash (c_1; c_2) : l} \ (\text{T-Cmd-Seq})$$

$$\frac{(x : l_c) \vdash e : l_e \quad l_e \leq lbl(ch) \quad l \leq lbl(ch)}{(x : l_c) \vdash \text{output } e \text{ to } ch : l} \ (\text{T-Cmd-Out})$$

$$\frac{(x : l_c) \vdash e : l_e \quad l_e \leq lbl(r) \quad l \leq lbl(r)}{(x : l_c) \vdash (r := e) : l} \ (\text{T-Cmd-Assign})$$

$$\frac{(x : l_c) \vdash e : l_e \quad (x : l_c) \vdash c_1 : l_1 \quad (x : l_c) \vdash c_2 : l_2 \quad l \leq l_1 \quad l \leq l_2 \quad l_e \leq l_1 \quad l_e \leq l_2}{(x : l_c) \vdash \text{if } e \text{ then } c_1 \text{ else } c_2 : l} \ (\text{T-Cmd-If})$$

$$\frac{(x : l_c) \vdash e : l_e \quad (x : l_c) \vdash c : l' \quad l \leq l' \quad l_e \leq l'}{(x : l_c) \vdash \text{while } e \text{ do } c : l} \ (\text{T-Cmd-While})$$

Fig. 7. Typing of commands

Rule (T-Cmd-Skip) says that skip can be given any level. The sequential composition of two commands must have a level that is below or equal to the levels of the two commands that are composed (T-Cmd-Seq). Rule (T-Cmd-Out) ensures two things. First, for an output command, the level of the expression that is output must be below or equal to the level of the channel on which it is output. Since l_e is an upper bound for the level the information that could have influenced e, this ensures no information leaks with this output. Second, the level l of the command itself must be a lower bound for the effects, and hence musy be below or equal to the level of the output channel. The rule for assignments (T-Cmd-Assign) is very similar: assignment to global variables is an effect that is similar to the effect of producing output. The rules for conditionals (T-Cmd-If) and (T-Cmd-While) make sure that no information leaks through the control flow and are needed to prevent implicit flows. Parts of the program that can only be reached dependent on information of level l_e (like the branches of an if-statement or the body of a while-statement) should only have effects that have l_e as lower bound. In other words, there should be no L effects in parts of the program whose reachability depends on H information.

Finally, we turn to programs (Figure 8). Each declared handler on $ch(x)$ c

$$\frac{}{\vdash \cdot} \text{ (T-Pgm-Empty)} \qquad \frac{(x : lbl(ch)) \vdash c : lbl(ch) \qquad \vdash p}{\text{on } ch(x) \ c; p} \text{ (T-Pgm)}$$

Fig. 8. Typing of programs

must be type-checked in a context that assigns the label of the channel ch to the bound variable x, and the side-effects of the resulting commands must be bounded by that same label; a H input event should not lead to L side effects.

Example 3. Consider again the JavaScript calculator:

on $KeyPress(x)$ $total := total + x$;
on $MouseClick(x)$ output $total$ on $Display$

If we define $lbl(total) = H$, this script passes type checking. The expression $total + x$ gets type H and the assignment $total := total + x$ can be given both types H and L (both these are lower bounds for the single effect of assigning to $total$). In a similar way, the output command in the second handler can be given both types H and L.

Example 4. The key logger script:

on $KeyPress(x)$ output x on $Network$

does not type check. The expression x must be given type H because it arrives on a H channel (rules (T-Pgm) and (T-Expr-Var)). As a consequence, the output command fails to type check as the level of $Network$ is L and rule (T-Cmd-Out) requires that the type of the expression being output is below or equal to the level of the output channel.

For similar reasons, the script below also does not type check:

on $KeyPress(x)$ $r := x$;
on $MouseClick(x)$ output r on $Network$

The first handler can only be type checked of r is given type H by defining $lbl(r) = H$. But then the second handler can not be type checked for the same reason as above.

Example 5. Finally, let us consider an example with conditionals. The program below:

$$\text{on } KeyPress(x) \text{ if } x = 100 \text{ then } r := 1 \text{ else skip};$$
$$\text{on } MouseClick(x) \text{ output } r \text{ on } Network$$

can not be type checked. Since the conditional of the if-statement depends on H information (x has type H), effects in the then and else branch must be bounded below by H (rule(T-CMD-IF)) . Hence, the r variable must be made H by defining $lbl(r) = H$. But then the second handler can not type check anymore.

One can prove that any program that type checks is noninterferent.

Theorem 1. *Suppose we are given a policy lbl that assigns security levels to I/O channels, and suppose that lbl can be extended to assign security levels to global variables such that $\vdash p$, then p is noninterferent under that policy.*

We refer the reader to [8] for a proof.

Note that the type system is *conservative*. It is easy to come up with example programs that are noninterferent but that fail to type check. For instance:

$$\text{on } KeyPress(x) \ r := x;$$
$$\text{on } MouseClick(x) \text{ output } r - r \text{ on } Network$$

is noninterferent since the expression $r - r$ always evaluates to 0. But the type system will treat the expression as H. The fact that type systems (and other static approaches) reject some good programs is one of the main motivations to also consider dynamic methods that can be more permissive [31].

5   Dynamic Enforcement

The first attempts at dynamically enforcing information flow also date back to the seventies [16], but for many years static enforcement techniques were considered more promising. The impression was that dynamic mechanisms are not a good match for information flow security, as they monitor only a single execution, and the definition of noninterference talks about two executions. Hence, for many years the emphasis was on the development of static methods.

In the last decade, we have seen a renewed interest in dynamic methods [31]. The most obvious dynamic approach is *monitoring* where the enforcement mechanism monitors an execution and blocks it as soon as it detects an information leak. Such a monitor for JavaScript was for instance developed by Hedin and Sabelfeld [17]. An alternative approach is the approach of *secure multi-execution (SME)* [15]. We illustrate dynamic enforcement by means of a secure multi-execution mechanism that is very close to the mechanism proposed by Bielova et al. [6].

The core idea of SME for reactive systems is to maintain two executions of the program (one for each security level, i.e. a low (L) and a high (H) execution), and to implement the following rules on the I/O performed by these executions. L input events are handled by both executions, and H input events are only handled by the H execution. Outputs on L channels are only performed in the L execution and outputs on H channels only in the H execution.

It is relatively easy to see that executing a program under this SME regime will guarantee non-interference: the execution that does output at level L only sees inputs of level L and hence the output could not have been influenced by inputs of level H.

Similarly, it is relatively easy to see that non-interferent programs run unmodified: if L outputs indeed only depend on L inputs, then the L execution will still perform the same outputs. The H execution gets all events and behaves exactly as the program would behave without SME so also the H outputs will remain the same. The only net effect that SME has on noninterferent programs is that – depending on how both executions are scheduled – outputs may happen in a different order (but outputs at the same security level remain in the same order). This is the *precision* property of SME. Rafnsson et al.[27] have shown that, if the program is noninterferent *and* low and high executions are scheduled correctly, then even ordering of outputs remains the same. However, in many cases it is sufficient to maintain order only within security levels. For instance, in the case of web scripts, if graphical outputs to the browser user are H and outputs to the network are L, it is sufficient to maintain order per security level. That is, the relative order of graphical outputs in relation to networks outputs is not important. This observation allows for simple schedulers which, for each input event, first perform the low execution (if the input event was low), and then the high execution. In this paper we focus on the case where the scheduler is simple, and only maintain output order per security level.

We formalize SME for web scripts by defining how to execute a script under SME. A program state under SME contains two program states of the original program $((\mu_L, c_L), (\mu_H, c_H))$, the state of the L execution (μ_L, c_L) and the state of the H execution (μ_H, c_H). We define the judgement $((\mu_L, c_L), (\mu_H, c_H)) \overset{ev}{\Rightarrow} ((\mu_L', c_L'), (\mu_H', c_H'))$ in Figure 9.

The rules (NEW-H-INPUT) and (NEW-L-INPUT) formalize that H inputs are only given to the H execution and L inputs are given to both executions. Then rules (L-INTERNAL) and (L-OUTPUT) are applicable until the L execution is finished with the current input event. These rules let the L execution run but suppress any H output events.

When the L execution is done, rules (H-INTERNAL) and (H-OUTPUT) kick in. The H execution can now run, but L outputs will be suppressed.

The *initial program state* is $((\mu_0, \texttt{skip}), (\mu_0, \texttt{skip}))$ and a program state is *passive* if it has the form $((\mu, \texttt{skip}), (\mu, \texttt{skip}))$. We define the notions of *execution under SME* and *event-complete* execution under SME in the obvious way (similar to how they were defined for the standard semantics in Section 2.2).

Note that SME does not *detect* insecure scripts, it automatically *fixes* them as they execute.

$$\frac{lbl(ch) = H \quad (p)(\mathbf{in}_{ch(n)}) \Downarrow c}{((\mu_L, \mathbf{skip}), (\mu_H, \mathbf{skip})) \xRightarrow{\mathbf{in}_{ch(n)}} ((\mu_L, \mathbf{skip}), (\mu_H, c))} \text{ (New-H-Input)}$$

$$\frac{lbl(ch) = L \quad (p)(\mathbf{in}_{ch(n)}) \Downarrow c}{((\mu_L, \mathbf{skip}), (\mu_H, \mathbf{skip})) \xRightarrow{\mathbf{in}_{ch(n)}} ((\mu_L, c), (\mu_H, c))} \text{ (New-L-Input)}$$

$$\frac{(\mu_L, c_L) \xrightarrow{o} (\mu_L', c_L') \quad o = \bullet \vee lbl(o) = H}{((\mu_L, c_L), (\mu_H, c_H)) \overset{\bullet}{\Rightarrow} ((\mu_L', c_L'), (\mu_H, c_H))} \text{ (L-Internal)}$$

$$\frac{(\mu_L, c_L) \xrightarrow{o} (\mu_L', c_L') \quad lbl(o) = L}{((\mu_L, c_L), (\mu_H, c_H)) \overset{o}{\Rightarrow} ((\mu_L', c_L'), (\mu_H, c_H))} \text{ (L-Output)}$$

$$\frac{(\mu_H, c_H) \xrightarrow{o} (\mu_H', c_H') \quad o = \bullet \vee lbl(o) = L}{((\mu_L, \mathbf{skip}), (\mu_H, c_H)) \overset{\bullet}{\Rightarrow} ((\mu_L, \mathbf{skip}), (\mu_H', c_H'))} \text{ (H-Internal)}$$

$$\frac{(\mu_H, c_H) \xrightarrow{o} (\mu_H', c_H') \quad lbl(o) = H}{((\mu_L, \mathbf{skip}), (\mu_H, c_H)) \overset{o}{\Rightarrow} ((\mu_L, \mathbf{skip}), (\mu_H', c_H'))} \text{ (H-Output)}$$

Fig. 9. Semantics of SME

Example 6. Consider again the key logger script:

$$\text{on } KeyPress(x) \text{ output } x \text{ on } Network$$

If this script is executed under SME, the occurrence of an input event on the *KeyPress* channel will be handled by the H execution only (rule New-H-Input). When that execution performs the output command on the *Network* channel, this output will be suppressed (rule H-Internal). SME fixes this example by never performing any of the insecure outputs.

Example 7. Consider again the script with the more subtle leaks:

$$\text{on } KeyPress(x) \ \text{ if } x = 100 \text{ then } r := 1 \text{ else skip};$$
$$\text{on } MouseClick(x) \text{ output } r \text{ on } Network$$

For this script, inputs on the *KeyPress* channel are only delivered to the H execution (rule New-H-Input). Hence the value of the global variable r can become 1 in μ_H, but it will always remain 0 in μ_L. On occurrence of an input on the *MouseClick* channel, this input is delivered to both executions (rule New-L-Input). The L execution runs first and outputs a 0 on *Network*. Then the H execution runs, but when it performs the output on *Network* (that could be 0 or 1 in this execution), this output is suppressed (rule H-Internal).

So we see that SME again fixes this example. The program becomes equivalent to the secure program that always outputs 0 to *Network* on a mouse click:

$$\text{on } KeyPress(x) \ \text{ if } x = 100 \text{ then } r := 1 \text{ else skip};$$
$$\text{on } MouseClick(x) \text{ output } 0 \text{ on } Network$$

The main security theorem about SME says that *any* script, when executed under the SME regime, is non-interferent.

Theorem 2. *Any program is noninterferent when executed under the SME semantics.*

For a proof, we refer the reader to [6].

Of course, since SME can change the behaviour of programs, we have to check that it does not change the behaviour of *secure* programs. We do not want an enforcement mechanism to do arbitrary changes to the semantics of secure programs. Fortunately, secure programs are more or less untouched.

Example 8. Consider again the (secure) JavaScript calculator:

$$\text{on } KeyPress(x) \; total := total + x;$$

$$\text{on } MouseClick(x) \; \text{output } total \text{ on } Display$$

If we execute this script under SME, the behaviour remains the same. Key presses are only delivered to the H execution, and the total is correctly computed in μ_H (The value of total remains 0 in μ_L). When an input arrives on the *MouseClick* channel, it is delivered to *both* executions (rule NEW-L-INPUT). The output produced on the *Display* channel by the L execution is suppressed (rule L-INTERNAL). The (correct) output produced by the H execution is performed (rule H-OUTPUT). We see that SME leaves the behaviour of this secure program untouched.

However, with the simple scheduling approach of first running the L execution and then running the H execution, it might happen that the order of outputs is changed even for secure programs.

Example 9. Consider the (secure) program:

$$\text{on } MouseClick(x) \; \text{output } x \text{ on } Display; \text{output } x \text{ on } Network$$

If we execute this script under SME, an input that arrives on the *MouseClick* channel, is delivered to *both* executions (rule NEW-L-INPUT). The L execution runs first (rules H-INTERNAL and H-OUTPUT can only fire once the L execution has finished; they state that the L execution must be passive). The output produced on the *Display* channel by the L execution is suppressed (rule L-INTERNAL), and the output on the *Network* channel is performed. Then the H execution runs. It performs the output on the *Display* channel, and the output on the *Network* channel is suppressed. The net effect is that the order of the *Display* and *Network* outputs is reversed.

Fortunately, this kind of reordering is the only change that SME does to secure programs. The *precision* theorem for SME says that the output, when projected on an arbitrary security level, remains the same. So the relative order of outputs on different security levels is the only thing that can change. For an exact statement of the theorem, and a proof, we refer the reader to [6].

If even this kind of reordering is undesirable, it is possible to schedule the L and H executions in a more interleaved way so that absolute ordering of outputs can be maintained for secure programs. We refer the reader to [37] for details.

6   Related Work

Information flow security is an established research area, and too broad to survey here. For many years, it was dominated by research into static enforcement techniques. We point the reader to the well-known survey by Sabelfeld and Myers [30] for a discussion of general, static approaches to information flow enforcement. Several static or hybrid techniques specifically for information flow security in web scripts or in browsers have been proposed. Bohannon et al. [8,7] define a notion of non-interference for reactive systems, and show how a model browser can be formalized as such a reactive system. Chugh et al. [10] have developed a novel multi-stage static technique for enforcing information flow security in JavaScript. Just et al. [19] propose a hybrid combination of dynamic information flow tracking and a static analysis to capture implicit flows within full (excluding exceptions) JavaScript programs, including programs calling eval.

Dynamic techniques have seen renewed interest in the last decade. Le Guernic's PhD thesis [22] gives an extensive survey up to 2007, but since then, significant new results have been achieved. Recent works propose run time monitors for information flow security, often with a particular focus on on the web scripts. Sabelfeld et al. have proposed monitoring algorithms that can handle DOM-like structures [29], dynamic code evaluation [2] and timeouts [28]. In a recent paper, Hedin and Sabelfeld [17] propose dynamic mechanisms for all the core JavaScript language features. Austin and Flanagan [3] have developed alternative, sometimes more permissive techniques.

Secure multi-execution (SME) was developed independently by several researchers [21,36,15]. Khatiwala et al. [21] proposed a technique called *Data Sandboxing*. They partition a program in two programs at source code level and use system call interposition to implement the SME I/O rules. In followup work, Capizzi et al. [9] avoid the need for source level partitioning by means of *shadow executions*: they run two executions of processes for the H (secret) and L (public) security level to provide strong confidentiality guarantees. Devriese and Piessens [15] independently came up with the closely related technique they called SME, and they were the first to prove the strong soundness and precision guarantees that SME offers.

These initial results were improved and extended in several ways: Kashyap et al. [20], generalize the technique of secure multi-execution to a family of techniques that they call *the scheduling approach to non-interference*, and they analyze how the scheduling strategy can impact the security properties offered. Barthe et al.[5] propose a program transformation that simulates SME. Bielova et al. [6] propose a variant of secure multi-execution suitable for reactive systems such as browsers. An implementation of SME in a real browser was done by De Groef et al. [12,13]. Austin and Flanagan [4] propose a more efficient implementation technique called multi-faceted evaluation. In a recent paper, Rafnsson and Sabelfeld [27] extend SME in several ways by showing (1) how to support policies that can distinguish presence of messages from content of messages, (2) how to perform declassification under SME and (3) how to make SME precise (or transparent in their terminology) even for observers that can observe more than one level. An alternative, more black-box approach to declassification was developed by Vanhoef et al. [33].

Information flow security is one promising approach to web script security, but two other general-purpose approaches have been applied to script security as well: isolation and taint-tracking.

Isolation or *sandboxing* based approaches develop techniques where scripts can be included in web pages without giving them (full) access to the surrounding page and the browser API. Several practical systems have been proposed, including Webjail [32], ADSafe [11], Caja [24], and JSand [1]. Maffeis et al. [23] formalize the key mechanisms underlying these techniques and prove they can be used to create secure sandboxes. They also discuss several other existing proposals, and we point the reader to their paper for a more extensive discussion of work in this area. Isolation is easier to achieve than non-interference, but it is also more restrictive: often access needs to be denied to make sure the script cannot leak the information, but it would be perfectly fine to have the script use the information locally in the browser.

Taint tracking is an approximation to information flow security, that only takes explicit flows into account. Several authors have proposed taint tracking systems for web security. Two representative examples are Xu et al. [35], who propose taint-enhanced policy enforcement as a general approach to mitigate implementation-level vulnerabilities, and Vogt et al. [34] who propose taint tracking to defend against cross-site scripting.

7   Conclusions

Information flow control is a widely studied information security mechanism. It makes sure that programs can not leak sensitive information that they receive for processing to output channels that might be observable by opponents that should not learn such sensitive information. Information flow control is an interesting security mechanism for web scripts, since these scripts need to process sensitive information as well as need to communicate over untrustworthy output channels.

We have described two information flow control mechanisms for web scripts, one static mechanism based on typing, and one dynamic mechanism based on multi-execution. We have explained the intuitions behind these mechanisms and illustrated them on examples.

Acknowledgments. This research is partially funded by the Research Fund KU Leuven, by the EU FP7 projects WebSand, Strews and NESSoS, and by the IWT project SPION. With the financial support from the Prevention of and Fight against Crime Programme of the European Union (B-CCENTRE). Mathy Vanhoef and Dominique Devriese hold a PhD fellowship of the Research Foundation - Flanders (FWO). Willem De Groef holds a PhD grant from the Agency for Innovation by Science and Technology in Flanders (IWT).

References

1. Agten, P., Van Acker, S., Brondsema, Y., Phung, P.H., Desmet, L., Piessens, F.: JSand: Complete Client-Side Sandboxing of Third-Party JavaScript without Browser Modifications. In: Proceedings of the Annual Computer Security Applications Conference, pp. 1–10 (2012)
2. Askarov, A., Sabelfeld, A.: Tight Enforcement of Information-Release Policies for Dynamic Languages. In: Proceedings of the IEEE Computer Security Foundations Symposium, pp. 43–59 (2009)
3. Austin, T.H., Flanagan, C.: Permissive Dynamic Information Flow Analysis. In: Proceedings of the ACM SIGPLAN Workshop on Programming Languages and Analysis for Security, pp. 3:1–3:12 (2010)
4. Austin, T.H., Flanagan, C.: Multiple Facets for Dynamic Information Flow. In: Proc. of the ACM SIGPLAN-SIGACT Symposium on Principles of Programming Languages, pp. 165–178 (2012)
5. Barthe, G., Crespo, J.M., Devriese, D., Piessens, F., Rivas, E.: Secure Multi-Execution through Static Program Transformation. In: Giese, H., Rosu, G. (eds.) FMOODS/FORTE 2012. LNCS, vol. 7273, pp. 186–202. Springer, Heidelberg (2012)
6. Bielova, N., Devriese, D., Massacci, F., Piessens, F.: Reactive non-interference for a browser model. In: Proc. of the International Conference on Network and System Security, pp. 97–104 (2011)
7. Bohannon, A., Pierce, B.C.: Featherweight firefox: Formalizing the core of a web browser. In: Proceedings of the 2010 USENIX Conference on Web Application Development, WebApps 2010, p. 11. USENIX Association, Berkeley (2010)
8. Bohannon, A., Pierce, B.C., Sjöberg, V., Weirich, S., Zdancewic, S.: Reactive Non-interference. In: Proceedings of the ACM Conference on Computer and Communications Security, pp. 79–90 (2009)
9. Capizzi, R., Longo, A., Venkatakrishnan, V., Sistla, A.: Preventing Information Leaks through Shadow Executions. In: Proc. of the Annual Computer Security Applications Conference, pp. 322–331 (2008)
10. Chugh, R., Meister, J.A., Jhala, R., Lerner, S.: Staged Information Flow for JavaScript. ACM SIGPLAN Notices 44(6), 50–62 (2009)
11. Crockford, D.: Adsafe (December 2009), http://www.adsafe.org/
12. De Groef, W., Devriese, D., Nikiforakis, N., Piessens, F.: FlowFox: a Web Browser with Flexible and Precise Information Flow Control. In: Proc. of the ACM Conference on Computer and Communications Security, pp. 748–759 (2012)
13. De Groef, W., Devriese, D., Nikiforakis, N., Piessens, F.: Secure multi-execution of web scripts: Theory and practice. Journal of Computer Security (2014)
14. Denning, D.E., Denning, P.J.: Certification of programs for secure information flow. Commun. ACM 20(7), 504–513 (1977)
15. Devriese, D., Piessens, F.: Noninterference Through Secure Multi-Execution. In: Proc. of the IEEE Symposium on Security and Privacy, pp. 109–124 (2010)
16. Fenton, J.S.: Memoryless subsystems. Comput. J. 17(2), 143–147 (1974)
17. Hedin, D., Sabelfeld, A.: Information-Flow Security for a Core of JavaScript. In: Proc. of the IEEE Computer Security Foundations Symposium, pp. 3–18 (2012)

18. Jang, D., Jhala, R., Lerner, S., Shacham, H.: An Empirical Study of Privacy-Violating Information Flows in JavaScript Web Applications. In: Proc. of the ACM Conference on Computer and Communications Security, pp. 270–283 (2010)
19. Just, S., Cleary, A., Shirley, B., Hammer, C.: Information Flow Analysis for JavaScript. In: Proc. of the ACM SIGPLAN International Workshop on Programming Language and Systems Technologies for Internet Clients, pp. 9–18 (2011)
20. Kashyap, V., Wiedermann, B., Hardekopf, B.: Timing- and Termination-Sensitive Secure Information Flow: Exploring a New Approach. In: Proc. of the IEEE Conference on Security and Privacy, pp. 413–428 (2011)
21. Khatiwala, T., Swaminathan, R., Venkatakrishnan, V.: Data Sandboxing: A Technique for Enforcing Confidentiality Policies. In: Proceedings of the Annual Computer Security Applications Conference (ACSAC), pp. 223–234 (2006)
22. Le Guernic, G.: Confidentiality Enforcement Using Dynamic Information Flow Analyses. Ph.D. thesis, Kansas State University (2007)
23. Maffeis, S., Mitchell, J.C., Taly, A.: Object Capabilities and Isolation of Untrusted Web Applications. In: Proceedings of the IEEE Symposium on Security and Privacy, pp. 125–140 (2010)
24. Miller, M.S., Samuel, M., Laurie, B., Awad, I., Stay, M.: Caja: Safe active content in sanitized javascript (January 2008),
    http://google-caja.googlecode.com/files/caja-spec-2008-01-15.pdf
25. Nikiforakis, N., Invernizzi, L., Kapravelos, A., Van Acker, S., Joosen, W., Kruegel, C., Piessens, F., Vigna, G.: You Are What You Include: Large-scale Evaluation of Remote JavaScript Inclusions. In: Proc. of the ACM Conference on Computer and Communications Security, pp. 736–747 (2012)
26. Nikiforakis, N., Kapravelos, A., Joosen, W., Kruegel, C., Piessens, F., Vigna, G.: Cookieless monster: Exploring the ecosystem of web-based device fingerprinting. In: Proceedings of the 34th IEEE Symposium on Security & Privacy, pp. 541–555 (May 2013)
27. Rafnsson, W., Sabelfeld, A.: Secure multi-execution: fine-grained, declassification-aware, and transparent. In: Proc. of the IEEE Computer Security Foundations Symposium, CSF (2013)
28. Russo, A., Sabelfeld, A.: Securing Timeout Instructions in Web Applications. In: Proceedings of the IEEE Computer Security Foundations Symposium, pp. 92–106 (2009)
29. Russo, A., Sabelfeld, A., Chudnov, A.: Tracking Information Flow in Dynamic Tree Structures. In: Backes, M., Ning, P. (eds.) ESORICS 2009. LNCS, vol. 5789, pp. 86–103. Springer, Heidelberg (2009)
30. Sabelfeld, A., Myers, A.C.: Language-Based Information-Flow Security. IEEE Journal on Selected Areas of Communications 21(1), 5–19 (2003)
31. Sabelfeld, A., Russo, A.: From dynamic to static and back: Riding the roller coaster of information-flow control research. In: Pnueli, A., Virbitskaite, I., Voronkov, A. (eds.) PSI 2009. LNCS, vol. 5947, pp. 352–365. Springer, Heidelberg (2010)
32. Van Acker, S., De Ryck, P., Desmet, L., Piessens, F., Joosen, W.: Webjail: Least-privilege integration of third-party components in web mashups. In: ACSAC (2011),
    https://lirias.kuleuven.be/handle/123456789/316291
33. Vanhoef, M., De Groef, W., Devriese, D., Piessens, F., Rezk, T.: Stateful declassification policies for event-driven programs. In: Proc. of the IEEE Computer Security Foundations Symposium, CSF (2014)
34. Vogt, P., Nentwich, F., Jovanovic, N., Kirda, E., Krügel, C., Vigna, G.: Cross Site Scripting Prevention with Dynamic Data Tainting and Static Analysis. In: Proceedings of the Network & Distributed System Security Symposium (2007)

35. Xu, W., Bhatkar, S., Sekar, R.: Taint-Enhanced Policy Enforcement: A Practical Approach to Defeat a Wide Range of Attacks. In: Proceedings of the USENIX Security Symposium, pp. 121–136 (2006)
36. Yumerefendi, A.R., Mickle, B., Cox, L.P.: TightLip: Keeping Applications from Spilling the Beans. In: Proceedings of the USENIX Symposium on Network Systems Design & Implementation, pp. 159–172 (2007)
37. Zanarini, D., Jaskelioff, M., Russo, A.: Precise enforcement of confidentiality for reactive systems. In: Proc. of the IEEE Computer Security Foundations Symposium, CSF (2013)

EasyCrypt: A Tutorial*

Gilles Barthe[1], François Dupressoir[1], Benjamin Grégoire[2], César Kunz[3],**,
Benedikt Schmidt[1], and Pierre-Yves Strub[1]

[1] IMDEA Software Institute, Madrid, Spain
{gilles.barthe,francois.dupressoir,benedikt.schmidt,
pierre-yves.strub}@imdea.org
[2] INRIA Sophia-Antipolis Méditerranée, France
benjamin.gregoire@inria.fr
[3] FireEye, Dresden, Germany
cesar.kunz@gmail.com

1 Introduction

Cryptography plays a key role in the security of modern communication and computer infrastructures; therefore, it is of paramount importance to design cryptographic systems that yield strong security guarantees. To achieve this goal, cryptographic systems are supported by security proofs that establish an upper bound for the probability that a resource-constrained adversary is able to break the cryptographic system. In most cases, security proofs are reductionist, i.e. they construct from an (arbitrary but computationally bounded) adversary that would break the security of the cryptographic construction with some reasonable probability another computationally bounded adversary that would break a hardness assumption with reasonable probability. This approach, known as provable security, is in principle able to deliver rigorous and detailed mathematical proofs. However, new cryptographic designs (and consequently their security analyses) are increasingly complex, and there is a growing emphasis on shifting from algorithmic descriptions to implementation-level descriptions that account for implementation details, recommendations from standards when they exist, and possibly side-channels. As a consequence, cryptographic proofs are becoming increasingly error-prone and difficult to check. One promising solution to address these concerns is to develop machine-checked frameworks that support the construction and automated verification of cryptographic systems. Although many such frameworks exist for the symbolic model of cryptography, comparatively little work has been done to develop machine-checked frameworks to reason directly in the computational model commonly used by cryptographers.

EasyCrypt[1] is an interactive framework for verifying the security of cryptographic constructions in the computational model. EasyCrypt adopts the code-based approach, in which security goals and hardness assumptions are modelled

---

* An up-to-date and living version of this document and the EasyCrypt formalization and proofs it refers to can be found at https://www.easycrypt.info/Tutorial
** Work performed while the author was working at IMDEA Software Institute.
[1] See http://www.easycrypt.info.

A. Aldini et al. (Eds.): FOSAD VII, LNCS 8604, pp. 146–166, 2014.

as probabilistic programs (called experiments or games) with unspecified adversarial code, and uses tools issued from program verification and programming language theory to rigorously justify cryptographic reasoning. Concretely, Easy-Crypt supports common patterns of reasoning from the game-based approach, which decomposes reductionist proofs into a sequence (or possibly tree) of small steps (sometimes called hops) that are easier to understand and to check. As each step relates two programs, one central component of EasyCrypt is a relational Hoare logic for probabilistic programs. The logic, called pRHL, reasons about judments of the form

$$[c_1 \sim c_2 : \Phi \Longrightarrow \Psi]$$

where c_1 and c_2 are probabilistic programs, and Φ and Ψ are relational assertions, i.e. first-order formulae which relate two memories; an instance of a relational assertion is $x\langle 1 \rangle = x\langle 2 \rangle$, which states that the value of x coincides in both memories. Although pRHL judgments do not explicitly refer to probabilities, it is possible to derive probability claims from valid judgments; indeed, the validity of pRHL judgments is based on a notion of lifting, inspired from probabilistic process algebra, and from which one can derive equalities and inequalities between two probabilities. Specifically, one can derive from valid pRHL judgments of the form

$$[c_1 \sim c_2 : \Phi \Longrightarrow E\langle 1 \rangle \rightarrow F\langle 2 \rangle]$$

that $\Pr[c_1, m_1 : E] \leq \Pr[c_2, m_2 : F]$ for every initial memories m_1 and m_2 that are related by Φ and events E and F. In addition, pRHL subsumes reasoning about equivalence of probabilistic programs: given a valid judgment of the form

$$\left[c_1 \sim c_2 : \Phi \Longrightarrow \bigwedge_{i=1}^{n} x_i\langle 1 \rangle = x_i\langle 2 \rangle \right]$$

we have $\Pr[c_1, m_1 : A] = \Pr[c_2, m_2 : A]$ for every initial memories m_1 and m_2 that are related by Φ and event A that only depends on $\{x_1, \ldots, x_n\}$. A useful generalization of observational equivalence is observational equivalence up to a failure event F:

$$\left[c_1 \sim c_2 : \Phi \Longrightarrow \neg F\langle 2 \rangle \rightarrow \bigwedge_{i=1}^{n} x_i\langle 1 \rangle = x_i\langle 2 \rangle \right]$$

It follows from the above judgment that for every initial memories m_1 and m_2 that are related by Φ and event A that only depends on $\{x_1, \ldots, x_n\}$, we have:

$$\Pr[c_1, m_1 : A] \leq \Pr[c_2, m_2 : A] + \Pr[c_2, m_2 : F]$$

In addition to relating the probability of events in different games, cryptographic proofs therefore require the computation of concrete upper bounds on the probability of some event, typically a failure event, in a game. A second component of EasyCrypt is a probabilistic Hoare logic to reason about the probability of events in games. The logic, called pHL, reasons about judgments of the form

$$[c : \varsigma \Longrightarrow \varphi] \diamond p$$

where c is a probabilistic program, ς and φ are (non-relational) assertions, $\diamond$ is a comparison operator and p is a probability expression.

Both pRHL and pHL are embedded into a higher-order logic in which one can define operators and their associated axioms. Reasoning in this ambient logic is supported by a core proof engine; the proof engine is heavily inspired by the SsReflect extension of Coq, but also enables the use of SMT solvers to discharge proof obligations.

A key challenge for the formalization of cryptographic proofs is to support compositional reasoning. Indeed, many cryptographic systems achieve their functionality by combining (often in intricate ways) different cryptographic constructions, which may themselves be built from several cryptographic primitives. In order to support reasoning about such cryptographic systems, EasyCrypt features a module system which allows the construction of modular proofs that respect the layered and modular design of the cryptographic system. The module system is also useful for structuring large and complex proofs that involve a large number of game hops and perform reductions at different levels.

1.1   Outline

We first recall useful concepts and notations, before presenting a high-level, mathematical overview of the construction and proof developed in this tutorial (Section 2). The objective of the rest of this document is to illustrate our preferred way of specifying cryptographic systems and their proof sketches by constructing a pseudo-random generator (PRG) from a pseudo-random function (PRF). We start by specifying the construction and the desired security notions (Section 3). Finally, we prove formally that our construction is a secure PRG if it is applied to a secure PRF (Section 4).

1.2   Preliminaries

Types, operators and data structures. EasyCrypt's expression language is a higher-order strongly typed functional language. We often view *types* as (non-empty) sets and *operators* as mathematical functions, sometimes using these terms interchangeably. In addition to some basic types (*unit*, *bool*, *int*, *real*), EasyCrypt's libraries provide specifications for some more advanced data structures that can be used when specifying cryptographic systems or when proving their security. We only mention here the types and operators relevant to our formalization.

First, we consider inductive lists, that may be the empty list [], or a value x::xs constructed inductively by prepending x to the list xs. We write |xs| to mean the length (or number of elements) of a list xs. We sometimes denote [x] the list x::[]. We define the boolean operator unique: α *list* $\rightarrow$ *bool* as the function that returns true if and only if its argument does not have any duplicates.

Our formalization also uses finite maps, that may be indexed by arbitrary types. We use mixfix notations for the map get (m[x]) and map set (m[x] = y) operations, denoting map0 the map that is everywhere undefined. We call the *domain* of a map m the (finite) set of indices on which m is defined.

Discrete probability sub-distributions. EasyCrypt features a type of *discrete probability sub-distributions* that is used to model probabilistic operations, including sampling from a distribution. Informally, a discrete probability distribution over a type A is a function $f : A \to \mathbb{R}$ such that: i. for every $a \in A$, $f\ a \geq 0$; ii. for every finite subset X of A, $\sum_{a \in X} f\ a \leq 1$; iii. the *support* of f, i.e. the set of elements a of A that have a non-zero probability (i.e. $f\ a > 0$) is discrete. Formally, we axiomatize discrete probability sub-distributions by defining for every type t a type t distr, and several operators, including an operator pr: $\alpha\ distr \to (\alpha \to bool) \to real$ that gives the probability of an event (modelled as a boolean-valued predicate over the carrier type). Moreover, we axiomatize various properties of discrete probability sub-distributions. We introduce some important properties of discrete probability sub-distributions:

- we call *full* sub-distributions whose support is the entire carrier type; conversely, we call *empty* sub-distributions whose support is the empty set,
- we call *lossless* sub-distributions in which the constantly true event has probability 1 (that is, proper distributions),
- we call *sub-uniform* sub-distributions that give the same probability to all elements in their support, using *uniform* to mean *lossless and sub-uniform*.

In the following, we often abuse terminology and use *distribution* to mean *discrete probability sub-distribution*.

2   High Level Description

We start by giving a high level description of the proof described in this tutorial. The idea is to prove that a concretely defined stateful random generator is a pseudo-random generator under the hypothesis that the underlying function is a pseudo-random function. We first introduce the construction, then the different security notions used in the proof.

A Stateful Random Generator. The stateful random generator we use in this chapter is a generic construction parameterized by a function Fc : seed $\to$ state $\to$ state $\times$ output The type seed represent the set of seeds, state is the set of states and output the set of the output returned by the random generator. The code of the construction is described in Figure 1. It is composed of two procedures: an initialization function that sample a seed and an initial state and a generator function generating an output. The generator uses Fc with the seed and the current state to obtain a new state, which is stored in place of the current, and an output which is returned to the caller. Concretely, one could, for example, instantiate the function Fc with AES, using appropriately-sized fixed-length

Game SRG =
  procedure init()
    $s \xleftarrow{\$} \mathsf{seed}$;
    $st \xleftarrow{\$} \mathsf{state}$;
  procedure next()
    $(st, r) \leftarrow F_c\ s\ st$;
    return r;

Fig. 1. Stateful random generator

bitstrings as seeds, states and outputs. The proof presented here would then directly apply to obtain a security result for this concrete instance.

We would like to prove that the concrete SRG construction is a secure pseudo-random generator (PRG) under reasonable assumptions on Fc. We now define the notion of PRG-security and formalize our assumption on Fc.

Pseudo-Random Generators (PRG). The notion of security for pseudo-random generators is expressed using games $\mathsf{Real}_{Fc}^{\mathrm{PRG}}$ and $\mathsf{Rand}_{output}^{\mathrm{PRG}}$ defined in Figure 2. Both games are parameterized by an adversary: a distinguisher D that, given oracle access to a next oracle, returns a bit representing its guess as to whether it is playing against the concrete PRG (game $\mathsf{Real}_{Fc}^{\mathrm{PRG}}$) or the ideal random generator (game $\mathsf{Rand}_{output}^{\mathrm{PRG}}$).

Game $\mathsf{Real}_{Fc}^{\mathrm{PRG}}(D)$	Game $\mathsf{Rand}_{output}^{\mathrm{PRG}}(D)$
procedure init()	procedure init()
$\quad s \xleftarrow{\$} \mathsf{seed}$;	
$\quad st \xleftarrow{\$} \mathsf{state}$;	
procedure next()	procedure next()
$\quad (st, r) \leftarrow \mathsf{Fc}\ s\ st$;	$\quad r \xleftarrow{\$} \mathsf{output}$;
$\quad$ return r;	$\quad$ return r;
procedure main()	procedure main()
$\quad$ init();	$\quad$ init();
$\quad b \leftarrow D_{\mathsf{next}}()$;	$\quad b \leftarrow D_{\mathsf{next}}()$;
$\quad$ return b;	$\quad$ return b;

Fig. 2. PRG security games

Definition 1 (PRG-advantage). *Let* Fc : seed → state → state × output *be a function. Let* D *be a distinguisher with an oracle access to a function* next *and returning a bit. The PRG-advantage of* D *against* Fc *is defined as*

$$\mathsf{Adv}_{Fc}^{\mathrm{PRG}}(D) = \Pr\left[\mathsf{Real}_{Fc}^{\mathrm{PRG}}(D) : \mathsf{res}\right] - \Pr\left[\mathsf{Rand}_{output}^{\mathrm{PRG}}(D) : \mathsf{res}\right]$$

Intuitively, a function Fc yields a stateful random generator that is secure when, for all "reasonable" distinguisher D, $\mathsf{Adv}_{Fc}^{\mathrm{PRG}}(D)$ is "small". Formally defining the notions of "reasonable" and "small" is not the objective of EasyCrypt: we rather aim at proving *concrete* bounds that can be used to prove security with respect to chosen definitions (for example, parameterizing the system by a security parameter η, "reasonable" adversaries might be algorithms that are p.p.t. in η, and "small" advantages might be negligible as functions of η). However, our proofs still require some restrictions to be placed on the adversaries considered. In particular, we will consider adversaries that make a bounded number of queries to their oracles.

Pseudo-Random Functions (PRF). In our example, the bound for $\mathsf{Adv}_{\mathsf{Fc}}^{\mathrm{PRG}}(D)$ is expressed in terms of the security of Fc seen as a pseudo-random function. We now introduce this notion.

A *function family* is a function $F : \mathcal{K} \times \mathcal{D} \to \mathcal{R}$, where $\mathcal{K}$ is the set (or type) of keys, $\mathcal{D}$ is the domain and $\mathcal{R}$ the range. We write $F_K(x)$ for $F(K, x)$. This allows us to view the function F as a family of functions from $\mathcal{D}$ to $\mathcal{R}$ indexed by $\mathcal{K}$.

A *pseudo-random function* is a function family that is computationally hard to distinguish from a random function when its key is chosen at random. Formally, this property is expressed using the games $\mathsf{Real}^{\mathrm{PRF}}$ and $\mathsf{Rand}^{\mathrm{PRF}}$ presented in Figure 3. Both games are parameterized by a distinguisher D which is given oracle access to a procedure Fn and returns a bit representing its guess as to which of the two games it is playing. In game $\mathsf{Real}^{\mathrm{PRF}}$, a key K is initially sampled in $\mathcal{K}$, and the procedure Fn is implemented using function F_K. In game $\mathsf{Rand}^{\mathrm{PRF}}$ the procedure Fn implements a lazily sampled random function: on each fresh query x a random value is sampled and stored into the (initially empty) map M, then the associated value is returned to the caller.

Game $\mathsf{Real}_F^{\mathrm{PRF}}(D)$	Game $\mathsf{Rand}_{\mathcal{R}}^{\mathrm{PRF}}(D)$
<u>procedure</u> init()	<u>procedure</u> init()
$K \xleftarrow{\$} \mathcal{K};$	$M \leftarrow \emptyset;$
<u>procedure</u> Fn(x)	<u>procedure</u> Fn(x)
return $F_K(x);$	if $M[x] = \bot$ then $M[x] \xleftarrow{\$} \mathcal{R};$
	return $M[x];$
<u>procedure</u> main()	<u>procedure</u> main()
init();	init();
$b \leftarrow D_{\mathsf{Fn}}();$	$b \leftarrow D_{\mathsf{Fn}}();$
return $b;$	return $b;$

Fig. 3. PRF security games

Definition 2 (PRF-advantage). *Let* $F : \mathcal{K} \to D \to R$ *be a function family. Let D be an adversary with oracle access to a procedure* Fn *and returning a bit. The PRF-advantage of D against F is defined as*

$$\mathsf{Adv}_F^{\mathrm{PRF}}(D) = \Pr\left[\mathsf{Real}_F^{\mathrm{PRF}}(D) : \mathsf{res}\right] - \Pr\left[\mathsf{Rand}_F^{\mathrm{PRF}}(D) : \mathsf{res}\right]$$

High level description of the security proof. The objective of the security proof is to bound, for all D in a certain class of algorithms, $\mathsf{Adv}^{\mathrm{PRG}}_{Fc}(D)$ as a function of $\mathsf{Adv}^{\mathrm{PRF}}_{Fc}(D')$ for some adversary D' constructed from D. More concretely, in Section 4.1, we prove the following abstract probability bound.

Theorem 1 (Abstract Security of our SRG). *For all PRG-distinguisher D, we construct a PRF-distinguisher D^{PRF}_D such that*

$$\mathsf{Adv}^{\mathrm{PRG}}_{Fc}(D) \leq \mathsf{Adv}^{\mathrm{PRF}}_{Fc}(D^{\mathrm{PRF}}_D) + \Pr\left[\mathsf{Rand}^{\mathrm{PRF}}_{\mathcal{R}}(D^{\mathrm{PRF}}_D) : \exists x, 1 < x \,\#\, \mathcal{Q}\right],$$

where $\mathcal{Q}$ is the multiset of queries made by D^{PRF}_D to the PRF oracle, and $x \,\#\, \mathcal{X}$ is the number of occurrences of element x in multiset $\mathcal{X}$.

In practice, the class of distinguishers considered is restricted to adversaries with access to bounded resources, taking into account running-time and number of queries to the oracles, and limiting the adversary's access to the real and ideal system's memory spaces. In Subsection 4.2, we restrict the class of distinguishers under consideration and compute concrete probability and resource bounds.

Theorem 2 (Concrete Security of our SRG). *For all PRG-distinguisher D that makes at most q_n queries to its* next *oracle, the constructed adversary D^{PRF}_D from Theorem 1 makes at most q_n queries to its PRF oracle, and we have*

$$\Pr\left[\mathsf{Rand}^{\mathrm{PRF}}_{\mathcal{R}}(D^{\mathrm{PRF}}_D) : \exists x, 1 < x \,\#\, \mathcal{Q}\right] \leq \frac{q_n^2}{|\mathsf{state}|},$$

where $|\mathsf{state}|$ is the cardinal of the set state.

Remark. The bound from Theorem 2 could be made slightly tighter. We choose to keep this weaker result in this tutorial to keep the proof clear. This and other generalizations and improvements are discussed in the online version of this tutorial.

3   EasyCrypt Specification

In this Section, we formalize in EasyCrypt the definitions given in Section 2. We start by formalizing our concrete SRG construction. We then formalize what it means for an abstract SRG to be a secure PRG, and what it means for a function family to be be a secure PRF. Finally, we instantiate these abstract definitions to our concrete construction and state our security theorem.

3.1   A Stateful Random Generator

First of all we need to declare the types and distributions on which our construction relies. As discussed in Section 2, those are kept abstract throughout this document but can later be instantiated, for example with bitstrings of various fixed lengths, *without having to re-prove anything*, simply by proving that the concrete instantiations given to types and operators fulfill the axioms specified in our formalization. We give an example of such an instantiation (although we do so on other theories) in Section 3.4.

```
type seed.

op dseed: seed distr.
axiom dseed_ll: islossless dseed.

type state.

op dstate: state distr.
axiom dstate_uf: isuniform dstate.
axiom dstate_fu: isfull dstate.

type output.

op dout: output distr.
axiom dout_uf: isuniform dout.

op Fc: seed → state → state * output.
```

Listing 1.1. Core Declarations

The first line declares a new *abstract type* seed representing the set of seeds. The second line declares an abstract operator dseed: a sub-distribution over seed, that we further restrict to be lossless (i.e. a proper distribution) with an axiom dseed_ll. The next lines introduce the types state and output, and uniform distributions over them, also requiring the distribution dstate to be full. Note that this combination of axioms defines dstate uniquely given a finite instantiation for type state. Finally, we declare an operator Fc representing a function family from type state to type state * output and indexed by the type seed.

```
module SRG = {
  var s : seed
  var st : state

  proc init(): unit = {
    s  $← dseed;
    st $← dstate;
  }

  proc next(): output = {
    var r;

    (st,r) = Fc s st;
    return r;
  }
}.
```

Listing 1.2. Our concrete Stateful Random Generator

Given these basic blocks, we define our stateful random generator as discussed in Section 2: during an initialization phase, a seed and an initial state are sampled from the specified distributions. Each query for a new random output then simply uses the function Fc applied to the seed and the old state to produce a new state and some output. The new state is stored for use in the next query, and the output is returned.

These procedures are defined as part of a *module*, which also specifies a *memory space*, here composed of two global variables: s of type seed and st of type state. All procedures in a module may access the module's entire memory space and there is no need to pass the current state of global variables around through the return values and arguments of the procedures that use them. EasyCrypt modules are used to formalize schemes, constructions and oracles, but also concrete adversaries, games and security experiments.

We now give generic formalizations of PRG-security and PRF-security that are independent of our concrete construction, as they might appear in Easy-Crypt's library of security notions. This library and the instantiation mechanism discussed in Section 3.4 often make it unnecessary to formalize security notions anew for each particular proof.

3.2 Pseudo-Random Generators

We first formalize PRG-security. To allow this notion to later be instantiated to the types declared in Listing 1.1 and our concrete SRG, we wrap the following definitions inside a *theory*: a collection of declarations and definitions, including types, operators, and modules, that can be restricted by axioms (assumptions) and extended with lemmas (derived from the axioms and the language's semantics).

```
theory PRG.
  type output.
  op dout: output distr.

  module type PRG = {
    proc init(): unit
    proc next(): output
  }.

  module type PRGA = { proc next(): output }.
```

Listing 1.3. Pseudo-Random Generators: Types

For any type output equipped with an arbitrary sub-distribution dout, we use a *module type* to define a random generator as a pair of algorithmes G = (init, next). A module type specifies a set of procedures that are expected to be provided by a module implementing it. A module is said to *implement* a module type if it provides *at least* all the procedures specified in the type, with the correct types. In particular, our construction from Listing 1.2 implements the PRG module type, but also the module type PRGA, that hides the existence of the init oracle. Module types can be used to quantify over adversaries, or prove generic results on abstract cryptographic constructions before applying them to concrete instances. In addition to quantification in lemmas, module types enable us to *parameterize* module definitions with abstract modules of a given type. Such module parameters can be used to define *generic constructions* of complex cryptographic schemes from abstract primitives, or to model that an adversary has *oracle access* to some procedure (that is, that it can query the procedure and get the corresponding reply, but cannot interfere with that procedure's internal state or its execution). For example, we consider adversaries that have only oracle access to the next algorithm, which can be formalized using the following set of definitions.

```
module type Distinguisher(G:PRGA) = { proc distinguish(): bool }.

module IND(G:PRG,D:Distinguisher) = {
  module D = D(G)

  proc main(): bool = {
    var b;

    G.init();
    b = D.distinguish();
    return b;
  }
}.

module PRGi:PRG,PRGA = {
  proc init(): unit = { }
  proc next(): output = { var r; r ←$ dout; return r; }
}.
end PRG.
```

Listing 1.4. Pseudo-Random Generators: Security

A PRG-distinguisher is an algorithm distinguish that, given no inputs, and oracle access to the next procedure of a PRG, returns a boolean. The module type Distinguisher is parameterized with an abstract module G implementing module type PRGA. This means that the implementation of its distinguish procedure may call the procedure G.next.

Given these module type definitions, we can now define an indistinguishability experiment as a module IND, parameterized by a PRG G and a PRG-distinguisher D. In this experiment, we first instantiate the distinguisher's module parameter, ensuring that any query it makes to next is answered using the implementation G.next, we then initialize G and run the distinguisher, returning its output. Security of a PRG G with respect to a given adversary D can then be defined using the standard notion of advantage. Formally, the advantage of an adversary D in distinguishing a PRG G from distribution dout in an initial memory m is written as follows:

$$\mathsf{Adv}_G^{\mathrm{PRG}}(D, m) = \Pr[\mathsf{IND}(G,D).\mathsf{main}() @ m: \mathsf{res}] - \Pr[\mathsf{IND}(\mathsf{PRGi},D).\mathsf{main}() @ m: \mathsf{res}].$$

Given a module M implementing procedure f, and an initial memory m, the expression Pr[M.f() @ m: res] is a real-valued expression whose value is the probability of procedure M.f() returning true when run in initial memory m. The formula appearing after the colon can be arbirary and may mention the global variables of any module currently in scope, as well as the special res variable, which is bound to the procedure's return value. In the rest of this document, we omit memories where irrelevant[2], and also omit the procedure name when it is main, simply writing, say, Pr[IND(G,D): res] for Pr[IND(G,D).main() @ m: res].

3.3   Pseudo-Random Functions

In EasyCrypt, we define pseudo-random functions using the following declarations, leading to the declaration of a function family F, and a module PRFr wrapping F so that it can be queried as an oracle, with a fixed key initially sampled in dK.

```
theory PRF.
 type D.

 type R.

 type K.

 op dK: K distr.
 axiom dK_ll: islossless dK.

 op F: K → D → R.

 module PRFr = {
   var k:K
   proc init(): unit = { k ⟵$ dK; }
   proc f(x:D): R = { return F k x; }
 }.
```

Listing 1.5. Pseudo-Random Functions

The security of a PRF F: K → D → R is defined, as shown below, with respect to a random function from D to R. We write it as expected, using the uniform distribution uR on the full range R to sample output values. The standard definition of a random function from D to R as a function sampled uniformly at random in R^D can be recovered if the domain D is finite.

---

[2] Formally, these probabilities may in fact depend on the initial memory. In practice, it is always possible to make sure that advantage expressions are in fact independent from the initial memory by initializing all variables before use, and we slightly abuse notations by omitting initial memories.

```
op uR:R distr.
axiom uR_uf: is_uniform uR.

module PRFi = {
  var m:(D,R) map

  proc init(): unit = { m = map0; }

  proc f (x:D): R = {
    if (x ∈ dom m) m[x] ⟵$ uR;
    return (oget m[x]);
  }
}.

module type PRF = {
  proc init(): unit
  proc f(x:D): R
}.

module type PRFA = {
  proc f(x:D): R
}.

module type Distinguisher (F:PRFA) = {
  proc distinguish(): bool
}.

module IND(F:PRF,D:Distinguisher) = {
  module D = D(F)

  proc main(): bool = {
    var b;

    F.init();
    b = D.distinguish();
    return b;
  }
}.
end PRF.
```

Listing 1.6. Pseudo-Random Functions: Security

The advantage of a given D in distinguishing the given PRF F (from Listing 1.5) from a random function in an initial memory m can be expressed as:

$$\mathsf{Adv}^{\mathrm{PRF}}_{\mathsf{F}}(\mathsf{D}) = \Pr[\mathsf{IND}(\mathsf{PRFr},\mathsf{D}): \mathsf{res}] - \Pr[\mathsf{IND}(\mathsf{PRFi},\mathsf{D}): \mathsf{res}].$$

3.4 Security of Our Stateful Random Generator

We now have enough definitions to properly express our desired security theorem. However, we first need to *instantiate* the abstract PRF and PRG theories with the types and definitions used in our stateful random generator. We do so using EasyCrypt's *theory cloning* mechanism.

```
clone PRF as PRFa
with
    type D ← state,
    type R ← state * output,
    type K ← seed,
    op dK ← dseed,
    op F ← Fc,
    op uR ← dstate * dout (* product distribution *)
proof *
    (* Proofs omitted *).

module IND_P^PRF = PRFa.IND(P).
module PRFc = PRFa.PRFr.
module PRFi = PRFa.PRFi.
```

Listing 1.7. Security of Fc

The clone instruction creates a copy of the PRF theory defined in Section 3.3, renaming it PRFa, and *instantiating* some of its declared types and operators. For example, we instantiate the abstract operator F from the theory with the function family Fc used in the construction of our SRG, instantiating the domain, range and keyspace accordingly. In addition to instantiating types and operators, the cloning instruction allows us to discharge assumptions about them made in the theory. Here, we discharge all axioms, ensuring that any lemma existing in the PRF theory are *unconditional* lemmas of its PRFa instantiation. After cloning and instantiating the PRF definitions, we define some shorthand notations for its instantiated modules. In particular, we call PRFc the PRFr module where Fc is used. PRF advantage notations in the rest of the paper refer to the advantage in the $\mathrm{IND}^{\mathrm{PRF}}$ game rather than the uninstantiated IND game. Also note that parameterized modules can be *partially applied*: given a module P implementing module type PRF, the partially applied module $\mathrm{IND}_P^{\mathrm{PRF}} = \mathrm{IND}^{\mathrm{PRF}}(P)$ is such that, given a PRF-distinguisher D, $\mathrm{IND}_P^{\mathrm{PRF}}(D) = \mathrm{IND}^{\mathrm{PRF}}(P,D)$. From now on, we often write the first parameter as an index when applying module expressions.

Similarly, we clone and instantiate the PRG theory with the types used in our construction to easily express the fact that PRGc is a secure PRG. Likewise, PRG advantage notations in the following refer to the instantiated $\mathrm{IND}^{\mathrm{PRG}}$ game.

```
clone PRG as PRGa
with
    type output ← output,
    op dout ← dout.

module IND_G^PRG = PRGa.IND(G).
module PRGi = PRGa.PRGi.
```

Listing 1.8. Security of PRGc

4   **EasyCrypt** Proof Sketch

4.1   Abstract Bounds for Arbitrary Distinguishers

We first bound the PRG advantage of D as abstract expressions that may not be very meaningful but hold for all D. This proof itself is done in two hops: i. the first hop transforms the SRG construction to make use of the random function PRFi to implement the next oracle instead of Fc; ii. the second hop shows that the PRFi-based implementation of the next oracle is equivalent, up to some well-defined failure event, to the ideal random generator PRGi. We now discuss both steps.

A simple reduction. We want to relate the probability of a distinguisher D to win the game $\mathsf{IND}^{\mathrm{PRG}}$ to the probability of another distinguisher $\mathsf{D}^{\mathrm{PRF}}$ to win the game $\mathsf{IND}^{\mathrm{PRF}}$. To do so we can simply use the game $\mathsf{IND}^{\mathrm{PRG}}$ itself as PRF distinguisher after rewriting SRG as a parameterized module PRGp that uses the PRF oracles instead of calling Fc directly. Anticipating on later proof steps, we also log the queries made by PRGp to the PRF oracle in a list $\mathsf{D}^{\mathrm{PRF}}$.log.

```
module D^PRF(D:PRGa.Distinguisher,F:PRFA) = {
  var log: state list

  module PRGp = {
    proc init(): unit = {
      SRG.st $← dstate;
      log = [];
    }

    proc next(): output = {
      var r;

      log = SRG.st::log;
      (SRG.st,r) = F.f(SRG.st);
      return r;
    }
  }.

  proc distinguish = IND^PRG_PRGp(D).main
}.
```

Note that the module PRGp does not declare its own memory space, but simply hijacks our initial SRG's global variables. Although this is not necessary, it simplifies invariants slightly by reducing the number of proof artefacts to consider. The following fact is now easy to prove.

Fact 1 *For any PRG distinguisher D whose memory space is disjoint from that of SRG and PRFc, we have*

$$\Pr\left[\mathit{IND}^{\mathrm{PRG}}_{SRG}(D):\mathsf{res}\right] = \Pr\left[\mathit{IND}^{\mathrm{PRF}}_{PRFc}(D^{\mathrm{PRF}}_D):\mathsf{res}\right]$$

Proof (Sketch). In EasyCrypt, the proof of this lemma makes use of the following pRHL judgment:

$$\mathsf{IND}^{\mathrm{PRG}}_{\mathsf{SRG}}(\mathsf{D}).\mathsf{main} \sim \mathsf{IND}^{\mathrm{PRF}}_{\mathsf{PRFc}}(\mathsf{D}^{\mathrm{PRF}}_{\mathsf{D}}).\mathsf{main}: =\{\mathsf{glob\ D}\} \implies =\{\mathsf{res}\}$$

The judgment itself is easily discharged by automated tactics after inlining all procedures. Indeed, the procedures are identical except for the fact that the program on the left uses variable SRG.s to store the seed whereas the one on the right uses PRFc.k. The main trick in this proof is to be able to prove the statement for all adversary D. Intuitively we have to compare two evaluations of D, the first uses the next function provided by the module SRG whereas the second uses the next function provided by the module PRGp. Assuming the memory space of D is equal in both evaluations, they can diverge only if: i. D can read values of variables SRG or PRFc but this is impossible due to memory restrictions; ii. the oracles return different results or dissimilar states even when called on identical arguments and in similar states. So, the only point that needs to be proved is that both oracles behave identically.

Once proved, this judgment can be used to prove the probability statement simply by using its semantic interpretation.   □

Fact 1 is written as follows in its full EasyCrypt notation.

lemma SRG_PRGp (D <: PRGa.Distinguisher {SRG,PRFc}) &m:
    Pr[IND^{PRG}(SRG,D).main() @ &m: res] =
    Pr[IND^{PRF}(PRFc,D^{PRF}(D)).main() @ &m: res].

Note that the quantification over the PRG-distinguisher D is made explicit in the lemma, the only restrictions on it being that it implements module type PRGa.Distinguisher and that its memory space (denoted glob D in pRHL statements) is disjoint from those of SRG and PRFc. We also prove this lemma for any initial memory: the variable &m denotes a universally quantified memory. We do not list full EasyCrypt notations for other lemmas, but rather refer the reader to the formalization itself.

Continuing the proof, and using Fact 1 we show:

$$\mathsf{Adv}^{\mathrm{PRG}}_{\mathsf{SRG}}(\mathsf{D}) = \Pr\left[\mathsf{IND}^{\mathrm{PRG}}_{\mathsf{SRG}}(\mathsf{D}) : \mathsf{res}\right] - \Pr\left[\mathsf{IND}^{\mathrm{PRG}}_{\mathsf{PRGi}}(\mathsf{D}) : \mathsf{res}\right] \qquad \text{by definition}$$

$$= \Pr\left[\mathsf{IND}^{\mathrm{PRF}}_{\mathsf{PRFc}}(\mathsf{D}^{\mathrm{PRF}}_{\mathsf{D}}) : \mathsf{res}\right] - \Pr\left[\mathsf{IND}^{\mathrm{PRG}}_{\mathsf{PRGi}}(\mathsf{D}) : \mathsf{res}\right] \qquad \text{by Fact 1}$$

$$= \Pr\left[\mathsf{IND}^{\mathrm{PRF}}_{\mathsf{PRFc}}(\mathsf{D}^{\mathrm{PRF}}_{\mathsf{D}}) : \mathsf{res}\right] - \Pr\left[\mathsf{IND}^{\mathrm{PRF}}_{\mathsf{PRFi}}(\mathsf{D}^{\mathrm{PRF}}_{\mathsf{D}}) : \mathsf{res}\right] +$$
$$\Pr\left[\mathsf{IND}^{\mathrm{PRF}}_{\mathsf{PRFi}}(\mathsf{D}^{\mathrm{PRF}}_{\mathsf{D}}) : \mathsf{res}\right] - \Pr\left[\mathsf{IND}^{\mathrm{PRG}}_{\mathsf{PRGi}}(\mathsf{D}) : \mathsf{res}\right]$$

$$= \mathsf{Adv}^{\mathrm{PRF}}_{\mathsf{Fc}}(\mathsf{D}^{\mathrm{PRF}}_{\mathsf{D}}) + \qquad\qquad\qquad \text{by definition}$$
$$\Pr\left[\mathsf{IND}^{\mathrm{PRF}}_{\mathsf{PRFi}}(\mathsf{D}^{\mathrm{PRF}}_{\mathsf{D}}) : \mathsf{res}\right] - \Pr\left[\mathsf{IND}^{\mathrm{PRG}}_{\mathsf{PRGi}}(\mathsf{D}) : \mathsf{res}\right]$$

Considering failure events. We now wish to bound the last term

$$\Pr\left[\mathsf{IND}^{\mathrm{PRF}}_{\mathsf{PRFi}}(\mathsf{D}^{\mathrm{PRF}}_{\mathsf{D}}) : \mathsf{res}\right] - \Pr\left[\mathsf{IND}^{\mathrm{PRG}}_{\mathsf{PRGi}}(\mathsf{D}) : \mathsf{res}\right].$$

It is clear from their definitions that the two games will only show different behaviours if a duplicate query is made to the PRF by D_D^{PRF}. Indeed, in this case, the value eventually returned to D is not sampled from dout but rather recalled from the random function's map, whereas the ideal random generator always samples its output freshly. We therefore expect the bound to be the probability of a duplicate query to the random function, which we expressed in Section 2 as $\Pr\left[\mathsf{IND}_{\mathsf{PRFi}}^{\mathsf{PRF}}(D_D^{PRF}) : \exists x, 1 < x \# \mathcal{Q}\right]$. Moving slightly away from this high-level description, we use the inductive list $D^{PRF}.\mathsf{log}$ to model multiset $\mathcal{Q}$, using the unique predicate (or rather its negation) to capture the desired event.

However, having the failure event occur only in the first (left) game of the transition would not yield the expected inequality. Indeed directly applying the semantics of equivalence upto failure as presented in Section 1 would lead to a lower-bound rather than the desired upper-bound. Still, an upper-bound can be obtained in this case if the failure event is known to happen with the same probability on both sides of the transitions. Therefore, we also instrument the PRGi module to construct a log of "intermediate states" that it does not otherwise use. In addition, we also make sure that the intermediate state and the output are sampled in the product distribution dstate * dout. This makes this complex game transition easier to prove, by separating two concerns.

```
module PRGi_log = {
  proc init(): unit = {
    SRG.st ←$ dstate;
    D^PRF.log = [];
  }

  proc next(): output = {
    var r;

    D^PRF.log = SRG.st :: D^PRF.log;
    (SRG.st,r) ←$ dstate * dout;
    return r;
  }
}.
```

First note that PRGi_log is indistinguishable from PRGi. Indeed, the additional log and state variables do not alter its control-flow and its output is the second component of a value sampled in the product distribution dstate * dout. In EasyCrypt, we in fact prove that oracles PRGi_log and PRGi define the same distribution on the type output regardless of initial state by proving

$\forall \&m1 \&m2\ o,$

$\quad \Pr\left[\mathsf{PRGi}_{log}.\mathsf{next}()@\ \&m1 : \mathsf{res} = o\right] = \Pr\left[\mathsf{PRGi}.\mathsf{next}()@\ \&m2 : \mathsf{res} = o\right].$

This is in fact sufficient to prove that, for any PRG-distinguisher D, we have

$$\Pr\left[\mathsf{IND}_{\mathsf{PRGi}_{log}}^{\mathsf{PRG}}(D) : \mathsf{res}\right] = \Pr\left[\mathsf{IND}_{\mathsf{PRGi}}^{\mathsf{PRG}}(D) : \mathsf{res}\right]$$

and we now only have to prove the following Fact.

Fact 2 (Equivalence upto failure) *For all PRG-distinguisher D whose memory space is disjoint from that of D^{PRF} and SRG, we have the following bound*

$$\Pr\left[\mathit{IND}^{\mathrm{PRF}}_{\mathit{PRFi}}(D^{\mathrm{PRF}}_D) : \mathsf{res}\right] - \Pr\left[\mathit{IND}^{\mathrm{PRG}}_{\mathit{PRGi}_{log}}(D) : \mathsf{res}\right] \leq$$
$$\Pr\left[\mathit{IND}^{\mathrm{PRF}}_{\mathit{PRFi}}(D^{\mathrm{PRF}}_D) : !\mathit{unique}\ D^{\mathrm{PRF}}.\mathit{log}\right]$$

Proof (Sketch). We prove in EasyCrypt a single pRHL statement:

$\mathsf{IND}^{\mathrm{PRF}}_{\mathsf{PRFi}}(D^{\mathrm{PRF}}_D).\mathsf{main} \sim \mathsf{IND}^{\mathrm{PRG}}_{\mathsf{PRGi}_{log}}(D).\mathsf{main}:$
$= \{\mathsf{glob}\ D\} \implies$
$(\mathsf{unique}\ D^{\mathrm{PRF}}.\mathsf{log}\{1\} = \mathsf{unique}\ D^{\mathrm{PRF}}.\mathsf{log}\{2\}) \wedge (\mathsf{unique}\ D^{\mathrm{PRF}}.\mathsf{log}\{2\} \Rightarrow =\{\mathsf{res}\}).$

This pRHL judgement implies two distinct probability relations. The first conjunct in the postcondition implies that the probability of the failure event in both games is equal

$$\Pr\left[\mathsf{IND}^{\mathrm{PRF}}_{\mathsf{PRFi}}(D^{\mathrm{PRF}}_D) : !\mathsf{unique}\ D^{\mathrm{PRF}}.\mathsf{log}\right] =$$
$$\Pr\left[\mathsf{IND}^{\mathrm{PRG}}_{\mathsf{PRGi}_{log}}(D) : !\mathsf{unique}\ D^{\mathrm{PRF}}.\mathsf{log}\right] \quad (1)$$

whereas the second conjunct implies the expected inequality

$$\Pr\left[\mathsf{IND}^{\mathrm{PRF}}_{\mathsf{PRFi}}(D^{\mathrm{PRF}}_D) : \mathsf{res}\right] - \Pr\left[\mathsf{IND}^{\mathrm{PRG}}_{\mathsf{PRGi}_{log}}(D) : \mathsf{res}\right] \leq$$
$$\Pr\left[\mathsf{IND}^{\mathrm{PRG}}_{\mathsf{PRGi}_{log}}(D) : !\mathsf{unique}\ D^{\mathrm{PRF}}.\mathsf{log}\right]$$

We then conclude easily.   □

Combining Fact 2 and Fact 1's corollary concludes the proof of Theorem 1. Note that this Theorem does not directly imply security in the concrete sense: although we did take care to ensure that our constructed PRF-distinguisher D^{PRF}_D did not have access to the internal memory of PRFc or PRFi (with which it could trivially distinguish the two constructions), we did not bound the number of oracle queries it makes, which may lead to large values of the PRF-advantage and to a large probability of the failure event occurring. We now bound these two quantitites more concretely.

4.2   Application to Resource-Bounded Adversaries

All proof steps seen so far hold regardless of the adversary's resource bounds (running time or number of oracle queries) and only place restrictions on the oracles the adversary can query (via its module type) and on the global variables it may access (via restrictions in the module quantification). However, computing probability and resource bounds requires us to restrict the adversary further, and in particular requires us to limit the number of oracle queries it can make.

Counting oracle queries. First, consider the following module wrappers, that simply count the number of queries made to the PRG (C^{PRG}) or PRF (C^{PRF}) oracles.

```
module C^PRG(G:PRG) = {
  var c:int

  proc init(): unit = {
    c = 0;
    G.init();
  }

  proc next(): output = {
    var r;

    r = G.next();
    c = c + 1;
    return r;
  }
}.
```

```
module C^PRF(F:PRF) = {
  var c:int

  proc init(): unit = {
    c = 0;
    F.init();
  }

  proc f(): output = {
    var r;

    r = F.f();
    c = c + 1;
    return r;
  }
}.
```

This wrapper allows us to easily restrict the number of queries made by an adversary to the oracle. In particular, all conditions of the form "D makes at most q queries to the PRG oracle" appearing below can be expressed in EasyCrypt using the following specification, which states that the distinguisher D playing the IND^{PRG} game against *any* appropriate G (note the restrictions ensuring that such a D exists) has a probability 1 of making *at most* q queries to the oracle G.next.

$$\forall \, (G <: PRG \, \{D,C^{PRG}\}),$$
$$\text{islossless } G.init \Rightarrow \text{islossless } G.next \Rightarrow$$
$$Pr[IND^{PRG}(C_G^{PRG},D): C^{PRG}.c \leq q] = 1$$

More complex conditions, for example relating the initial value of the counter to its final value even when $D(C_G^{PRG})$.distinguish is run independently of the experiment, can also be expressed in similar ways.

Bounding the failure event. We can now bound the probability of the failure event from Theorem 1 for any PRG-distinguisher D that makes at most q queries to its next oracle.

Lemma 1 (Probability of the failure event). *For all positive integer q, and all PRG-distinguisher D whose memory space is disjoint from those of C^{PRG}, PRFc, PRFi and D^{PRF} and that makes at most q queries to its next oracle, we have*

$$\Pr\left[IND_{PRFi}^{PRF}(D_D^{PRF}) : !unique \; D^{PRF}.log\right] \leq \frac{q^2}{|state|},$$

where $|state|$ is the cardinal of type state.

Proof (Sketch). To prove this, we make use of the *failure event lemma*, that intuitively states that, if an event occurs with probability at most p, regardless of state and adversary inputs, during each execution of the oracle, and if the adversary may call this oracle at most q times, then the probability of the event occurring during a full run of the adversary is bounded by $p \cdot q$.

To ease the computation of the probability that the failure event is triggered during a given execution of the oracle, we simplify the computation in two ways: i. we first observe that, from equality (1) obtained during the proof of Fact 2, it is in fact sufficient to bound the probability $\Pr\left[\mathsf{IND}^{\mathrm{PRG}}_{\mathsf{PRGi}_{log}}(\mathsf{D}) : !\mathsf{unique}\ \mathsf{D}^{\mathrm{PRF}}.\mathsf{log}\right]$; and ii. we soundly approximate the failure event with a more general one, triggered as soon as a state that already appears in the log is sampled, rather than when it is added to the log.

```
proc next(): output = {
    var r;

    log = SRG.st::log;
    (SRG.st,r) ←$ dstate * dout;
    bad = bad ∨ mem SRG.st log;
    return r;
}
```

Clearly, if bad is initially unset, we can prove that bad has to be set for the log to have duplicates. This implication is sufficient to prove, in pRHL:

$$\Pr\left[\mathsf{IND}^{\mathrm{PRG}}_{\mathsf{PRGi}_{log}}(\mathsf{D}) : !\mathsf{unique}\ \mathsf{D}^{\mathrm{PRF}}.\mathsf{log}\right] \leq \Pr\left[\mathsf{IND}^{\mathrm{PRG}}_{\mathsf{PRGi}_{log}}(\mathsf{D}) : \mathsf{bad}\right].$$

In this latest variant of the next oracle, it becomes clear that the probability of the bad event being triggered during a given query knowing that it was not true beforehand is exactly the probability that a freshly sampled state already appears in the log. Since the log until that point does not have duplicates and dstate is uniform and full, this probability is exactly $\frac{|\mathsf{log}|}{|\mathsf{state}|}$. Given that the log's size is bounded by q, we obtain the desired bound.   □

Bounding the resources of the PRF-distinguisher. Finally, we prove that for any bounded PRG-distinguisher D with no access to the memory of the primitive modules, the generic construction $\mathsf{D}^{\mathrm{PRF}}$ and both $\mathsf{C}^{\mathrm{PRG}}$ modules, the constructed PRF-distinguisher $\mathsf{D}^{\mathrm{PRF}}_{\mathsf{D}}$ makes at most as many queries to the PRF as D did to the PRG.

Lemma 2 (Number of PRF queries). *For all positive integer q, and all PRG-distinguisher D whose memory space is disjoint from those of $\mathsf{C}^{\mathrm{PRG}}$, $\mathsf{C}^{\mathrm{PRF}}$, PRFc, PRFi and SRG, and that makes at most q oracle queries, the constructed PRF-distinguisher $\mathsf{D}^{\mathrm{PRF}}_{\mathsf{D}}$ makes at most q oracles queries.*

Proof (Sketch). Given an integer q and PRG-distinguisher D as constrained above, we prove the following equality, which states that (for all initial memory) the probability that the constructed D_D^{PRF} makes at most q queries to PRFc.f during a run of the IND^{PRF} experiment is 1.

$$\Pr\left[IND^{PRF}_{C^{PRF}(PRFc)}(D_D^{PRF}) : C^{PRF}.c \leq q\right] = 1.$$

We do so by proving the following statement, inlining all functions and noting that the counters remain synchronized through the execution.

$$\Pr\left[IND^{PRF}_{C^{PRF}(PRFc)}(D_D^{PRF}) : C^{PRF}.c \leq q\right] = \Pr\left[IND^{PRG}_{C^{PRG}(SRG)}(D) : C^{PRG}.c \leq q\right]$$

We conclude by applying the assumption on D, rewriting the right-hand-side of this equality into 1.   □

This concludes the proof of Theorem 2.

5   Further Reading and Concluding Remarks

EasyCrypt provides tool-assisted support for building and verifying machine-checked cryptographic proofs. Its foundations are based on a probabilistic relational Hoare logic, pRHL, that was first introduced in [5], and a verification condition generator that was first presented in [4]. Another key component of EasyCrypt is its module system, which supports the formalization of complex and layered proofs and has been used for instance to verify the security of protocols for secure function evaluation and verifiable computation [2]. One main motivation for the development of EasyCrypt is to close the gap between security proofs and implementations; an approach based on certified compilers is presented in [1]. Beyond EasyCrypt, it is possible to develop and apply fully automated verification techniques for analyzing the security of classes of cryptographic constructions; for instance, one can use customized logics to reason about the security of padding-based encryption schemes, i.e. public-key encryption schemes built from one-way trapdoor permutations and random oracles [3]. Deduction rules of the logic capture high-level reasoning principles that can be formalized in EasyCrypt, and contribute to building an extensive library of common reasoning patterns in cryptography. It is our hope that the development of the library will somewhat shift the focus of EasyCrypt proofs to reduce the emphasis on proving pRHL judgments and to bring them closer to the high level reasoning steps used by cryptographers.

References

1. Almeida, J.B., Barbosa, M., Barthe, G., Dupressoir, F.: Certified computer-aided cryptography: efficient provably secure machine code from high-level implementations. In: ACM Communications and Computer Security (CCS), pp. 1217–1230. ACM (2013)

2. Almeida, J.B., Barbosa, M., Barthe, G., Davy, G., Dupressoir, F., Grégoire, B., Strub, P.-Y.: Verified implementations for secure and verifiable computation. Cryptology ePrint Archive, Report 2014/456 (2014), http://eprint.iacr.org/
3. Barthe, G., Crespo, J.M., Grégoire, B., Kunz, C., Lakhnech, Y., Schmidt, B., Béguelin, S.Z.: Fully automated analysis of padding-based encryption in the computational model. In: ACM Communications and Computer Security (CCS), pp. 1247–1260. ACM (2013)
4. Barthe, G., Grégoire, B., Heraud, S., Béguelin, S.Z.: Computer-aided security proofs for the working cryptographer. In: Rogaway, P. (ed.) CRYPTO 2011. LNCS, vol. 6841, pp. 71–90. Springer, Heidelberg (2011)
5. Barthe, G., Grégoire, B., Zanella-Béguelin, S.: Formal certification of code-based cryptographic proofs. In: ACM Principles of Programming Languages (POPL), pp. 90–101. ACM (2009)

Cryptographic Voting — A Gentle Introduction

David Bernhard and Bogdan Warinschi

University of Bristol, UK

Abstract. These lecture notes survey some of the main ideas and techniques used in cryptographic voting systems. The write-up is geared towards readers with little knowledge of cryptography and it focuses on the broad principles that guide the design and analysis of cryptographic systems, especially the need for properly designed security models.

We use a system proposed by Fujioka, Okamoto and Ohta as starting example to introduce some basic building blocks and desirable security properties. We then slowly build towards a comprehensive description of the Helios voting system, one of the few systems deployed in practice and briefly discuss a few of its security properties.

1 Introduction

A potential solution to the problem of decrease turn-out in elections is the use of remote voting systems. The increased comfort that permits voters to cast their ballot from anywhere and at any time (as long as they have an internet connection) should translate in higher voter participation and even reduce the costs of running elections. Just like with any advanced technology, bringing electronic voting[1] to widespread practice faces both technological and societal challenges.

The latter is well illustrated by Norway's recent decision, that follows a couple of trials, not to expand internet voting to nationwide elections because of the impact that public's trust in this technology may have on the democratic process. Related problems raised questions regarding the constitutionality of internet voting in Germany. While the deployment and usability issues (e.g. dealing with malware on user's voting device, overcoming social inertia, gaining public trust) still need to be solved, it is fair to say that the cryptographic technology that goes into electronic voting is by now in a reasonably stable condition. In particular existing schemes build upon a powerful and versatile toolbox of cryptographic techniques which are combined to achieve the desired functionality and security.

These notes survey some of the most commonly used cryptographic primitives used in electronic voting. We explain and motivate the functionality and security they achieve through their use within electronic voting schemes. In this context, perhaps the most important message we wish to convey is the crucial

---

[1] We remark that in this write-up we use the term electronic voting to refer to online voting schemes. The term is also used to refer to kiosk-voting that involves some form of digital recording machine, potentially combined with other mechanisms like optical scanners, paper-based recording, etc.

A. Aldini et al. (Eds.): FOSAD VII, LNCS 8604, pp. 167–211, 2014.

role that rigorous models play in the development of secure systems. For protocols with complex security requirements, as is the case of electronic voting, models are necessary for understanding the security these protocols offer and for enabling rigorous security proofs. Most of the discussion is driven by two voting schemes from the literature, one of which is in current use. We aim to provide a comprehensive overview of the latter.

These notes are intended for readers with little to no knowledge of cryptography, but who wish to understand some of the underpinnings of cryptographic voting. We assume some familiarity with basic abstract algebra and ease in using mathematics.

Primitives and models. One of the main goals of this write-up is to present the building blocks used in voting systems. Our presentation is not exhaustive but it includes some of the most used primitives: digital and blind signatures, homomorphic encryption, threshold techniques and zero-knowledge proofs. For each of the primitives we present a rigorous security model where we clarify what is an adversary, how it can interact with the primitive, and what constitutes a breach against the primitive. To ease understanding, we find it useful to define the functionality and security of these primitives by analogy with systems which achieve similar levels of security in the physical world. In addition, for increased clarity but at the expense of some precision, we chose not to give the typical fully formal cryptographic definitions.

We remark that, perhaps surprisingly, not all of the (many) security properties that voting systems should satisfy have formal definitions. Indeed, most of the recent research on cryptographic voting focuses on the design of such models and the analysis of existing schemes. In these notes we recall ballot privacy, a security notion that captures the idea that users' votes stay private. In addition, we briefly comment on the equally important property of verifiability.

Instantiations and Helios. For all of the primitives that we cover we show how they can be (securely) instantiated; each instantiation is preceded by the necessary mathematical background. In particular, we show how to realize all of the primitives that go into the design of the Helios voting systems, one of the few voting systems that are actually used in practice. For pedagogical reasons we present an incremental design of Helios: we start with a basic voting system which is functional but not secure, then we identify attacks against the scheme which we show how to defend against via cryptographic techniques. The resulting design together with the instantiations of the different primitives that we present yield a scheme which has ballot privacy. We briefly discuss (informally) its verifiability properties.

Conventions. To allow the reader to zoom-in on the parts that may be of more interest to him/her we separate and clearly indicate the following. Sections giving mathematical background information are marked with a frame and a large Σ. Sections that introduce basic cryptographic primitives are marked with a lock symbol (🔒). Sections giving applications specific to the Helios voting scheme are marked with a ☼ symbol.

2   First Steps

2.1   Example

Here is one way to run a poll. Voters enter a polling station and pick up a voting card on which the candidates standing for election or choices in a referendum are printed. They fill in their card by placing crosses in boxes. Then they take their card and put it in an opaque envelope which they seal. In keeping with the cryptographic constructions we will describe later, we call such an envelope containing a filled in vote card a "ballot". This completes the first step, ballot creation.

To cast their ballots, voters present them to an official along with some identification. The official checks that the voter is registered at this polling station and has not cast a vote yet, but the official does not get to see the vote itself. Then the official places the ballot-envelope in a stamping machine and stamps the envelope, in such a way that the imprint of the stamp is not only visible on the envelope but also transferred to the vote card within.

Voters post their ballots to a counting centre. The postal service agrees to send any correctly stamped envelope free of charge from anywhere in the country so voters can post their envelope anonymously in any post box that they choose. The counting centre shuffles all received envelopes, opens them and counts all vote cards that contain an imprint of the official stamp.

2.2   🔒 Digital Signatures

We will now start to develop the tools that we will use to build a cryptographic version of the protocol sketched in the last section. Along the way we will introduce the cryptographer's method of defining and reasoning about security of schemes and protocols.

Digital signatures are the cryptographer's replacement for signatures or stamps. If we know what someone's signature looks like and believe that it would be hard for anyone but the owner to produce such a signature, the presence of such a signature on a document attests that the owner has seen and signed it. Similarly, the imprint of a stamp on a document attests that someone with the appropriate stamp has stamped the document — although as we will see soon this does not have to mean that the stamp-owner has seen the document.

Digital signatures differ from physical ones in that they are not placed on an original document, modifying the original, but are separate objects that can be provided alongside the original. As a consequence, to prevent someone from transferring a signature from one document to another, digital signatures for different documents will be completely different objects.

We follow the cryptographic convention of first defining a class of schemes (that is, digital signature schemes) and then, in a later step, defining what we mean when we say that a member of this class is "secure". Keeping functionality and security separate has many advantages including that we can reason about several different levels of security for the same class of schemes. We will give some examples of this relating to signature schemes in particular.

To be able to create digital signatures, a signer first has to generate a pair of keys called the signing key (or secret key) and verification key (or public key). To do this, a digital signature scheme defines a key generation algorithm. The signing key is like a stamp with which the signer can stamp documents. Such a stamp on a document does not mean much on its own (anyone can create their own stamps) but if you know what a particular person's or organisation's stamp looks like, you can verify any stamped document to see if it was really stamped by the person or organisation you know, by comparing the imprint on the document with the imprint you know to be theirs. The verification key plays a similar role for digital signatures.

A digital signature scheme comes with two more algorithms. The signing algorithm takes a document and a signing key as input and returns a signature for the document. The verification algorithm takes a document, a signature and a verification key and outputs 1 if the signature is valid for the given key and document, otherwise 0.

It is the signer's responsibility that all verifiers have an authentic copy of the verification key. For example, in some government e-ID card schemes every citizen gets a smartcard containing a signing key and the government maintains a public database of verification keys. For a digital election, if the election authorities need to sign ballots they can publish their verification key as part of the election specification.

Definition 1. *A digital signature scheme Σ is a triple of algorithms*

$$\Sigma = (\mathtt{KeyGen}, \mathtt{Sign}, \mathtt{Verify})$$

known as the key generation, signing and verification algorithms and satisfying the correctness condition below.

The key generation algorithm takes no input and produces a pair of keys $(sk, vk) \leftarrow \mathtt{KeyGen}()$ known as the signing and verification keys. The signing algorithm takes a signing key sk and a message m as inputs and produces a signature $\sigma \leftarrow \mathtt{Sign}(sk, m)$. The verification algorithm must be deterministic. It takes a verification key vk, a message m and a signature σ as inputs and returns 0 or 1. We say that σ is a (valid) signature for m under key vk if $\mathtt{Verify}(vk, m, \sigma) = 1$.

A digital signature scheme must satisfy the following correctness condition which means that correctly generated signatures are always valid. For any message m, if you run the following sequence of algorithms then you get $b = 1$:

$$(sk, vk) \leftarrow \mathtt{KeyGen}(); \quad \sigma \leftarrow \mathtt{Sign}(sk, m); \quad b \leftarrow \mathtt{Verify}(vk, m, \sigma)$$

We will present a concrete digital signature scheme later in this work when we have developed the necessary mathematics to motivate it. For now, we briefly change our focus to talk about security notions and models.

2.3   Security Models

We introduce the cryptographer's viewpoint of security using digital signatures as an example. Security means that an certain kind of attacker can not do certain things, like create a signature on a document that verifies under someone else's key.

Cryptographic Games. The core of a security notion, at least in this work, is a cryptographic game. A game formalises two main aspects of a notion. First, it defines exactly what we want an attacker not to be able to do: a scheme will be called secure (w.r.t. a notion or game) if we can show that no attacker can win the given game. Secondly, a game specifies what we assume the attacker can do, by giving a set of moves allowed in the game and conditions on when and how often the attacker can use them.

Security games are defined in three parts. First, the game begins with some setup algorithm. Secondly, we give one or more moves that the attacker can play in the game. Finally, we state the winning conditions for the attacker.

For example, the two security notions for digital signatures that we use in this work both start by having the game playing the role of a signer and creating a signature key pair. They also both end by saying that the attacker wins if she can forge a signature but they differ in what other signatures the attacker may legitimately obtain: the security notion for "no-message" attackers considers attackers that never see any valid signatures whereas "chosen message" attackers may ask the signer to sign any message of their choice and win if they can forge a signature on a message that was never signed by the signer.

Cryptographers use two kinds of security games. The first, which could be called "trace games", are games in which the attacker wins if she does something that should be impossible in a secure system (like obtain someone's secret key or forge a signature). Here, the security definition calls a scheme secure if no attacker can win the game. The second type of game is the indistinguishability game where the attacker is asked to guess which of two things the game did. In an indistinguishability game, the attacker can always make a guess at random so the security definition says that a scheme is secure if no attacker can win the game with more than the probability 1/2 of guessing at random. It will always be clear from our description of games and their winning conditions which type of game is meant.

From Games to Security Notions. The second main ingredient in a security notion is the definition of the resources available to a hypothetical attacker. These resources are composed of two factors: first, the moves available to the attacker in the game and secondly, the computational resources that the attacker can use "during her turns". Thus, the difference between a security game and a security notion is that a game specifies an interface with which the attacker can interact but says nothing about the attacker herself whereas a security notion describes both a game and a class of attackers, usually in a statement of the form "no attacker of a given class can win the given game (with more than a certain probability)".

There are two principal classes of attackers. The first are computationally un-bounded attackers who may have unlimited resources; only a very small number of cryptographic constructions can be secured against unbounded attackers. This does not include digital signatures or indeed any scheme using a fixed-length se-cret key — an unbounded attacker can always break such schemes by trying all possible keys. Commitment schemes which we will introduce later can however be made secure even if one of the two players involved has unbounded resources.

The second class of attackers is that of polynomially bounded attackers, com-monly called efficient attackers. This class follows the notion of efficiency from complexity theory: an algorithm taking a bitstring s as input if there is some polynomial $p(x)$ such that on input a string s, the algorithm completes in at most $p(|s|)$ steps where $|s|$ is the length of s in bits. This allows us to introduce cryptographic keys since an n-bit key can be chosen in 2^n possible ways and 2^n grows much faster than any polynomial in n.

A fully formal treatment of this approach, which can be called asymptotic security, gets complex very quickly. We cannot talk about the security of any one fixed scheme but instead have to reason about families of schemes indexed by a so-called security parameter, which can very informally be thought of as the bit-length of keys in a scheme. Further, an asymptotic security notion typically says that the attacker's probability of winning the game is smaller than the inverse of any polynomial in the security parameter, what complexity theorists would call a negligible function[2].

In this work, we largely sweep such considerations under the carpet in favour of a more readable (we hope) introduction to the concepts and high-level con-nections that make up a cryptographic voting scheme. For the same reason we omit all formal security proofs which we could not present without fully formal definitions.

2.4   Security of Digital Signatures

An obvious property that signatures should have is that you cannot forge a signature on a message that verifies under someone else's key. We call such a forgery an existential forgery and we call an attacker that produces such a forgery a no-message attacker (we will see why in a moment). The security game and notion for this property have the game create a key pair and give the adversary the verification key, which is supposed to be public. The adversary wins if she produces a forgery:

Definition 2. *A digital signature scheme is existentially unforgeable under no-message attacks (EF-NMA) if no attacker can win the following game.*

Setup *The game creates a key pair* $(sk, vk) \leftarrow$ KeyGen() *and saves them; the attacker gets the verification key* vk.
Moves *None in this game.*

---

[2] A negligible quantity is not the same thing as an exponentially small one like 2^{-n}, but an exponentially small quantity is always negligible.

Winning conditions *The attacker wins the game if she provides a message/ signature pair (m^*, sk^*) such that this pair verifies under the game's key:* $\texttt{Verify}(vk, m^*, \sigma^*) = 1.$

This definition is considered necessary but not sufficient. The attacker may be a participant in some system using digital signatures in which she gets to see messages legitimately signed by some other person; she should still not be able to forge anyone else's signature on any message they did not sign. This includes such attacks as taking a signature off one message and claiming that the signer actually signed some other message. Cryptographers model this with the chosen-message attack game. Here the adversary gets an extra move: she may ask the game to sign any messages of her choice and wins if she can forge a signature on any message that the game did not sign.

Definition 3. *A digital signature scheme is existentially unforgeable under chosen message attacks (EF-CMA) if no attacker can win the following game.*

Setup *The game creates a key pair $(sk, vk) \leftarrow \texttt{KeyGen}()$ and saves them; the attacker gets the verification key vk. The game also makes an empty list L of signed messages.*

Moves *The attacker may, any number of times, send the game a message m of her choice. The game signs this message producing a signature $\sigma \leftarrow \texttt{Sign}(sk, m)$, adds m to L and returns σ to the attacker.*

Winning conditions *The attacker wins the game if she provides a message/ signature pair (m^*, sk^*) such that (1) this pair verifies under the game's key: $\texttt{Verify}(vk, m^*, \sigma^*) = 1$ and (2) the game never signed the message m^*, i.e. $m^* \notin L$.*

In neither of the above games would it make any difference if we gave the attacker an extra move to verify signatures: she already knows the verification key vk so she can do this herself.

🔒 **One-Time Signatures.** There are several reasons why it is useful to define several security notions of increasing strength for the same class of scheme, rather than just go with the strongest known definition. For signature schemes in particular, some protocols use a construction called a one-time signature: a signer who has a personal signing key pair (pk, sk) of some signature scheme generates, for each action that she performs in the protocol, a new key pair (pk', sk') of a one-time signature scheme and uses sk' to sign exactly one message whereas she signs the one-time public key pk' under her long-term key pk. One reason why one might do such a construction is for greater anonymity: in a voting scheme, a voter could send her ballot with a one-time signature under sk' to the ballot counting authority and her signature on pk' to another, independent authority. The ballot is now anonymous in the sense that it is not linked to the voter's public key pk but in the case of a dispute, the information held by the two authorities together can be used to trace the ballot. Since sk' is only ever used once, a scheme secure under no-message attacks is sufficient for this application

and in some cases this allows one to choose a more efficient signature scheme
and/or reduce the signature size.

2.5 🔒 Blind Signatures

Voting is one of several applications where it is useful to be able to sign messages without knowing their content. To ensure that only authorized voters cast
ballots, one could ask voters to authenticate themselves with an authority who
holds a signing key and signs the ballots of authorized voters. Unfortunately, a
straightforward use of digital signatures here would reveal everyone's votes to
the authority. Instead, one can use blind signatures: each voter fills in her ballot
and blinds it — we will define this formally in a moment but think of blinding
for now as placing the ballot in an envelope — then authenticates herself to the
authority, who signs the blinded ballot without knowing its contents. The voter
then turns the signature on the blinded ballot into a signature on the real ballot
and casts this ballot along with the signature.

Blind signatures will require two security properties. Security for the signer
requires that no-one can forge signatures on messages that the signer has not
blind-signed, even though the signer will not usually know which messages she
has signed. Security for the user (in our case, the voter) requires that the signer
cannot learn which messages she has signed. We follow Fujioka et al. [FOO92] in
the definition of blind signatures and Schröder and Unruh [US11] in the definition
of security properties.

Definition 4. *A blind signature scheme is a tuple*

$$BS = (\mathtt{KeyGen}, \mathtt{Blind}, \mathtt{Sign}, \mathtt{Unblind}, \mathtt{Verify})$$

of algorithms where Verify *is deterministic and the rest may be randomized.
The key generation algorithm outputs a keypair* $(sk, vk) \leftarrow \mathtt{KeyGen}()$. *The blinding algorithm takes a message* m *and a verification key* vk *and outputs a blinded
message* b *and an unblinding factor* u: $(b, u) \leftarrow \mathtt{Blind}(m, vk)$. *The signing algorithm takes a signing key* sk *and a blinded message* b *and outputs a blinded
signature* $s \leftarrow \mathtt{Sign}(b, sk)$. *The unblinding algorithm takes a verification key
vk, a blinded signature s and an unblinding factor u and outputs a signature
$\sigma \leftarrow \mathtt{Unblind}(vk, s, u)$. The verification algorithm finally takes a verification key
vk, a message m and a signature σ and outputs a bit $v \leftarrow \mathtt{Verify}(vk, m, \sigma)$ that
is 1 if the signature verifies.*

A blind signature scheme is correct if the following outputs $v = 1$ *for any
message* m, *i.e. a correctly generated signature verifies:*

$$(sk, vk) \leftarrow \mathtt{KeyGen}(); \ (b, u) \leftarrow \mathtt{Blind}(vk, m); \ s \leftarrow \mathtt{Sign}(sk, b);$$
$$\sigma \leftarrow \mathtt{Unblind}(vk, s, u); \ v \leftarrow \mathtt{Verify}(vk, m, \sigma)$$

Definition 5. *A blind signature scheme is unforgeable (secure for the signer) if
no attacker can win the following game.*

Setup *The game creates a key pair $(sk, vk) \leftarrow \mathtt{KeyGen}$ and saves them. It also creates a list L of signed messages which starts out empty. The attacker gets vk.*

Moves *The attacker may submit a message m for signing as long as $m \notin L$. The game runs $(b, u) \leftarrow \mathtt{Blind}(vk, m)$; $s \leftarrow \mathtt{Sign}(sk, b)$; $\sigma \leftarrow \mathtt{Unblind}(vk, s, u)$, adds m to L and returns the signature σ. The attacker may use this move as many times as she likes.*

Winning Conditions. *The attacker wins if she can output a list of message/ signature pairs*

$$((m_1, \sigma_1), (m_2, \sigma_2), \ldots, (m_{k+1}, \sigma_{k+1}))$$

satisfying the following conditions: (1) all messages are distinct: $m_i \neq m_j$ for all pairs (i, j) with $i \neq j$ (2) all pairs verify i.e. $\mathtt{Verify}(vk, m_i, \sigma_i) = 1$ for all i and (3) the attacker has made at most k signature moves, i.e. fewer than the number of messages she returns.

The list L here serves a slightly different purpose than for plain digital signatures: it prevents the attacker from submitting the same message twice. The winning condition is that the attacker has produced signatures on more messages than she has used in signing moves, so at least one of her output pairs is a genuine forgery. The reason for this formulation is that some blind signature schemes allow you to take a message/signature pair (m, σ) and create a new signature $\sigma' \neq \sigma$ on the same message such that (m, σ') is still a valid message/signature pair on the same key.

In the blindness game, the attacker takes the role of the signer. She may interact with two users bringing messages of the attacker's choice to be signed; her aim is to guess which order the users come in.

Definition 6. *A blind signature scheme is blind (secure for the user) if no attacker can guess the bit b in the following game with better probability than one half.*

Setup. *The game picks a bit b at random from the set $\{0, 1\}$.*

Moves. *The attacker has only one move and she may use it only once. First, the attacker may send the game a verification key vk. The attacker may then choose a pair of messages (m_0, m_1) and send them to the game. The game runs $(b_0, u_0) \leftarrow \mathtt{Blind}(vk, m_0)$ and $(b_1, u_1) \leftarrow \mathtt{Blind}(vk, m_1)$ and sends (b_b, b_{1-b}) to the attacker. If the attacker returns a pair (s_b, s_{1-b}) then the game sets $\sigma_0 \leftarrow \mathtt{Unblind}(vk, s_0, u_0)$ and $\sigma_1 \leftarrow \mathtt{Unblind}(vk, s_1, u_1)$. If both σ_0 and σ_1 are valid, the game sends (σ_0, σ_1) to the attacker.*

Winning Conditions. *The adversary may make a guess for b at any time. This stops the game. The adversary wins if the guess is correct.*

Our presentation of blind signatures is that of Fujioka et al. [FOO92] that was used in their voting protocol which we are working towards. There is a more general notion of blind signatures where the $\mathtt{Blind}$, $\mathtt{Unblind}$ and $\mathtt{Sign}$ algorithms are replaced by interactive algorithms for the user and signer, however not all blind signatures of the more general type can be used to construct a voting protocol in the manner that we do in this work.

We now turn our attention to a possible implementation of standard and blind digital signatures based on the famous RSA construction.

RSA. In 1978, Rivest, Shamir and Adleman constructed the first public-key encryption scheme [RSA78]. In 1985, Chaum used RSA to propose and construct a blind signature scheme which we will present in the next section; let us first describe the RSA construction.

Pick two prime numbers p, q and multiply them together to get $N = pq$. The RSA construction lives in the ring $\mathbb{Z}_N^*$: the elements are the integers $\{1, 2, \ldots, N-1\}$ with the operation of multiplication modulo N. This ring is not a field (p, q are zero-divisors after all) but for large N, if we pick a random element x from $\{1, \ldots, N-1\}$ the chance of hitting a non-invertible element is small. One idea behind RSA is that if you know N but not p and q, you can treat $\mathbb{Z}_N^*$ as if it were a field. Specifically, you can try and invert any element with Euclid's algorithm and if you find a non-invertible element then you can factor N (you've found a multiple of p or q that's coprime to the other factor of N) and vice versa. Factoring is arguably the most famous computationally hard problem in mathematics.

If you pick an element $x \in \mathbb{Z}_N^*$ coprime to N (not a multiple of p or q) and look at the subgroup $\{x^k \pmod{N} \mid k \in \mathbb{N}\}$ that it generates then this subgroup has order exactly $\phi(N) = (p-1)(q-1)$ where ϕ is the Euler totient function, i.e. $x^{(\phi(N))} = 1 \pmod{N}$. The RSA construction makes use of exponentiation modulo N as its basic operation. The idea is that if you pick a pair of integers e, d satisfying $e \cdot d = 1 \pmod{\phi(N)}$ then for any invertible $x \in \mathbb{Z}_N^*$ the equation $(x^e)^d = x^{e \cdot d} = x \pmod{N}$ holds, i.e. exponentiating with e and d are mutually inverse operations. Crucially, given N and any e that is coprime to N, it is considered hard to find the corresponding d or to compute $x^d \pmod{N}$ for random x. A cryptographer would say that $x \mapsto x^e \pmod{N}$ is a trapdoor one-way function: one-way because it is easy to compute yet hard to invert; "trapdoor" because given d it becomes easy to invert. Upon such a function one can construct much of modern cryptography. While it is clear that if you can factor N you can also invert the function $x \mapsto x^e \pmod{N}$ for any $e > 0$, it is less clear whether an attack on RSA implies the ability to factor N. However, RSA has stood the test of time in that no-one has managed to attack properly generated RSA keys of decent key sizes, either through factoring or any other means, since the system was first proposed.

To generate an RSA keypair (whether for encryption, signing or many other applications), the key generation algorithm `KeyGen` performs the following steps:

1. Pick large enough primes p and q and compute $N = pq$. The bitlength of N is your key length.
2. Pick any unit e of $\mathbb{Z}_N^*$ — choices such as $e = 3$ are common as they are efficient to work with.
3. Find d such that $ed = 1 \pmod{(p-1)(q-1)}$ (since you know p, q this can be done with a variation on Euclid's algorithm).
4. The public key is the pair (N, e). People can share e but everyone gets their own N. The private key is the tuple (N, e, d, p, q) — most of the time, the pair (N, d) suffices to work with though.

2.6   A Blind Signature Based on RSA

We start with the construction of a digital signature scheme, which then we show how to turn into a blind one. The scheme is based on the RSA group described above and is as follows. The private signing key is (N, d) and public verification key is (N, e). To sign a message $m \in \mathbb{Z}_N^*$ (without blinding) with key (N, d), one computes

$$\texttt{Sign}((N, d), m) := H(m)^d \pmod{N}$$

and to verify a signature σ, check that the following returns 1:

$$\texttt{Verify}((N, e), m, \sigma) := \begin{cases} 1, \text{ if} & \sigma^e = H(m) \pmod{N} \\ 0, \text{ otherwise} \end{cases}$$

Here, H is a hash function that serves two purposes. First, it allows a signature of constant size on a message of any length. Secondly, the hash function is a necessary part of the security of this construction: without it, you could take any value x, compute $y = x^e \pmod{N}$ and claim that x is a signature on y.

Chaum's blind signature has the user blind the message m (or, more precisely, the value of $H(m)$) with a random value r before sending it to the signer and strip this factor out again afterwards:

KeyGen: Standard RSA key generation.
Blind$((N, e), m)$: pick a random r from $\mathbb{Z}_N^*$ and set $b := H(m) \cdot r^e \pmod{N}$, $u := r$.
Sign: as for the basic RSA signature.
Unblind$((N, e), s, u)$: Compute $\sigma := s/u \pmod{N}$.
Verify: as for the basic RSA signature.

Let us check correctness of the blind signature. We have

$$\sigma^e = (s/u)^e = ((H(m) \cdot r^e)^d)^e = H(m)^{e \cdot d}(r^{e \cdot d})^e = 1 \cdot 1^e = 1 \pmod{N}$$

Note that σ is exactly the standard RSA signature on m for verification key (N, e). The analysis for this scheme is due to Bellare et al. and [BNPS03] and we omit it in this work.

2.7 🔒 Commitment Schemes

A commitment scheme is the cryptographer's equivalent of placing a message in an opaque envelope and placing this envelope on the table: no-one else can can read your message until you open the envelope but you cannot change the message that you have placed in the envelope either: you are committed to the message.

Definition 7. *A commitment scheme CS is a triple of algorithms*

$$CS = (\texttt{Setup}, \texttt{Commit}, \texttt{Open})$$

called the setup, commitment and opening algorithms. The setup algorithm outputs some commitment parameter $p \leftarrow \texttt{Setup}()$. The commitment algorithm takes a parameter p and a message m and returns a commitment c and an opening key k: $(c, k) \leftarrow \texttt{Commit}(p, m)$. The opening algorithm takes a parameter p, a message m, a commitment c and a key k and returns a bit b to indicate whether the commitment matches the message: $b \leftarrow \texttt{Open}(p, m, c, k)$. The opening algorithm must be deterministic.

A commitment scheme must satisfy the following correctness property. For any message m, if you run

$$p \leftarrow \texttt{Setup}(); \;\; (c, k) \leftarrow \texttt{Commit}(p, m); \;\; b \leftarrow \texttt{Open}(p, m, c, k)$$

then $b = 1$ i.e. correctly commited messages also open correctly.

Security of commitment schemes has two parts. A commitment is hiding if you cannot extract a committed message from a commitment until it is opened. A commitment is binding if you cannot change it once committed.

In more detail, the hiding property says that for any two messages of your choice, if you are given a commitment to one of them then you cannot guess better than at random which message was committed to.

Definition 8. *A commitment scheme $CS = (\texttt{Setup}, \texttt{Commit}, \texttt{Open})$ is hiding if no attacker can win the following game with better probability than one half.*

Setup *The game picks a bit b at random and creates a parameter $p \leftarrow \texttt{Setup}()$. The attacker gets p.*
Moves *The attacker may, once only, send a pair of messages m_0, m_1. The game runs $(c, k) \leftarrow \texttt{Commit}(p, m_b)$ and returns c to the attacker.*
Winning conditions *The attacker wins if she guesses b. A guess stops the game.*

The binding property asks the attacker to produce one commitment c and two different messages m, m' to which she can open the commitment, i.e. keys k, k' (which may or may not be the same) such that $\texttt{Open}$ returns 1 on both triples involved.

Definition 9. *A commitment scheme* $CS = (\mathtt{Setup}, \mathtt{Commit}, \mathtt{Open})$ *is binding if no attacker can win the following game.*

Setup. *The game creates parameters* $p \leftarrow \mathtt{Setup}()$. *The attacker gets* p.
Moves. *No moves.*
Winning Conditions. *The attacker may provide a string* c, *two messages* m, m' *and two keys* k, k'. *She wins if (1)* $m \neq m'$ *and (2) both* $\mathtt{Open}(p, c, m, k)$ *and* $\mathtt{Open}(p, c, m', k')$ *return 1.*

Commitment is one of the few cryptographic primitives that can be built securely against attackers with unlimited resources, however a commitment scheme can only be either "perfectly hiding" or "perfectly binding", not both at once. All decent commitment schemes are both hiding and binding against computationally bounded attackers.

2.8   The FOO Protocol

The cryptographic tools we introduced above allow us to describe the voting scheme presented by Fujioka, Okamoto and Ohta at Auscrypt 1992 [FOO92]. This scheme was also the one that we motivated in the informal example above and has the convenient abbreviation FOO.

The FOO protocol uses two administrators, a counter who publishes all ballots sent to her and an authority who checks voters' eligibility and can produce blind signatures. Voters must be able to talk anonymously to the counter; this requirement could be achieved with cryptographic tools that we will introduce later such as mix-nets.

The FOO protocol assumes that there is some public-key infrastructure in place in which each voter has a digital signature keypair and the association of verification keys to voters is public. FOO requires each voter to perform four steps:

1. Prepare a ballot on her own, sign it and save a private random value.
2. Authenticate herself to the authority and get a blind signature on the ballot.
3. Submit the ballot and authority signature anonymously to a ballot counter (this is equivalent to publishing the ballot).
4. After voting has closed, submit the private random value from step 1 to the counter, also anonymously.

Definition 10. *The FOO protocol is the following protocol for voters, an authority and a ballot counter.*

Tools. The FOO protocol requires a digital signature scheme Σ, a blind signature scheme BS and a commitment scheme CS. We write algorithms with the scheme name as prefix, for example $BS.\mathtt{Sign}$, to avoid ambiguity. We assume that some commitment parameters $p \leftarrow CS.\mathtt{Setup}()$ have been generated.
Voter. The voter starts out with a digital signature keypair (sk_V, vk_V) for Σ, a vote v and the authority's blind signature verification key vk_A.

1. She creates a commitment $(c, k) \leftarrow CS.\texttt{Commit}(p, v)$, blinds it as $(b, u) \leftarrow BS.\texttt{Blind}(vk_A, c)$ and signs this as $\sigma_V \leftarrow \Sigma.\texttt{Sign}(sk_V, b)$.
2. She then sends (ID_V, b, σ_V) to the authority and expects a blinded signature s in return. Here ID_V is some string describing the voter's identity.
3. On receipt of s, she creates the blind signature $\sigma_A \leftarrow \texttt{Unblind}(vk_A, s, u)$ and sends her ballot (c, σ_A) anonymously to the counter. The counter replies with some random identifier i.
4. After voting has closed and the counter has invited the voters to open their ballots, the voter sends (i, v, k) anonymously to the counter.

Authority. The authority has a keypair (sk_A, vk_A) for a blind signature scheme. She also has access to a table T of the identities and verification keys of all eligible voters: (ID_V, vk_V) for all voters V. Further, the authority has a list L of the identities, blinded ballots and signatures of all voters who have already voted (this list starts out empty of course). When a voter sends the authority a triple (ID_V, b, σ_V) the authority checks that the voter is eligible to vote, i.e. $ID_V \in T$, and retrieves the corresponding verification key vk_V. The authority then checks that the signature is valid: $\Sigma.\texttt{Verify}(vk_V, b, \sigma_V) = 1$. If this is correct, the authority checks that the voter has not already voted, i.e. ID_V does not appear in L. The authority then adds (ID_V, b, σ_V) to L and returns a blind signature $s \leftarrow BS.\texttt{Sign}(sk_A, b)$ to the voter.

At the end of the voting phase, the authority publishes the list L.

Counter. The ballot counter starts out with the authority's verification key vk_A. The counter holds no secrets and performs no secret operations: the entire protocol for the counter can be performed in public and therefore checked by anyone.

During the voting phase, the counter anonymously receives ballots (c, σ). She checks that each incoming ballot is valid, i.e. $BS.\texttt{Verify}(vk_A, c, \sigma) = 1$ and publishes all accepted ballots along with their signatures and a unique identifier i, i.e. the counter maintains a list of entries (i, c, σ). The identifiers could be randomly chosen or simply sequence numbers.

At the end of the election, the counter invites all voters to open their ballots. On receipt of an anonymous message (i, v, k) the counter retrieves the entry (i, c, σ) and if such an entry exists, she computes $x \leftarrow CS.\texttt{Open}(p, v, c, k)$. If this returns 1, the ballot is valid and the counter adds the vote v to the set of valid votes. Finally, the counter tallies all valid votes.

Privacy of FOO. The FOO protocol was published in 1992, before any formal models for voting schemes had been developed. Consequently, the original paper only offers a "proof sketch" for privacy; no-one has presented a formal analysis of privacy in FOO to date although there is no reason to suspect that this property would not hold. The modelling of anonymous channels is also not standardised; one could use mix-nets (discussed in Section 6) to achieve anonymity in which case the anonymity offered is well understood.

We give a brief sketch of why FOO is private. Before the tallying phase, each voter submits a pair (c, σ). c is a commitment and thus hides the contained vote;

σ is a signature on the commitment so it cannot leak more information on the vote than the commitment itself. Even the authority only sees the commitment and not the vote in clear, so votes are kept private.

After tallying, the votes are revealed and FOO argue that no-one, not even the authority and vote counter together, can link a voter to a vote. This is because the items on the board are posted anonymously and the only non-anonymous communication that might link a voter to a ballot occurs when the voter obtains a signature from the authority. However, the authority only sees a blinded commitment and the returned signature is a blind signature, so the authority cannot link the ballots on the board to the commitments that she has signed.

Verifiability of FOO. To date, no formal models for verifiability exist that could be usefully applied to FOO. We will briefly argue informally why FOO is a verifiable protocol. Specifically, we check the following properties.

Individual verifiability Voters can check that their ballot was counted.

Universal verifiability Anyone can check that all ballots were counted correctly.

Ballot verifiability Anyone can check that all ballots correspond to correct votes.

Eligibility verifiability Anyone can check that only eligible voters have voted, and only once each.

For individual verifiability, since the counter just publishes all ballots the voter can check if her ballot is included among the published ones. Better still, in case of a dispute the voter can expose a cheating counter if the counter refuses to accept a correctly signed ballot.

Universal verifiability is easy since the counter holds no secrets: anyone can repeat the count of all opened ballots. The same holds for ballot verifiability since the ballots are opened individually.

Indeed, the nature of the FOO protocol is that only eligibility is assured by cryptographic means alone; the other verifiability properties follow from the public nature of the bulletin board and counting operation. This comes at the cost of practicality: voters must interact with the system twice, once to cast their ballots and once again to open them. Later systems such as Helios only require voters to interact with the system once; verifiability will become a more involved matter here.

For eligiblility, first note that anyone can verify that only correctly signed ballots are counted. If we assume that the authority is honest then only eligible voters will receive a signature from the authority and only once each. Even if the authority is dishonest, its log L would show if it had ever blind- signed a ballot that was not accompanied by a correct signature from a legitimate voter key, or if the authority had signed two ballots with a signature from the same voter.

Dispute Resolution in FOO. In addition to verifiability, the FOO protocol provides a digital audit trail that can be used to resolve many disputes which could arise. We mention some cases that were addressed in the original paper; we imagine that all these disputes could be brought before a judge or election official. In the following we assume that honest parties' keys are not available to cheaters. This means that in any dispute between a honest and a dishonest party, the honest party will be able to convince a judge that the other side is cheating - more precisely, that either the other side is cheating or her signature has been forged. In the following we give a list of possible accusations and how a judge should respond.

- The authority refuses to give a legitimate voter a signature, or provides her with an invalid signature.

  The voter can publish a blinded ballot and her digital signature on it; a judge can now ask the authority to either sign this ballot or give a reason for refusing to do so. If the judge asks to see the authority's blinded signature, the voter can reveal her vote and blinding factor to the judge who can then check the unblinding step and verify the resulting signature. This way, a cheating authority will always be exposed.

- The authority claims that a voter has already voted.

  A judge can ask for the voter's previous blinded ballot and digital signature as proof. If the authority fails to produce this, she is exposed - if she does produce this, the voter must explain why said blinded ballot carries a signature under her key.

- The authority signs a ballot that does not come from a legitimate voter, or more than one ballot from the same voter.

  The judge checks the counter's published ballots against the authority's list L for any signed ballots that do not have a valid voter-signature in L, or two ballots with the same voter's signature.

- The authority signs something that is not a legitimate ballot.

  If the illegitimate ballot is never opened, it does not contribute to the result and can be ignored. Once a ballot is opened, the judge can check its contents. It is not the authority's fault if its signature is discovered on an invalid ballot: since the authority's signature is blind, the authority has no way of knowing the contents of what it signs.

- A voter tries to vote more than once.

  The judge checks that all the counter's ballots are also referenced in the list L and then checks the list L for two different ballots with the same voter's signature.

- The counter refuses to accept a legitimate ballot.

  The judge checks the signature on the disputed ballot; if it verifies and the counter still refuses then the counter is exposed as a cheater. The same applies to opening keys k where the judge checks using the opening algorithm.

- The counter accepts an illegitimate ballot (without a valid signature).

  The judge checks the signature; if it fails the counter is exposed as a cheater. The same applies to opening information.

– The counter produces a false result.

The judge recomputes the result and disqualifies the counter if the results do not match.

3 Homomorphic Voting

The FOO protocol from the last section scores well on privacy, verifiability and dispute resolution but has one major drawback: voters need to interact with the voting system at two different times, once to cast their ballot and once again after the voting period has ende to open their ballot. A different approach to cryptographic voting removes this drawback.

3.1 Motivation and Example

Here is another sketch of a "physical" voting protocol. Consider a yes/no referendum. Each voter gets two balls of the same size and appearance except that one weighs 1 lb[3]and the other 2 lb. To vote no, the voter writes her name on the lighter of two balls and places it on a tray; to vote yes she does the same for the heavier one. This allows anyone to check that only eligible voters have voted and only once each by comparing the names on the cast ball(ot)s with a list of eligible voters. To tally the election, one first counts the number of balls cast, then weighs the entire tray and derives the number of light and heavy balls from the total amount and weight of the balls. This way, the amount that each individual ball(ot) contributed to the tally is hidden from everyone except the voter who cast it. One point that we will have to take care of in the cryptographic protocol based on this idea is how we prevent a voter from casting a forged ball weighing more than 2 lb to gain an unfair advantage.

The cryptographic tool that we will use to build the equivalent of the balls above goes by the name of "homomorphic asymmetric encryption". The adjective "homomorphic" describes a scheme where ciphertexts (or commitments, signatures etc.) can be added together to create a new ciphertext for the sum of the original messages. Before we can define homomorphic asymmetric encryption, we first need to define what asymmetric encryption is in the first place.

3.2 🔒 Asymmetric Encryption

Asymmetric or "public key" encryption is perhaps the best-known invention of modern cryptography. It is certainly one of the oldest: it was first suggested by Diffie and Hellman in 1976 [DH76] and implemented successfully by Rivest, Shamir and Adleman in 1978 [RSA78].

There are many ways to explain asymmetric encryption using physical terms: our favourite example is a letter-box. Anyone can send you letters by placing them in your letter-box but only you can get letters out of the box again[4].

---

[3] One pound, abbreviated lb, is around 0.454 kg.

Indeed, once someone has placed a letter in your letter-box, even they can't get it out again.

As for digital signatures, we define the types of algorithms required and the security requirements.

Definition 11. *An asymmetric encryption scheme E is a triple of algorithms*

$$E = (\texttt{KeyGen}, \texttt{Encrypt}, \texttt{Decrypt})$$

where the key genration algorithm takes no input and returns a pair $(pk, sk) \leftarrow$ KeyGen() *known as the public and secret key. The encryption algorithm takes a public key pk and a message m and returns a ciphertext* $c \leftarrow$ Encrypt(pk, m). *The decryption algorithm takes a secret key sk and a ciphertext c and outputs either a decrypted message* $d \leftarrow$ Decrypt(sk, c) *or declares the ciphertext invalid, which we indicate with the special output symbol* $\perp$. *The decryption algorithm must be deterministic.*

The correctness condition is that for any message m, the following operations result in $d = m$:

$$(pk, sk) \leftarrow \texttt{KeyGen}(); \ \ c \leftarrow \texttt{Encrypt}(pk, m); \ \ d \leftarrow \texttt{Decrypt}(sk, c)$$

3.3 Security of Encryption

It took the community of cryptographers some time to come up with the definitions of security for asymmetric encryption that are in use today. The first obvious condition is that given a ciphertext, you should not be able to tell the contained message. Unfortunately this is not sufficient, here is an example why. Alice, a famous cryptographer, wishes to announce the birth of her child to her family while keeping its gender secret from the world at large for now. She encrypts the good news under her family's public keys and sends out the ciphertexts. Eve, an eavesdropper from the press, obtains Alice's ciphertexts. This should not matter — this is exactly what encryption is for, after all.

Eve guesses that Alice's message is either "It's a boy!" or "It's a girl!". Instead of trying to decrypt a completely unknown message, Eve would already be happy if she could tell which of two messages (that she already knows) Alice has encrypted. Further, Eve might be able to obtain Alice's family's public keys from a directory — they are meant to be public as their name suggests — and Eve can encrypt both her guessed messages herself under these public keys and check if either of her ciphertexts matches the one sent by Alice. If so, Eve has effectively broken Alice's secret.

This story gives rise to two more requirements: given a ciphertext and two candidate messages, you should be unable to guess which of the two messages was

---

[4] The design of letter-boxes varies a lot between countries; we have in mind the continental European style where letterboxes have a flap to insert letters and the owner can open a door on the letter-box with a key to retrieve letters.

encrypted; given two ciphertexts you should not be able to tell if they encrypt the same message or not. The first common security requirement for encryption is known as indistinguishability under chosen plaintext attack, abbreviated IND-CPA. Here, the attacker may chose any two messages, send them to the security game and get an encryption of one of them back; a scheme is called IND-CPA secure if she cannot tell which message the security game chose to encrypt.

Definition 12. *An asymmetric encryption scheme E is IND-CPA secure if no attacker can win the following game with better probability than $1/2$, the probability of guessing at random.*

Setup. *The game creates a keypair $(pk, sk) \leftarrow \mathtt{KeyGen}()$ and gives the attacker the public key pk. The game also picks a bit b randomly from $\{0, 1\}$ and keeps this secret.*

Moves. *Once in the game, the attacker may pick a pair of messages m_0 and m_1 of the same length[†] and send them to the game. The game encrypts $c \leftarrow \mathtt{Encrypt}(pk, m_b)$ and returns this to the attacker.*

Winning Conditions. *The attacker may make a guess at b which ends the game. The attacker wins if she guesses correctly.*

([†]) The condition that the two messages be of the same length is to avoid the attacker guessing the message from the ciphertext length. In the example above, "boy" has three letters but "girl" has four so any encryption scheme that returns a ciphertext with the same number of characters as the message is vulnerable to such an attack and Alice should pad both her messages to the same length to be safe. In practice, many encryption schemes work not on characters but on blocks of characters in which case the restriction can be weakened to both messages producing the same number of ciphertext blocks; the ElGamal scheme which we will consider later operates on messages in a fixed group where all messages have the same length "1 group element" and this condition is vacuous.

There are stronger notions of security for encryption that we will introduce at the appropriate point later in this work and explain how they relate to keeping encrypted votes private.

3.4 🔒 Homomorphic Encryption

A homomorphic encryption scheme offers an additional algorithm Add that takes two ciphertexts and a public key and produces a new ciphertext for the "sum" of the two messages in the original ciphertexts. We put "sum" in quotes because the principle can be applied to different operations such as multiplication as well.

Definition 13. *An asymmetric encryption scheme*

$$E = (\mathtt{KeyGen}, \mathtt{Encrypt}, \mathtt{Decrypt})$$

is homomorphic if there are these additional operations:

− An operation $+$ on the message space.

– An algorithm Add *that takes a public key pk and two ciphertexts c_1, c_2 and outputs another ciphertext s.*

The correctness condition is that for any messages m_1, m_2 the following returns $d = m_1 + m_2$:

$(pk, sk) \leftarrow$ KeyGen(); $c_1 \leftarrow$ Encrypt(pk, m_1); $c_2 \leftarrow$ Encrypt(pk, m_2);
$c \leftarrow$ Add(pk, c_1, c_2); $d \leftarrow$ Decrypt(sk, c)

Actually, we require a slightly stronger condition as the presentation above does not exclude the following degenerate construction: a "ciphertext" is a list of ciphertexts, the encryption algorithm returns a list with one element and Add just returns a list containing its two input ciphertexts. The decryption algorithm takes a list, decrypts each element individually and returns the sum of all decryptions. What we require in particular is that sums of ciphertexts look just like ordinary ones and even the legitimate decryptor cannot tell a sum from a simple ciphertext. For example, if a ciphertext decrypts to 2, the decryptor should not be able to tell if this was a direct encryption of 2, a sum of encryptions of 0 and 2 or of 1 and 1 etc.

$\sum$ **Prime-Order Groups.** We are now working towards the ElGamal encryption scheme that we will use to build a toy voting scheme called "minivoting" and then extend this to get the Helios voting scheme. ElGamal uses a prime-order group, we sketch a number-theoretic construction. To set up such a group, one typically picks a prime p such that $q = (p-1)/2$ is also prime (this is even more essential than for RSA, to avoid "small subgroup" problems). The group $\mathbb{Z}_p^*$ with multiplication modulo p has $p - 1$ elements; since p is a large prime and therefore is odd there will be a factor 2 in $p - 1$. If $(p - 1)$ factors as $2 \cdot q$ where q is also prime and we pick an element $g \in \mathbb{Z}_p^*$ of order q then the subgroup $G := \langle g \rangle \subset \mathbb{Z}_p^*$ is itself a cyclic group of order q. Since q is prime, G has no true subgroups, i.e. apart from the identity, there is no extra "structure" to be discovered by examining the traces of individual group elements[5].

The ElGamal encryption scheme lives in such a group G given by parameters (p, q, g). Since G is isomorphic to $\mathbb{Z}_q$, we have an inclusion $\mathbb{Z}_q \rightarrow G, (x \mapsto g^x \pmod{p})$. This map is efficient to compute (square-and-multiply and variations) but is considered to be hard to invert on randomly chosen points. Its inverse is known as taking the discrete logarithm of a group element. Further, given two group elements h and k, there are unique integers $a, b \in \mathbb{Z}_q$ such that $h = g^a \pmod{p}$ and $k = g^b \pmod{p}$. The group operation sends such (h, k) to $h \cdot k = g^{a+b} \pmod{p}$. We can define a further operation $\otimes$ that sends such (h, k) to $g^{a \cdot b} \pmod{p}$. This turns out to be a bilinear map on G called the Diffie-Hellman product and it is considered to be hard to compute in general; computing it for random h, k is the computational Diffie-Hellman problem. For random h, k and another group element z, it is even considered hard to tell whether $z = h \otimes k$ or z is just another random group element, this is called the decisional Diffie-Hellman problem. However, if you are given the integer a (from which you could easily compute $h = g^a$ in G) then you can easily take the Diffie-Hellman product with any k as $h \otimes k = k^a \pmod{p}$.

Definition 14. *A Diffie-Hellman group is a group $\langle g \rangle \subset \mathbb{Z}_p^*$ of order q for p, q primes with $(p-1)/2 = q$. Such a group is given by parameters (p, q, g) and such parameters can be public and shared among all users of a cryptosystem.*

To generate a Diffie-Hellman keypair, pick parameters if required and pick an x at random from $\mathbb{Z}_q$, then set $y = g^x \pmod{p}$. Your secret key is x and your public key is y.

Two comments on this scheme are in order. First, the group has order q but is represented as a subgroup of $\mathbb{Z}_p^*$. The rule to remember is, always reduce group elements modulo p and integers (exponents) modulo q. This is why you pick your secret key from $\mathbb{Z}_q$ (it's an integer) and then compute the public key (a group element) modulo p.

Secondly, there are other possible realisations of cryptographically useful prime-order groups in which the Diffie-Hellman product and discrete logarithms are assumed to be hard. The most popular alternative uses a representation on an elliptic curve over a finite field; we will not go into details of the construction in this work but the ElGamal encryption scheme works identically whether you are using a $\mathbb{Z}_p^*$ group or an elliptic curve group.

3.5   ElGamal

The ElGamal encryption scheme [E85] was invented in 1985. It encrypts a message $m \in G$ as a pair (c, d):

Definition 15. *The ElGamal encryption scheme is the encryption scheme given by the algorithms below.*

KeyGen Pick or obtain parameters (p, q, g). Pick sk at random from $\mathbb{Z}_q$ and set $pk = g^{sk} \pmod{p}$, return (pk, sk).

Encrypt(pk, m) Pick r at random from $\mathbb{Z}_q$ and set $c = g^r \pmod{p}, d = m \cdot pk^r \pmod{p}$. Return (c, d).

Decrypt$(sk, (c, d))$ Compute $m = d/c^{sk} \pmod{p}$.

The message is multiplied with a random group element, resulting in a uniformly distributed group element d. Since r was random in $\mathbb{Z}_q$, so is $pk^r \pmod{p}$ for any group element pk, thus d on its own is independent of m. To allow the key-holder, and her only, to decrypt, an additional element c is provided. Since $m = d/(c \otimes y)$, the decryptor can compute m with her secret key; for anyone else extracting the message given both c and d is equivalent to solving the computational Diffie-Hellman problem. Telling which of two messages was encrypted (the IND-CPA security game) is equivalent[6] to solving the decisional Diffie-Hellman problem.

 Exponential ElGamal. ElGamal is homomorphic but the operation is not as useful as we would like: for ciphertexts (c, d) and (c', d') we can set

$$\texttt{Add}((c, d), (c', d')) := (c \cdot c' \pmod{p}, d \cdot d' \pmod{p})$$

such that for messages m, m' in G we get a ciphertext for $m \cdot m' \pmod{p}$. What we would really like for voting is a scheme where messages lie in the additive group $\mathbb{Z}_q$ and we can perform homomorphic addition, rather than multiplication, of ciphertexts. If our messages are restricted to small integers (indeed, in our ballots they will be wither 0 or 1) then we can use a variation called exponential ElGamal: to encrypt an integer m, replace the d-component with $g^m \cdot pk^r \pmod{p}$. For two ciphertexts (c, d) for m and (c', d') for m' the $\texttt{Add}$ operation now produces a ciphertext that decrypts to $g^{m+m' \pmod{q}}$ as desired. While getting the exponent back from an arbitrary group element is hard (the discrete logarithm problem), for small enough exponents this can be done just by trying $g^0, g^1, g^2, \ldots$ until we find the correct decryption. This is the approach taken by Helios, which we will replicate in our minivoting scheme as a first step towards constructing Helios.

Other Homomorphic Schemes. Besides ElGamal, there are numerous other homomorphic encryption schemes. The DLIN scheme of Boneh et al. [BBS04] works on similar principles to ElGamal but uses a different security assumptioni and is thus applicable to different kinds of groups. The Paillier scheme [P99] operates in composite-order RSA-type groups and offers additive instead of multiplicative homomoprhism, but is much less efficient than ElGamal. There are also many extensions of ElGamal such as Signed ElGamal (a.k.a. TDH0) and TDH2 [SG98] from which an ElGamal ciphertext with homomorphic properties can be extracted.

3.6   Minivoting

We will develop the concept of homomorphic voting in several steps, ending up with Helios as an example. The first step is a scheme called "minivoting" by Bernhard et al. from Esorics 2011 [BC+11]. Minivoting is not verifiable and indeed is only secure against passive attackers who cannot send malformed ciphertexts. In a later step we will add further components to minivoting in order to obtain a fully secure scheme.

---

[6] Ignoring some details.

Definition 16. *Minivoting is the following voting scheme for a yes/no question, based on a homomorphic asymmetric encryption scheme E with a message space $\mathbb{Z}_n$ for some n larger than the number of voters.*

Participants. *Minivoting requires one authority, a public bulletin board to which everyone can post authenticated messages and any number of voters smaller than n.*

Setup. *The authority creates a key pair $(pk, sk) \leftarrow E.\mathsf{KeyGen}$ and posts pk to the bulletin board.*

Voting. *Voters read the public key pk off the board. They choose $v = 1$ for "yes" and $v = 0$ for "no" and create a ballot $b \leftarrow E.\mathsf{Encrypt}(pk, v)$ which they post on the board.*

Tallying. *The authority uses the $E.\mathsf{Add}$ operation to add all ballots, creating a final ballot s which she decrypts as $d \leftarrow E.\mathsf{Decrypt}(sk, s)$. The authority then counts the number m of ballots submitted and posts the result "d yes, $m - d$ no" to the board.*

4   Vote Privacy

We give a notion of ballot privacy against observers for voting schemes, following the principles set out by the IND-CPA game for encryption. The attacker can choose two votes for each voter and the voters will either cast the first or second vote (all voters make the same choice which of the two to cast). The attacker's aim is to tell which choice the voters made, just like the IND-CPA game asks the attacker to tell which of two messages was encrypted. Since the two results that this game produces may differ, which would immediately tell the attacker what is going on, the game will always report the first result.

Definition 17. *A voting scheme has ballot privacy against observers if no attacker can do better in the following game than guess at random (with probability $1/2$).*

Setup. *The game picks a bit b at random and keeps it secret. The game then sets up the voting scheme and plays the voters, authorities and bulletin board.*

Moves. *Once for each voter, the attacker may choose two votes v_0 and v_1. The game writes down both votes. If $b = 0$, the game lets the voter vote for v_0; if $b = 1$ the game lets the voter vote for v_1.*
The attacker may ask to look at the bulletin board at any point in the game. When all voters have voted, the game gives the attacker the result computed as if everyone had cast their first (v_0) vote.

Winning Conditions. *At any point in the game, the attacker may submit a guess for b. This ends the game immediately. The attacker wins if her guess is correct.*

Although we do not prove it here, we could show that if there is an attacker with a better than random chance of winning this game for the minivoting scheme (based on some homomorphic encryption scheme E) then we can build an attacker who wins the IND-CPA game for the same encryption scheme E with better than one half probability too. The rough idea is that any attacker guessing better than at random for the ballot privacy game must have selected at least one voter and given her different votes v_0 and v_1, so we could run the IND-CPA game with messages v_0 and v_1 and use the attacker's guess to make our guess at which one was encrypted. The crux of the proof is that the IND-CPA game allows only one challenge move whereas the ballot privacy game allows many voters. This gives us the following proposition.

Proposition 18. *For any IND-CPA secure homomorphic asymmetric encryption scheme, the derived minivoting scheme has ballot privacy against observers.*

In particular this holds for the minivoting scheme based on ElGamal.

4.1 🔒 Threshold Encryption

Minivoting used a single authority which is bad for two reasons. First, a dishonest authority could decrypt individual ballots. Secondly, if the authority loses her key, the election cannot be tallied. (We will deal with the authority trying to claim a false result in a later section.)

Threshold schemes aim to mitigate these risks. In a k-out-of-n threshold scheme, there are n authorities and any subset of at least k can tally the election. In this way, a coalition of up to $k-1$ dishonest authorities cannot decrypt individual ballots (or obtain early results) whereas up to $n-k$ of the authorities can drop out and the election can still be tallied.

In our definition of threshold schemes, the authorites run an interactive protocol to generate keys, as a result of which each authority obtains a public key share and a secret key share. A user of the scheme can run a key combination algorithm to obtain a single public key and encrypt messages with this. To decrypt, each authority that takes part in the decryption process produces a decryption share with her secret key and anyone can combine at least k decryption shares to recover the message.

Definition 19. *A (k, n) threshold encryption scheme consists of a key generation protocol* KeyGen *for n authorities and four algorithms*

$$(\text{CombineKey}, \text{Encrypt}, \text{DecryptShare}, \text{Combine})$$

The key generation protocol results in all participants obtaining a public key share pk_i and a secret key share sk_i. The key combination algorithm takes a list of n public key shares and returns a public key $pk \leftarrow \text{CombineKey}(pk_1, \ldots, pk_n)$ or the special symbol $\perp$ to indicate invalid shares. The encryption algorithm works just like non-threshold encryption: $c \leftarrow \text{Encrypt}(pk, m)$. The decryption share algorithm takes a secret key share sk_i and a ciphertext c and outputs a decryption share $d_i \leftarrow \text{DecryptShare}(sk_i, c)$. The recombination algorithm takes a ciphertext c, a set $D = \{d_i\}_{i \in I}$ of at least k decryption shares and outputs either a message m or the symbol $\perp$ to indicate failure.

The correctness condition is that for any message m and any set I of at least k authorities, the following yields d = m:

$((pk_1, \ldots, pk_n), (sk_1, \ldots, sk_n)) \leftarrow \texttt{KeyGen}();$
$pk \leftarrow \texttt{CombineKey}(pk_1, \ldots, pk_n); \quad c \leftarrow \texttt{Encrypt}(pk, m);$
$\text{for } i \in I : \quad d_i \leftarrow \texttt{DecryptShare}(sk_i, c); \quad d \leftarrow \texttt{Combine}(c, \{d_i\}_{i \in I});$

Threshold ElGamal for $k = n$. Here is an implementation of threshold encryption for $k = n$, i.e. all authorities must be present to decrypt. ElGamal can also be used for arbitrary (k, n) thresholds but the construction is more complex. The definition below is secure against up to $n - 1$ authorities as long as they follow the protocol, i.e. they may compute and communicate freely "on the side" but can not deviate from the key generation protocol. We will adapt the system to be secure against misbehaving authorities in a later section once we have introduced the necessary tools.

KeyGen All authorities agree on or obtain common parameters (p, q, g). Each authority then simply generates an ElGamal keypair under these parameters.
CombineKey Take all n shares $pk_1, \ldots, pk_n$ and multiply them together: $pk \leftarrow \prod_{i=1}^{n} pk_i \pmod{p}$.
Encrypt This is standard ElGamal encryption with the public key.
DecryptShare(sk_i, c) An ElGamal ciphertext is a pair $c = (a, b)$. Return the share $d_i := a^{sk_i} \pmod{p}$.
Combine On input a ciphertext $c = (a, b)$ and a set of n decryption shares $\{d_i\}_{i=1}^{n}$ set $d := b / \prod_{i=1}^{n} d_i \pmod{p}$.

This works because

$$d = b / \prod_{i=1}^{n} d_i = b / \prod_{i=1}^{n} a^{sk_i} = b / a^{\sum_{i=1}^{n} sk_i \pmod{q}} = b / a^{sk} \pmod{p}$$

where $sk := \sum_{i=1}^{n} sk_i \pmod{q}$ is the secret key corresponding to the public key pk, so this is just a normal ElGamal decryption. We draw the reader's attention to the correct use of ps and qs: the group elements are taken modulo p whereas the integers in the exponent are taken modulo $q = (p - 1)/2$.

4.2 Problems with Minivoting

Minivoting (even with threshold encryption) is not a secure scheme if some of the participants misbehave. For example,

1. A voter may encrypt g^2 to get an unfair advantage. For more complex ballots than yes/no questions, voters have even more ways to cheat.
2. A voter can stall the election by submitting a ballot for g^r for some random r — no-one will be able to decrypt the result anymore.
3. You have to trust the authorities that they have announced the correct result.

Luckily, cryptographers have found solutions to all these problems. They are:

1. Zero-knowledge proofs.
2. Zero-knowledge proofs.
3. Zero-knowledge proofs.

Zero-knowledge proofs are a technique to turn any protocol secure against observers into a protocol secure against misbehaving participants. The idea is that whenever a participant submits some information (say, a ballot) they must submit two things: first, the ballot and secondly, a proof that they have made a correct ballot. "Zero-knowledge" means that these proofs reveal nothing beyond that the ballot is correct. In particular, a proof that your ballot is correct does not leak your vote.

4.3 🔒 Zero-knowledge Proofs

Zero-knowledge proofs[7] are tools that allow you to prove that you have done a certain operation correctly, without revealing more than that fact. In this section we develop the mathematical theory of zero-knowledge proofs based on so-called Σ-protocols and then give the protocols used in Helios. Our development and presentation of Σ-protocol theory follows the work of Bernhard [B14]; we present the Schnorr [S91], Chaum-Pedersen [CP92] and disjunctive Chaum-Pedersen (DCP) protocols.

Proofs in Helios. Helios uses zero-knowledge proofs in three ways:

- Each voter proves that she has cast a ballot for a valid vote, without revealing her vote.
- The authorities prove that they know their secret keys (that match the election public keys), without revealing their secret keys.
- At the end of the election, the authorities prove that they have tallied correctly (decrypted the result correctly), again without revealing their secret keys.

Consider an ElGamal keypair $(sk, pk = g^{sk} \pmod{p})$ for a group defined by parameters (p, q, g). Suppose you want to prove that you know the secret key matching the public key. One paper-based protocol, following the ideas in earlier sections, could work like this: prepare 100 keypairs. Write the secret keys on pieces of paper and place them in opaque envelopes; write the matching public keys on the outside of the envelopes. Let someone pick 99 of the envelopes, open them and check that the keys inside match those outside (i.e. that $g^{sk_i} =$

---

[7] Formally, one can distinguish zero-knowledge "proofs" from "arguments" and "proofs of knowledge" from "proofs of facts". We ignore these distinctions here.

pk_i (mod p) for each pair (pk_i, sk_i) opened). If this holds for randomly chosen envelopes, then with probability at least $99/100$ the last envelope is also correct and you can use the key written on the outside as your public key. This protocol has two slight drawbacks. First, it is wasteful with envelopes — especially if you want a really high security margin like $1 - 2^{100}$ — which is not good for the environment. Secondly, you only convince one person that your key is correct: an observing third party cannot know if you have not agreed in advance which envelope your accomplice will not pick, in which case you could easily cheat and claim someone else's public key as your own, for which you do not know the secret key.

To address the first problem we note that the map turning secret keys into public keys, $(sk \mapsto g^{sk}$ (mod p)), is linear if you look at it the right way. If you have two key pairs (sk, pk) and (sk', pk') then $sk + sk'$ (mod q) is the secret key matching the public key $pk \cdot pk'$ (mod p). Note that the operation on public keys is written as a multiplication instead of an addition but the secret and public keys live in isomorphic groups so they are really both just group operations. The map taking a secret key to a public key is an isomorphism, its inverse is the discrete logarithm operation which is (hopefully) hard to compute but a well-defined map nonetheless. Further, if you rerandomise a secret key sk with an integer r to get $sk' = r \cdot sk$ (mod q) then the corresponding public key is $pk' = pk^r$ (mod p) where pk was the public key corresponding to sk.

$$\sum$$

On Linearity. To speak of a linear map we actually need a vector space over a field; since we are working in a prime-order cyclic group $\mathbb{Z}_q$ for the exponents we may embed this into the finite field $\mathbb{F}_q$ by adjoining the obvious field multiplication structure to get our field. Any field is a one-dimensional vector space over itself so the secret key space can be interpreted as a $\mathbb{F}_q$–vector space. The public key space is isomorphic to the secret key space, so we can really speak of the isomorphism $(sk \mapsto g^{sk}$ (mod p)) as an $\mathbb{F}_q$–linear map. The statement that you can add secret keys is saying that our map commutes with vector addition; rerandomising a key is field multiplication and together these two properties show linearity. Why we do all this should become clear later when we construct Σ-protocols on statements involving vectors which are tuples of group elements.

With these foundations in place, here is a protocol to prove that you know a secret key sk matching a given public key pk. Pick a second keypair (sk', pk') and reveal pk'. Let someone pick a number c between 0 and $n - 1$ (for $n \leq q$, to be exact) and compute the linear combination $pk'' = pk' \cdot pk^c$ (mod p). You then reveal $sk'' := sk' + c \cdot sk$ (mod q) and your challenger checks that $g^{sk''} = pk''$ (mod p). This protocol does the same (and some more) than the one above with n envelopes. To see why, consider the point of view of the challenger who knows pk and pk' and has just picked c. Unless you know the correct sk, or are able to compute such a sk, there is only one single value of c for which you have any hope of providing the correct answer that will convince your challenger. The probability of cheating is bounded by $1/n$ and n can be chosen as large as you like (up to $q - 1$).

Suppose that there are two distinct values of c, namely c_1 and c_2, for which you have some nonzero probability of finding a correct answer and call these answers sk_1'' and sk_2''. By a bit of linear algebra, since both answers are correct we must have

$$g^{sk_1''} = pk' \cdot pk^{c_1} \pmod{p} \tag{1}$$

$$g^{sk_2''} = pk' \cdot pk^{c_2} \pmod{p} \tag{2}$$

which suggests that we divide the two, cancelling pk':

$$g^{sk_1''}/g^{sk_2''} = pk^{c_1}/pk^{c_2} \pmod{p} \tag{3}$$

$$g^{sk_1''-sk_2'' \pmod{q}} = pk^{c_1-c_2 \pmod{q}} \pmod{p} \tag{4}$$

but the exponent space is a field and c_1, c_2 are distinct so we can rearrange to get

$$g^{\frac{sk_1''-sk_2''}{c_1-c_2} \pmod{q}} = pk \pmod{p} \tag{5}$$

and this exponent is exactly the secret key sk such that $g^{sk} = pk \pmod{p}$. In other words, if you can find the answers sk_1'', sk_2'' to two different challenges c_1, c_2 then from this information you can compute a secret key $sk = \frac{sk_1''-sk_2''}{c_1-c_2}$ $\pmod{q}$ yourself. This property is called "special soundness". Conversely, if you do not know the secret key sk then you cannot hope to answer any two different challenges c_1, c_2 in the same protocol so your probability of cheating is at most $1/n$. This inability for Alice to cheat (except with a tiny probability) is called "soundness" of the protocol. Special soundness implies soundness.

This protocol is Schnorr's protocol [S91] for proof of knowledge of a discrete logarithm. An additional advantage of this protocol over the envelope-based one is that you can pick one keypair (pk, sk) and re-run the protocol to convince many different people that you know your secret key, picking a new (pk', sk') keypair for each person you run the protocol with but keeping the same public key pk all the time. (If you ever re-use a pk', the two people that you did the protocol with using the same pk' can get together and compute your secret key exactly as described above, unless they both happened to pick the same challenge which is very unlikely for large n.) A cryptographer would say that Schnorr's protocol is a "proof of knowledge" of a value sk such that $g^{sk} = pk \pmod{p}$ because the protocol satisfies the following condition:

Proposition 20. *Any person that can convince a challenger with more than $1/n$ probability in Schnorr's protocol (for challenges from $\{0, \ldots, n-1\}$ and public key pk) can also compute a secret key sk that matches pk.*

Suppose that Alice is using Schnorr's protocol to prove to Bob that she knows her secret key. We have just established that Alice cannot cheat Bob (except with probability at most $1/n$). Can Bob cheat? That is, can Bob use the Schnorr protocol to gain more information about Alice's secret key than he could if he only got her public key pk in the first place?

The answer is of course "no" — at least if Bob picks his challenge randomly. What Bob gets to see in this protocol is a new public key pk' and a secret key sk'' for a c of his choice; we argue that Bob could just as well create these elements himself if Alice didn't want to run the protocol with him.

1. Bob picks a value c at random from $\{0, 1, \ldots, n - 1\}$.
2. Bob picks a value sk'' at random from $\{0, 1, \ldots, q - 1\}$ and computes $pk'' := g^{sk''} \pmod{p}$.
3. Bob sets $pk' = pk''/pk^c \pmod{p}$ where pk is Alice's public key.

The triple (pk', c, sk'') looks exactly like one that would be generated if Bob did Schnorr's protocol with Alice; in particular the verification equation holds: $g^{sk''} = pk' \cdot pk^c \pmod{p}$ from the definition of pk' and c, pk', sk'' are uniformly random subject to this equation holding. So Schnorr's protocol gives Bob no more information about Alice's key than he could already compute by himself, if Bob chooses his challenge randomly. This property of the protocol is called "honest verifier zero-knowledge".

Proposition 21. *If Bob picks his challenge c randomly, he gains no information from a run of Schnorr's protocol with Alice.*

Another way of phrasing this argument is that if Alice does the protocol with Bob and Carol observes this, the protocol convinces Bob but it cannot convince Carol: Alice and Bob could be working together to cheat Carol. To do this, Alice could pick any public key for which she does not know the secret key, Bob could create values as above and agree them with Alice beforehand and they could run the protocol together on these values.

The bit about honest verifiers — Bob picking his challenge randomly — is not just a technicality. For sure, it cannot help Bob to choose his challenge in a way that Alice could predict (this just allows Alice to cheat, but not Bob). Bob can however throw a spanner in the works by choosing his challenge as the value of a pseudorandom or hash function on input the values he has seen so far, pk and pk'. This breaks the "simulation" argument above because Bob had to choose his c before he picked pk'. This is exactly why Alice needs to know sk to convince Bob but Bob does not need to know sk to simulate the protocol: when Alice is talking to Bob, she has to send him pk' before he chooses c but on his own, Bob can do it "backwards".

Before we go on to fix this problem, we slightly abstract Schnorr's protocol which will come in useful when we discuss other protocols along similar lines such as Chaum-Pedersen. The flow of messages in Schnorr's protocol can be drawn to look like the Greek letter Σ which prompted Cramer [C96] to call such protocols "Σ-protocols".

Definition 22. *A Σ-protocol is a protocol after the following template for Alice to prove knowledge of a preimage $x : y = \phi(x)$ of a value y to Bob.*

1. *Alice samples a random a from the domain of ϕ, sets $b := \phi(a)$ and sends b to Bob. We assume that Bob already knows y, alternatively Alice could send y to Bob too.*
2. *Bob picks a challenge c randomly from the set $\{0, 1, \ldots, n-1\}$ which must form part of the field $\mathbb{F}$. Bob sends c to Alice.*
3. *Alice computes $d := a + cx$ in the field $\mathbb{F}$ and sends d to Bob.*
4. *Bob checks that $\phi(d) = b + c \cdot y$ where this calculation is done in the $\mathbb{F}$–vector space of which y is an element ($c \cdot y$ is scalar multiplication; c is a field element).*

A Σ-protocol gives Alice no more than a $1/n$ probability of cheating and Bob, if he chooses his challenge randomly, no advantage in finding Alice's preimage.

Proposition 23. *A Σ-protocol derived from the template above is a honest verifier zero-knowledge proof of knowledge of a preimage of a linear map ϕ (over some field $\mathbb{F}$).*

We have a second problem beyond Bob not choosing a random c. If Alice wants to use a zero-knowledge proof to convince everyone that her ballot is valid, using an interactive proof like the one above would mean that everyone must be able to challenge Alice to run a protocol with them, even after the election has closed. This is clearly impractical. What we want is a non-interactive proof, where Alice can once and for all time convince every possible Bob that her ballot is valid. And, almost paradoxically, the way Alice can do this is by doing exactly what we just argued that no Bob can be allowed to do: choose the challenge c herself as a hash value on pk and pk'. This technique is usually attributed to and named after Fiat and Shamir[8][FS86].

Definition 24. *The Fiat-Shamir transformation of a Σ-protocol is the protocol in which Bob's choice of a challenge c is replaced by Alice computing the challenge as $c := H(y, b)$ where y is the value of which she is proving a preimage and b is her "commitment", the message that she would send to Bob immediately before getting his challenge. H is a cryptographic hash function with range $\{0, 1, \ldots, n-1\}$. This is a non-interactive proof of knowledge.*

To verify a proof $\pi = (y, b, c, d)$ you first check that $c = H(y, b)$. If this holds, check that $\phi(d) = b + c \cdot y$ for the function ϕ in question and accept the proof if this is the case.

 Key generation in Helios. These are the exact steps that a Helios authority performs to generate her key share. Helios uses n-out-of-n threshold keys as we described earier.

---

[8] The attribution is not uncontested: others prefer to credit Blum with the technique [BR93].

1. Obtain parameters (p, q, g) or agree these with the other authorities.
2. Generate a key pair by picking sk_i randomly from $\mathbb{Z}_q$ and setting $pk_i := g^{sk_i r} \pmod{p}$. Here i is some identifier.
3. Pick another keypair $(a, b = g^a \pmod{p})$ for the proof.
4. Compute $c := H(pk_i, a) \pmod{q}$ where H is a hash function (Helios uses SHA-256).
5. Compute $d := a + c \cdot sk_i \pmod{q}$.
6. Your public key component is pk_i and its proof of correctness is $\pi_i = (c, d)$. Your public key share is (pk_i, π_i).

The value a is omitted from the proof as the verifier can recompute it using the verification equation as $a = g^d/(pk_i)^c \pmod{p}$ and then check that $c = H(pk_i, a)$. This variation is equivalent to the one we gave above, i.e. zero-knowledge and a proof of knowledge, but saves one group element per proof.

4.4 Chaum-Pedersen: Proving Correct Decryption

To prove that you have decrypted a ciphertext correctly, you need to show that you have produced a value d such that $d = a^{sk_i} \pmod{p}$ where sk_i is your secret key share satisfying $g^{sk_i} = pk_i \pmod{p}$, the value a is the first component of the ciphertext and pk_i is the key component of your public key share. Put another way, you have to show knowledge of an sk_i satisfying

$$a^{sk_i} = d \pmod{p} \wedge g^{sk_i} = pk_i \pmod{p}$$

All constants appearing in this formula (a, d, g, pk_i, p) are public. In the notation that we have just introduced, you have to show knowledge of

a preimage x of (d, g) under $\phi(x) = (a^x \pmod{p}, g^x \pmod{p})$

this function is conveniently also linear. Here we start to see why linearity and vector spaces are the correct way to understand Σ-protocols abstractly: for the finite field $\mathbb{F}_q$, our function signature is $\phi : \mathbb{Z}_q \to G^2$, mapping integers (1-dimensional vectors) into 2-dimensional vectors over the group G.

The protocol for this particular ϕ-function was invented by Chaum and Pedersen [CP92]. We give the exact steps to prove a decryption share correct:

1. Inputs: ciphertext (a, b), public key share pk_i, secret key share sk_i.
2. Pick a random r from $\mathbb{Z}_q$. Compute

$$(u, v) := \phi(r) = (a^r \pmod{p}, g^r \pmod{p})$$

3. Compute a challenge as $c := H(pk_i, a, b, u, v)$.
4. Let $s := r + c \cdot sk_i \pmod{q}$.
5. Compute the decryption factor $d := a^{sk_i} \pmod{p}$.
6. Reveal d and the proof $\pi := ((u, v), s)$.

To check such a proof, your inputs are a, b, pk_i, u, v and s. Compute the hash value $c := H(pk_i, a, b, u, v)$ and check that

$$a^s = u \cdot d^c \pmod{p} \quad \wedge \quad g^s = v \cdot (pk_i)^c \pmod{p}$$

There is an important difference between Schnorr's protocol and that of Chaum and Pedersen. In the former, Bob already knows that whatever Alice claims as her public key has a discrete logarithm — all group elements do, by definition. Alice is only trying to convince Bob that she knows the discrete logarithm of her public key. By contrast, in the Chaum-Pedersen protocol the focus is less on convincing Bob that you know how to decrypt but that you have done so correctly. Indeed, if a ciphertext decrypts to d but you claim some $d' \neq d$ instead, the pair (pk, d') will not lie in the image of ϕ so there will be no x with which you can convincingly run the protocol. For the interactive Chaum-Pedersen protocol, someone who has decrypted incorrectly cannot cheat (with more than $1/n$ probability) even if they have unlimited resources and can even take discrete logarithms. For the non-interactive protocol, the security analysis depends on the hash function but we still get the property that no realistic attacker can produce a proof of a false decryption. This property is called "soundness".

Proposition 25. *In a Σ-protocol following our construction, it is infeasible to produce a proof (whether interactive or non-interactive) for a value not in the image of the ϕ-function.*

4.5   DCP: Proving That a Vote Is Valid

We come to our third and final Σ-protocol. This one is for the voter to prove that she encrypted a valid vote in her ballot (namely 0 or 1), without revealing the vote. ElGamal encryption of a message m with random value r, in the exponential version used by Helios, can be expressed by the formula

$$c = \phi(m, r) := (g^r \pmod{p}, g^m pk^r \pmod{p})$$

which is linear in m and r as a function with signature $\phi : (\mathbb{Z}_q)^2 \to G^2$ where g, p, q and pk are taken to be constants. This immediately yields a Σ-protocol to prove knowledge of your vote and randomness but does not prove that your vote m lies in a particular range. Let us consider how Alice would prove that she had voted for a particular value of m. If her ciphertext is $(a, b) = (g^r \pmod{p}, g^m pk^r \pmod{p})$ then she could divide out g^m again to get $(a, b') = (a, b/g^m \pmod{p})$ which is the image of the linear function

$$\phi' : \mathbb{Z}_q \to G^2, r \mapsto (g^r \pmod{p}, pk^r \pmod{p})$$

In other words, to prove that (a, b) is a ciphertext for m Alice can prove that she knows a preimage r of $(a, b/g^m \pmod{p})$ under the function ϕ'. This is of course exactly the protocol of Chaum and Pedersen with pk playing the role of the second basis (instead of a in our last discussion).

There is a general construction for Alice to prove that she knows a preimage of (at least) one of two linear functions for given images, without revealing which. Given linear functions ϕ_0, ϕ_1 and values y_0, y_1 in their respective domains, to prove that she knows $x_0 : \phi_0(x_0) = y_0$ or $x_1 : \phi_1(x_1) = y_1$ Alice runs the following protocol.

- Start running the Σ-protocols for both functions.
- Get Bob to pick a single challenge c from $\{0, 1, \ldots, n-1\}$.
- For each of the two protocols, produce a new challenge c_i and a final value x_i'' such that both protocols are correct individually and $c = c_1 + c_2 \pmod{n}$.

The trick is that Alice cheats and picks c and x'' first for the function where she does not have a preimage. The condition $c = c_1 + c_2$ where c is chosen by the challenger lets Alice cheat in one of the two protocols but not both. In more detail, here is the general construction.

1. For the value i where you know a preimage $x_i : \phi_i(x_i) = y_i$, pick a new pair $(x_i', y_i' = \phi_i(x_i'))$ as you would to start the Σ-protocol for this function.
2. For the value j where you do not know a preimage, run the cheating protocol: pick c_j at random from $\{0, 1, \ldots, n\}$ and x_j'' at random from the domain of ϕ_j. Then set $y_j' := \phi(x_j'') - c_j \cdot y_j$, where these operations are done in the vector space that contains the range of ϕ_j, i.e. $c_j \cdot y_j$ is scalar multiplication with the scalar c_j.
3. Send y_0' and y_1' to the challenger and obtain a c in return.
4. Set $c_i := c - c_j \pmod{n}$ and complete the protocol for ϕ_i by setting $x_i'' := x_i' + c_i \cdot x_i$. These operations are done in the vector space that contains the range of ϕ_i.
5. Send c_0, c_1, x_0'', x_1'' to the challenger to complete the protocol.

From Bob's point of view, there are two Σ-protocols running in parallel:

1. Bob knows functions ϕ_0, ϕ_1 and claimed images y_0, y_1. He gets a pair of further values y_0', y_1' from Alice.
2. Bob chooses a single value c at random from $\{0, 1, \ldots, n-1\}$.
3. Alice sends Bob values c_0, c_1, x_0'', x_1''. Bob checks the following equations. The first two check the individual Σ protocols and the final one ensures that Alice can cheat on at most one of the protocols:

$$\phi_0(x_0'') = y_0' + c_0 \cdot y_0 \tag{6}$$
$$\phi_1(x_1'') = y_1' + c_1 \cdot y_1 \tag{7}$$
$$c = c_0 + c_1 \pmod{n} \tag{8}$$

The argument that Alice cannot cheat in both protocols is as follows. Suppose Alice knows neither a preimage of y_0 nor of y_1. If there are two values of c, c' for which she could both convince Bob then there must be some values c_0, c_1, c_0', c_1' that she could use to convince Bob, i.e. $c_0 + c_1 = c$ and $c_0' + c_1' = c'$ (all modulo n). But $c \neq c'$ so at least one of $c_0 \neq c_0'$ or $c_1 \neq c_1'$ must hold, which implies that Alice can already cheat in one of the two individual Σ-protocols on its own.

Of course this protocol can be made non-interactive with a hash function just like any Σ-protocol. The items that need to be hashed here are y_0, y_1, y_0', y_1' and any other constants appearing in the two protocols. Similarly, the same technique can be used for three or more functions — what Alice is proving in each case is that she knows at least one preimage, without revealing which. The resulting Σ-protocol is called a "disjunctive proof" or an "OR-proof". Applied to Chaum-Pedersen proofs, the resulting protocol is called disjunctive Chaum-Pedersen or DCP.

Proofs in Helios ballots. In Helios, a voter uses this technique to prove that she either knows a random value r_0 with which she can do a Chaum-Pedersen proof that her ballot is an encryption of 0, or she knows a value r_1 with which she can do a Chaum-Pedersen proof that she has encrypted 1. The voter must produce one such proof for each ciphertext in her ballot.

If the election format demands that the voter choose a certain minimum/maximum number of options in a question (e.g. vote for at most one candidate) then the voter additionally takes the homomorphic sum of all her ciphertexts for the question and performs an additional DCP proof on the sum, showing that it is in the allowed range. This proof is known as the overall proof for the question.

Definition 26. *The following is the voter's protocol for proving that a ciphertext is an encryption of 0 or 1. The voter's inputs are the parameters (p, q, g), the election public key pk, the voter's ciphertext $(a, b) = (g^r, g^v \cdot pk^r)$, her vote $v \in \{0, 1\}$ and the random value r that she used to encrypt her vote.*

If your vote is $v = 0$:

1. Simulate the protocol for proving $v = 1$. Pick c_1 randomly from $\{0, 1, \ldots, n\}$ and r_1'' from $\mathbb{Z}_q$ at random. Set

$$b' := b/g^1 \pmod{p}$$
$$a_1' := g^{r_1''}/a^{c_1} \pmod{p}$$
$$b_1' := pk^{r_1''}/(b')^{c_1} \pmod{p}$$

2. Set up the proof that $v = 0$. Create a value r_0' from $\mathbb{Z}_q$ at random and set

$$a_0' := g^{r_0'} \pmod{p}$$
$$b_0' := pk^{r_0'} \pmod{p}$$

3. Get the challenge for the $v = 0$ proof. Compute

$$c := H(pk, a, b, a_0', b_0', a_1', b_1')$$
$$c_0 := c_1 - c \pmod{n}$$

4. Complete the $v = 0$ proof. Compute

$$r_0'' := r_0' + c_0 \cdot r \pmod{q}$$

5. Your proof π is the tuple

$$(a_0', a_1', b_0', b_1', c_0, c_1, r_0'', r_1'')$$

If your vote is $v = 1$:

1. Simulate the protocol for proving $v = 0$. Pick c_0 randomly from $\{0, 1, \ldots, n\}$ and r_0'' from $\mathbb{Z}_q$ at random. Set

$$a_0' := g^{r_0''}/a^{c_0} \pmod{p}$$
$$b_0' := pk^{r_0''}/b^{c_0} \pmod{p}$$

2. Set up the proof that $v = 1$. Create a value r_1' from $\mathbb{Z}_q$ at random and set

$$a_1' := g^{r_1'} \pmod{p}$$
$$b_1' := pk^{r_1'} \pmod{p}$$

3. Get the challenge for the $v = 1$ proof. Compute

$$c := H(pk, a, b, a_0', b_0', a_1', b_1')$$
$$c_1 := c_0 - c \pmod{n}$$

4. Complete the $v = 1$ proof. Compute

$$r_1'' := r_1' + c_1 \cdot r \pmod{q}$$

5. Your proof π is the tuple

$$(a_0', a_1', b_0', b_1', c_0, c_1, r_0'', r_1'')$$

To verify such a proof, the following equations need to be checked.

$$g^{r_0''} = a_0' \cdot a^{c_0} \pmod{p} \tag{9}$$
$$g^{r_1''} = a_1' \cdot a^{c_1} \pmod{p} \tag{10}$$
$$pk^{r_0''} = b_0' \cdot b^{c_0} \pmod{p} \tag{11}$$
$$pk^{r_1''} = b_1' \cdot (b/g^1)^{c_1} \pmod{p} \tag{12}$$
$$c_0 + c_1 = H(pk, a, b, a_0', b_0', a_1', b_1') \pmod{n} \tag{13}$$

The Helios ballot format. Homomorphic ballots are possible not just for yes/no questions but for a number of voting/election setups including first-past-the-post, approval voting and top-k-of-n elections. All these formats have in common that a voter answers a question by ticking some (or all, or none)

of a predefined set of checkboxes and the election result is essentially a list, for each box, of how many voters ticked this box. Homomorphic voting in the above sense cannot handle write-in votes or ranked (Instant runoff etc.) counts.

For example, in a first-past-the-post election for three candidates A, B and C, voters will be presented with three boxes — obviously labelled A, B and C — and must tick exactly one box each (or possibly none, to cast a blank vote). The election result is the number of votes that A, B and C each got, from which one can form the sum and determine the turnout and the percentage of votes that each candidate got.

Helios supports such elections: a ballot contains one ciphertext for each checkbox. These ciphertexts are encryptions of either 0 or 1. In addition, each ciphertext is accompanied by a proof that it really contains 0 or 1; these proofs are known as individual proofs. If the election specification sets limits on the numbers of boxes you can/must check, there is one further proof per ballot attesting to this known as the overall proof. A ballot can be composed of several structures as just described, allowing for multiple questions in a poll or multiple races in an election.

Attacks against the Ballot Format and Ballot Weeding. Cortier and Smyth [CS13] pointed out the following problem with bulletin board based elections. Suppose there are three voters, Alice, Bob and Eve. Alice and Bob both cast ballots. Next, Eve reads Alice's ballot off the board and submits a copy of it as her own ballot. The election result is now announced as 2 yes, 1 no: Eve knows that Alice must have voted yes and Bob no, since the two copied ballots must encrypt the same vote. However, in a truly private election, Eve should never be able to tell whether Alice votes yes and Bob no or the other way round, since these two scenarios both make the same contribution to the result. If the result is that everybody voted yes then Eve can deduce that Alice voted yes too, which is unavoidable — the problem with ballot copying is that Eve can find out more than she could by just observing the result.

A first reaction to this problem could be to introduce ballot weeding in the following sense: we reject any ballot that is an exact copy of a ballot already on the board. If ballots are non-malleable ciphertexts, this is actually sufficient — however, homomorphic ciphertexts can never be non-malleable as Eve can always Add an encryption of g^0 to an existing ciphertext. Eve will still know that the two ciphertexts encrypt the same vote but no-one else, even the decryptor, can tell such a "rerandomised" ciphertext from a genuine ballot by a voter who just happened to vote for the same choice as Alice.

We can solve this problem and the problem of Eve voting for g^2 in one go by adding a non-malleable zero-knowledge proof to each ciphertext. Ballot weeding will now reject any ballot that shares a proof with a previous ballot.

In fact we even fix one more problem that Cortier and Smyth identified with the original ballot format. Consider a poll for choices A, B and C so ballots take the form

$$(c_A, \pi_A, c_B, \pi_B, c_C, \pi_C, \pi_O)$$

where c_A is the ciphertext for choice A, π_A is the individual proof that c_A is well-formed and π_O is the overall proof (that at most one of c_A, c_B, c_C encrypts a 1). If the above is Alice's ballot, Eve can submit the following modified ballot:

$$(c_B, \pi_B, c_A, \pi_A, c_C, \pi_C, \pi_O)$$

The result is that Eve has swapped the A- and B-components of Alice's ballot around but she knows exactly what the relations between the original and modified ballot are and can use this knowledge to attack Alice's privacy. In Helios version 3, after you submitted a ballot, the hash of your ballot was sent to you as a confirmation value and the hashes of all ballots were displayed on a "short board", with the "full board" of all ballots also available. The point here is that Eve's ballot will have a completely different hash value to Alice's and while Helios prevented Eve from submitting a ballot with the same hash value as Alice's (i.e. making an exact copy), this modified ballot was accepted by Helios without complaint. It could be detected by auditing the full board but code for this was not available in Helios at the time.

4.6 Ballot Privacy

With zero-knowledge proofs in ballots, everyone can be assured that voters are casting ballots for valid votes. To model what security level this yields, we give the full ballot privacy game that protects against dishonest voters. It differs from the previous notion of privacy against observers in that the attacker can declare any voters she likes to be dishonest and provide them with arbitrary ballots. This accounts for both attempts at making "bad ballots" and ballot-copying or modifying existing ballots and resubmitting them as your own.

Definition 27. *A voting scheme has ballot privacy if no attacker can do better in the following game than guess at random (with probability 1/2).*

Setup *The game picks a bit b at random and keeps it secret. The game then sets up the voting scheme and plays the voters, authorities and bulletin board.*
Moves *Once for each voter, the attacker may perform one of two moves.*
- *The attacker declares this voter to be honest. She may then choose two votes v_0 and v_1. The game writes down both votes. If $b = 0$, the game lets the voter vote for v_0; if $b = 1$ the game lets the voter vote for v_1.*
- *The attacker declares this voter to be dishonest and may provide an arbitrary ballot b for the voter, which the game processes.*

The attacker may ask to look at the bulletin board at any point in the game. When all voters have voted, the game individually decrypts all dishonest voters' ballots. It then gives the attacker the result computed as follows: for each honest voter, it takes the first (v_0) vote and for each dishonest voter, it takes the vote obtained by decrypting the submitted ballot.

Winning conditions *At any point in the game, the attacker may submit a guess for b. This ends the game immediately. The attacker wins if her guess is correct.*

4.7 Achieving Ballot Privacy with Non-Malleability

We sketch how one would show that minivoting with zero-knowledge proofs added to key shares, ballots and decryption shares achieves ballot privacy. The main issue is that the attacker may derive one of her own ballots from that of an honest voter. Bernhard et al. [BPW12a, BS13] have explored the connection between ballot privacy and ballot independence — the property that there are no "unexpected" relations between the votes in ballots of different voters — and concluded that the two are essentially the same, i.e. to achieve privacy one must ensure that ballots are independent.

The model that we use to capture independence is that of non-malleable encryption. This can be expressed by taking the IND-CPA game and letting the attacker, once in the game, produce any number of ciphertexts she likes and ask the game to decrypt them. If the attacker has already obtained a challenge ciphertext, she cannot ask for the challenge ciphertext to be decrypted however.

Definition 28. *An asymmetric encryption scheme E is non-malleable if no attacker can win the following game with better probability than $1/2$, the probability of guessing at random.*

Setup. *The game creates a keypair $(pk, sk) \leftarrow \mathsf{KeyGen}()$ and gives the attacker the public key pk. The game also picks a bit b randomly from $\{0, 1\}$ and keeps this secret.*

Moves. *Once in the game, the attacker may pick a pair of messages m_0 and m_1 of the same length and send them to the game. The game encrypts $c \leftarrow \mathsf{Encrypt}(pk, m_b)$ and returns this to the attacker.*

Once in the game, the attacker may send the game a list of any number of ciphertexts $(c_1, \ldots, c_n)$. If the attacker has already obtained a challenge ciphertext c, she must not include this ciphertext in her list. The game decrypts each ciphertext in the list and sends the attacker back the decrypted messages.

Winning Conditions. *The attacker may make a guess at b which ends the game. The attacker wins if she guesses correctly.*

This notion captures non-malleability in the following sense. Suppose that a scheme is malleable in that the attacker can take a ciphertext c and somehow turn it into a different ciphertext c' for a message that has some relation to the message in c — for example, the two ciphertexts encrypt the same message. Then the attacker can win the non-malleability game as follows:

- Pick any messages m_0, m_1 and ask for a challenge ciphertext c.
- Turn c into c' and ask for c' to be decrypted.
- If the decrypted message is m_0, guess $b = 0$, otherwise guess $b = 1$.

The exact form of the game has been shown be Bellare and Sahai [BS99] to imply that the attacker is unable to construct any number of ciphertexts that have an "unexpected" relation with the challenge message. By "unexpected", we mean that we are glossing over the following problem: the attacker can always make two fresh ciphertexts c_0 and c_1 for m_0 and m_1 herself, this pair (c_0, c_1) will then have the relation "one of the two encrypted messages matches that in the challenge ciphertext". Informally, what we want is that the attacker cannot construct any relation that helps her decide what is in the challenge ciphertext. The formal argument can be found in the cited paper [BS99].

ElGamal on its own is homomorphic and therefore not non-malleable: an attacker can always add an encryption of 0 to a challenge ciphertext to get a new ciphertext for the same message. ElGamal with a Σ-protocol based zero-knowledge proof however is non-malleable. As proven by Bernhard, Pereira and Warinschi [BPW12b]:

Proposition 29. *The encryption scheme obtained by combining ElGamal with a DCP proof that the encrypted message lies in a certain range is non-malleable.*

Side Note — CCA Security. Non-malleability is a strictly stronger notion of security than IND-CCA. There is a further, even stronger notion that is often cited as "the correct notion" for security of asymmetric encryption called CCA, security against "chosen-ciphertext attacks". In this notion, the attacker can use the decryption move as many times as she likes, as long as she never asks to decrypt the challenge ciphertext. The game is usually presented in a form where the attacker asks one decryption at a time instead of a list at once which makes no difference (whereas the fact that the attacker only gets one decryption move is a central part of the non-malleability notion). For the purposes of building ballot private voting schemes, non-malleability is sufficient.

Ballot Privacy of Minivoting. To obtain ballot privacy we need two ingredients. The first is non-malleability which prevents Eve from submitting a modified version of Alice's ballot as her own. The second ingredient is ballot weeding, a way to catch Eve if she tries to submit an exact copy of Alice's ballot. In a scheme with ballot weeding, whenever anyone submits a ballot, the bulletin board checks the ballot against all previous ballots and rejects it if it finds a relation. If ballots are non-malleable, this relation can be "the ballot is an exact copy of a previous one". This leads to the following proposition attesting to ballot privacy of minivoting with proofs.

Proposition 30. *Minivoting with non-malleable ballots and ballot weeding for exact copies has ballot privacy.*

The non-malleability of ElGamal with DCP gives non-malleable ballots if each ballot contains only a single ciphertext. Otherwise, as explained in the section on the Helios ballot format, Cortier/Smyth attacks [CS13] in which the ciphertexts in a ballot get permuted might still be possible. The correct way to weed ballots containing multiple ElGamal+DCP ciphertexts is to check for repeated proofs. This extends to show ballot privacy of the version of Helios that we present in this work.

Proposition 31. *Minivoting with ElGamal+DCP ciphertexts/proofs has ballot privacy if the ballot weeding rejects any ballot re-using a proof from an earlier ballot.*

On ballot privacy in Helios. The original Helios security result by Bernhard et al. [BC+11] showed that Helios would have ballot privacy if it employed CCA secure encryption. The combination of ElGamal and a DCP proof (or any other Σ-protocol with special soundness w.r.t the encryption randomness r and the Fiat-Shamir transformation for the challenge) has not been shown CCA secure in a widely accepted model and indeed there is evidence suggesting that it is not CCA secure, although no proof of this has been published to date.

CCA security is not necessary for ballot privacy however: the latest proofs [BPW12a, BPW12b] achieve privacy from non-malleability alone and ElGamal + DCP definitely is non-malleable.

However, Bernhard, Pereira and Warinschi [BPW12b] have also shown that the currently available version 3 of Helios does not perform the zero-knowledge proofs of knowledge correctly, as a result of which Helios currently does not satisfy our notion of ballot privacy and can even be attacked in practice. The Helios described in this paper is a fixed version; the Helios authors have assured us that the upcoming Helios version 4 will contain fixed proofs.

4.8   ☼ Helios

We now have all the building blocks to describe the Helios electronic voting scheme.

To generate an election or poll, the authorities agree on the questions and options and generate parameters (p, q, g). They each generate an ElGamal keypair with a Schnorr proof to obtain their threshold keys. One of the authorities then combines the public key and publishes the election specification, parameters, public key shares and the public key itself on a bulletin board.

To vote, voters obtain and check the public key. By check, we mean that they check the authorities' Schnorr proofs and re-run the key combination step. For each option "checkbox", the voter encrypts g^0 to leave the box empty and g^1 to check it. She accompanies each ciphertext with a DCP proof that she has indeed encrypted either g^0 or g^1. If the election specification restricts the maximum or minimum number of boxes that a voter must check for a question, she also makes an overall proof that the number of boxes checked lies in the allowed range. The voter's ballot contains her ciphertexts, individual proofs and if required and overall proof for each question; she posts this ballot to the bulletin board. Typically, a board will require voters to authenticate themselves before accepting any ballots. The board never sees the actual votes however.

To tally an election, the authorities check all proofs in the ballots and discard any ballots with invalid proofs. Further, they reject any ballot that has copied a proof from an earlier ballot[9]. These checks can also be done by the board itself when ballots are submitted so invalid ones never end up on the board but for security reasons, the authorities always need to repeat these checks to protect against a dishonest board collaborating with a dishonest voter. One authority sums all ciphertexts for each individual question and posts the sum-ciphertexts back on the board. Each authority then produces a decryption share for each sum-ciphertext and posts this to the board. One authority completes the tally by combining the decryption shares for each sum and posting this on the board and computing the result in the correct format, for example each option's count as a percentage of the total number of ballots cast.

5 Verifiability

Anyone can verify a Helios election. Taking the board of a completed election, they should perform the following steps.

1. Check that the Schnorr proofs on the public key shares are correct and that the public key was combined correctly.
2. Check that each ballot meets the election format (correct number of cipher-texts and proofs) and that all proofs in the ballots verify, or that all invalid ballots have been marked as such and excluded from the tally.
3. If ballots contain voter information, check that this is consistent, i.e. only eligible voters have voted and no-one has cast more votes than allowed.
4. Check that no ballot re-uses a proof from an earlier ballot, or that all ballots that do so have been marked as invalid.
5. Recompute the sum-ciphertexts and check that they are correct. In particular, the sums should be over only those ballots not marked as invalid.
6. Check the zero-knowledge proofs on all decryption shares.
7. Recombine all decryptions and check that they are correct.
8. Check that the announced result matches the decryptions.

From this procedure, we can check whether Helios meets the following verifiability criteria.

Individual Verifiability. Each voter can save a copy of her ballot and check that it is included in the final bulletin board. This property is satisfied.

---

[9] At least, this is the way Helios should check ballots and will do in a future version. The current version (v3) is still susceptible to some ballot-copying attacks.

Eligibility Verifiability. This depends on the election setting as eligibility information must be available to check this (such as a list of all eligible voters) and a method is required to verify that ballots really come from who they claim to come from. If voters are all equipped with digital signature keypairs and the public keys are available in a public directory, voters could be asked to sign their ballots as part of the authentication process.

Universal Verifiability. This was the key design aim of Helios and is satisfied. All the steps in the protocol that use secret information are protected by zero-knowledge proofs: key generation, ballot creation (the vote is secret) and decryption. These proofs are available on the bulletin board for anyone to audit.

Ballot Verifiability. Ballots are protected by zero-knowledge proofs attesting to the fact that they contain correct votes. These votes are available on the bulletin board to audit. This property is satisfied[10].

As the reader will have noted, this too is an informal analysis — no formal model for verifiability of Helios-type schemes[11] exists yet, in contrast to ballot privacy. Creating a suitable model and proving Helios secure in such a model (or finding an attack) is one of the open challenges of cryptographic voting.

6   Mix-Nets

In this section we give a brief overview of mix-nets, the other main technique (beside blind signatures and homomorphic encryption) to achieve private and verifiable cryptographic voting schemes. An advantage of mix-nets over homomorphic voting is that they can handle arbitrary ballot formats including write-in votes.

Suppose that every voter encrypts their vote with normal ElGamal (not the exponential variant) and posts the ciphertext on the board, along with some identification information (or even a digital signature) to ensure eligibility. Normal ElGamal can handle arbitrary bitstrings (of a fixed length) as messages as long as the basic group is chosen cleverly[12]. Since we can no longer do homomorphic tallying, we need another way to anonymize ballots. Here is one: a trusted authority takes all ballots, randomly shuffles them and re-encrypts each one, that is for a ciphertext (a, b) the authority generates a random r from $\mathbb{Z}_q$ and sets $(a', b') := (a \cdot g^r \pmod{p}, b \cdot pk^r \pmod{p})$. These shuffled ciphertexts

---

[10] This analysis refers to the version of Helios described in this work — the current (v3) Helios does not satisfy ballot verifiability due to a bug in the implementation of the proofs.

[11] There is a model for verifiability by Kuesters et al. [KTV11] but it coniders voting schemes from a highly abstract point of view and has, to our knowledge, never been successfully applied to a fully cryptographic scheme such as Helios.

[12] The kind of groups we presented in this work are not suitable for this kind of scheme, since our messages have to start out as group elements. ElGamal in groups defined over elliptic curves does work and is typically faster (for the same key-size) too.

contain the same set of votes as the originals but the link between voter and ballot is hidden, so the shuffled ciphertexts can be decrypted individually.

This also removes the need for zero-knowledge proofs to assert correctness of ballots: if someone has encrypted a 2 in an 0/1 question, since ballots are decrypted individually such invalid ballots can be discarded individually too. This technique does not prevent the need for non- malleable encryption to combat ballot-copying however so ElGamal will still need some kind of proof protecting the ciphertexts.

If one does not have a trustworthy authority, once can take several authorities who each shuffle and re-encrypt all ballots in turn. As long as any one of the authorities is honest, this protects voters' privacy from all other authorities. The system is also resilient to mixers failing: a mixer who does not complete a mix can be simply replaced by another.

Unfortunately, the scheme as described is not verifiable and in fact completely insecure against a cheating mixer substituting ballots of her own instead of returning a shuffled, re-encrypted version of her inputs. In this way, a dishonest mixer can arbitrarily manipulate the election results. The solution to this problem is clear: zero-knowledge proofs!

In a real mix-net, each mixer takes a list of ciphertexts $(c_1, \ldots, c_n)$ as input and outputs a mix $(c'_1, \ldots, c'_n)$ together with a proof π that the outputs are a mix of the inputs. Different mix-nets differ in the kind, size and efficiency of the proof: proofs of correct mixing are typically quite expensive to compute. Some mix-nets offer an "online/offline" mode where most of the work in computing a mix and a proof can be done "offline" before or during the election. This work involves choosing random values $r_1, \ldots, r_n$ for some upper bound n of the number of ballots expected and a permutation p on the set $\{1, \ldots, n\}$, then pre-computing as much of the proof as possible without the actual ciphertexts. At the end of the election, the pre-computed values can then be applied more efficiently to the ciphertexts forming the ballots in an "online" phase, returning the permuted and rerandomised ballots and the proof of correct mixing.

7   Conclusion

We have presented several cryptographic schemes and techniques for voting, introduced the building blocks from which they are constructed and given an overview of how cryptographers work with security properties and models. The state of the art is that we have (albeit imperfect) models for ballot privacy and proofs for that the (fixed) Helios scheme satisfies these models; while these models and proofs were developed, their authors discovered subtle problems with the existing Helios which shows the importance of a detailed and formal approach to security. While Helios is widely believed to be verifiable, which is one of its design goals if not the key selling point, a formal model in which this claim can be justified has not been published at the time of writing.

References

[DH76]   Diffie, W., Hellman, M.: New Directions in Cryptography. IEEE Transactions on Information Theory 22(6), 644–654 (1976)

[RSA78]   Rivest, R., Shamir, A., Adleman, L.: A method for obtaining digital signatures and public-key cryptosystems. Communications of the ACM 21(2), 120–126 (1978)

[C85]   Chaum, D.: Security without Identification: Transaction Systems to make Big Brother obsolete. Communications of the ACM 28(10) (October 1985)

[E85]   ElGamal, T.: A public key cryptosystem and a signature scheme based on discrete logarithms. IEEE Transactions on Information Theory 31, 469–472 (1985)

[FS86]   Fiat, A., Shamir, A.: How to prove yourself: Practical solutions to identification and signature problems. In: Odlyzko, A.M. (ed.) CRYPTO 1986. LNCS, vol. 263, pp. 186–194. Springer, Heidelberg (1987)

[S91]   Schnorr, C.P.: Efficient signature generation for smart cards. Journal of Cryptology 4, 161–174 (1991)

[CP92]   Chaum, D., Pedersen, T.P.: Wallet Databases with Observers. In: Brickell, E.F. (ed.) CRYPTO 1992. LNCS, vol. 740, pp. 89–105. Springer, Heidelberg (1993)

[FOO92]   Fujioka, A., Okamoto, T., Ohta, K.: A Practical Secret Voting Scheme for Large Scale Elections. In: Zheng, Y., Seberry, J. (eds.) AUSCRYPT 1992. LNCS, vol. 718, pp. 244–251. Springer, Heidelberg (1993)

[BR93]   Bellare, M., Rogaway, P.: Random Oracles are Practical: A Paradigm for Designing Efficient Protocols. In: Proceedings of the 1st ACM Conference on Computer and Communications Security (CCS 1993), pp. 62–73 (1993)

[C96]   Cramer, R.: Modular Design of Secure yet Practical Cryptographic Protocols. PhD thesis, University of Amsterdam (1996)

[SG98]   Shoup, V., Gennaro, R.: Securing Threshold Cryptosystems against Chosen Ciphertext Attack. In: Nyberg, K. (ed.) EUROCRYPT 1998. LNCS, vol. 1403, pp. 1–16. Springer, Heidelberg (1998)

[P99]   Paillier, P.: Public-Key Cryptosystems Based on Composite Degree Residuosity Classes. In: Stern, J. (ed.) EUROCRYPT 1999. LNCS, vol. 1592, pp. 223–238. Springer, Heidelberg (1999)

[BS99]   Bellare, M., Sahai, A.: Non-Malleable Encryption: Equivalence between Two Notions, and an Indisinguishability-Based Characterization. In: Wiener, M. (ed.) CRYPTO 1999. LNCS, vol. 1666, pp. 519–536. Springer, Heidelberg (1999)

[BNPS03]   Bellare, M., Namprempre, C., Pointcheval, D., Semanko, M.: The One-More-RSA-Inversion Problem and the Security of Chaum's Blind Signature Scheme. J. of Cryptology 16(3), 185–215 (2003)

[BBS04]   Boneh, D., Boyen, X., Shacham, H.: Short Group Signatures. In: Franklin, M. (ed.) CRYPTO 2004. LNCS, vol. 3152, pp. 41–55. Springer, Heidelberg (2004)

[BC+11]   Bernhard, D., Cortier, V., Pereira, O., Smyth, B., Warinschi, B.: Adapting Helios for Provable Ballot Privacy. In: Atluri, V., Diaz, C. (eds.) ESORICS 2011. LNCS, vol. 6879, pp. 335–354. Springer, Heidelberg (2011)

[US11]   Schröder, D., Unruh, D.: Security of Blind Signatures Revisited. Eprint, report 2011/316 (2011)

[KTV11]   Küsters, R., Truderung, T., Vogt, A.: Verifiability, Privacy, and Coercion-Resistance: New Insights from a Case Study. In: IEEE Symposium on Security and Privacy (S&P 2011). IEEE Computer Society (2011)

[BPW12a] Bernhard, D., Pereira, O., Warinschi, B.: On Necessary and Sufficient Conditions for Private Ballot Submission. Eprint,
          http://eprint.iacr.org/2012/236

[BPW12b] Bernhard, D., Pereira, O., Warinschi, B.: How Not to Prove Yourself: Pitfalls of the Fiat-Shamir Heuristic and Applications to Helios. In: Wang, X., Sako, K. (eds.) ASIACRYPT 2012. LNCS, vol. 7658, pp. 626–643. Springer, Heidelberg (2012)

[BS13]   Smyth, B., Bernhard, D.: Ballot secrecy and ballot independence coincide. In: Crampton, J., Jajodia, S., Mayes, K. (eds.) ESORICS 2013. LNCS, vol. 8134, pp. 463–480. Springer, Heidelberg (2013)

[CS13]   Cortier, V., Smyth, B.: Attacking and fixing Helios: An analysis of ballot secrecy. Journal of Computer Security 21(1), 89–148 (2013)

[B14]   Bernhard, D.: Zero-Knowledge Proofs in Theory and Practice. PhD thesis, University of Bristol (2014)

Encryption and Fragmentation
for Data Confidentiality in the Cloud

Sabrina De Capitani di Vimercati[1], Robert F. Erbacher[2], Sara Foresti[1],
Sushil Jajodia[3], Giovanni Livraga[1], and Pierangela Samarati[1]

[1] Dipartimento di Informatica, Università degli Studi di Milano
Via Bramante 65, 26013 Crema, Italy
firstname.lastname@unimi.it
[2] U.S. Army Research Laboratory, USA
2800 Powder Mill Road, Adelphi, MD 20783, USA
robert.f.erbacher.civ@mail.mil
[3] Center for Secure Information Systems, George Mason University
4400 University Drive, Fairfax, VA 22030-4422, USA
jajodia@gmu.edu

Abstract. Cloud computing has emerged as a successful paradigm allowing individual users as well as companies to resort to external providers for storing/processing data or making them available to others. Together with the many benefits, cloud computing introduces however new security and privacy risks. A major issue is that the data owner, storing data at external providers, loses control over them, leaving them potentially exposed to improper access, use, or dissemination. In this chapter, we consider the problem of protecting confidentiality of sensitive information when relying on external cloud providers for storing and processing data. We introduce confidentiality requirements and then illustrate encryption and data fragmentation as possible protection techniques. In particular, we discuss different approaches that have been proposed using encryption (with indexing) and fragmentation, either by themselves or in combination, to satisfy confidentiality requirements.

1 Introduction

Cloud computing has brought enormous benefits to individual users as well as companies, enabling them to enjoy convenient and flexible availability of on demand storage and computational resources for storing, processing and share data with others. While these advantages are appealing, the price to pay for them is a loss of control of the data owners on their data, whose confidentiality and integrity could then be put at risk [20,32]. Security issues may vary depending on the considered cloud scenario. In fact, the term cloud refers to a variety of distributed computing environments, which differ in the architectural or trust assumptions. Specifically, different deployment models can be identified [36], ranging from *private cloud*, which operates for a single organization and the infrastructures and services are maintained on a private network, to a

A. Aldini et al. (Eds.): FOSAD VII, LNCS 8604, pp. 212–243, 2014.
© Springer International Publishing Switzerland 2014

public cloud, where the cloud infrastructure is owned by a cloud provider that offers its services to everybody. Ownerships and operation models between these two extremes are also possible, such as in a *community cloud*, where the cloud infrastructure is shared among a set of organizations with similar needs, and a *hybrid cloud*, where an organization with a private cloud wants to use it in conjunction with a public or community cloud for a given purpose (e.g., critical applications and data are managed in the private cloud while other less critical applications can be managed in a public cloud). In all models above, the consideration of (not fully trusted/trustworthy) providers introduces potential risks on the protection of data that are stored or processed by external providers. In particular, while providers could typically be assumed to be trustworthy with respect to the proper management of the data, they might not be trusted for data confidentiality. In other words, data should be protected from the providers themselves (considered *honest-but-curious*) that, while providing data storage, management, and processing, should not be authorized to know the actual data content.

In this chapter, we address the problem of guaranteeing data confidentiality when relying on external cloud providers for storing and processing data and illustrate possible solutions for it. In particular, a natural solution for protecting data confidentiality is *encryption*: data are protected by applying an encryption layer wrapping them before outsourcing them to external cloud providers. However, while effective, encryption makes query execution more complex. In fact, the external provider cannot decrypt the data for query execution, and must execute queries directly on encrypted data (not always applicable in practice) or rely on indexing information that can be associated with encrypted data. An additional/alternative solution is data *fragmentation*: when what is sensitive is the association among data (rather than the individual data themselves), confidentiality can be provided by storing different chunks of the data in separate non-linkable fragments.

The remainder of this chapter is organized as follows. Section 2 introduces the protection requirements to be enforced as a set of confidentiality constraints, and describes encryption and fragmentation as basic techniques that can be used to preserve the confidentiality of stored data. It also introduces the different data protection paradigms given by the disjoint or combined application of encryption and fragmentation, which are illustrated in more details in subsequent sections. Section 3 illustrates protection via data encryption (and indexing). Section 4 illustrates an approach departing from encryption in favor of data fragmentation whenever possible and assuming two data fragments and the availability of two independent and non-communicating providers for storing them. Section 5 illustrates a similar approach assuming an arbitrary number of non-linkable data fragments, which can be stored at an arbitrary number (including one) of providers on which no specific assumption is required. Section 6 illustrates an approach completely departing from encryption relying instead only on fragmentation and assuming the owner's involvement in storing (and processing) a limited amount of data. Finally, Section 7 concludes the chapter.

2   Protection Requirements and Techniques

In this section, we first discuss confidentiality requirements that may need to be satisfied when moving the data to the cloud (Section 2.1), and then describe the protection techniques that can adopted for their enforcement (Section 2.2). Finally, we illustrate the data protection paradigms resulting from different combinations of these protection techniques (Section 2.3).

2.1   Confidentiality Constraints

Protection requirements express what is sensitive and should be therefore maintained confidential when storing data at external providers. For simplicity and concreteness, most existing proposals assume data to be organized as a relation r over relational schema $R(A_1, \ldots, A_n)$, where A_i, $i = 1, \ldots, n$, are the different attributes of the relation, with the note that the proposed protection techniques could however be applied to different data models. Similarly, they assume protection requirements to be defined at the schema level, meaning at the level of attributes (in contrast to specific attribute values). This assumption simplifies the management and the application of the protection techniques, ensuring the applicability of the solutions.

Operating at the schema level, we can distinguish the following two kinds of confidentiality requirements that can apply to the data, corresponding to the fact that a given attribute is sensitive or that the association among some attributes is sensitive.

- *Sensitive attributes.* Some attributes are sensitive and their values should be maintained confidential. Simple examples of such attributes are SSN, credit card numbers, emails or telephone numbers and similar attributes whose values should not be released.
- *Sensitive associations.* In some cases, what is sensitive is the association among attributes values rather than the values of an attribute. For instance, the names of patients in a hospital may be considered not sensitive, and so the diseases treated by the hospital; however the specific association between individual patients and their illnesses is sensitive and should be maintained confidential.

A simple, yet conveniently expressive, way to capture the confidentiality requirements of sensitive attributes/associations is the specification of confidentiality constraints as set of attributes whose joint visibility should be avoided [1]. Singleton sets correspond to sensitive attributes; non-singleton sets correspond to sensitive associations.

Definition 1 (Confidentiality constraint). *Let $R(A_1, \ldots, A_n)$ be a relation schema. A confidentiality constraint c over R is a subset of attributes in R (i.e., $c \subseteq \{A_1, \ldots, A_n\}$)*

PATIENTS

SSN	Name	Race	Job	Disease	Treatment	Ins
123-45-6789	Alice	white	teacher	flu	paracetamol	160
234-56-7890	Bob	while	farmer	asthma	bronchodilators	100
345-67-8901	Carol	asian	nurse	gastritis	antacids	100
456-78-9012	David	black	lawyer	angina	nitroglycerin	200
567-89-0123	Eric	black	secretary	flu	aspirin	100
678-90-1234	Fred	asian	lawyer	diabetes	insulin	180

(a)

$\mathcal{C}$

$c_1 = \{\text{SSN}\}$
$c_2 = \{\text{Name, Disease}\}$
$c_3 = \{\text{Name, Ins}\}$
$c_4 = \{\text{Disease, Ins}\}$
$c_5 = \{\text{Race, Job, Ins}\}$

(b)

Fig. 1. An example of a relation (a) and of confidentiality constraints over it (b)

As an example, consider relation PATIENTS in Figure 1(a), reporting the information about hospitalized patients. Figure 1(b) illustrates an example of confidentiality constraints over it stating that:

- c_1: the Social Security Numbers of the patients are sensitive and should be maintained confidential (sensitive attribute);
- c_2, c_3: the disease suffered from a patient and the medical insurance she pays are sensitive and should be maintained confidential (sensitive associations);
- c_4: the association between the disease of a patient and the medical insurance she pays is sensitive (sensitive association);
- c_5: the association among the race of a patient, her job, and the insurance she pays is confidential (sensitive association).

Note that the protection of a confidentiality constraint c_i implies the protection of any confidentiality constraint c_j such that $c_i \subset c_j$ (if observers do not have visibility of the attribute/association c_i they clearly do not have visibility of the association including it); making the consideration of c_j redundant. A set $\mathcal{C}$ of confidentiality constraints over R is *well-defined* if it does not include *redundant* constraints, that is, $\forall c_i, c_j \in \mathcal{C}$, $i \neq j$: $c_i \not\subset c_j$. The set of constraints in Figure 1(b) is well-defined.

2.2   Encryption and Fragmentation

Two natural protection techniques that have been proposed for satisfying confidentiality requirements are *encryption* and *fragmentation*.

Encryption consists in encrypting the data before outsourcing them to external providers so to make them intelligible only to users holding the decryption keys, and protecting them from unauthorized eyes (including the provider itself). Although in principle both symmetric and asymmetric encryption schemas can be adopted, for performance reasons, most proposals assume the adoption of symmetric encryption. Encryption could be enforced at different levels of granularity: table, column, tuple, and individual cell. Encrypting at the level of table implies that the whole relation needs to be returned to the client for access, requiring heavy communication and leaving the whole query processing work to the client. Such a drawback is also present in case of encryption at the level of column as the only operation that the provider could perform is projection, with the whole column of interest for a query being always returned. On the other hand, encrypting at the level of individual cells would introduce many encryption/decryption operations and issues related to possible inferences on the encrypted data. Encrypting at the level of tuple appears then the preferable option, providing some ability for fine-grained retrieval (returning only a subset of the tuples) while not requiring too many encryption/decryption operations.

Since the provider is not trusted for confidentiality, encrypted data cannot be decrypted for query execution. Queries need therefore to be evaluated on the encrypted data themselves. There are typically two lines of approaches for providing this functionality: performing queries directly on encrypted data, possibly with the use of specific cryptographic techniques (e.g., [6,13,25,34]), or attaching to the encrypted data some metadata representing indexes that are then exploited for query execution (e.g., [5,14,22,26]). These approaches however support evaluation of only specific kinds of queries.

Fragmentation consists in splitting the attributes of a relation R producing different vertical views (fragments) in such a way that these views stored at external providers do not violate confidentiality requirements (neither directly nor indirectly). Intuitively, fragmentation protects the sensitive association represented by an association constraint c when the attributes in c do not appear all in the same (publicly available) fragment, and fragments cannot be joined by non authorized users. Note that singleton constraints are correctly enforced only when the corresponding attributes do not appear in any fragment that is stored at a cloud provider. In this chapter, we illustrate fragmentation solutions assuming attributes to be independent. Fragmentation can however take into account also the case of possible correlations among attributes (which could introduce inferences or enable linking) [16].

2.3 Data Protection Paradigms

Different approaches have been proposed for protecting confidentiality of data stored at external providers by applying encryption and fragmentation, by themselves or in combination. We distinguish four different protection paradigms that have been proposed.

- *Encryption/indexing.* Data are encrypted before being outsourced to external providers, with encryption typically applied at the level of tuple. Encryption does not distinguish between attributes or association constraints, applying instead the wrapping protection layer to all the attributes in a tuple. For query purposes, the encrypted data are associated with some metadata (indexes) that can be used by the cloud provider for executing queries.
- *Two can keep a secret.* It assumes the availability of two independent, non-communicating, providers each storing a portion of the data. Whenever possible, sensitive associations are protected by partitioning the involved attributes among the two providers (any way would do, as long as none of the two providers has complete visibility of all the attributes in a sensitive association). Sensitive attributes are always encrypted. Other attributes may

be stored in encrypted form whenever storing them in the clear at any of the two providers would violate at least one confidentiality constraint. The two fragments have a key attribute in common, making them joinable by the owner and by authorized users, who are the only parties who have access to both providers.

– *Multiple fragments.* It employs encryption for protecting sensitive attributes and fragmentation for protecting sensitive associations. It does not make assumptions on the nature/number of providers and on the number of fragments. Employing an arbitrary number of fragments allows sensitive associations to always be satisfied with fragmentation. Fragments are complete (all attributes are stored in each fragment in either encrypted or plaintext form) and not linkable (they have no attribute in common). Being fragments unlinkable, there is no need of assuming absence of communication between the providers.

– *Keep a few.* It assumes the involvement of a trusted party (typically the owner) for storing, and hence participating in the processing of, a limited amount of data. No encryption is applied. Sensitive attributes are stored at the owner side. Sensitive associations are protected by storing at least one of their attributes at the owner side (trying to minimize storage/computation required to the owner).

In the following sections, we describe more in details these four data protection paradigms. For the encryption/indexing paradigm, we will present the data model and describe how to execute queries directly on the encrypted data. For the fragmentation-based paradigms, we will present: *i)* the fragmentation model; *ii)* the metrics for evaluating the quality of a fragmentation; *iii)* the algorithms developed for computing an optimal fragmentation; and *iv)* the techniques to efficiently evaluate queries on the fragmentation.

3   Encryption and Indexing

We first describe how data confidentiality can be guaranteed by encrypting the data before storing them in the cloud [14,26] (Figure 2), and then illustrate how indexes can be defined and adopted for supporting the execution of queries.

Encryption Model. A relation r, defined over schema $R(A_1, \ldots, A_n)$, is represented at the cloud provider as an encrypted and indexed relation r^e, defined over schema $R^e(\underline{tid}, enc, I_i, \ldots, I_j)$, where:

– tid is a randomly generated tuple identifier;
– enc is the encrypted tuple;
– $\{I_i, \ldots, I_j\}$ is the set of indexes defined over attributes $\{A_i, \ldots, A_j\} \subseteq R$.

Each tuple t in r is represented by an encrypted tuple t^e in r^e, where: $t^e[tid]$ is a randomly generated value; $t^e[enc] = Enc(t,k)$, with Enc a symmetric encryption function with key k; and $t^e[I_l] = \iota_l(t[A_l])$, with ι_l an index function defined for

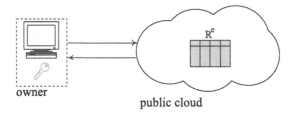

Fig. 2. Encryption and indexing

PATIENTS^e

tid	enc	I_r	I_j	I_d	I_i
1	4tBf	α	δ	ζ	σ
2	lkG7	α	δ	η	ρ
3	wF4t	β	ϵ	θ	ρ
4	m;Oi	γ	ϵ	κ	σ
5	n:8u	γ	δ	λ	ρ
6	xF-g	β	ϵ	μ	σ

Fig. 3. An example of encrypted and indexed version of relation PATIENTS in Figure 1(a)

attribute A_l. Note that not all the attributes in R are associated with an index in the corresponding encrypted relation R^e. Typically, indexes are defined only for those attributes on which conditions need to be evaluated in query execution. Figure 3 illustrates the encrypted version of relation PATIENTS in Figure 1(a), with indexes over attributes Race, Job, Disease, and Ins. In the figure, for simplicity, index values are represented with Greek letters.

Depending on how the index function ι maps plaintext values into the corresponding index values, most of the existing indexing techniques can be classified as follows [22].

- *Direct index*: maps each value in the attribute domain to a different index value and viceversa. Encryption-based indexes (e.g., [14]) represent an example of direct index. In fact, the index function maps plaintext value $t[A]$ to index value $\iota(t[A]) = E_k(t[A])$, for each tuple t in r. For instance, index I_r in relation PATIENTS^e in Figure 3 is a direct index over attribute Race of relation PATIENTS in Figure 1(a).

- *Bucket-based index*: maps different values in the attribute domain to the same index value (i.e., generates collisions), but each value in the attribute domain is mapped to one index value only. Partition-based and hash-based indexes are examples of bucket-based indexes. Partition-based indexes (e.g., [26]) split the domain D of attribute A into non-overlapping subsets of contiguous values and associate a label with each of them. The index value representing $t[A]$, for each tuple t in r, is the label of the partition to which $t[A]$ belongs. For instance, index I_i in relation PATIENTS^e in Figure 3 is a partition-based index over attribute Ins of relation PATIENTS in Figure 1(a), where the domain has been partitioned in two intervals: [100, 150] with label

ρ, and [151,200] with label σ. Hash-based indexes (e.g., [14]) instead adopt a secure hash function h that generates collisions. Hence, the index value representing $t[A]$ is computed as $h(t[A])$, for each tuple t in r. For instance, index I_j in relation PATIENTS^e in Figure 3 is a hash-based index over attribute Job of relation PATIENTS in Figure 1(a), where the hash function is defined as follows: h(teacher)=h(farmer)=h(secretary)=δ and h(nurse)=h(lawyer)=ϵ.

– *Flattened index*: maps each value in the attribute domain to a set of index values, in such a way that all the index values have the same number of occurrences (flattening). Each index value however represents one value in the attribute domain only. An example of flattened index applies direct encryption to the values in the attribute domain and a post-processing to flatten the distribution of index values. For instance, index I_d in relation PATIENTS^e in Figure 3 represents a flattened index over attribute Disease of relation PATIENTS in Figure 1(a), where each index value has one occurrence.

Besides these approaches, indexing techniques have been proposed for supporting the evaluation of specific conditions and SQL clauses [21]. As an example, solutions that exploit homomorphic encryption have been developed to support aggregate functions and the basic arithmetic operators (e.g., [24,27]). Techniques based on the Order Preserving Encryption schema have been instead studied to support range conditions and ordering (e.g., [2,35]). A different class of indexing techniques rely on the definition of specific data structures (e.g., $B+$-tree) to support the evaluation at the provider-side of specific operations. These indexes are however not represented as attributes of the encrypted relation, but they translate into additional relations stored together with r^e at the cloud provider [14].

Query Evaluation. Since moving data to the cloud should be transparent for final users, they formulate their queries over the original relation schema. These queries are then translated into equivalent queries operating on the encrypted and indexed relation r^e. The translation of a query q operating on the original relation into an equivalent set of queries exploiting indexes depends on the indexing techniques adopted by the data owner.

Consider, for simplicity, a query q of the form "SELECT *Att* FROM R WHERE *Cond*", with *Att* a set of attributes in R and *Cond*= $\bigwedge_i cond_i$ is the conjunction of equality conditions of the form $A=v$, with $A \in R$ and v a value in its domain. To partially delegate the query evaluation to the cloud provider storing r^e, q is translated into two queries: q_p executed by the provider and q_u executed by the user. Query q_p contains only the equality conditions in the WHERE clause of q that operate on indexes. Query q_u operates on the result of q_p and contains all the other conditions. To translate q into an equivalent pair of queries $\{q_p,q_u\}$, *Cond* is first split in sub-conditions *Cond$_p$*, *Cond$_u$*, and *Cond$_{pu}$* as follows:

– *Cond$_p$* is the conjunction of conditions *cond* in *Cond* involving attributes that are represented by an index in r^e that fully support equality conditions (e.g., direct and flattened indexes);

Original query	Translated queries

$q := $ SELECT Att
      FROM R
      WHERE $Cond$
	$q_p := $ SELECT tid, enc
	      FROM R^e
	      WHERE $Cond_p{}^e$ AND $Cond_{pu}{}^e$
	$q_u := $ SELECT Att
	      FROM $Decrypt(R_p.enc,k)$
	      WHERE $Cond_u$ AND $Cond_{pu}$

$q := $ SELECT Name
      FROM   Patients
      WHERE Race='white' AND
          Job='teacher' AND
          Treatment='paracetamol'
	$q_p := $ SELECT tid, enc
	      FROM Patients^e
	      WHERE $I_r = \alpha$ AND $I_j = \delta$
	
	$q_u := $ SELECT Name
	      FROM $Decrypt(R_p.enc,k)$
	      WHERE Job='teacher' AND
	          Treatment='paracetamol'

Fig. 4. An example of query translation in the encryption and indexing scenario

- $Cond_u$ is the conjunction of conditions *cond* in *Cond* that involve attributes that are not represented by an index in r^e;
- $Cond_{pu}$ is the conjunction of conditions *cond* in *Cond* that involve attributes that are represented by any index in r^e that only partially supports the evaluation of equality conditions (e.g., bucket-based indexes, due to collisions).

For instance, consider the encrypted and indexed version of relation PATIENTS in Figure 1(a) reported in Figure 3, and query "SELECT Name FROM Patients WHERE Race='white' AND Job='teacher' AND Treatment='paracetamol'". In this case, $Cond_p = \{$Race='white'$\}$, $Cond_u = \{$Treatment='paracetamol'$\}$, and $Cond_{pu} = \{$Job='teacher'$\}$.

After conditions in *Cond* have been classified in $Cond_p$, $Cond_u$, and $Cond_{pu}$, query q is translated in q_p and q_u, as illustrated in Figure 4. Query q_p, evaluated by the provider, operates on r^e and evaluates the conditions in $Cond_p$ and in $Cond_{pu}$, properly translated to operate on indexes. That is, each condition $(A_i = v)$ is represented in q_p by condition $(I$ IN $\iota(v))$, with I the index defined over A and ι the corresponding index function. When the user receives the result R_p of query q_p, it decrypts attribute enc and evaluates, on the resulting tuples, query q_u. Query q_u evaluates conditions in $Cond_u$ and $Cond_{pu}$ and projects the attributes Att. Consider, as an example, the encrypted and indexed version of relation PATIENTS in Figure 1(a) reported in Figure 3, and query "SELECT Name FROM Patients WHERE Race='white' AND Job='teacher' AND Treatment='paracetamol'". Figure 4 illustrates the translation of q in the corresponding sub-queries operating at the provider (i.e., q_p) and at the user (i.e., q_u) sides.

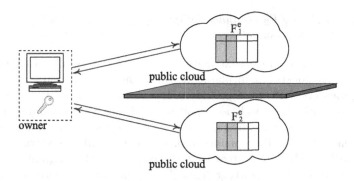

Fig. 5. Two can keep a secret

4 Two Can Keep a Secret

We present a solution based on encryption and fragmentation where data are split into two fragments, with each fragment stored at a different provider (Figure 5). The two providers are assumed to be non-communicating [1].

Fragmentation Model The satisfaction of confidentiality constraints is guaranteed by proper combination of vertical fragmentation and encryption, and relies on the assumption that the two cloud providers storing fragments do not communicate with each other (see Figure 5). Note that in the original proposal [1] encryption is considered as one of the techniques that can be used for encoding (i.e., obfuscating) attributes. Given an attribute A, the encoding of A consists in splitting its value in two (or more) attributes, say A^i and A^j, whose combined knowledge is necessary to reconstruct A (i.e., $A = A^i \otimes A^j$ with $\otimes$ a non-invertible composition operator). Encoding an attribute using encryption means therefore that A^i contains the ciphertext, A^j contains the encryption key, and $\otimes$ is the encryption function adopted by the data owner. For the sake of readability, in the remainder of this section we will consider encryption as the specific technique adopted to enforce encoding.

According to the proposal in [1], the original relation r is fragmented generating a fragmentation $\mathcal{F}=\{F_1,F_2,E\}$, where F_1 and F_2 are two fragments that are stored at two providers and E is the set of encrypted attributes. Singleton constraints are satisfied by encrypting sensitive attributes. Association constraints are satisfied by splitting the involved attributes between the two providers. Since relation r can be split in two fragments only, it may happen that an attribute cannot be stored at any of the two providers without violating a confidentiality constraint. In this case, the confidentiality constraint can be satisfied by encrypting one (or more) of its attributes. A fragmentation $\mathcal{F}=\{F_1,F_2,E\}$ is *correct* if it satisfies all the confidentiality constraints defined by the data owner, as formally stated below.

Definition 2 (Correct Fragmentation). *Let $R(A_1,\ldots,A_n)$ be a relation schema and $\mathcal{C}$ be a set of confidentiality constraints over it. A fragmentation $\mathcal{F} = \{F_1, F_2, E\}$ is* correct *iff:*

- $\forall c \in \mathcal{C}$: $c \not\subseteq F_1$, $c \not\subseteq F_2$ (*confidentiality*),
- $F_1 \cup F_2 \cup E = R$ (*completeness*).

The first condition requires that neither F_1 nor F_2 store all the attributes in a confidentiality constraint in plaintext. Since the two fragments are stored at different providers, and these providers do not communicate with each other, sensitive associations as well as sensitive attribute values cannot be reconstructed by non authorized users. The second condition instead demands that the fragments store (either plaintext or encrypted) all the attributes in the original relation. This guarantees that the content of the original relation can always be reconstructed starting from $\mathcal{F}$. For instance, a correct fragmentation $\mathcal{F}$ of relation PATIENTS in Figure 1(a) with respect to the confidentiality constraints in Figure 1(b) is $\mathcal{F}=\{F_1, F_2, E\}$, with $F_1=\{\texttt{Name,Race,Job}\}$, $F_2=\{\texttt{Disease,Treatment}\}$, and $E=\{\texttt{SSN,Ins}\}$.

At the physical level, fragments F_1 and F_2 are represented by *physical fragments* F_1^e and F_2^e, respectively. Each physical fragment F_i^e stores the attributes in F_i in plaintext, and all the attributes in E encrypted. The two physical fragments representing relation r must have a common attribute, to allow authorized users to correctly reconstruct the content of r (lossless join property). Therefore, physical fragment F_i^e representing fragment F_i has schema $F_i^e(\underline{tid}, A_{i_1}, \ldots, A_{i_n}, A_{e_1}^i, \ldots, A_{e_m}^i)$, where:

- tid is a randomly generated tuple identifier;
- $\{A_{i_1}, \ldots, A_{i_n}\}$ is the set of attributes composing fragment F_i;
- $\{A_{e_1}^i, \ldots, A_{e_m}^i\}$ is the set of attributes resulting from the encryption of the attributes in $E=\{A_{e_1}, \ldots, A_{e_m}\}$, that is, for each A_{e_i} in E, either $A_{e_i}^1$ represents encrypted attribute A_{e_i} and $A_{e_i}^2$ represents the corresponding encryption key, or viceversa.

Each tuple t in r is represented by a tuple t_1^e in F_1^e and a tuple t_2^e in F_2^e, where: $t_1^e[tid]=t_2^e[tid]$ is a randomly generated value; $t_1^e[A]=t[A]$, $\forall A \in F_1$ and $t_2^e[A]=t[A]$, $\forall A \in F_2$; and attributes $t_1^e[A^1]$, $t_2[A^2]$ are the encrypted version and the encryption key of attribute $t[A]$, $\forall A \in E$ (i.e., $Enc(t[A], t_1^e[A^1]) = t_2^e[A^2]$ or $Enc(t[A], t_2^e[A^2]) = t_1^e[A^1]$).

Figure 6 illustrates the physical fragments representing fragmentation $\mathcal{F}=\{F_1, F_2, E\}$, with $F_1=\{\texttt{Name,Race,Job}\}$, $F_2=\{\texttt{Disease,Treatment}\}$, and $E=\{\texttt{SSN,Ins}\}$ of relation PATIENTS in Figure 1(a). In this example, for simplicity, we assume that F_1^e stores the encrypted attribute values and F_2^e stores the corresponding encryption keys for all the tuples in r and for both attributes SSN and Ins.

Fragmentation Metrics. Given a relation schema R and a set $\mathcal{C}$ of confidentiality constraints over it, the data owner needs to compute a correct fragmentation. However, there may exist different fragmentations that satisfy all the constraints. As a simple example, fragmentation $\mathcal{F}=\{F_1, F_2, E\}$ with $E=R$ and $F_1=F_2=\emptyset$ is clearly correct but undesirable, since no query can be evaluated

$$F_1^e$$

tid	Name	Race	Job	SSN^1	Ins^1
1	Alice	white	teacher	$Enc(123\text{-}45\text{-}6789, k_{SSN}^1)$	$Enc(150, k_{Ins}^1)$
2	Bob	while	farmer	$Enc(234\text{-}56\text{-}7890, k_{SSN}^2)$	$Enc(100, k_{Ins}^2)$
3	Carol	asian	nurse	$Enc(345\text{-}67\text{-}8901, k_{SSN}^3)$	$Enc(100, k_{Ins}^3)$
4	David	black	lawyer	$Enc(456\text{-}78\text{-}9012, k_{SSN}^4)$	$Enc(200, k_{Ins}^4)$
5	Eric	black	secretary	$Enc(567\text{-}89\text{-}0123, k_{SSN}^5)$	$Enc(100, k_{Ins}^5)$
6	Fred	asian	lawyer	$Enc(678\text{-}90\text{-}1234, k_{SSN}^6)$	$Enc(180, k_{Ins}^6)$

$$F_2^e$$

tid	Disease	Treatment	SSN^2	Ins^2
1	flu	paracetamol	k_{SSN}^1	k_{Ins}^1
2	asthma	bronchodilators	k_{SSN}^2	k_{Ins}^2
3	gastritis	antacids	k_{SSN}^3	k_{Ins}^3
4	angina	nitroglycerin	k_{SSN}^4	k_{Ins}^4
5	flu	aspirin	k_{SSN}^5	k_{Ins}^5
6	diabetes	insulin	k_{SSN}^6	k_{Ins}^6

Fig. 6. An example of a correct fragmentation of relation PATIENTS in Figure 1(a) in the two can keep a secret scenario

by the providers storing F_1^e and F_2^e. Aiming at leaving as much computational effort as possible to the cloud providers, it is then necessary to define a metric to measure the *quality* of a fragmentation in terms of the query overhead required to users for evaluating their queries over the fragmentation $\mathcal{F}$. The metric proposed in [1] is based on the knowledge of the query workload $\mathcal{Q}$ (i.e., a set of representative queries that are expected to be frequently executed) characterizing the system. In fact, the query workload describes how frequently attributes appear together in queries, and then permits to estimate the computational overhead that a fragmentation that splits these attributes may cause to users. To assess the quality of a fragmentation, the query workload is modeled as an *affinity matrix*, which is a symmetric matrix with a row and a column for each attribute in R, and where each cell $M[A_i, A_j] = M[A_j, A_i]$ $(i \neq j)$, represents the cost (i.e., the computation overhead for users) of having attributes A_i and A_j stored in different fragments. Each cell $M[A, A]$ (i.e., cells along the diagonal) instead represents the cost of having attribute A encrypted. For instance, the affinity matrix in Figure 7 states that the cost of having attributes Name and Disease stored in two different fragments is $M[\text{Name}, \text{Disease}] = 10$, and that of encrypting attribute Ins is $M[\text{Ins}, \text{Ins}] = 15$. The cost of a fragmentation $\mathcal{F}$ is computed by summing the costs of the attributes encrypted in $\mathcal{F}$, and the costs of the pairs of attributes not stored together in a fragment in $\mathcal{F}$. Formally, the cost of a fragmentation $\mathcal{F} = \{F_1, F_2, E\}$ is defined as:

$$\sum_{A_i \in F_1, A_j \in F_2} M[A_i, A_j] + \sum_{A_i \in E} M[A_i, A_i]$$

As an example, consider relation PATIENTS in Figure 1(a), the fragmentation in Figure 6, and the affinity matrix in Figure 7 (since the matrix is symmetric, we report the values only for the cells in the upper half of the matrix). The quality of $\mathcal{F}$ is computed as: $M[\text{Name}, \text{Disease}] + M[\text{Name}, \text{Treatment}] + M[\text{Race}, \text{Disease}] + M[\text{Race}, \text{Treatment}] + M[\text{Job}, \text{Disease}] + M[\text{Job}, \text{Treatment}] + M[\text{SSN}, \text{SSN}] + M[\text{Ins}, \text{Ins}] = 10 + 15 + 32 + 40 + 14 + 23 + 10 + 15 = 159$.

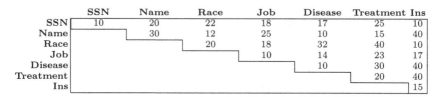

	SSN	Name	Race	Job	Disease	Treatment	Ins
SSN	10	20	22	18	17	25	10
Name		30	12	25	10	15	40
Race			20	18	32	40	10
Job				10	14	23	17
Disease					10	30	40
Treatment						20	40
Ins							15

Fig. 7. An example of affinity matrix

Computing an Optimal Fragmentation. The problem of computing a fragmentation that minimizes the cost of query evaluation is NP-hard (the minimum hypergraph coloring problem reduces to it in polynomial time [1]). Hence, in [1] the authors propose to adopt an heuristic approach to compute a good, although non optimal, solution. The proposed solution is based on a graph modeling of the fragmentation problem, where each attribute in R is represented as a vertex in a *complete graph* G whose edges and vertices are weighted according to M (i.e., $weight(A)=M[A,A]$ and $weight(A_i,A_j)=M[A_i,A_j]$). The graph has an additional set H of hyperarcs, modeling the confidentiality constraints in $\mathcal{C}$. The proposed heuristic combines two approximation techniques, traditionally used to find a good solution to the following well known hard problems.

- *Min-Cut.* Assuming that $\mathcal{C}$ is empty, the problem of computing an optimal fragmentation can be translated into the problem of computing a minimum cut for G. A minimum cut for a graph G is a partitioning of the set of vertices in G in two subsets, V_1 and V_2, that minimizes the weight of the edges with one vertex in V_1 and vertex in V_2. Intuitively, the heuristic approaches proposed for the Min-Cut problem can be used to compute different cuts that are nearly minimal, and then we can choose the one that satisfies the highest number of confidentiality constraints.
- *Weighted Set Cover.* If we do not consider the cost of splitting attributes between F_1 and F_2, the problem of computing a correct fragmentation can be translated into the minimum set cover problem. Intuitively, each confidentiality constraint is a set whose elements are the attributes composing it. The weight of each attribute A is $M[A,A]$ and the minimum set cover is the set C' of attributes with minimum weight that includes (at least) one attribute for each constraint. Confidentiality constraints can be satisfied by encrypting all the attributes in C'.

By combining these two approaches, it is possible to compute a good fragmentation in polynomial time. In fact, the Min-Cut heuristic algorithm guarantees to compute a good split of the attributes between F_1 and F_2, while the weighted set cover guarantees constraint satisfaction. The corresponding heuristic algorithm works as follows. First, it computes a minimum set cover E through a greedy strategy, to guarantee that all the constraints are satisfied by encrypting the attributes in E. Then, it computes a minimum cut for the attributes in $R \backslash E$, to split them between F_1 and F_2 minimizing the cost of the fragmentation.

Finally, for each attribute A in E, it moves A to F_1 (F_2, respectively) if no confidentiality constraint is violated.

Query Evaluation. A query q formulated over the original relation r is translated into a set of queries operating over the two fragments stored at the two cloud providers. A naive solution would download from the two providers both F_1^e and F_2^e, and locally evaluate q at the user side on the joined fragments. However, this solution would not be acceptable due to the high computational and communication overhead for users. The translation of original queries to operate on fragments should then limit the computational overhead for the user (i.e., moving as much as possible the query evaluation process to the providers).

Consider, for simplicity, a query q of the form "SELECT Att FROM R WHERE $Cond$", with Att a set of attributes in R and $Cond = \bigwedge_i cond_i$ a conjunction of basic conditions of the form $(A_i\ op\ v)$, $(A_i\ op\ A_j)$, or $(A_i$ IN $\{v_i, \dots, v_k\})$, where $A_i, A_j \in R$, $\{v, v_1, \dots, v_k\}$ are constant values in the domain of A_i, and op is a comparison operator in $\{=, \neq, >, <, \geq, \leq\}$. For the sake of readability, in the following, we will use notation $Attr(cond)$ to denote the set of attributes in the basic condition $cond$. To partially delegate the computation of the query to the providers storing F_1^e and F_2^e, q is translated into a set $\{q_1, q_2, q_u\}$ of queries operating at the provider storing F_1^e, at the provider storing F_2^e, and at the user side, respectively. This translatwion is based on the observation that the evaluation of basic conditions involving only attributes plaintext represented in F_1^e (F_2^e, respectively) can be delegated to the provider storing F_1^e (F_2^e, respectively). Conditions operating on encrypted attributes or on two attributes, say A_1 and A_2, with $A_1 \in F_1$ and $A_2 \in F_2$, must be evaluated by the user. Given query q, condition $Cond$ in the WHERE clause is then split into three sub-conditions as follows:

- $Cond_1 = \bigwedge_i cond_i$: $Attr(cond_i) \subseteq F_1$ is the conjunction of basic conditions that involve only attributes in fragment F_1;
- $Cond_2 = \bigwedge_i cond_i$: $Attr(cond_i) \subseteq F_2$ is the conjunction of basic conditions that involve only attributes in fragment F_2;
- $Cond_u = \bigwedge_i cond_i$: $Attr(cond_i) \not\subseteq F_1$ and $Attr(cond_i) \not\subseteq F_2$ is the conjunction of basic conditions that either involve encrypted attributes or are of the form $(A_i\ op\ A_j)$, where $A_i \in F_1$ and $A_j \in F_2$ (or viceversa).

For instance, consider relation PATIENTS in Figure 1(a), its fragmentation in Figure 6 and query $q=$"SELECT `Name` FROM `Patients` WHERE `Job`='lawyer' AND `Disease`='flu' AND `Ins`=100." $Cond_1$ includes basic condition `Job`='lawyer'; $Cond_2$ includes basic condition `Disease`='flu'; and $Cond_u$ includes basic condition `Ins`=100.

The evaluation of a query q on R can follow different strategies, depending on whether $Cond_1$ and $Cond_2$ are evaluated in parallel (Figure 8(a)) or in sequence (Figure 8(b)), as illustrated in the following.

- *Parallel strategy.* The two providers evaluate in parallel queries q_1 and q_2, which are in charge of returning the tuples in F_1^e and F_2^e satisfying conditions

Original query	Translated queries
$q :=$ SELECT Att FROM R WHERE $Cond$	$q_1 :=$ SELECT $tid, (Att \cup Attr(Cond_u)) \cap (F_1 \cup E)$ FROM F_1^e WHERE $Cond_1$ $q_2 :=$ SELECT $tid, (Att \cup Attr(Cond_u)) \cap (F_2 \cup E)$ FROM F_2^e WHERE $Cond_2$ $q_u :=$ SELECT Att FROM R_1 JOIN R_2 ON $R_1.tid = R_2.tid$ WHERE $Cond_u$
$q :=$ SELECT Name FROM Patients WHERE Job='lawyer' AND Disease='flu' AND Ins=100	$q_1 :=$ SELECT tid, Name, Ins[1] FROM F_1^e WHERE Job='lawyer' $q_2 :=$ SELECT tid, Ins[2] FROM F_2^e WHERE Disease='flu' $q_u :=$ SELECT Name FROM R_1 JOIN R_2 ON $R_1.tid = R_2.tid$ WHERE $Decrypt(\text{Ins}[1], \text{Ins}[2])$=100

(a) PARALLEL STRATEGY

Original query	Translated queries
$q :=$ SELECT Att FROM R WHERE $Cond$	$q_1 :=$ SELECT $tid, (Att \cup Attr(Cond_u)) \cap (F_1 \cup E)$ FROM F_1^e WHERE $Cond_1$ $q_2 :=$ SELECT $tid, (Att \cup Attr(Cond_u)) \cap (F_2 \cup E)$ FROM F_2^e WHERE $(tid$ IN $R_1.tid)$ AND $Cond_2$ $q_u :=$ SELECT Att FROM R_1 JOIN R_2 ON $R_1.tid = R_2.tid$ WHERE $Cond_u$
$q :=$ SELECT Name FROM Patients WHERE Job='lawyer' AND Disease='flu' AND Ins=100	$q_1 :=$ SELECT tid, Name, Ins[1] FROM F_1^e WHERE Job='lawyer' $q_2 :=$ SELECT tid, Ins[2] FROM F_2^e WHERE (tid IN $\{4,6\}$) AND Disease='flu' $q_u :=$ SELECT Name FROM R_1 JOIN R_2 ON $R_1.tid = R_2.tid$ WHERE $Decrypt(\text{Ins}[1], \text{Ins}[2])$=100

(b) SEQUENTIAL STRATEGY

Fig. 8. An example of query translation in the two can keep a secret scenario

$Cond_1$ and $Cond_2$, respectively. Query q_1 (q_2, respectively) returns the tuple identifier tid, which is necessary to join its result R_1 (R_2, respectively) with the result of q_2 (q_1, respectively), and all those attributes included in F_1 (F_2, respectively) and in E that appear either in the SELECT clause of q, or in $Cond_u$. When the user receives both R_1 and R_2, she executes query q_u that computes the join between them, decrypts encrypted attributes, evaluates $Cond_u$, and projects the attributes in the SELECT clause of q. Figure 8(a) illustrates the translation of query $q=$ "SELECT Name FROM Patients WHERE Job='lawyer' AND Disease='flu' AND Ins=100" formulated over relation PATIENTS in Figure 1(a) into an equivalent set of queries operating on the fragments in Figure 6.

- *Sequential strategy.* With this strategy, one among the two queries q_1 and q_2 is sent to the corresponding provider first. Let us assume that the provider storing F_1^e goes first (the case where the provider managing F_2^e goes first is symmetric) and executes query q_1, which evaluates condition $Cond_1$ retuning attribute tid and all those attributes included in F_1 and in E that appear either in the SELECT clause of q, or in $Cond_u$. Upon receiving R_1, the user sends to the provider storing F_2^e the identifiers of the tuples in R_1. The provider then executes q_2, which evaluates $Cond_2$ on the tuples in F_2^e whose identifier is among the ones received from the user. The user finally computes the join between R_1 and R_2, evaluates $Cond_u$ and projects the attributes of interest. Figure 8(b) illustrates the translation of query $q=$ "SELECT Name FROM Patients WHERE Job='lawyer' AND Disease='flu' AND Ins=100" formulated over relation PATIENTS in Figure 1(a) into an equivalent set of queries operating on the fragments in Figure 6. (Values $\{4,6\}$ in the WHERE clause of q_2 are the identifiers of the tuples satisfying $Cond_1$.)

The choice between the parallel and the sequential strategies depends on the performance they guarantee and on the resource that the user considers more valuable. In fact, the parallel strategy has the advantage of reducing the response time, while causing a higher communication cost than the sequential strategy (R_2 is likely to be composed of a higher number of tuples). The choice of the provider that goes first in the sequential strategy instead depends only on the selectivity of $Cond_1$ and $Cond_2$, since it is preferable to evaluate the most selective condition first.

5   Multiple Fragments

We present a solution based on encryption and fragmentation where data can be splitted among an arbitrary number of fragments [7,10], which may be possibly stored at the same provider (Figure 9).

Fragmentation Model. The goal of the proposal in [7] is to remove the limiting assumption of absence of collusion between the two providers characterizing the solution in [1]. The idea is therefore to compute a fragmentation (with no limits

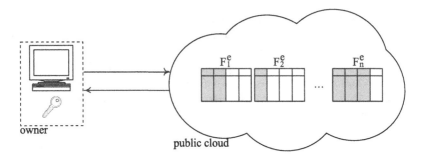

Fig. 9. Multiple fragments

on the number of fragments composing it) in such a way that its fragments are not linkable, meaning that it is not possible for parties different from the data owner and authorized users to reconstruct the original relation and then also the sensitive values and associations. Being non linkable, fragments can be stored at a different providers, but also at the same provider, with no confidentiality risk.

The approach in [7] couples vertical fragmentation with encryption to satisfy confidentiality constraints. In particular, each singleton constraint $c=\{A\}$ is satisfied by encrypting the involved attribute A. Each association constraint $c=\{A_1,\ldots,A_n\}$ can instead be satisfied by either encrypting at least one among the $A_1,\ldots,A_n$ attributes, or by storing these attributes in different fragments. To prevent indirect violation of confidentiality constraints by joining fragments, fragments must be disjoint (i.e., no attribute can appear in more than one fragment). More formally, a *correct* fragmentation is defined as follows.

Definition 3 (Correct Fragmentation). *Let $R(A_1,\ldots,A_n)$ be a relation schema and $\mathcal{C}$ be a set of confidentiality constraints over it. A fragmentation $\mathcal{F} = \{F_1,\ldots,F_m\}$ is correct iff:*

- *$\forall c \in \mathcal{C}, \forall F \in \mathcal{F}: c \nsubseteq F$ (confidentiality);*
- *$\forall F_i, F_j \in \mathcal{F}, i \neq j: F_i \cap F_j = \emptyset$ (unlinkability).*

The first condition states that a fragment in $\mathcal{F}$ cannot contain all the attributes composing a confidentiality constraint. The second condition states that fragments must be disjoint. This approach has two advantages: *i)* being disjoint, all fragments $F_1,\ldots,F_n$ composing a fragmentation $\mathcal{F}$ are not linkable and can therefore be stored at the same provider; and *ii)* not imposing any limit on the number of fragments, association constraints can always be satisfied without encryption, thus increasing the *visibility* over data, with clear advantages for query evaluation. In fact, the plaintext representation of an attribute A in a fragment F permits the evaluation of conditions over A at the cloud provider storing F. For this reason, the approach in [7] aims at computing fragmentations that maximize visibility. A fragmentation maximizes visibility if each attribute A in R not appearing in a singleton constraint is plaintext represented in *at least* one fragment. Note however that, to satisfy the unlinkability condition, each attribute

F_1^e			
salt	enc	Name	Job
s_1^1	xTb:	Alice	teacher
s_1^2	o;!G	Bob	farmer
s_1^3	Ap'L	Carol	nurse
s_1^4	.u7t	David	lawyer
s_1^5	y"e3	Eric	secretary
s_1^6	(11!	Fred	lawyer

F_2^e			
salt	enc	Disease	Treatment
s_2^1	hg5=	flu	paracetamol
s_2^2	mB71	asthma	bronchodilators
s_2^3	:k?2	gastritis	antacids
s_2^4	Ql4,	angina	nitroglycerin
s_2^5	-kGd	flu	aspirin
s_2^6	p[Mz	diabetes	insulin

F_3^e			
salt	enc	Race	Ins
s_3^1	bP5	white	160
s_3^2	*Cx	white	100
s_3^3	1Bny	asian	100
s_3^4	Oj)6	black	200
s_3^5	vT7/	black	100
s_3^6	11fY	asian	180

Fig. 10. An example of correct fragmentation of relation PATIENTS in Figure 1(a) in the multiple fragments scenario

not appearing in a singleton constraint can belong to *at most* one fragment in a correct fragmentation. For instance, $\mathcal{F}=\{\{\mathtt{Name,Job}\}, \{\mathtt{Disease,Treatment}\},$ $\{\mathtt{Race,Ins}\}\}$ is a correct fragmentation of relation PATIENTS in Figure 1(a) with respect to the constraints in Figure 1(b). This fragmentation maximizes visibility as all the attributes but SSN, which is sensitive per se (c_1), are plaintext represented in exactly one fragment.

At a physical level, each fragment $F_i = \{A_{i_1}, \ldots, A_{i_n}\}$ of a fragmentation $\mathcal{F}$ is represented by a *physical fragment* $F_i^e(\underline{salt}, enc, A_{i_1}, \ldots, A_{i_n})$, where:

- *salt* is the primary key of the relation and contains a randomly chosen value;
- *enc* is an attribute storing the encrypted attributes in $R \setminus \{A_{i_1}, \ldots, A_{i_n}\}$;
- $\{A_{i_1}, \ldots, A_{i_n}\}$ is the set of attributes composing fragment F_i.

Each tuple t in r is represented by a tuple in each of the physical fragments $\{F_1^e, \ldots, F_m^e\}$ corresponding to the fragments $\{F_1, \ldots, F_m\}$ in $\mathcal{F}$. Tuple t^e representing t in F_i^e is such that: $t^e[salt]$ is a random value; $t^e[enc]$ is computed as $Enc(t[R \setminus F_i] \oplus t[salt], k)$, with $\oplus$ the binary XOR operator; and $t^e[A]=t[A]$, $\forall A \in F$. Note that the attributes not appearing in plaintext in F^e are combined with a random salt before encryption to prevent frequency attacks [33]. Since each physical fragment stores (either plaintext or encrypted) all the attributes in R, every query can be evaluated on a single fragment. Figure 10 illustrates the physical fragments representing fragmentation $\mathcal{F}=\{\{\mathtt{Name,Job}\},$ $\{\mathtt{Disease,Treatment}\}, \{\mathtt{Race,Ins}\}\}$ of relation PATIENTS in Figure 1(a).

Fragmentation Metrics. Given a relation schema R and a set $\mathcal{C}$ of confidentiality constraints over it, there may be different correct fragmentations that maximize visibility. As an example, a fragmentation $\mathcal{F}$ where each attribute in R that does not appear in a singleton constraint is stored in a different fragment is correct and maximizes visibility. However, this solution causes an excessive fragmentation making the evaluation of queries involving more than one attribute expensive. We now present different metrics (see Figure 11) that can be used to assess the quality of a fragmentation in terms of the query evaluation overhead caused to users.

- *Minimal fragmentation* (e.g., [7]). A simple metric for evaluating the quality of a fragmentation consists in minimizing the number of fragments thus

Metric	Quality function
Number of fragments	$card(\mathcal{F})$
Affinity	$\sum\limits_{k=1}^{n} \mathit{aff}(F_k)$ where $\mathit{aff}(F_k) = \sum_{A_i,A_j \in F_k, i<j} M[A_i,A_j], \; k=1,\dots,n$
Query evaluation cost	$\sum\limits_{i=1}^{m} \mathit{freq}(q_i)\cdot cost(q_i,\mathcal{F})$ where $cost(q_i,\mathcal{F})=Min(cost(q_i,F_j), \; j=1,\dots,n)$ and $cost(q_i,F_j)=S(q_i,F_j)\cdot|r|\cdot size(t_j), \; i=1,\dots,m$ and $j=1,\dots,n$

Fig. 11. Classification of the metrics in the multiple fragments scenario

avoiding excessive fragmentation. Intuitively, a fragmentation with a lower number of fragments is likely to store more attributes in the same fragment, clearly favoring the evaluation of queries that involve these attributes (also together). For instance, both $\mathcal{F}=\{\{\texttt{Name,Job}\}, \{\texttt{Disease,Treatment}\}, \{\texttt{Race,Ins}\}\}$ and $\mathcal{F}'=\{\{\texttt{Name,Job}\}, \{\texttt{Disease}\},\{\texttt{Treatment}\}, \{\texttt{Race,Ins}\}\}$ are correct fragmentations of relation PATIENTS in Figure 1(a). However, $\mathcal{F}$ is preferable to $\mathcal{F}'$ because it efficiently supports the evaluation of queries involving, both Disease and Treatment. Two different notions of minimality have been proposed: *minimality* (i.e., composed of the minimum number of fragments [3,12]) and *local minimality* (i.e., composed of fragments that cannot be merged without violating constraints [7,12]). We note that, while a locally minimal fragmentation might not be composed of the minimum number of fragments, a minimal fragmentation is indeed also locally minimal (i.e., merging any of its fragments violates at least a constraint).

– *Maximum affinity* (e.g., [10]). A more precise assessment of the quality of a fragmentation is based on the *affinity* between attributes. The affinity between two attributes quantifies the performance advantage in query evaluation that can be obtained by storing them in the same fragment [31]. Attributes with high affinity are expected to be frequently involved together in queries. Therefore, the higher the affinity, the higher the advantage in query evaluation of having the attributes stored in the same fragment. Attribute affinity can be modeled by an *affinity matrix* M, which is a symmetric matrix with a row and a column for each attribute that do not appear in a singleton constraint. Each cell $M[A_i,A_j]$, with $i \neq j$, represents the benefit obtained by storing attributes A_i and A_j in the same fragment. For instance, Figure 12 illustrates an example of affinity matrix for relation PATIENTS in Figure 1(a). Fragmentations that keep in the same fragment attributes with high affinity are to be preferred over fragmentations that split them in different fragments. The quality of a fragmentation $\mathcal{F}$ is measured as the sum of the affinity of the fragments composing it, where the affinity of a fragment F is obtained by summing the affinities of the pairs of attributes in F. As an example, consider relation PATIENTS in Figure 1(a), the fragmentation in Figure 10, and the affinity matrix in Figure 12. The quality of $\mathcal{F}$ is computed as: $M[\texttt{Name, Job}] + M[\texttt{Disease, Treatment}] + M[\texttt{Race, Ins}] = 30 + 25 + 40 = 95$.

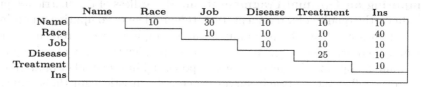

	Name	Race	Job	Disease	Treatment	Ins
Name		10	30	10	10	10
Race			10	10	10	40
Job				10	10	10
Disease					25	10
Treatment						10
Ins						

Fig. 12. An example of affinity matrix

- *Minimum query evaluation cost* (e.g., [8]). Another possible metric is based on the definition of a query cost model, which can be used to evaluate the cost of executing a representative set of queries over fragments. This metric, compared with the affinity metric, has the advantage of taking into consideration also the benefit of storing in the same fragment arbitrary sets of attributes (instead of pairs thereof). The adoption of this metric requires the availability of the query workload Q of the system, which is a set $\{q_1, \ldots, q_m\}$ of queries along with their execution frequency $freq(q_i)$, $i = 1, \ldots, m$. The proposal in [8] assumes that queries in Q are of the form "SELECT $A_{i_1}, \ldots, A_{i_n}$ FROM R WHERE $\bigwedge_{j=1}^{n} (A_j$ IN $V_j)$" with V_j a set of values in the domain of attribute A_j. The quality of a fragmentation $\mathcal{F}$ then depends on the cost of executing the queries in Q, properly weighted by their frequency, over the fragments in $\mathcal{F}$. Since each physical fragment stores, either plaintext or encrypted, all the attributes in R, the cost of evaluating a query q over $\mathcal{F}$ is the minimum among the costs of evaluating q over each physical fragment F^e in $\mathcal{F}$. The cost of evaluating q on F^e is estimated by the size of the result returned to the user, because the costs of communication, decryption, and evaluation of conditions on encrypted attributes at the user side are more expensive than the computational costs at the provider side. Hence, the cost $cost(q_i, F_j)$ of executing q_i on F_j is computed as $S(q_i, F_j) \cdot |r| \cdot size(t_j)$, where $S(q_i, F_j)$ is the selectivity of query q_i, $|r|$ is the number of tuples in r, and $size(t_j)$ is the size of the attributes appearing in the SELECT clause of q_i and the size of attribute *enc* if there is the need of accessing attributes not appearing in plaintext in F_j. The selectivity of condition A IN $V = \{v_1, \ldots, v_n\}$ is an estimate of the ratio of the number of tuples in F that satisfy the condition over the total number of tuples in r. If attribute A does not appear in plaintext in F, the selectivity is set to 1. Consider, as an example, a query workload composed of two queries: $q_1 =$ "SELECT * FROM **Patients** WHERE **Job**='teacher' AND **Race**='asian'", with frequency 30; and $q_2 =$ "SELECT * FROM **Patients** WHERE **Job**='lawyer' AND **Disease**='flu'", with frequency 70. The fragmentation in Figure 10 implies a query evaluation cost $cost(Q, \mathcal{F}) = cost(q_1, \mathcal{F}) \cdot freq(q_1) + cost(q_2, \mathcal{F}) \cdot freq(q_2) = 1/6 \cdot 6 \cdot 1 \cdot 30 + 1/3 \cdot 6 \cdot 1 \cdot 70 = 170$. In fact, assuming that the size of the tuples is the same for all the fragments and is equal to 1, the fragment that minimizes query evaluation cost for q_1 is F_1, and are both F_1 and F_2 for q_2. Indeed, the most selective condition in q_1 operates on attribute **Job**, while the two conditions in q_2 are equally selective.

Computing an Optimal Fragmentation. Regardless of the metric adopted to evaluate the quality of a fragmentation, the problem of computing an optimal fragmentation is NP-hard (the minimum hypergraph coloring problem reduces to it in polynomial time [10]). Hence, the time complexity of any algorithm able to compute an optimal fragmentation is exponential in the number of attributes in R. In the following, we briefly survey exact and heuristic algorithms proposed for efficiently computing a correct and optimal (according to a chosen metric) fragmentation.

– *Minimal fragmentation* (e.g., [3,7,12]). Both exact and heuristic algorithms have been proposed to the aim of avoiding an excessive fragmentation and producing minimal or locally minimal fragmentations. The exact algorithms in [3,12], proposed to produce a minimal fragmentation, rely on a logical modeling of the problem. The attributes in R are interpreted as Boolean variables, and each confidentiality constraint $c=\{A_1,\dots,A_n\}$ in $\mathcal{C}$ as a Boolean formula representing the conjunction $A_1 \wedge \dots \wedge A_n$ of the attributes composing it. A fragment F of R is a truth assignment that assigns *true* to the variables representing the attributes in the fragment, and *false* to the other variables. A fragmentation $\mathcal{F}$ is a set of truth assignments that satisfy all the constraints in $\mathcal{C}$, and such that each variable A is assigned *true* in at most one fragment F in $\mathcal{F}$. Two approaches have been studied to compute a set of truth assignments representing a correct fragmentation that use a SAT (SATisfiability) and an OBDD (Ordered Binary Decision Diagram) formulation of the fragmentation problem. The adoption of SAT solvers has been proposed in [3] to compute a fragmentation composed of the minimum the number of fragments. To this aim, a SAT solver able to compute a correct fragmentation composed of n fragments is iteratively invoked. At the first iteration, n is set to 1. It is then incremented by 1 at each iteration. The iteration stops when the SAT solver finds a correct fragmentation. The adoption of the OBDD data structure to represent confidentiality constraints and efficiently compute fragments (i.e., truth assignments) satisfying constraints has been proposed in [12]. The problem of computing a fragmentation composed of the minimum number of fragments is translated into the problem of computing a maximum weighted clique over a *fragmentation graph*. The fragmentation graph models fragments, efficiently computed using OBDDs, that satisfy all the confidentiality constraints and a subset of the visibility constraints (i.e., required views over the data) defined in the system. Another heuristic approach for computing a locally minimal fragmentation has been proposed in [7]. The algorithm starts from an empty fragmentation $\mathcal{F}$ and tries to insert each attribute A in R (non involved in a singleton constraint) into a fragment $F \in \mathcal{F}$. If A cannot be inserted into any fragment in $\mathcal{F}$ without violating constraints, a new fragment $F'=\{A\}$ is created and inserted into $\mathcal{F}$. The attributes are considered in decreasing order of the number of constraints in which they are involved (i.e., attributes appearing in a higher number of constraints are considered first).

- *Maximum affinity* (e.g., [10]). The greedy approach proposed in [10] takes advantage of the affinity matrix M previously illustrated in this section to compute a fragmentation that maximizes affinity. The proposed technique starts with a fragmentation $\mathcal{F}$ where each attribute A that does not appear in a singleton constraint belongs to a different fragment $F \in \mathcal{F}$. At each iteration, the algorithm merges the pair of fragments $\langle F_i, F_j \rangle$ with highest affinity according to M, provided no constraint is violated. The algorithm terminates when no further merge is possible.
- *Minimum query evaluation cost* (e.g., [8]). The exact algorithm proposed in [8] to minimize the cost of query execution is based on an efficient visit of the solution space of the fragmentation problem, which is represented through a lattice $(S_F, \preceq)$. Set S_F includes all the fragmentations of relation R composed of disjoint fragments; $\preceq$ is a dominance relationship between fragmentations where $\mathcal{F} \preceq \mathcal{F}'$ iff $\mathcal{F}$ can be obtained by merging fragments in $\mathcal{F}'$. The visit of the fragmentation lattice is based on two nice properties of the dominance relationship: *i)* given a non-correct fragmentation $\mathcal{F}'$, any fragmentation $\mathcal{F}$ such that $\mathcal{F} \preceq \mathcal{F}'$ is not correct; and *ii)* given two fragmentations $\mathcal{F}$ and $\mathcal{F}'$ such that $\mathcal{F} \preceq \mathcal{F}'$, the query evaluation cost of $\mathcal{F}'$ is higher than the cost of $\mathcal{F}$ (i.e., the cost is monotonic with the dominance relationship). A heuristic algorithm exploiting the fragmentation lattice has also been proposed [8].

Query Evaluation. Since each physical fragment stores (either plaintext of encrypted) all the attributes in R, a query q can be evaluated on any physical fragment. However, the performance clearly depends on the fragment that is chosen to evaluate q. Given the set Att of attributes involved in q, it is intuitively more convenient to evaluate q over a physical fragment F_i^e that stores attributes in Att (or a subset thereof) in the clear, rather than over a fragment F_j^e where attributes in Att are encrypted. In fact, choosing F_j^e would require the user to download the whole fragment from the cloud and to locally evaluate the query (after the encrypted attributes have been decrypted). Instead, resorting to F_i^e permits to (partially) delegate to the provider the query evaluation task.

The solution in [7] considers queries q of the form SELECT Att FROM R WHERE $Cond$, with Att a set of attributes in R and $Cond = \bigwedge_i cond_i$ a conjunction of basic conditions of the form $(A_i\ op\ v)$, $(A_i\ op\ A_j)$, or $(A_i\ \text{IN}\ \{v_i, \ldots, v_k\})$, where $A_i, A_j \in R$, $\{v, v_1, \ldots, v_k\}$ are constant values in the domain of A_i, and op is a comparison operator in $\{=, \neq, >, <, \geq, \leq\}$. Let us assume that query q is evaluated over physical fragment F^e. The basic conditions in the WHERE clause of q operating on attributes in F (i.e., attributes appearing in plaintext in F^e) can be evaluated by the provider while the basic conditions operating on attributes not included in F (i.e., encrypted attributes in F^e) must be evaluated by the user who knows the encryption key. To translate q into an equivalent set of queries operating on F^e, $Cond$ is split in sub-conditions $Cond_p$ and $Cond_u$, as follows:

Original query	Translated queries

q := SELECT Att
    FROM R
    WHERE $Cond$
	q_p := SELECT $salt, enc, Att\cap F$
	    FROM F^e
	    WHERE $Cond_p$
	
	q_u := SELECT Att
	    FROM $Decrypt(R_p.enc\oplus salt,k)$
	    WHERE $Cond_u$

q := SELECT Name
    FROM   Patients
    WHERE Disease='flu' AND
          Job='teacher'
	q_p := SELECT salt, enc, Name
	    FROM F^e_1
	    WHERE Job='teacher'
	
	q_u := SELECT Name
	    FROM $Decrypt(R_p.enc\oplus salt,k)$
	    WHERE Disease='flu'

Fig. 13. An example of query translation in the multiple fragments scenario

- $Cond_p = \bigwedge_i cond_i : Attr(cond_i) \subseteq F$ is the conjunction of the basic conditions involving only attributes plaintext stored in the chosen fragment;
- $Cond_u = \bigwedge_i cond_i : Attr(cond_i) \not\subseteq F$ is the conjunction of the basic conditions that involve at least one attribute that appears encrypted in the chosen fragment.

For instance, consider the fragmentation in Figure 10, and assume that query "SELECT Name FROM Patients WHERE Disease='flu' AND Job='teacher'" is evaluated over fragment F^e_1. In this case, $Cond$ includes conditions Disease='flu' and Job='teacher'. Since attribute Job belongs to F_1 while attribute Disease does not, $Cond_p$ includes condition Job='teacher', and $Cond_u$ includes condition Disease='flu'.

After conditions in $Cond$ have been classified between $Cond_p$ and $Cond_u$, query q is translated in two queries, as illustrated in Figure 13. Query q_p, executed at the provider side, operates on the selected physical fragment F^e and evaluates condition $Cond_p$. When the user receives the result R_p of query q_p, it decrypts attribute enc and evaluates, on the resulting tuples, query q_u. Query q_u evaluates condition $Cond_u$ and projects the attributes in Att. Note that if $Cond_u$ is empty and all the attributes in the SELECT clause of q belong to F, then q_u does not need to be executed and q_p does not need to return attributes $salt$ and enc (since the result R_p returned by q_p already coincides with the result of the original query q). Consider, as an example, relation PATIENTS in Figure 1(a), the fragmentation in Figure 10, and query $q=$"SELECT Name FROM Patients WHERE Disease='flu' AND Job='teacher'", returning the names of the teachers suffering from flu. While, in principle, the query might be evaluated using any of the three fragments, F^e_1 and F^e_3 are more convenient than F^e_2 because F^e_2 does not include any of the attributes involved in the conditions of q. Figure 13 illustrates the translation of q in the corresponding sub-queries operating at the provider side (i.e., q_p) and at the user side (i.e., q_u) using F^e_1.

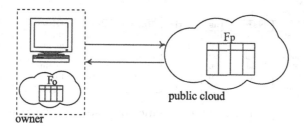

Fig. 14. Keep a few

6 Keep a Few

We present a solution completely departing from encryption where a trusted party (the owner) is involved in storing a portion of the data (Figure 14). Specifically, data are splitted into two fragments, one stored at the data owner side, and one stored at an external provider so that the fragment managed by the provider does not violate the confidentiality constraints [4,9,11].

Fragmentation Model. Sensitive associations are protected by the approaches discussed in previous sections by encrypting (a portion of) the original relation and/or by splitting its content into non-linkable fragments. The approach in [9] departs from encryption, and protects sensitive associations relying on owner-side storage to satisfy confidentiality constraints. According to this proposal, relation R is fragmented generating a pair $\mathcal{F} = \langle F_o, F_p \rangle$ of fragments, with F_o stored at the data owner and F_p stored at a cloud provider. This solution satisfies singleton constraints $c=\{A\}$ by storing A at the owner. Similarly, it satisfies association constraints $c=\{A_1, \ldots, A_n\}$ by storing at least one among $\{A_1, \ldots, A_n\}$ at the owner. Formally, a *correct fragmentation* is defined as follows.

Definition 4 (Correct Fragmentation). *Let $R(A_1, \ldots, A_n)$ be a relation schema and C be a set of confidentiality constraints over it. A fragmentation $\mathcal{F} = \langle F_o, F_p \rangle$ is correct iff:*

- *$\forall c \in C, c \nsubseteq F_p$ (confidentiality);*
- *$F_o \cup F_p = R$ (losslessness).*

The first condition states that fragment F_p cannot contain all the attributes composing a confidentiality constraint. This condition must hold only for F_p, since F_o is stored at the data owner and is therefore accessible to authorized users only. The second condition demands that all attributes in R are represented at the data owner or at the cloud provider, thus guaranteeing losslessness of the fragmentation. Although, in principle, F_o might include attributes appearing in F_p, this redundancy is not necessary and might be expensive for the data owner (both in terms of storage and computation). Fragments are then required to be disjoint (i.e., $F_o \cap F_p = \emptyset$). For instance, $\mathcal{F} = \langle F_o, F_p \rangle$ with $F_o = \{\texttt{SSN,Name,Ins}\}$

	F_o^e				F_p^e			
tid	SSN	Name	Ins	tid	Race	Job	Disease	Treatment
1	123-45-6789	Alice	160	1	white	teacher	flu	paracetamol
2	234-56-7890	Bob	100	2	while	farmer	asthma	bronchodilators
3	345-67-8901	Carol	100	3	asian	nurse	gastritis	antacids
4	456-7 8-9012	David	200	4	black	lawyer	angina	nitroglycerin
5	567-89-0123	Eric	100	5	black	secretary	flu	aspirin
6	678-90-1234	Fred	180	6	asian	lawyer	diabetes	insulin

Fig. 15. An example of a correct fragmentation of relation PATIENTS in Figure 1(a) in the keep a few scenario

and $F_p=\{$Race,Job,Disease,Treatment$\}$ represents a correct fragmentation of relation PATIENTS in Figure 1(a) with respect to the confidentiality constraints in Figure 1(b).

At the physical level, fragments F_o and F_p must have a common key attribute to permit authorized users to correctly reconstruct the content of relation r. This attribute can be either the primary key of relation R, if it is not sensitive, or an attribute that does not belong to the schema of R and that is added to both F_o and F_p to this purpose. Assuming that the primary key of R cannot be publicly released, a fragmentation $\mathcal{F} = \langle F_o, F_p \rangle$, with $F_o = \{A_{o_1}, \ldots, A_{o_i}\}$ and $F_p = \{A_{p_1}, \ldots, A_{p_j}\}$, is translated into physical fragments $F_o^e(\underline{tid}, A_{o_1}, \ldots, A_{o_i})$ and $F_p^e(\underline{tid}, A_{p_1}, \ldots, A_{p_j})$, where tid is a randomly generated tuple identifier. Figure 15 illustrates the physical fragments representing fragmentation $\mathcal{F} = \langle F_o, F_p \rangle$ with $F_o=\{$SSN,Name,Ins$\}$ and $F_p=\{$Race,Job,Disease,Treatment$\}$ of relation PATIENTS in Figure 1(a). Note that at least one attribute of each constraint in Figure 1(b) is in F_o.

Fragmentation Metrics. Given a relation schema R and a set $\mathcal{C}$ of confidentiality constraints over it, there may exist different correct fragmentations that are non-redundant. For instance, consider a fragmentation $\mathcal{F} = \langle F_o, F_p \rangle$ where $F_o = R$ and $F_p = \emptyset$. This fragmentation is correct and non-redundant, but it does not take advantage of outsourcing as no storage and/or computation is delegated to the cloud provider. To maximize the advantages for the data owner, she must push to the cloud provider as much as possible of the storage and computation workload necessary for the management of her data. To this aim, it is necessary to properly measure the storage, computation, and communication overhead caused to the data owner by the storage and management of fragment F_o. In the following, we illustrate the metrics that can be adopted to assess the quality of a fragmentation, depending on the resource that the data owner values more and on the information available about the system workload at initialization time [9].

- *Minimal fragmentation.* The most straightforward metric consists in counting the number of attributes in F_o. Intuitively, a fragment composed of a lower number of attributes is likely to be smaller (reducing the storage occupation), and to be involved in a lower number of queries (reducing the computation and communication overhead).

Attribute A	$size(A)$
SSN	10
Name	20
Race	5
Job	18
Disease	18
Treatment	30
Ins	8

(a)

Query q	$freq(q)$	$Attr(q)$	$Cond_q$
q_1	20	Job, Disease	$\langle$Job$\rangle$, $\langle$Disease$\rangle$
q_2	30	Disease, Treatment	$\langle$Disease$\rangle$, $\langle$Treatment$\rangle$
q_3	40	Job, Ins	$\langle$Job$\rangle$, $\langle$Ins$\rangle$
q_4	10	SSN, Ins, Disease	$\langle$SSN$\rangle$, $\langle$Ins$\rangle$, $\langle$Disease$\rangle$

(b)

Fig. 16. An example of size of attributes (a) and query workload (b) for relation PATIENTS in Figure 1(a)

- *Minimal size of attributes.* If the data owner aims at limiting the storage occupation at the provider side, the most effective metric to assess the quality of a fragmentation measures the size of F_o. The storage occupation of F_o is computed as the sum of the size of the attributes composing it. For instance, suppose that the size of the attributes of relation PATIENTS in Figure 1(a) is as summarized in Figure 16(a). The size of fragment F_o in Figure 15 is $size(\mathtt{SSN})+size(\mathtt{Name})+size(\mathtt{Ins}) = 10 + 20 + 8 = 38$.

- *Minimal number of queries.* The computation and communication overhead at the data owner side can be measured as the number of queries whose evaluation requires the owner's intervention (i.e., queries involving at least one attribute in F_o). The adoption of this metric requires the knowledge of the query workload $\mathcal{Q}$ characterizing the system that, in this scenario, is a set $\{q_1,\ldots,q_m\}$ of representative queries, along with their frequency $freq(q_i)$, $i = 1,\ldots,m$. For instance, the first three columns in Figure 16(b) represent a query workload for relation PATIENTS in Figure 1(a). The cost of a fragmentation $\mathcal{F} = \langle F_o, F_p \rangle$ is computed as the sum of the frequencies of the queries including at least one attribute in F_o. With respect to the workload in Figure 16(b), the fragmentation in Figure 15 requires the evaluation of $freq(q_3)+freq(q_4) = 50$ queries at the data owner, since q_3 and q_4 involve attributes in F_o.

- *Minimal number of conditions.* A more precise metric measuring the computation overhead of the data owner considers, instead of the number of queries, the number of conditions she should evaluate. In fact, the presence of multiple conditions in the same query operating on F_o causes a higher computation overhead for the data owner. To adopt this metric, it is necessary to know, besides the frequency $freq(q_i)$ of each query q_i in the query workload $\mathcal{Q}$, also the conditions, denoted $Cond(q_i)$, composing it. The quality of $\mathcal{F} = \langle F_o, F_p \rangle$ is then computed as the sum of the frequencies of the conditions in $\mathcal{Q}$ involving attributes in F_o. For instance, the first, second, and fourth column of Figure 16(b) represent a possible workload profile for relation PATIENTS in Figure 1(a). With respect to this workload, the fragmentation in Figure 15 requires the evaluation of $freq(\langle\mathtt{SSN}\rangle)+freq(\langle\mathtt{Ins}\rangle)$ $= 10 + (40 + 10) = 60$ conditions at the data owner side.

	Metric	Quality function
Storage	Number of attributes	$card(F_o)$
	Size of attributes	$\sum_{A \in F_o} size(A)$
Computation and communication	Number of queries	$\sum_{q \in \mathcal{Q}} freq(q)$ s.t. $Attr(q) \cap F_o \neq \emptyset$
	Number of conditions	$\sum_{cond \in Cond(\mathcal{Q})} freq(cond)$ s.t. $cond \cap F_o \neq \emptyset$

Fig. 17. Classification of the metrics in the keep a few scenario

Figure 17 summarizes the formal definition of the metrics illustrated above. Note that the adoption of each metric is subject to the knowledge of different information about relation r and the query workload expected for the system.

Computing an Optimal Fragmentation. The problem of computing an optimal fragmentation that minimizes the storage or the computation and communication costs for the data owner is NP-hard (the minimum hitting set problem reduces to it in polynomial time [9]). The heuristic approach proposed to compute a good fragmentation is based on the nice property that all the metrics illustrated above are monotonic in the number of attributes in F_o (i.e., the cost of a fragmentation $\mathcal{F}$ increases when an attribute is moved from F_p to F_o). Hence, the same heuristics applies to all the four metrics in Figure 17. The algorithm proposed in [9] aims at computing a *locally minimal fragmentation* $\mathcal{F} = \langle F_o, F_p \rangle$, which is defined as a fragmentation where no attribute can be moved from F_o to F_p without violating confidentiality constraints. The algorithm first inserts into F_o all the attributes that are considered sensitive per se (i.e., the attributes involved in singleton constraints). The remaining attributes, which initially belong to F_p, are organized in a priority queue. The priority of an attribute A depends on: *i)* the number of constraints that would be solved moving A to F_o, and *ii)* the cost that the data owner would pay to move A to F_o. The algorithm iteratively extracts from the queue the attribute A with highest priority (i.e., the attribute with minimum cost per solved constraint) and inserts it into F_o. The iteration stops when either all the constraints are satisfied or the queue is empty (i.e., $F_o=R$ and $F_p=\emptyset$). The algorithm finally tries to move each attribute in F_o to F_p, to guarantee minimality of the computed fragmentation.

Query Evaluation. A query q formulated over the original relation r must be translated into an equivalent set of queries operating on $\mathcal{F} = \langle F_o, F_p \rangle$. The solution in [9] considers queries q of the form SELECT *Att* FROM R WHERE *Cond*, with *Att* a set of attributes in R and *Cond*$= \bigwedge_i cond_i$ a conjunction of basic conditions of the form $(A_i \ op \ v)$, $(A_i \ op \ A_j)$, or $(A_i \ \text{IN} \ \{v_i, \dots, v_k\})$, where $A, A_i, A_j \in R$, $\{v, v_1, \dots, v_k\}$ are constant values in the domain of A_i, and op is a comparison operator in $\{=, \neq, >, <, \geq, \leq\}$. Although in principle the data owner can evaluate, any query q formulated by the users, such a solution should be avoided when possible as it would reduce the advantages of resorting to a cloud provider for partial data storage and management. In fact, the cloud provider shluld be delegated for the evaluation of all those conditions operating on attributes in F_p. Given query q, the approach in [9] first splits $Cond$ in three sub-conditions, $Cond_o$, $Cond_p$, and $Cond_{po}$, depending on the attributes involved in each basic condition, as follows:

- $Cond_o = \bigwedge_i cond_i : Attr(cond_i) \subseteq F_o$ is the conjunction of basic conditions that involve only attributes stored at the data owner, which can be evaluated only by the owner;
- $Cond_p = \bigwedge_i cond_i : Attr(cond_i) \subseteq F_p$ is the conjunction of basic conditions that involve only attributes stored at the cloud provider, which can be evaluated by the provider;
- $Cond_{po} = \bigwedge_i cond_i : Attr(cond_i) \cap F_o \neq \emptyset$ and $Attr(cond_i) \cap F_p \neq \emptyset$ is the conjunction of basic conditions of the form $(A_i \; op \; A_j)$, where $A_i \in F_o$ and $A_j \in F_p$, which can be evaluated only by the data owner, with the support of the provider.

For instance, consider relation PATIENTS in Figure 1(a), its fragmentation in Figure 15 and query $q=$"SELECT Name FROM Patients WHERE Disease='flu' AND Ins=100". $Cond_p$ includes condition Disease='flu'; $Cond_o$ includes condition Ins=100; and $Cond_{po}$ is empty.

The evaluation of a query q on R can follow the *provider-owner* or the *owner-provider* strategies, depending on the order in which $Cond_p$, $Cond_o$, and $Cond_{po}$ are evaluated (see Figure 18).

- *Provider-Owner strategy.* This strategy first evaluates condition $Cond_p$ at the provider side and then evaluates both $Cond_o$ and $Cond_{po}$ at the data owner side. Query q is translated into two equivalent queries q_p and q_o, as illustrated in Figure 18(a). Query q_p operates on F_p^e and evaluates condition $Cond_p$. It returns to the data owner the tuple identifier tid (which is necessary to join the result R_p of q_p and F_o^e) and the attributes in F_p^e that appear in the SELECT clause of q or in $Cond_{po}$. When the data owner receives R_p, she executes query q_{po} that computes the join between R_p and F_o^e, evaluates $Cond_o$ and $Cond_{po}$, and projects the attributes in the SELECT clause of q. The data owner finally returns the result R_{po} of q_{po} to the user. As an example, Figures 18(a) illustrate the translation of query $q=$"SELECT Name FROM Patients WHERE Disease='flu' AND Ins=100" formulated over relation PATIENTS in Figure 1(a) into an equivalent set of queries operating on the fragmentation in Figure 15.
- *Owner-Provider strategy.* This strategy first evaluates $Cond_o$ at the data owner, then evaluates condition $Cond_p$ at the provider side, and finally evaluates $Cond_{po}$ again at the data owner side. Query q is then translated into three queries, as illustrated in Figure 18(b). Query q_o operates on F_o^e, evaluates condition $Cond_o$, and projects attribute tid only. The result R_o of this query, computed by the data owner, is sent to the cloud provider that

Original query	Translated queries

$q :=$ SELECT Att
       FROM R
       WHERE $Cond$
	$q_p :=$ SELECT $tid, (Att \cup Attr(Cond_{po})\})) \cap F_p$
	        FROM F_p^e
	        WHERE $Cond_p$
	
	$q_o :=$ SELECT Att
	        FROM F_o^e JOIN R_p ON $F_o^e.tid{=}R_p.tid$
	        WHERE $Cond_o$ AND $Cond_{po}$

$q :=$ SELECT Name
       FROM   Patients
       WHERE Disease='flu' AND
             Ins=100
	$q_p :=$ SELECT tid, Name
	        FROM F_p^e
	        WHERE Disease='flu'
	
	$q_o :=$ SELECT Name
	        FROM F_p^e JOIN R_p ON F_p^e.tid$=R_p$.tid
	        WHERE Ins=100

(a) PROVIDER-OWNER STRATEGY

Original query	Translated queries

$q :=$ SELECT Att
       FROM R
       WHERE $Cond$
	$q_o :=$ SELECT tid
	        FROM F_o^e
	        WHERE $Cond_o$
	
	$q_p :=$ SELECT $(Att \cup Attr(Cond_{po})) \cap F_p$
	        FROM F_p^e
	        WHERE $(tid$ IN $R_o)$ AND $Cond_p$
	
	$q_{po} :=$ SELECT Att
	         FROM F_o^e JOIN R_p ON $F_o^e.tid{=}R_p.tid$
	         WHERE $Cond_{po}$

$q :=$ SELECT Name
       FROM   Patients
       WHERE Disease='flu' AND
             Ins=100
	$q_o :=$ SELECT tid
	        FROM F_o^e
	        WHERE Ins=100
	
	$q_p :=$ SELECT tid, Name
	        FROM F_p^e
	        WHERE $(tid$ IN $\{2,3,5\})$ AND Disease='flu'
	
	$q_{po} :=$ SELECT Name
	         FROM F_o^e JOIN R_p ON F_o^e.tid$=R_p$.tid

(b) OWNER-PROVIDER STRATEGY

Fig. 18. An example of query translation in the keep a few scenario

executes query q_p on the join between R_o and F_p^e. Query q_p evaluates condition $Cond_p$, and returns attribute tid and the attributes in F_p^e that appear in the SELECT clause of q or in $Cond_{po}$. The provider returns the result R_p of q_p to the data owner, who evaluates q_{po} on the join between R_p and F_o^e. Query q_{po} evaluates $Cond_{po}$ and projects the attributes in the SELECT clause of q. The data owner finally returns the result R_{po} of q_{po} to the user. As an example, Figures 18(b) illustrate the translation of query $q=$ "SELECT Name FROM Patients WHERE Disease='flu' AND Ins=100" formulated over relation PATIENTS in Figure 1(a) into an equivalent set of queries operating on the fragmentation in Figure 15 (values {2,3,5} in the WHERE clause of q_p represent the identifiers of the tuples satisfying $Cond_o=$Ins$=100$).

In the choice between these two strategies, it is necessary to take into consideration (besides performance) the risk of leakage of sensitive information that the Owner-Provider strategy may cause. In fact, if the provider knows the query q formulated by the user, this strategy reveals to the provider which are the tuples in F_p that satisfy $Cond_o$, even if the provider is not authorized to see the content of attributes in F_o.

7   Conclusions

Users as well as private and public organizations are more and more often relying on cloud providers to store and manage their data, enjoying economic advantages and high data availability. Although appealing, outsourcing the storage and management of data to the cloud introduces risks for data confidentiality, which could still represent a major obstacle to the wide adoption of cloud computing. In this chapter, we focused on the problem of protecting the confidentiality of data stored at external cloud providers. We first described the confidentiality requirements that may need to be considered and enforced before moving the data in the cloud. We then surveyed different approaches that have been proposed for enforcing such confidentiality requirements, using data encryption and fragmentation, either by themselves or in combination. In addition to the data confidentiality issue treated in this chapter, other issues that might need to be addressed when relying on external cloud providers for data storage or computation include: data integrity, and availability; protection against external attacks; selective access to the data; fault tolerance management; the specification of security requirements on task/resource allocation in a cloud; query privacy; and query and computation integrity (e.g., [15,17,18,19,23,28,29,30]).

Acknowledgements. This work was supported in part by the European Commission under the project "ABC4EU" (FP7-312797) and the Italian Ministry of Research within PRIN 2010-2011 project "GenData 2020" (2010RTFWBH).

References

1. Aggarwal, G., Bawa, M., Ganesan, P., Garcia-Molina, H., Kenthapadi, K., Motwani, R., Srivastava, U., Thomas, D., Xu, Y.: Two can keep a secret: A distributed architecture for secure database services. In: Proc. of CIDR 2005, Asilomar, CA, USA (January 2005)
2. Agrawal, R., Kierman, J., Srikant, R., Xu, Y.: Order preserving encryption for numeric data. In: Proc. of SIGMOD 2004, Paris, France (June 2004)
3. Benedikt, M., Bourhis, P., Ley, C.: Querying schemas with access restrictions. Proc. of VLDB Endowment 5(7), 634–645 (2012)
4. Biskup, J., Preuß, M., Wiese, L.: On the inference-proofness of database fragmentation satisfying confidentiality constraints. In: Lai, X., Zhou, J., Li, H. (eds.) ISC 2011. LNCS, vol. 7001, pp. 246–261. Springer, Heidelberg (2011)
5. Ceselli, A., Damiani, E., De Capitani di Vimercati, S., Jajodia, S., Paraboschi, S., Samarati, P.: Modeling and assessing inference exposure in encrypted databases. ACM TISSEC 8(1), 119–152 (2005)
6. Chang, Y.-C., Mitzenmacher, M.: Privacy preserving keyword searches on remote encrypted data. In: Ioannidis, J., Keromytis, A.D., Yung, M. (eds.) ACNS 2005. LNCS, vol. 3531, pp. 442–455. Springer, Heidelberg (2005)
7. Ciriani, V., De Capitani di Vimercati, S., Foresti, S., Jajodia, S., Paraboschi, S., Samarati, P.: Fragmentation and encryption to enforce privacy in data storage. In: Biskup, J., López, J. (eds.) ESORICS 2007. LNCS, vol. 4734, pp. 171–186. Springer, Heidelberg (2007)
8. Ciriani, V., De Capitani di Vimercati, S., Foresti, S., Jajodia, S., Paraboschi, S., Samarati, P.: Fragmentation design for efficient query execution over sensitive distributed databases. In: Proc. of ICDCS 2009, Montreal, Canada (June 2009)
9. Ciriani, V., De Capitani di Vimercati, S., Foresti, S., Jajodia, S., Paraboschi, S., Samarati, P.: Keep a few: Outsourcing data while maintaining confidentiality. In: Backes, M., Ning, P. (eds.) ESORICS 2009. LNCS, vol. 5789, pp. 440–455. Springer, Heidelberg (2009)
10. Ciriani, V., De Capitani di Vimercati, S., Foresti, S., Jajodia, S., Paraboschi, S., Samarati, P.: Combining fragmentation and encryption to protect privacy in data storage. ACM TISSEC 13(3), 22:1–22:33 (2010)
11. Ciriani, V., De Capitani di Vimercati, S., Foresti, S., Jajodia, S., Paraboschi, S., Samarati, P.: Selective data outsourcing for enforcing privacy. JCS 19(3), 531–566 (2011)
12. Ciriani, V., De Capitani di Vimercati, S., Foresti, S., Livraga, G., Samarati, P.: An OBDD approach to enforce confidentiality and visibility constraints in data publishing. JCS 20(5), 463–508 (2012)
13. Curtmola, R., Garay, J., Kamara, S., Ostrovsky, R.: Searchable symmetric encryption: Improved definitions and efficient constructions. In: Proc. of CCS 2006, Alexandria, VA, USA (October-November 2006)
14. Damiani, E., De Capitani di Vimercati, S., Jajodia, S., Paraboschi, S., Samarati, P.: Balancing confidentiality and efficiency in untrusted relational DBMSs. In: Proc. of CCS 2003, Washington, DC, USA (October 2003)
15. De Capitani di Vimercati, S., Foresti, S., Jajodia, S., Livraga, G., Paraboschi, S., Samarati, P.: Enforcing dynamic write privileges in data outsourcing. Computers & Security 39, 47–63 (2013)
16. De Capitani di Vimercati, S., Foresti, S., Jajodia, S., Livraga, G., Paraboschi, S., Samarati, P.: Fragmentation in presence of data dependencies. IEEE TDSC (to appear, 2014)

17. De Capitani di Vimercati, S., Foresti, S., Jajodia, S., Paraboschi, S., Samarati, P.: Encryption policies for regulating access to outsourced data. ACM TODS 35(2), 12:1–12:46 (2010)
18. De Capitani di Vimercati, S., Foresti, S., Jajodia, S., Paraboschi, S., Samarati, P.: Integrity for join queries in the cloud. IEEE TCC 1(2), 187–200 (2013)
19. De Capitani di Vimercati, S., Foresti, S., Paraboschi, S., Pelosi, G., Samarati, P.: Efficient and private access to outsourced data. In: Proc. of ICDCS 2011, Minneapolis, MN, USA (June 2011)
20. De Capitani di Vimercati, S., Foresti, S., Samarati, P.: Managing and accessing data in the cloud: Privacy risks and approaches. In: Proc. of CRiSIS 2012, Cork, Ireland (October 2012)
21. De Capitani di Vimercati, S., Foresti, S., Samarati, P.: Protecting data in outsourcing scenarios. In: Das, S., Kant, K., Zhang, N. (eds.) Handbook on Securing Cyber-Physical Critical Infrastructure. Morgan Kaufmann (2012)
22. De Capitani di Vimercati, S., Foresti, S., Samarati, P.: Selective and fine-grained access to data in the cloud. In: Jajodia, S., Kant, K., Samarati, P., Swarup, V., Wang, C. (eds.) Secure Cloud Computing. Springer (2014)
23. Gamassi, M., Piuri, V., Sana, D., Scotti, F.: Robust fingerprint detection for access control. In: Proc. of RoboCare Workshop 2005, Rome, Italy (May 2005)
24. Gentry, C.: Fully homomorphic encryption using ideal lattices. In: Proc. of STOC 2009, Bethesda, MA, USA (May 2009)
25. Goh, E.J.: Secure indexes. Tech. Rep. 2003/216, Cryptology ePrint Archive (2003), http://eprint.iacr.org/
26. Hacigümüs, H., Iyer, B., Mehrotra, S.: Providing database as a service. In: Proc. of ICDE 2002, San Jose, CA, USA (February 2002)
27. Hacıgümüş, H., Iyer, B., Mehrotra, S.: Efficient execution of aggregation queries over encrypted relational databases. In: Lee, Y., Li, J., Whang, K.-Y., Lee, D. (eds.) DASFAA 2004. LNCS, vol. 2973, pp. 125–136. Springer, Heidelberg (2004)
28. Jhawar, R., Piuri, V.: Fault tolerance management in IaaS clouds. In: Proc. of ESTEL 2012, Rome, Italy (October 2012)
29. Jhawar, R., Piuri, V.: Fault tolerance and resilience in cloud computing environments. In: Vacca, J. (ed.) Computer and Information Security Handbook, 2nd edn., pp. 125–141. Morgan Kaufmann (2013)
30. Jhawar, R., Piuri, V., Samarati, P.: Supporting security requirements for resource management in cloud computing. In: Proc. of CSE 2012, Paphos, Cyprus (December 2012)
31. Özsu, M., Valduriez, P.: Principles of distributed database systems, 2nd edn. Prentice-Hall, Inc. (1999)
32. Samarati, P.: Data security and privacy in the cloud. In: Huang, X., Zhou, J. (eds.) ISPEC 2014. LNCS, vol. 8434, pp. 28–41. Springer, Heidelberg (2014)
33. Schneier, B.: Applied Cryptography, 2nd edn. John Wiley & Sons (1996)
34. Wang, C., Cao, N., Ren, K., Lou, W.: Enabling secure and efficient ranked keyword search over outsourced cloud data. IEEE TPDS 23(8), 1467–1479 (2012)
35. Wang, H., Lakshmanan, L.: Efficient secure query evaluation over encrypted XML databases. In: Proc. of VLDB 2006, Seoul, Korea (September 2006)
36. Winkler, V.: Securing the Cloud: Cloud Computer Security Techniques and Tactics. Syngress (2011)

Location Privacy in WSNs: Solutions, Challenges, and Future Trends

Ruben Rios[1], Javier Lopez[1], and Jorge Cuellar[2]

[1] Network, Information and Computer Security (NICS) Lab,
Universidad of Málaga, Spain
[2] Siemens AG, Munich, Germany
{jlm,ruben}@lcc.uma.es,
jorge.cuellar@siemens.com

Abstract. Privacy preservation is gaining popularity in Wireless Sensor Network (WSNs) due to its adoption in everyday scenarios. There are a number of research papers in this area many of which concentrate on the location privacy problem. In this paper we review and categorise these solutions based on the information available to the adversary and his capabilities. But first we analyse whether traditional anonymous communication systems conform to the original requirements of location privacy in sensor networks. Finally, we present and discuss a number of challenges and future trends that demand further attention from the research community.

Keywords: Wireless sensor networks, location privacy, traffic analysis, survey.

1 Introduction

The miniaturisation of electro-mechanical systems has led to the creation of tiny, inexpensive computers capable of feeling their environment in the same way as humans experience the world through our senses. These matchbox-sized computers are called sensor nodes and they can cooperate and communicate wirelessly with other nodes nearby forming a wireless sensor network (WSN). The data collected by the sensor nodes are transmitted to a powerful device called the base station or data sink, which serves as an interface to the network.

These systems have been successfully applied to numerous application scenarios where sensor nodes are unobtrusively embedded into systems for monitoring, tracking and surveillance operations [13]. However, sensor nodes are highly vulnerable to a number of threats and attacks [45] due to their hardware limitations, which may limit their applicability to scenarios where security and privacy are essential properties. Particularly sensitive scenarios are those involving individuals, businesses and relevant assets.

A first line of defence against attacks is to protect the data traversing the network from modifications and eavesdropping but even if secure confidentiality and integrity mechanisms are in place, an adversary can attack the network

A. Aldini et al. (Eds.): FOSAD VII, LNCS 8604, pp. 244–282, 2014.

in another way. By silently observing and analysing the communications, the adversary can obtain contextual information associated with the measuring and transmission of data [33]. These metadata are inherently more difficult to protect than the data contained in the packets' payload. Indeed, the mere presence of messages may reveal sensitive information related to the application scenario. For example, the transmission of messages by a sensor node used for monitoring the structural health of a fuel pipeline is an indicator of internal corrosion.

A noteworthy piece of contextual information that may be leaked to the attacker is the location of relevant nodes in the network. The location of data sources reveals the area where special phenomena are being observed. These phenomena may be related to individuals, endangered animals, valuable cargo, etc., and as a result, the adversary obtains the location of those entities and goods. On the other hand, the location of the base station is relevant for several reasons. The base station is the most critical device in the network and if the adversary is able reach it, he may be able take control of the network or even render it completely useless by destroying it. Besides its importance for the survivability of the network, the location of the base station is strategically significant because it is most likely housed in a highly-sensitive facility. In a scenario where a WSN is deployed to monitor the behaviour of whales in the middle of the ocean, finding the base station leads to the ship where the biologists are analysing the results.

Location privacy schemes can be categorised following two main criteria, which are (a) what information is available to the adversary, and (b) what are the capabilities of the adversary to be countered. There are basically two items of interest which may help the adversary to locate targets, namely the identities of the nodes and the traffic pattern. Packet headers contain the identifiers of the source and destination of a transaction, therefore obscuring this information is the first step in achieving location privacy. Although these data are effectively protected, the attacker can still obtain location information by analysing the traffic generated by the network. The strategy of the adversary is determined by his goal and capabilities. The literature usually considers an external and passive attacker with either local or global eavesdropping capabilities. Occasionally, the attacker is also capable of compromising a small portion of the sensor nodes, thus becoming an internal adversary. As a result, we propose a taxonomy of solutions (see Fig. 1) that will guide the exposition of subsequent sections.

The rest of this work is organised as follows. Prior to the analysis of location privacy solutions in WSNs, Section 2 studies whether traditional anonymous communication systems devised for computer networks can adjust to the specific requirements and adversaries considered in sensor networks. Then, Section 3 examines two approaches to node identity protection based on the creation and use of pseudonyms. Section 4 dives into source-location privacy solutions, paying attention both to external and internal adversaries. Similarly, Section 5 analyses solutions for the protection of the base station against local and global observers. Finally, Section 6 presents and discusses a number of open issues and future areas of research, and Section 7 concludes this paper.

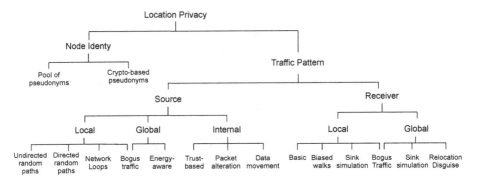

Fig. 1. Taxonomy of Location Privacy Solutions in WSNs

2 Computer-Based Anonymity Systems

Anonymous communication systems for computer networks were originally devised to hinder traffic analysis attacks. Therefore, it appears feasible to use these solutions to protect location privacy in sensor networks as this problem is caused by the peculiar traffic pattern of this networks. First, we need to analyse the anonymity requirements in both scenarios. After that, we select several renowned anonymous communication systems to study whether these can be implemented in resource-constrained sensor nodes and also whether the deployment of these solutions limit in any way, the usability or functionality of the network.

2.1 Anonymity Requierements

There are several anonymity properties that may help entities to preserve their privacy when communicating with other entities [34]. These properties provide different levels of anonymity ranging from avoiding the identification of a given subject within a set of other subjects to the impossibility of proving the participation of a specific subject in a given communication. The most usual property implemented by traditional anonymous communication systems is the *unlinkability* of senders and receivers, which is intended to prevent an adversary from identifying which entities are communicating with whom, since this allows him to learn the habits and interests of a specific individual. However, this property is not necessary in WSNs since an external adversary already knows that all sensor nodes communicate with the base station.

Some other solutions focus on providing sender *anonymity* with respect to the receiver. The goal is to prevent ill-intentioned service providers from collecting data from users for the purpose of tracking and profiling. In WSNs, the enforcement of this property is not only unnecessary but also detrimental to the normal operation of the network. The reason is that the base station needs to know the identities of the nodes generating data messages in order to faithfully identify the location of relevant events in the field. Nevertheless, source anonymity is also suitable for systems where the communications traverse some potentially malicious (i.e., honest but curious) nodes interested in learning the actual data sender. This type of anonymity is important in WSNs where some nodes are compromised by the attacker and try to obtain the source node identifier. Therefore, source anonymity is only necessary in certain circumstances.

While *unobservability* is a very strong notion of privacy and is only rarely necessary in computer networks, it becomes the most natural way of protecting location privacy in WSNs. It is imperative to hide the existence of the nodes reporting on or receiving event data. If the adversary cannot sufficiently detect the presence of data messages in the network, he will be unable to determine the location of the nodes taking part in the communication. Consequently, if the attacker is not able to ascertain the existence of messages, he will not be able to determine who is the sender or recipient of that message by simply performing traffic analysis attacks.

In general, we can state that some anonymity properties are unsuitable or unnecessary for protecting location privacy in WSNs, in fact, they might even be counterproductive in particular cases.

2.2   Overhead Analysis

The aforementioned properties have been satisfied by anonymous communication schemes through different techniques, which incur notorious computational and communication overhead to the system. These techniques range from simple identity renaming to more complex operations such as layered encryption, fake traffic injection, and tightly-synchronised broadcast communications. Moreover, anonymous communications systems can be categorised based on their architecture as centralised or decentralised, depending on whether the users are members of the system that collaborate in the anonymisation process or not. Here we have selected three solutions that not only cover a wide range of techniques and features but also pursue different anonymity properties and architectures.

Mix-nets [6] are high-latency centralised systems composed of a set of store-and-forward devices (i.e., mixes) that prevent the correlation between incoming and outgoing messages. Whenever a user wants to communicate with another user, he selects a series of mixes and recursively adds a layer of (public-key) encryption to the message for each mix in reverse order. In this way, each mix device only knows its predecessor and successor in the path. This scheme is extremely effective for ensuring unlinkability in delay-tolerant applications but its is not suitable for WSNs, where real-time monitoring capabilities are usually necessary. Moreover, there are some other limitations with respect to the memory and computational requirements imposed by the scheme. Data sources are required to perform $n+1$ public-key operations per data packet, being n the path length, but they also need to have a complete knowledge of the topology of the mix-net in order to apply the layers of encryption in the right order. Additionally, each intermediate node is required to not only perform one decryption per packet but also to store a number of packets for a long period of time. Finally, a centralised scheme cannot protect from global adversaries and, for the particular case of mix-nets, it cannot protect itself from local adversaries either because the attacker can eventually reach the edge of the mix-net and from there locate the data sources.

Crowds [38] is a decentralised scheme where a set of users collaborate to issue requests to servers in order to provide anonymity to its members. After joining the crowd, any of its members can initiate requests to different servers, which are delivered by a random member. Whenever a crowd member wants to send a message, it chooses a random member, possibly itself, to act as an intermediary. The recipient decides, based on some biased probability, whether to forward the data to another member or to finally submit it to the destination. Subsequent requests from the same data source and same destination follow the same path. Messages are re-encrypted and the sender identity is replaced at every hop. Although this model is far less complex than the previous one from a computational point of view, it still has high memory demands. Each node must hold $n - 1$ shared keys (i.e., one key per crowd member) and a translation table containing all the paths that have the node as an intermediary, as paths are static. This is, indeed, an important drawback to its application in WSNs because static paths can be easily traced back by local adversaries. Even though this is a decentralised solution, global adversaries might be able to identify data sources since new traffic is only generated in the presence of real events, and also, the base station as all the traffic is addressed to it. However, this scheme does provide some means of protection against Internal adversaries due to the identity renaming mechanism.

DC-nets [7] is a decentralised solution based on simple calculations that allows a group of users to share information while hiding the actual sender (and recipient) of messages even from other protocol participants. To this end, each member shares bitwise keys with any other participant and all members simultaneously broadcast the result of the bitwise sum of their secrets. The key point is that if a participant has something to say he inverts this result before broadcasting it. Each secret is used twice so the final result must be zero if no one has inverted his result. Since the initial shared bits are secret, there is no way to determine the actual sender. Although the original protocol considers the transmission of a single data bit, the DC scheme can be easily extended to transmit string messages by sharing random numbers instead of random bits. The application of the DC-nets model in WSNs has several impediments. First, the need for a tight and reliable broadcast channel that covers all sensor nodes and the base station. Second, the high memory overhead required to store one-time secrets for multiple protocol rounds and the high waste of bandwidth and energy due to the continuous rounds even when no participant is willing to transmit. Another substantial problem has to do with simultaneous communications. The scheme does not support multiple transmissions at the same time, which would highly constrain the usability and nature of sensor networks.

Table 1 presents a summary of the this analysis. It indicates that even though some solutions are sufficiently lightweight to run in sensor nodes, the true weak

Table 1. Suitability of some Anonymous Communication Systems

	Limitations	Adversary		
		Global	Local	Internal
Mix-nets	high	×	×	✓
Crowds	low	×	×	≈
DC-nets	high	✓	✓	✓

point is that the solutions do not fit the requirements and the adversarial models under consideration. Similarly, another group of solutions are suitable for the protection of location privacy in WSNs but they are rather expensive or they present important limitations. As a result, new tailored solutions have been designed specifically for WSNs.

3   Node Anonymity

Packet headers consist of various data fields containing, among other things, the identifiers of the data sender and the destination. These data are sent in clear text to enable intermediate nodes to perform routing tasks. Thus, after a sufficient number of observations, an attacker can elaborate a map of the network relating node identifiers to locations in the field. Being in possession of such a network map, the attacker may simply wait next to the base station for incoming messages and easily obtain the location where events occur.

Several techniques have been proposed to provide node anonymity, most of which are based on the use of dynamic pseudonyms. Some authors have approached the management of pseudonyms by means of pools of pseudonyms while others have turn to cryptographic mechanisms for the same purpose. Note that most of the solutions fall into the second category since the use of cryptographic techniques for the creation of pseudonyms have several benefits over the use of network pools. Next, we review these solutions in detail.

3.1   Pool of Pseudonyms

Misra and Xue [26] were the first authors to provide a set of solutions for node identity protection. The Simple Anonymity Scheme (SAS) is based on a network-wide pool of pseudonyms which the base station divides into subranges of l bits and provides each node with a random set of them (see Fig. 2a). Each node builds a pseudonyms table where it stores pseudonym ranges for incoming and outgoing messages for each neighbour and their corresponding secret keys. When the node wants to communicate with a specific neighbour, it selects a random value from the range of pseudonyms belonging to that node and concatenates the index of the row from where it picked the pseudonym. The recipient node checks whether the received pseudonym belongs to the incoming range corresponding to the given index and, that being the case, it uses the shared key to decrypt the message. The principal limitation to SAS is the large memory space necessary

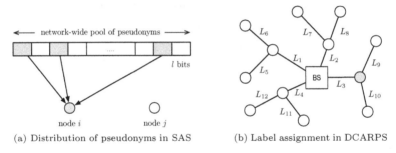

(a) Distribution of pseudonyms in SAS   (b) Label assignment in DCARPS

Fig. 2. Pool-Based Approaches

to store a sufficiently large pseudonym space, especially in densely populated networks.

Nezhad et al. [27,28] proposed a label switching protocol as part of their DCARPS anonymous routing protocol. After each topology discovery phase, the base station obtains an updated map of the network and assigns labels (i.e., identifiers) to each and every network link, as depicted in Fig. 2b. These labels serve as pseudonyms and whenever a node has to send a packet to the base station, it uses the label assigned to the link connecting it to a neighbour that is closer to the base station. Upon the reception of the packet, the neighbour node, checks whether the label corresponds to one of its input labels. If the label is known to the node, it replaces the input label with its own output label. For example, the grey node in Fig. 2b checks whether an incoming message has either label L_9 or L_{10} and, in the case it does, it forwards the packet after changing the original label with L_3. The main drawback to this labelling solution is that labels are modified only after a topology change has been discovered, which allows the attacker to correlate labels with specific nodes, thus completely compromising anonymity.

3.2   Cryptographic Pseudonyms

The second solution by Misra and Xue [26] is intended to reduce the amount of memory needed by SAS at the expense of increased computational overhead. The Cryptographic Anonymity Scheme (CAS) uses a keyed hash function to generate the pseudonyms. Before the deployment of the network, each node is assigned a pseudo-random function, a secret key and a random seed shared with the base station. After deployment, each pair of neighbours agree upon a random seed and a hash key that they store together with a sequence number. Whenever a node wants to send data to the base station, using a neighbour as intermediary, it creates a message $M = \{sID, rID, EncryptedPayload, seq\}$, where sID and rID are the pseudonyms generated after applying the keyed hash functions to the random seed and the sequence number shared with the base station and the intermediary, respectively. This scheme is more memory efficient but it imposes a computational overhead, not only to the intended recipient but also to any neighbour receiving the packet which need to compute a keyed hash value before discovering it is not addressed to them.

The CAS scheme assume that an attacker cannot compromise the secrets shared between the nodes. To reduce the impact of secrets being compromised, Ouyang et al. [31] propose two methods based on keyed hash chains. The Hashing-based ID Randomisation (HIR) scheme, uses the result of applying a keyed hash function to the true identifier of the node as pseudonym. More precisely, each node shares pairwise keys with uplink and downlink neighbours and creates, for each link, the keyed hash identifier of the uplink node of that neighbour. After the transmission or reception of a message on a particular link, the node rehashes the value contained in the table to generate a fresh pseudonym. Additionally, packets convey another identifier used for the base station to be able to identify the original data source. This value is also an element of a hash chain keyed with a secret shared with the base station. Since hash values are assumed to be non-invertible, this solution provides backwards secrecy, but if the adversary compromises the key used by the hash functions, he can generate future pseudonyms. The second solution, Reverse HIR (RHIR), attempts to reduce this problem by creating the hash chain during the initialisation and then using the elements of the chain in reverse order. Once a pseudonym has been used, it is no longer needed and it can be deleted from the memory. In this way, the attacker cannot generate any fresh pseudonyms even if he compromises the key. The main drawback to this solution with respect to the previous one lies in the need for increased memory space to accommodate a lengthy hash chain.

Later, Jiang et al. [16] introduced the Anonymous Path Routing (APR) protocol. One of the elements of this scheme, namely the anonymous one-hop communication, introduces an enhancement that improves the resilience against secret compromise attacks compared to previous solutions. In this scheme each node creates a table to keep the uplink and downlink hidden identities of each neighbour. These identities are calculated by hashing the values of the secret keys, identities, a sequence number and a nonce shared by the nodes. The novelty of this approach is that not only the hidden identities are updated (i.e., rehashed) after each successful transmission between neighbouring nodes but also the keys shared between the nodes. The same idea has been developed by Chen et al. [9] in the Efficient Anonymous Communication (EAC) protocol. The problem with this is scheme is that, nodes exchange with their neighbours the keys and nonces they share with the base station to update the pseudonyms used for one-hop communications. This allows any node to determine whether the true source of the packet is a neighbouring node as well as to impersonate any of its neighbours.

Finally, it is important to highlight that node anonymity is only a first line of defence to preserve location privacy. An adversary can perform more sophisticated attacks to obtain location information from the analysis of traffic patterns. In the following sections we concentrate on the most important solutions that have been developed to diminish the threat of different types of adversaries.

4   Source-Location Privacy

Source-location privacy refers to the ability to hide the location of data sources, which results in the protection of the physical location of the events being monitored since they may be related to individuals or valuable resources. This problem has drawn the attention of the research community and plenty of solutions have been devised for countering passive adversaries with a local or a global view of the communications, but only a few authors have concentrated on the threat of internal attackers.

4.1   Local Adversaries

A local adversary can only monitor a small portion of the network, typically the equivalent of the hearing range of an ordinary sensor node. Therefore, they must turn to moving in the field using a *traceback attack* in an attempt to reach the target by moving along the path of messages from the source to the base station in reverse order. This attack is successful because data packets tend to follow the same path over and over again. Consequently, most of the solutions to this problem are based on the randomisation of routes although some schemes also take advantage of bogus traffic to mislead the adversary. Note that some solutions may belong to more than one category.

Undirected Random Paths.   The first solution to provide source-location privacy was devised by Ozturk et al. and is called Phantom Routing [32]. Phantom Routing proposes making each packet undergo two phases, a walking phase and a flooding phase. In the walking phase, the packet is sent on a random walk for h hops until it reaches a node, which is called the phantom source. Then, in the next phase, the phantom source initiates a baseline or probabilistic flooding, which eventually delivers the packet to the base station. This two-phase process picks random phantom sources for each new message thereby originating different paths. Later, a new version of protocol, called Phantom Single-Path Routing [17] replaced the flooding in the second phase by a single-path routing, which results in even longer safety periods due to the fact that the adversary misses some packets. Fig. 3 depicts the transmission of two messages using this solution, where dashed arrows represent the walking phase and the ordinary arrows represent the single-path phase. The grey node is the phantom source. The main limitation to Phantom Routing protocols is in the walking phase. Pure random walks tend to stay close to the source node and the definition of a larger value of h does not provide a direct improvement in the safety period, it only increases the energy waste. This problem is represented in Fig. 3, where phantom sources are within a distance of two or three hops regardless of the definition of a 5-step random walk.

Xi et al. [49] state that using pure random walks is desirable because routing decisions are independent from the source location but also impractical since the average delivery time of messages goes to infinity. The idea behind GROW is

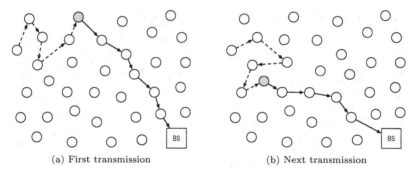

(a) First transmission   (b) Next transmission

Fig. 3. Phantom Single-Path Routing with $h = 5$

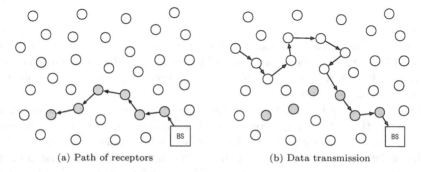

(a) Path of receptors   (b) Data transmission

Fig. 4. Operation of the GROW Scheme

using two random walks as the probability of them not intersecting decreases exponentially in time. First, it creates a permanent path of receptors by transmitting a special packet on a random walk from the base station. Then, the source nodes send data packets on a greedy random walk that will eventually hit a node from the path of receptors. From there, the packet is forwarded to the base station following the established path in reverse order. This process is illustrated in Fig. 4. Despite being designed as a greedy algorithm, one of the main limitations of GROW is the substantial delivery time of the packets.

Cross-layer routing [42] was designed to further mitigate the problem of random walks staying close to the data source. This approach is basically a Phantom Routing that hides the walking phase by routing data using the beacon frames from the data link layer. Since beacons are transmitted regardless of the occurrence of events, the attacker is unable to distinguish legitimate beacons from those containing event data. At the end of the walking phase, event data reaches a pivot node that sends the data to the base station using the implemented routing protocol. The operation of the protocol is depicted in Fig. 5a, where the dotted arrows represent the beacon frames, solid arrows represent the routing phase, and the black and grey circles represent the source and the pivot node,

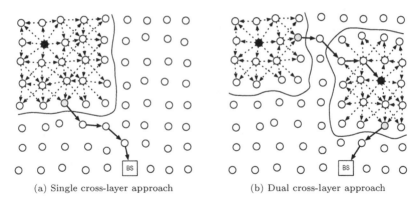

(a) Single cross-layer approach   (b) Dual cross-layer approach

Fig. 5. Cross-Layer Routing Schemes

respectively. The main limitation to this approach lies in the tradeoff between the level of protection it can provide and the delay introduced by large beaconing areas[1]. Therefore, the larger the beaconing area is the better the protection but also the longer the delay.

An attacker may be able to reach the edge of the beaconing area and, from there, reach the data source if the network administrator turns to small values for h to boost the delivery time. A double cross-layer solution is proposed to further enhance location privacy in these circumstances. In this version of the protocol, instead of sending the data directly to the base station, the pivot node sends the data to another randomly chosen node using the routing layer. Then, this random node chooses a new pivot node and starts a second beaconing phase. Thus, the attacker cannot easily reach the edge of the beacon area to which the original data source belongs. The dual cross-layer approach is represented in Fig. 5b.

Based on the same idea of hiding the walking phase, Mahmoud and Shen propose creating a cloud of fake traffic around the data source to hinder traceback attacks [23]. During the network setup, sensor nodes choose a group of nodes at different distances to later become fake source nodes, similar to phantom sources or pivot nodes. Also, each node divides its immediate neighbours in several groups in such a way that the neighbours from the same group are in different directions. During the data transmission phase, for each message, the source node chooses one of its fake sources and sends the message to the group where there is a member which knows how to reach it. As the packet travels to the fake source, it generates fake traffic to cover the route. A node from the addressed group that does not know where the fake source is, generates a fake message and picks one of its groups at random to broadcast it. The fake message lasts for h hops, generating clouds with dynamic shapes. Compared to

---

[1] Beacon frames are sent out at intervals ranging from milliseconds to hundreds of seconds.

the previous scheme, this solution consumes substantially more energy but it reduces the delivery time.

Directed Random Paths. Instead of simply sending packets at random, some authors have proposed using mechanisms to guide the walking phase. The first solution to have considered this is Phantom Routing itself [32]. The authors suggest changing the pure random walk in favour of a directed random walk. To that end, each node separates its neighbours into two groups depending on whether they are in the same direction or in the opposite direction to the base station. Thus, during the walking phase, the next hop in the path is still selected uniformly at random but only from the set of nodes in the direction of the base station. By introducing this simple mechanism they prevent packets from looping in the vicinity of the source thereby increasing the level of protection.

Yao and Wen devised the Directed Random Walk (DROW) in [53]. The idea behind this solution is quite simple, any sensor node having a data packet to transmit must send it to any of its parent nodes (i.e., a node closer to the sink) with equal probability. Therefore, the level of protection is highly dependent on the connectivity of the network. In 2010, Yao alone published another paper describing the Directed Greedy Random Walk (DGRW) [52], which is basically a copy of DROW with a different name. Also, the Forward Random Walk (FRW) [8] does exactly the same thing. However, the Chen and Lou argue that this solution cannot obtain a high level of protection and it would be necessary to inject dummy messages in the network to reduce the chances of the adversary.

Interestingly, Wei-Ping et al. [48] observed that long random walks do not necessarily increase the protection unless the phantom sources are not placed close to the straight line between the data source and the sink. The reason is that if phantom sources are close to this line too often, the single paths originated by them will be very similar to each other and thus the attacker has more opportunity to overhear packets. This problem is depicted in Fig. 6a, where the curly lines represent directed random walks from the source node to the phantom sources and the dashed lines represent the single-path routing phase. To prevent this situation, in Phantom Routing with Locational Angle (PRLA) a sensor node assigns its neighbours forwarding probabilities based on their inclination angles in such a way that neighbours with larger angles will be more likely to receive messages. A major downside to this work is that it is not fully clear how the nodes obtain the inclination angles[2] of their neighbours without built-in geolocation devices or directional antennas.

Wang et al. [46] devised a solution, called the Weighted Random Stride (WRS), which is similar to PRLA in the sense that both of them make routing decisions probabilistically based on the inclination angle of its neighbours. Data paths are guided by two parameters, a forwarding angle and a stride. The forwarding angle determines the next neighbour in the path while the stride defines the number of hops for a particular forwarding angle. The node receiving a expired stride selects a new forwarding angle and starts a new stride. In practice,

---

[2] The authors claim that the inclination angle is calculated in terms of the hop count.

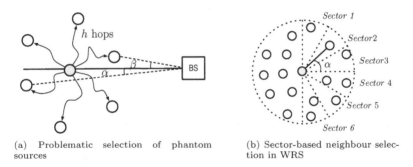

(a) Problematic selection of phantom sources

(b) Sector-based neighbour selection in WRS

Fig. 6. Angle-based privacy solutions

sensor nodes divide their neighbours into closer and further nodes and these into sectors. Sectors with larger inclination angles are prioritised. For example, in Fig. 6b, sectors 1 and 6 are more likely to be chosen than sectors 2 and 5, and sectors 3 and 4 are the least likely. The main difference between this approach and PRLA is that in WRS there are no phantom sources from where the packets are finally routed to the base station using a single-path approach.

Besides the WRS routing, Wang et al. [46] designed the Random Parallel routing, which assigns each sensor node n parallel routing paths to the base station. Messages are evenly distributed to different paths in such a way that the adversary traceback time is the same at any path. The underlying idea is that once the adversary chooses one of the paths he is forced to stay on that path. This increases the traceback time, which is now equivalent to the sum of all the parallel paths, without delaying message delivery. In a real-world setting, the generation of n truly parallel paths is a complex task, especially in large-scale sensor network deployments. Moreover, since the paths are parallel to each other, retrieving several packets from any of the paths provides a good idea of the direction to the source. This would significantly reduce the expected traceback time for the adversary.

Li et al. [19] proposed Routing through a Random selected Intermediate Node (RRIN) to the problem of selecting phantom sources close to the data source. The authors assume that the network is divided into a grid and that each node knows its relative location (i.e., cell position) as well as the grid dimensions. In this way, the source node can pick a random point in the field and send the packet to that location. The node closest to that location becomes the intermediate node. They devised two versions of RRIN. In the first version, the intermediate point is chosen uniformly at random but it is forced to be placed at least at a distance d_{min} from the source as shown in Fig. 7a. The main drawback to this scheme is that the probability of being selected as an intermediate node is proportional to the distance to the data source. Additionally, no mechanism prevents them from being picked from the proximities of the source-destination shortest path, which was one of the problems addressed by PRLA and WRS. In the second version of RRIN, any location in the network has the same probability of being selected

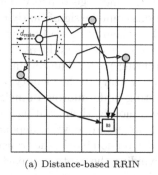

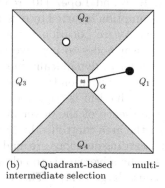

(a) Distance-based RRIN

(b)   Quadrant-based   multi-intermediate selection

Fig. 7. Routing through Random selected Intermediate Nodes

as the random intermediate point. The consequence is that some intermediate nodes will be very close to the data source thus exposing its location while some others will be extremely far resulting in energy-intensive paths.

The RRIN scheme has been extended and used in several other papers. The Sink Toroidal Routing (STaR) routing protocol [22] is also designed to improve upon the initial RRIN designs. More precisely, the goal is to reduce the energy cost associated with the selection of pure random intermediate nodes in the field. To that end, the source node picks random points within a toroidal region around the base station, which guarantees that intermediate nodes are, at most, a given distance from the destination but also not too close in order to prevent traceback attacks. The main drawback to this solution again has to do with the selection of problematic intermediate nodes not only between the source and the base station but also behind it.

In [20], Li et al. propose two schemes that use multiple random intermediate nodes instead of a single one. In the angle-based multi-intermediate node selection, the source node selects a maximum angle β to limit the location of the last intermediate node within the range $(-\beta, \beta)$. Once the maximum angle has been determined, the source node uniformly chooses a random angle θ between itself and the node with respect to the base station, such that $\theta \in (-\beta, \beta)$. Then, the data source selects the rest of the n intermediate nodes to be evenly separated between itself and the final intermediate node. In the quadrant-based multi-intermediate node selection, each sensor node divides the network into four quadrants in such a way that it is placed in the first quadrant and the base station is in the middle. The source node location is determined within the first quadrant based on a random angle α. The last intermediate node is selected to be somewhere within its adjacent quadrants, namely quadrant 2 and 4 as shown in Fig. 7b. Both extensions ensure that nodes are neither selected from behind the base station nor close to the shortest-path between the data source and the destination. However, it is not fully clear why it is necessary to use multiple intermediate nodes instead of a single intermediary.

Finally, Rios and Lopez [40] realised that the message delivery delay and energy consumption incurred by existing solutions could be significantly reduced. The Context-Aware Location Privacy (CALP) scheme takes advantage of the ability of sensor nodes to perceive the presence of a mobile adversary in their vicinity in order to dynamically modify the routing paths. The routing process operates as usual but upon the detection of an adversary in the vicinity of a node the CALP mechanism is triggered. The detecting node informs its neighbours about the presence of the adversary and they modify their routing tables to circumvent the area controlled by him. Two strategies are devised depending on the way forwarding decisions are made. The strict version blocks the transmission of packets if the adversary is too close, thus avoiding the capture of packets but it might cause large delays. The second version is more permissive as it only penalises the transmission of packets within an area close to the adversary but it reduces the delay.

Network Loop Methods. A completely different approach to deceive local adversaries consists of the creation of network loops. A network loop is basically a sequence of nodes that transmit messages in a cycle in order to keep the adversary away from the real direction towards the data source.

The Cyclic Entrapment Method (CEM) [30] sets traps in the form of decoy messages to distract the adversary from the true path to the data source for as long as possible. After the deployment of the network, each sensor node decides whether it will generate a network loop with a given probability. Then, the node selects two neighbouring nodes and sends a loop-creation message that travels h hops from the first to the other neighbour. All the nodes receiving this message become loop members. During the normal operation of the network, a loop remains active as long as a loop member receives a real packet. Interestingly, when CEM is used in conjunction with single-path routing (see Fig. 8a), real traffic reaches the base station in the shortest time possible without incurring extra delays. During a traceback attack, when reaching a fork in the path the adversary must decide which packet to follow. If he picks the fake message he is trapped in the loop for h hops. However, an skilled adversary might avoid loops since packets with a larger inclination angle are more likely to lead to a loop.

In the information Hiding in Distributed Environments (iHIDE) scheme [18] the sensor network consists of a set of ring nodes which are inter-connected with each other and with the base station by means of a network bus. This arrangement is similar to the one depicted in Fig. 8a but in iHIDE all sensor nodes are either bus or ring nodes. During the data transmission period, a source node that wishes to communicate data to the sink first sends the data to the next ring member in a (counter-)clockwise direction[3]. When the bus node receives the packet, it forwards it to the next bus node closer to the sink but the packet continues to loop in the same ring for a random number of hops. As the packet travels through the bus, each bus node decides, based on a given probability, to

---

[3] In the case that the sensor node belongs to multiple rings simultaneously it randomly selects one of them to forward the message.

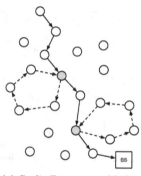

(a) Cyclic Entrapment Method

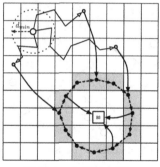

(b) Network Mixing Ring

Fig. 8. Network Loops Methods

forward the packet into its own ring or to directly submit it to the next bus node. The main limitation to iHIDE is that the adversary can wait until he observes that a bus node just forwards a message to the next bus node. This implies that somewhere in a previous ring there is a data source.

The Network Mixing Ring (NMR) scheme [21] creates a virtual ring of nodes surrounding the base station whose aim is to mix up real messages with fake traffic in order to mislead the adversary. This scheme consists of two phases. In the first phase, the source nodes picks an intermediate node using the RRIN approach (see Section 4.1). In the second phase, the intermediate sends the packet to the network mixing ring. Once there, the packet is relayed clockwise for a random number of hops before being finally submitted to the base station. Within the mixing ring there are a few nodes that generate vehicle messages, which are re-encrypted at every hop. These messages carry several bogus data units, which are replaced as real messages enter the ring. The whole process is depicted in Fig. 8b, where the grey cells represent the area defining the network mixing ring. A major limitation to this scheme is that ring nodes are likely to deplete their batteries soon, thus isolating the sink from the rest of the network.

To diminish the energy imbalance between ordinary sensor nodes and ring nodes, the authors propose predefining several rings and activating only one at a time according to the residual energy of their members. Additionally, they briefly discuss the possibility of having several active rings simultaneously to improve the level of protection of the data sources. This idea have been continued by Yao et al. [54]. Whenever a sensor nodes has something to transmit it picks two random rings (one closer and one farther), and an angle α between zero and π. Then, it sends out the packet to the farther ring and once there it is relayed counterclockwise until the angle is reached. From this point, the packet is sent to the closer ring and once more travels counterclockwise for an angle $\beta = \pi - \alpha$. Finally, the packet is routed directly to the base station. During this process, fake packets are injected by the nodes on contiguous rings to further complicate traffic analysis. Clearly, these ring-based solutions require the network to be densely populated in order to enable the creation of full rings.

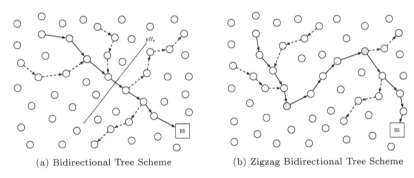

(a) Bidirectional Tree Scheme   (b) Zigzag Bidirectional Tree Scheme

Fig. 9. Bidirectional Tree Schemes

Fake Data Sources. The idea of using fake data sources was first suggested by Ozturk et al. [32]. They proposed two strategies, namely Short-lived and Persistent Fake Source, to simulate the presence of real events in the field by making some sensor nodes to behave as true data sources. In the first strategy, whenever a sensor node receives a real message it decides, based on a particular probability distribution, whether to generate a fake message and flood the network with it. This scheme provides a poor privacy protection since fake data sources are ephemeral. The second strategy aims to prevent this by creating persistent sources of fake messages. Each sensor node decides with a probability to become a fake data source. The efficiency of this strategy is very much dependent on the positioning of the fake data source. If fake data sources are far from a real data source it helps, otherwise it may lead the adversary to the real data source.

Chen and Lou [8] designed several solutions to protect location privacy based on the use of fake messages, namely the Bidirectional Tree (BT) scheme, the Dynamic Bidirectional Tree (DBT) scheme, and the Zigzag Bidirectional Tree (ZBT) scheme. These solutions are intended to protect both source- and receiver-location privacy simultaneously but we cover them here in full detail to avoid the duplication of contents across different sections. In the BT scheme, real messages travel along the shortest path from the source to the sink and several branches of fake messages flow into and out of the path. To that end, before the transmission of data messages, the source node sends a packet containing its own hop count H_s along the shortest path. Those nodes in the path whose distance to the sink is greater than $(1-p)H_s$, being p a network-wide parameter, will generate an input branch[4] with a given probability. Similarly, the nodes satisfying pH_s will choose whether to generate an output branch. This solution is depicted in Fig. 9a, where dashed arrows represent (input or output) fake branches. The idea behind the creation of fake branches is to misdirect the adversary from the real path but is not difficult for a skilled adversary to realise that nodes deviating from the already travelled path are fake branches.

To prevent the adversary from easily obtaining directional information, the DBT scheme suggests that when a node receives a real message it must decide the

---

[4] The authors do not specify how sources of fake input data are selected.

next hop uniformly at random its neighbours closer to the base station. Similar to the BT scheme, fake branches are created but in this case, input branches are generated with a given probability when the hop count is smaller than $H_s/2$, and output branches otherwise. In the ZBT real packets zigzag along three segments: from the source node to a source proxy, from there to a sink proxy, and finally to the real sink. During the data transmission phase, each node in the path generates fake branches with a given probability. In the segment from the source node to the source proxy, the fake packets flow into the path, and in the segment from the sink proxy to the sink, the packets flow out. No branches are generated in the segment connecting the source and sink proxies. The operation of the ZBT scheme is depicted in Fig. 9b, where grey nodes represent the source and sink proxy nodes. This scheme presents the same limitation as the original BT scheme, that is, fake branches can be eventually discarded. Either the attacker discards a fake branch after tracing it or due to a unusual inclination angle.

Jhumka et al. [14] developed two solutions, namely fake source (FS) 1 and 2, to investigate the effectiveness of using fake data sources. Both solutions are built on top of a baseline flooding protocol. In FS1, the data source floods the network with a message containing the event data and a hop count. When this packet reaches the base station, it generates an away message containing the distance between itself and the data source, and floods the network with it. The away message is intended to reach all nodes at the same distance as the source to the sink and make them transmit a choose message. This new message is forwarded to nodes further away, which decide to forward it based on a given probability. When the hop count of the choose message reaches 0, it generates a random number and, if above a given threshold, the node becomes a fake data source. The FS2 protocol is very similar to FS1, the difference is that in FS2 all the nodes that receive a message forward it, while in FS1 the forwarding of messages is determined by a given probability. Consequently, more nodes are likely to become fake data sources in FS2 and thereby the level of protection achieved by this scheme is better at the expense of increased energy consumption.

4.2   Global Adversaries

The aforementioned techniques are only effective against adversaries performing traceback attacks with a limited hearing range. Global adversaries are capable of monitoring all the traffic generated and forwarded in the network. Such adversaries can easily detect the data sources among mere intermediaries because sensor nodes are programmed to report event data to the base station as soon as it is detected.

There are two main approaches to hide the location of data sources from global adversaries, either using fake packets or introducing significant delays in the transmissions. Most solutions have concentrated on the injection of bogus traffic and a huge research effort has been devoted to making these solutions as energy-efficient as possible.

Bogus Traffic. The threat of global adversaries was first considered by Mehta et al. in [24], where they proposed the Periodic Collection scheme. This scheme hides the presence of events in the field by making every node transmit fake messages at regular intervals. However, it is not as simple as sending fake messages at a constant rate because the occurrence of an event message would change the transmission pattern, as shown in Fig. 10a. This figure depicts a timeline where the transmissions of real and fake packets are represented by arrows with white or black heads, respectively. In the Periodic Collection scheme, sensor nodes transmit messages at a given rate $\mathcal{R}$ regardless of the presence of events. Instead of transmitting a message immediately after the detection of an event, the message is temporarily stored until the next scheduled transmission time, as shown in Fig. 10b. Since real and bogus traffic are indistinguishable from each other, this method provides perfect event source unobservability because the transmission rate is not altered by the presence of events.

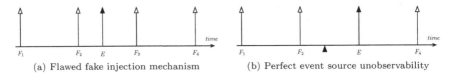

(a) Flawed fake injection mechanism   (b) Perfect event source unobservability

Fig. 10. Periodic Fake Packet Injection

As event messages need to be delayed until the next scheduled transmission time, this poses a serious limitation in time-critical applications. Intuitively, the delivery delay can be reduced by changing scheduling in order to have shorter inter-transmission times. However, this impacts negatively on the energy waste of the network. Therefore, the transmission rate must be carefully adjusted in order to ensure the durability of the network without incurring an excessive delay.

Energy-Aware Approaches. There has been an extensive body of research which focuses on reducing the overhead imposed by the injection of fake messages at regular intervals. These proposed solutions have approached the problem in different ways: simulating the presence of events in the field, filtering out fake traffic, using already existing traffic to convey event data, and sending messages according to a given probability distribution.

The Source Simulation scheme [24] is based on the idea of saving energy by reducing the number of nodes transmitting fake messages. Instead of making all nodes send out messages at regular intervals, the network simulates the presence of real events in the field. During network deployment, a set of L nodes are preloaded, each with a different token. These nodes generate fake traffic during the data transmission phase and after a predefined period of time, the token is passed to one of its neighbours (possibly itself) depending on the behaviour

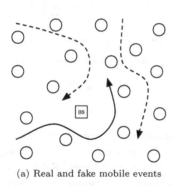 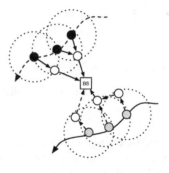

(a) Real and fake mobile events   (b) Modelling of event propagation

Fig. 11. Unobservable Handoff Trajectory

of real objects. The size of L determines the level of protection as well as the energy consumed by the network. The main problem with this approach lies in the difficulty of accurately modelling the movement of an object so it appears as real to the adversary.

The Unobservable Handoff Trajectory (UHT) [29] is another solution that simulates the presence of objets in the field. The UHT is a decentralised and self-adaptive scheme that generates fake mobile events with the same probability distribution as real events. Real events follow a Poisson distribution and fake events are generated in such a way that the overall distribution is not affected. The generation of dummy events starts at the perimeter of the network and propagates for a number of hops according to the length of real events (see Fig. 11a). Each perimeter node decides to generate a new dummy event independently based on the number of perimeter nodes and the number of real events they observe over a time window. After being created, fake messages must be propagated. This process is based on the fact that all the neighbours of a fake node receive the fake packets sent towards the base station. This packet contains who will be the next fake source in the path and also the length of the current event. The propagation is represented in Fig. 11b, where fake sources are shaded in grey and real sources in black while fake and real messages are represented with dashed and ordinary arrows, respectively.

Besides the cross-layer scheme described in Section 4.1, Shao et al. [42] proposed another version of the same solution that can protect against global adversaries. This alternative protocol is very similar to the Periodic Collection proposed by Mehta et al. but the main difference is that instead of using ordinary network traffic it takes advantage of the beaconing phase. This scheme also provides perfect event source unobservability at no additional cost since event data is hidden within beacon frames, which are periodically broadcast regardless of the occurrence or not, of events in the field. However, since the time between consecutive beacons is relatively large, the solution is only practical for some applications where no tight time restrictions exist.

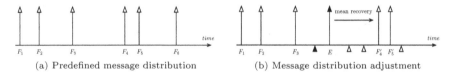

(a) Predefined message distribution   (b) Message distribution adjustment

Fig. 12. Statistically strong source unobservability

In order to reduce network traffic while maintaining source unobservability, Yang et al. [50] proposed a bogus traffic filtering scheme. In this solution, any node sends real or fake messages at a given rate and some nodes operate a filtering proxies. Proxy nodes discard bogus traffic and temporarily buffer and re-encrypt real traffic before forwarding it. If there are no real messages available, a proxy node sends encrypted dummy messages. In the Proxy-based Filtering Scheme (PFS) selects a number of proxies and traffic is filtered by only them. In the Tree-based Filtering Scheme (TFS) packets can be processed by several proxy nodes as the move towards the base station, thus reducing fake traffic at the expense of increased network delay. A drawback to this solution is that an attacker can still use rate monitoring techniques to identify the proxy nodes, which are important for the operation of the network.

Another branch of research has concentrated on the concept of statistically strong source unobservability. This concept was introduced by Shao et al. [43] to relax the tight requirements of perfect event source unobservability while maintaining a statistical assurance on the protection of data source. Before deployment, sensor nodes are configured to transmit according to a message distribution F_i, as depicted in Fig. 12. During the data transmission phase, when an event E occurs, the real message can be transmitted before the next scheduled transmission, F_4, without altering the parameters (e.g., the mean and variance) of the distribution. This process is depicted in Fig. 12b. Sensor nodes keep a sliding window of previous inter-message delays $\{\delta_1, \delta_2, ..., \delta_{n-1}\}$ and, upon the occurrence of an event, δ_n is set to a value very close to 0 and gradually incremented by a small random number until the whole sliding window passes a goodness of fit test. Thus, the real event transmission can be sent ahead of the scheduled time without alerting the adversary even if he performs statistical tests on inter-message delays. The solution includes a mean recovery mechanism which delays subsequent transmissions because the presence of bursts of real messages might skew the mean of the distribution.

Recently, Alomair et al. [2] showed that a global adversary has more efficient ways of breaking statistically strong unobservability. Instead of focusing on the inter-message delays of a single sliding window, the attacker might try to spot differences between any two sliding windows (i.e., intervals) in order to detect the presence of real events. The strategy of the adversary is to identify short inter-message delays followed by long inter-message delays. These patterns are common in intervals containing real events because the delay of real messages is usually shorter than the mean in order to reduce the latency, and subsequent

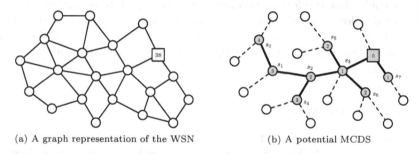

(a) A graph representation of the WSN   (b) A potential MCDS

Fig. 13. Minimum Connected Dominating Set

messages are delayed in order to adjust the mean of the distribution, as proposed in [43]. To the contrary, inter-message delays are independent identically distributed random variables in fake intervals. Consequently, by counting the number of short-long inter-message delays an attacker might be able to distinguish intervals containing real events. The solution proposed by Alomair et al. is to make fake intervals resemble intervals with real events by introducing some statistical interdependence between fake inter-message delays.

Proano and Lazos [36] pointed out that since a global vision is obtained by means of an adversarial network, the attacker cannot exactly determine the transmission rate of each and every sensor node. As a result, not all sensor nodes need to be active sources of fake traffic to deceive the adversary. They suggest reducing the number of fake data sources by partitioning the network into a minimum connected dominating set (MCDS) rooted at the base station. In a MCDS each node either belongs to the MCDS or is one hop away from it, as depicted in Fig. 13. In this way, the nodes in the MCDS transmit (real or fake) traffic at a given rate and the rest of the nodes regulate their transmissions in order to conform to the statistical traffic properties observed by an eavesdropper. Later, in [37], the same authors added a deterministic assignment scheme for coordinating sensor transmissions and thus reduce end-to-end delay for real packets. Nodes deeper in the MCDS are scheduled to transmit sooner, so that any real packet reaches the sink at the end of each interval. For example, in Fig. 13b, each time interval is divided into four subintervals since the maximum depth of the MCDS is four. Sensor node s_0 transmits at the first subinterval, node s_1 at the next subinterval, and so on.

Previous solutions have countered a passive global attacker. Yang et al. [51] consider a global attacker who, upon detecting suspicious cells devises an optimal route to visit these spots. Tthey propose two potential strategies to find a (pseudo-)optimal route to visit all suspicious cells. The first strategy is based on a greedy algorithm, which ends in polynomial time but is not globally optimal, and the second one is a dynamic programming algorithm, which finds the optimal solution but requires an exponential time to finish. Subsequently, the authors evaluate the impact of the proposed attacker model to two existing solutions: statistically strong source unobservability and source simulation.

They conclude that the former behaves well when the rate of real messages to be delivered is low while the latter approach is suitable when the rate is high. As a result, Yang et al. propose a dynamic approach that combines the merits of both solutions by switching from the one to the other based on the load of the network.

4.3 Internal Adversaries

Some adversaries might be able to compromise and control a subset of nodes from the legitimate network. These nodes become internal adversaries since they can participate in the same tasks performed by any other network node and provide the attacker with any information contained in the packets they forward. The solutions devised to deal with these types of attackers are very limited and their approaches rather diverse.

The Identity, Route and Location privacy (IRL) algorithm [41] is as a network-level privacy solution. The primary goal of this solution is to provide source anonymity and location privacy as well as provide assurance that packets reach their destination. Although the authors do not consider the threat of internal adversaries, one of its features is suitable for just this purpose. The authors introduce the notion of trust and reputation to prevent routing through mis-behaving adversaries. First, each node classifies its neighbours into four groups depending on their position with respect to the base station. Additionally, each node classifies its neighbours as either trustworthy or untrustworthy. When a node wants to transmit, it selects random trustworthy nodes which are closer to the base station. If no trustworthy nodes are found it tries with nodes at the same distance or in the opposite direction. In the case no trustworthy nodes are found, the node simply drops the packet. Therefore, each message follows a random path composed of trustworthy nodes only. Additionally, dishonest en-route nodes are unable to determine whether the sender is the real data source or a mere intermediary since nodes replace the identifier of received packets with their own at every hop.

Pongaliur and Xiao [35] propose to modify packets headers at dynamically selected nodes in the route to the base station to protect the identity of the data source from internal adversaries. When a node creates a packet it includes a pseudonym instead of its real identifier. This pseudonym is a value from a hash chain used in reverse order obtained from the real identifier of the node. The packets also include a random value that is used by intermediate nodes to determine whether to replace the identifier carried in the packet by their own pseudonym[5]. Additionally, a rehashing node concatenates the replaced identifier to the payload and encrypts it with its own shared with the base station. An extra field is used for verifying the validity of the modifications. To that end, the base station needs to keep track of the hash chains of all the nodes in order to find the key corresponding to each of concatenated the hash values. Another

---

[5] A hash function is applied to the random value and the result is used as input to a mapping function which returns 0 or 1 with a given probability.

limitation to this approach is that an internal adversary can estimate its distance to the data source based on the rehashing probability and the size of the payload.

The last solution is called *p*DCS [44] and its aim is to provide security and privacy in Data-Centric Sensor (DCS) networks, where the data collected by sensing nodes is forwarded and kept at storage node until the base station queries for them. Sensing nodes know where to send the data by means of a a publicly known mapping function. Since this function is public an attacker can easily determine which nodes to compromise to obtain a particular type of data. After compromising such nodes, he can also identify the location where the data was originally collected. *p*DCS is intended to protect against this type of threat. The scheme is based on the use of a secure mapping function[6] and the storage of encrypted data in a remote location. In the case the adversary compromises a storage node he is not able to decrypt the data contained in it because these data are encrypted with the key of the sensing nodes which collected them. If a sensing node is compromised, the attacker cannot determine where previous data was stored because the secure mapping function prevents this from happening. Moreover, when a node is found to be compromised there is a node revocation mechanism in order to prevent the attacker from obtaining the location of future event data. Finally, the authors suggest protecting the flow of data from the sensing to the storage node by means of any existing source-location privacy solution.

5   Receiver-Location Privacy

Receiver-location privacy refers to the protection of the destination of messages but it primarily concentrates on hiding the location of the base station. The location of the base station is exposed due to the peculiar communication pattern of WSNs: each sensor node transmits data messages to this single point. Intuitively, the solution is to normalise the traffic load by making each sensor node transmit, on average, the same number of messages but this incurs a prohibitive network overhead. In the following we analyse proposals dealing with local adversaries followed by solutions considering the threat of global adversaries. To the best of our knowledge, there are no solutions in the literature that study the threat of internal adversaries.

5.1   Local Adversaries

A local attacker usually starts at a random position in the network[7] and moves around until he overhears some transmissions in the area surrounding him. The typical types of attacks performed by an adversary who wishes to find the sink are: content analysis, time correlation, and rate monitoring. Content analysis tries to obtain information from the packet headers or payload. Additionally, an

---

[6] A secure mapping function is basically a keyed hash function that uses as input the type of event and other secret information shared by a group of nodes.

[7] Starting at the edge of the network is, in our opinion, more realistic.

attacker can observe the packet sending times of neighbouring nodes in order to determine the direction to the base station.Finally, in a rate monitoring attack, the strategy of the adversary is to move in the direction of those nodes with higher transmission rates since nodes in the vicinity of the base station receive more packets than remote nodes.

Next we analyse some basic countermeasures against the aforementioned attacks followed by a set of more advanced solutions. Most of these solutions aim to balance the amount of traffic between all network nodes by selecting the next hop based on some probability while other solutions attempt to disguise or emulate the presence of the base station at different locations. Again, some solutions may fall into several categories depending on the features analysed.

Basic Countermeasures. Some basic countermeasures have been proposed in [12] to prevent the aforementioned attacks. First, content analysis can be hindered by applying secure data encryption on a hop-by-hop basis. This process should be applied throughout the whole lifetime of the network but it is not easy to satisfy this requirement until each node shares pairwise keys with all its neighbours. Thus, they propose an ID confusion technique to conceal the source and destination during the route discovery phase. This technique is based on reversible hash functions so that when a node x sends a message to node y, it randomly selects an element from $C_x = \{h_x : x = H(x)\}$ as the source address, and an element from $C_y = \{h_y : y = H(y)\}$ as the destination address. Finally, it encrypts the whole packet with a network-wide shared key pre-loaded on all sensor nodes. A receiving node decrypts the message and, by reverting the hash function, it obtains the true sender and intended recipient.

During data transmission, sensor nodes must ensure that packets change their appearance as they move towards the base station. Each node in the path must decrypt any received packet and then re-encrypt it with the key shared with the next node in the route. However, even if the attacker cannot observe the contents of the packets, he can learn some information from packet sending times and eventually infer the relationship between parent and child (i.e., closer and further) nodes. To prevent this, Deng et al. [11] propose applying random delays to the transmission of packets. Additionally, the authors suggest creating a uniform sending rate to prevent rate monitoring attacks. This can be achieved by making a parent node accept packets from a child node only if its own packet has been forwarded. In the case the parent node has nothing new to send, it can simply continue to send the same packet or inject dummy traffic.

There are some limitations to these basic countermeasures that require the development of further solutions. The following schemes aim to reduce these limitations.

Biased Random Walks. This category brings together solutions where the routing process is random but somehow biased towards the base station. The first solution is also presented by Deng et al. [11] and is called Multi-Parent Routing (MPR). The MPR consists of making each sensor node pick the next

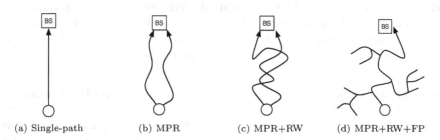

| (a) Single-path | (b) MPR | (c) MPR+RW | (d) MPR+RW+FP |

Fig. 14. Schematic of Several Multi-Parent Routing Techniques

element in the path uniformly at random from its set of parent nodes. See in Fig. 14 a comparison between a single-path routing and a MPR scheme. In Fig. 14a all transmissions use the same transmission path, which is represented by a straight arrow, while in Fig. 14b the paths followed by two different packets are represented. The MPR scheme obtains a better load balance as data packets spread within a band of nodes next to the shortest path from the data source to the base station. However, the traffic flow still points to the base station as the next communication hop is always selected from the list of parent nodes. To further diversify routing paths, the authors suggest combining MPR with a random walk (RW) routing scheme. In this version of the protocol, nodes forward packets to a parent node with probability p_r and to a randomly chosen neighbour with probability $1 - p_r$. Consequently, packets may not only travel towards the base station but in any other direction. In Fig. 14c we depict two routing paths which at some points move in the opposite direction to the base station. This scheme provides better security at the cost of a higher message delivery delay.

Similarly, Jian et al. [15] propose to make every sensor node divide its neighbours two groups. The first group contains nodes which are closer to the base station and the second group contains the rest of their neighbours. So, nodes forward packets to further nodes with probability $P_f < 1/2$ and to closer nodes with probability $1 - P_f$. This implies that the transmission is biased and the attacker is able to infer the direction to the data sink. To prevent this, the authors inject fake packets in the opposite direction to the base station with probability P_{fake} after receiving a real packet. This packet travels for several hops away from the base station. In general, the adversary cannot distinguish real from fake traffic which makes this solution secure since packets flow in any direction with an even probability. However, if the adversary observes a node that does not forward a packet he knows that it is a fake packet. As fake packets are sent to further neighbours exclusively, the adversary learns that the base station is in the opposite direction.

Rios et al. [39] devised an new strategy that solves the previous problem. They suggest to send a pair of messages (real and fake) for every transmission in such a way that real traffic is more likely to be sent towards the base station and fake traffic is used to compensate the message rate for every neighbour. When fake traffic is received by a node, it continues sending two messages, both of which are fake, for a number of hops that depends on the hearing range of the adversary. The branches of fake traffic must reach out of the hearing range of the adversary. Now, if the adversary observes a node that drops a received packet he knows that this packet is fake but he is unable to determine the direction to the base station since fake packets are sent in any possible direction.

Fake Traffic Injection. Deng et al. [11] proposed new ways of improving MPR based on the injection of fake traffic. Fractal Propagation (FP) was designed to be used in conjunction with MPR and RW. When a sensor node observes that a neighbouring node is forwarding a data packet to the base station, it generates a fake packet with probability p_c and forwards it to one of its neighbours. The durability of fake packets is controlled by means of a global time-to-live parameter K. Also, if a node observes a fake packet with parameter k $(0 < k < K)$ it propagates another fake packet with time-to-live parameter $k - 1$. Fig. 14d shows the trace resulting from the transmission of a single packet using the three mechanisms together. The main problem of the FP scheme is that nodes in the vicinity of the base station generate much more fake traffic than remote nodes. To address this problem, the authors propose the Differential Fractal Propagation (DFP), where sensor nodes adjust their probability of generating fake traffic p_c according to the number of packets they forward. Besides reducing the energy waste, this scheme provides better privacy protection because it balances the network traffic load more evenly.

Yao et al. propose in [55] a new fake packet injection scheme. Real packets are sent to the base station using the shortest path and when two paths of real messages intersect at some point, the node receiving these packets sends two fake packets to two fake data sinks after a timer expires or a packet counter reaches a certain threshold. In this way, real and fake data sinks receive a similar number of packets. Moreover, when a packet reaches subsequent intersection points, the intersection node sends N_f packets to some random destinations. This process is depicted in Fig. 15, where dark grey nodes represent intersection nodes, light grey nodes are fake sinks or some random data destinations. Ordinary arrows symbolise real data packets while dashed arrows represent fake packets. In Fig. 15a the first intersection node transmits fake traffic to both fake data sinks. Meanwhile, the second intersection node introduces fake traffic to other random destinations as well. The main problem of Yao et al.'s approach is an attacker starting from a data source and tracing packets can trivially reach the first intermediate node. From that point, he can distinguish fake paths since they may imply an abrupt change in the angle of transmission. This problem has already been discussed for other solutions.

Sink Simulation. Some approaches try to emulate the presence of the base station at different points in the field. Simulation techniques are based on the generation of fake traffic but, instead of being transmitted in random directions, it is addressed to particular network locations. This results in a concentration of high volumes of fake traffic, called hotspots, the objective of which is to draw the adversary away from the true data sink. The main challenge is to create

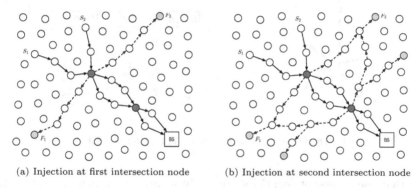

(a) Injection at first intersection node   (b) Injection at second intersection node

Fig. 15. Yao et al. Fake Packet Injection Scheme

hotspots that are evenly distributed throughout the network with a minimum overhead.

Maelstrom [5] is one of such solutions that generates a number of fake data sinks. After deployment, the base station sends N special configuration packets, each of which is configured to travel H_s hops away from the base station. After that, each of these packets travel H_r random hops to any node on the same level or further away. The final recipients of these packets become the centre of a maelstrom area and announce this by sending a discovery packet to nearby nodes. During data transmission, when a node receives a real packet it generates, with a probability, a fake message and forwards it to its closest maelstrom. However, once an intelligent attacker reaches a maelstrom area he can discard it as the true data sink.

A similar approach is proposed by Biswas et al. [3]. The idea is to evenly distribute multiple fake data sinks with the largest number of neighbours, since this implies more incoming traffic. During data transmission, each node is configured to transmit a fixed number of messages either real or fake so that after a given time period all nodes have sent the same amount of traffic. Fake traffic is directed to fake data sink by its neighbours except for nodes which are not immediate neighbours, where the selection of a fake destination is done in a round-robin fashion. The result should be that fake base stations receive at least the same amount of traffic as the actual base station. This approach may deal with naive rate monitoring adversaries but it can be defeated by informed adversaries.

Finally, Deng et al. [11] refined their fractal propagation solutions and created a new scheme called Differential Enforced Fractal Propagation (DEFP) that is capable of creating hotspots in a decentralised and dynamic way. Sensor nodes keep track of the number of fake packets forwarded to each neighbour and new fake traffic is more likely to be sent to neighbours who have previously received more fake traffic, as shown in Fig. 16. In this way there is no need for a central authority or a complex coordination system to establish where the hotspots should be placed. Another interesting feature of this solution is that the hotspots can be deactivated by simply resetting the forwarding probabilities of each node.

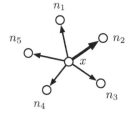

neighs(x)	tickets	Probability
n_1	1	1/8
n_2	4	1/2
n_3	1	1/8
n_4	1	1/8
n_5	1	1/8

Fig. 16. Decentralised Hotspot Generation in DEFP

After that, new hotspot locations are likely to appear, which prevents smart attackers from discarding fake data sinks (i.e., hotspots) until they find the real base station.

5.2   Global Adversaries

The aforementioned techniques are considered to be effective only in a local adversarial model but some of them may also provide some means of protection against global adversaries. As a matter of fact, they can be useful if the global adversary has no real-time analysing capabilities.

Again, the injection of fake traffic is one of the main approaches for protecting from global adversaries. Making the base station mimic the behaviour of sensor nodes, simulating the presence of several data sinks, and moving the base station to a different location might also be useful solutions.

Bogus Traffic. As mentioned in Section 5, flooding the network with messages is a simple yet efficient mechanism to protect the location of the base station. The main drawback to flooding is the high communication cost associated with the retransmission of the same message to every corner of the network. Backbone flooding [25] reduces the communication cost by limiting the transmissions within a backbone area. The backbone area consists of a sufficient number of adjacent nodes to achieve a desired level of privacy. Any data packet generated in the network is addressed to the backbone, where it spreads to all its members. Since data sinks must be located at least within the range of a backbone member, they overhear all messages. A major limitation to this approach is that the backbone is static. The authors suggest to alleviated this problem by (a) periodically rebuilding the backbone or (b) defining several backbones from the beginning. Fig. 17 illustrates the transmission of a data packet and its propagation within the backbone area.

The scheme called Concealing Sink Location (CSL) [56] follows a different strategy. The idea is to make each sensor node transmit at the same rate regardless of its distance to the base station. This rate is calculated for nodes at distance i from the sink by counting the number of nodes at distance greater than i and dividing it by the number of nodes at distance i. This ratio represents

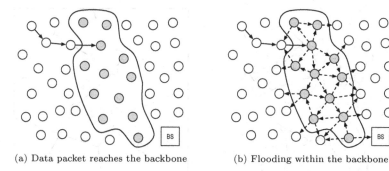

(a) Data packet reaches the backbone   (b) Flooding within the backbone

Fig. 17. Backbone Flooding

that each node must send its own traffic and forward the traffic from nodes further away. The number of nodes at a given distance i is estimated via geometric analysis considering the size of the deployment area and a uniform distribution of the nodes in the field. However, these estimations may differ significantly from the reality. Also, it is important to note that the authors assume that sensor nodes have a similar transmission rate for real messages but this might not be the case in the presence of bursts of messages.

A similar approach is followed in [57], where the transmission rate of nodes is calculated based on the number of child nodes an immediate neighbour of the sink has. The idea is to make all sensor nodes transmit as many messages as a sink neighbour has to since they are the busiest nodes. When a sensor node receives a fake packet it simply drops it, while if the packet is real, it buffers it temporarily. In the meantime the sensor node generates fake traffic to satisfy the overall transmission rate. The authors claim that by generating that much traffic the lifetime of the network is not reduced. The argument is that all nodes in the network will deplete their batteries at the same time and not only the sink neighbours. However, they have not considered that in this way the transceivers of the nodes are active most of the time and they need to decrypt much more messages. Also, they have not considered collisions and packet retransmissions.

Sink Simulation. Sink simulation has also been suggested as a mechanism to protect from global adversaries. Mehta et al. [25] propose simulating the presence of several data sinks in the field. During the deployment k of sensor nodes are picked as fake data sinks and the true data sinks are manually placed within the communication range of some of these. The number of fake sinks must outnumber the number of true sinks. When a source node detects event data, it send them to all the fake data sinks, which on reception broadcast the message locally. This process is illustrated in Fig. 18a, where the data source S sends messages to $F_1, \ldots, F_2$ and each of them broadcast the message locally. Since all fake sinks receive the same amount of traffic, they are all equally likely to be next to a true data sink. The larger the value of k the better the protection but the higher the volume of traffic in the network.

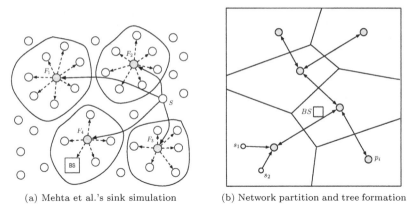

(a) Mehta et al.'s sink simulation   (b) Network partition and tree formation

Fig. 18. Examples of Sink Simulation Approaches

The solution in [4] is also based on the concept of k-anonymity. The idea is to have at least k nodes with a communication pattern similar to the nodes around the base station. To that end, the network is partitioned into k Voronoi regions, each of which contains a node that collects all the information sensed in that region. These nodes p_i are organised as an Euclidean minimum-spanning tree and the data they received from their own region is forwarded to all other tree members. Fig. 18a shows a Voronoi partition of the network for the designated nodes p_i, in grey. Note that all nodes connecting the designated nodes see all the network traffic and thus the base station simply needs to be placed close to one of them. As a result, the uncertainty of the attacker is much greater than in the previous scheme for the same value of k. However, the nodes forming the tree are highly likely to deplete their batteries much sooner than the rest of the nodes.

Wang and Hsiang [47] propose another solution that starts by generating a shortest-path tree rooted at the base station. After that, neighbouring leaf nodes establish communication links to generate network cycles. During data transmission, the shortest-path tree is used to transmit data to the base station and, simultaneously, fake packets are injected into the cycles. Fake traffic continues moving along the cycle until it is completed. When several cycles intersect at a node it creates a hotspot since it receives all the bogus traffic from the cycles. The authors include a mechanism to limit the number of cycles by allowing leaf nodes to establish links only if their least common ancestor is at least h hops away from both nodes. In this way, each of the hotspots receive more traffic. Even though the authors assume a global adversarial model, this solution does not seem suitable for that purpose. The main problem is that the true sink behaves differently from the rest of the artificial hotspots. While the transmission rate of the base station is negligible, fake hotspots must forward the real data packets coming from its child nodes.

Relocation and Disguise. As far back as 2003, Deng et al. [12] suggested the reallocation of the base station for enhanced security. They assume that the base

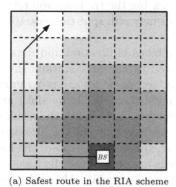
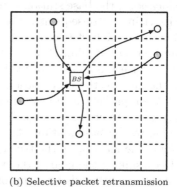

(a) Safest route in the RIA scheme   (b) Selective packet retransmission

Fig. 19. Relocation and Disguise Examples

station has complete knowledge of the topology of the network and thus it may calculate an optimal future location that maximises its security. Actually, they do not address a global eavesdropper but a compromised node dropping packets. Therefore, we refer the reader to their paper for further details.

Possibly motivated by the approach just mentioned, Acharya and Younis propose the Relocation for Increased Anonymity (RIA) scheme [1], where the base station finds a new location by considering both the impact over network performance and its own level of protection. The base station calculates a score for each cell based on the node density and the threat level (i.e., transmission rate). The rationale behind this scoring mechanism is that by moving the base station to a cell with a low threat , the cells with high activity need to send packets to remote areas, which increases the delivery time and consumes more energy. Likewise, if there is a low transmission rate due to a reduced node density, moving the base station to that cell would cause the few nodes in the cell to become overwhelmed with traffic. Once the base station knows which is the most suitable cell to reside in, it follows the safest route to reach the final destination. In Fig. 19a we depict the path selected by the base station for relocation based on the scores of each of its cells, the cells with higher scores are depicted in a lighter colour.

Mimicking the behaviour of ordinary sensor nodes is another way of hiding the base station from global adversaries. The Base-station Anonymity increase through selective packet Re-transmission (BAR) [1] suggests to make the base station decide whether to forward the packets it receives for several hops. The length of the walk is dynamically adjusted based on the level of threat perceived by the base station. If the base station needs to increase its level of protection it defines longer walks. The general idea is that by doing this, the number of transmissions in remote cells increase and thus the attacker cannot clearly identify the actual location of the base station based on the transmission rate of a cell. An example of this approach is illustrated in Fig. 19b, where source nodes and destination nodes are represented as grey and white circles, respectively. The main problem with this approach is that by forwarding packets to random remote locations, the base station is also increasing the transmission rate of the cells in its vicinity. Consequently, the attacker may still spot the base station as the cell with the highest transmission rate.

Finally, the Decoy Sink Protocol [10] combines indirection and data aggregation to reduce the amount of traffic received by the base station. Instead of sending the data to the base station directly, sensor nodes are programmed to transmit their packets to an intermediate node (i.e., the decoy sink) and, on their way, the data are aggregated. Finally the decoy sink sends the result of the aggregation to the base station. Although this may prevent the attacker from determining the location of the true data sink, this scheme exposes the location of the decoy sink. If the goal of the attacker is to compromise the base station, he obtains a similar result by compromising the decoy sink. Also, if he destroys it the protocol stops working. This problem is contemplated by the authors and they suggest picking several random nodes during the initialisation of the network to operate as decoy sinks. During the transmission period, sensor nodes send all their readings to a particular decoy sink for a pre-established period of time. This version of the protocol adds robustness to the network and balances the traffic load but the attacker is still able to ultimately achieve his original goal.

6   Challenges and Future Trends

Privacy preservation in WSNs has proven to be an extremely challenging task and regardless of the number of solutions that have been devised there are several open questions that need further attention:

- **Cost-Effective Solutions.** The main approach to location privacy is to increase the number of transmissions in order to mislead the adversary from the target in some way. However, sending more packets implies more energy waste and increased delays. This overhead is normally related to the level of protection provided by the solutions but sending more packets does not always increase privacy, as shown by angle-based privacy solutions. Moreover, many solutions are incapable of completely deceiving the adversary and can only guarantee a longer safety period until the adversary eventually finds the target. Consequently, it is necessary to devise and develop new solutions that keep to a reasonable energy budget without sacrificing the level of protection. Some solutions based on innovative techniques already exist (e.g., cross-layer routing and context-aware location privacy) but there is still room for original research in the area.
- **Holistic Privacy.** Despite the number of solutions existing in the literature devoted to protecting source- and receiver-location privacy, there is no single scheme capable of effectively and efficiently providing an integral solution to both problems simultaneously. While source-location privacy can be achieved by hiding the transmissions of real packets, receiver-location privacy demands a homogeneous traffic load in the network. Therefore, a naive

solution to these problems is to use baseline flooding together with fake data sources. However, this approach is too energy consuming for ordinary sensor networks, where the energy budget is rather limited. How to solve this problem in an energy-efficient way demands further attention from the research community.

– **Interoperability Framework.** Another open problem in the literature is the lack of a unified framework for quantifying location privacy for comparing different solutions. Currently, different authors resort to different approaches such as measuring entropy, game theory, evidence theory, numerical analysis, and simulations. However, it is not trivial to provide a formal model that accurately represents the behaviour of the system, especially in the context of a local adversary. Although it is possible to measure the privacy loss in one step, the information leak accumulates in a way that remains intractable as the adversary moves in the field. Probably, this is the reason why simulations is the most common approach to proving the correctness of solutions. But simulation results are not easily reproducible because either the simulator is not standardised or the code is not made publicly available, or both. Thus, defining an interoperability framework is a challenging area of research that may help to devise new contrasted solutions.

– **More Skilled Adversaries.** Also in relation with the previous issue, it is necessary to formally and faithfully define the capabilities and actions that may be performed by the adversary. The traditional approach is to define an adversary with a predefined strategy that remains unaltered. An appropriate model for representing the knowledge of the adversary does not exist. At most, the adversary knows whether he has visited a specific node before or not. The adversary does not use or infer new information based on previously known data or additional sources of information. For example, the adversary might use the routing tables of the nodes to compromise receiver-location privacy. In this regard, the adversarial model considered in the literature is mostly passive and does not interfere with the normal operation of the network. Particular attention must be paid to adversaries who can inject, modify, reply, or block messages from a portion of the network given the hardware limitations of sensor nodes. Also, more research must be conducted to devise solutions against internal adversaries, which are not only capable of obtaining contextual information but also payload contents.

– **Dynamic Environments and Future Scenarios.** All the solutions analysed here only consider static networks. Once placed, sensor nodes are not reallocated to another location. However, the Internet of Things opens the door to new scenarios where everyday objects are fitted with computational power and limited batteries. This will result in one of the most promising areas for innovation. In this landscape, mobility is of paramount importance but it may also imply intermittent network connectivity and the use of untrustworthy data relays to reach the base station. Moreover, it is possible that not only the base station has a connection to the outside world, but the sensor nodes could also be directly connected to the Internet. Similarly, new

278 R. Rios, J. Lopez, and J. Cuellar

types of adversaries might appear. Therefore, we believe that the integration of sensor networks with the Internet will result in a prolific area of study.

Note that this paper has focused on location privacy but there are more metadata that may be leaked from the operation of the network. For example, it is important to hide the moment in time when an event takes place (i.e., temporal privacy) since it allows an adversary to predict future behaviours of the elements being monitored by the network. Also, there is also room for innovation and research in content-oriented privacy, which is primarily aimed to hide packets contents while enabling data-aggregation. Finally, another related issue that requires further attention is query privacy, namely, preventing the disclosure of a query based on the nodes that respond to it.

7   Conclusions

This paper has presented a taxonomy of solutions for location privacy in Wireless Sensor Networks. The taxonomy is organised based on the information to be protected and the capabilities of the adversary that may want to compromise location privacy. More than 50 papers have been analysed including solutions for node anonymity, source-location privacy, and receiver-location privacy. In general, local adversaries are countered by means of random walk routing solutions, which are ineffective against global adversaries. Dummy traffic injection is the typical approach to provide protection against more powerful adversaries but the overhead imposed by these solutions is overly high. Internal adversaries have not received sufficient attention yet.

Prior to analysing solutions we have studied whether traditional anonymous communication systems are suitable for protecting location privacy in WSNs. This study has first considered which anonymity requirements are desirable for the sensors' domain and then we have studied the overhead and limitations imposed by some renowned anonymous communication systems. From this, we have shown that some of these solutions are sufficiently lightweight to run in sensor nodes but either the anonymity requirements or the adversarial model differ from the ones considered in WSNs. To the contrary, other solutions are suitable for the location privacy problem but impose a high overhead or limit the usability of the network.

At the end of this paper we present a number of challenges and open issues that must be addressed by the research community to facilitate the acceptance of sensor networks and other foreseeable technologies.

Acknowledgements. This work has been partially funded by the European Commission through the FP7 project NESSoS (FP7 256890), the Spanish Ministry of Science and Innovation through the ARES project (CSD2007-00004) and the Andalusian Government PISCIS project (P10-TIC-06334).

References

1. Acharya, U., Younis, M.: Increasing base-station anonymity in wireless sensor networks. Ad Hoc Networks 8(8), 791–809 (2010)
2. Alomair, B., Clark, A., Cuellar, J., Poovendran, R.: Towards a Statistical Framework for Source Anonymity in Sensor Networks. IEEE Transactions on Mobile Computing 12(2), 248–260 (2012)
3. Biswas, S., Mukherjee, S., Mukhopadhyaya, K.: A Countermeasure against Traffic-Analysis based Base Station Detection in WSN (2008),
   http://citeseerx.ist.psu.edu/viewdoc/summary?doi=10.1.1.98.948
4. Chai, G., Xu, M., Xu, W., Lin, Z.: Enhancing sink-location privacy in wireless sensor networks through k-anonymity. International Journal of Distributed Sensor Networks 2012, 16 (2012)
5. Chang, S., Qi, Y., Zhu, H., Dong, M., Ota, K.: Maelstrom: Receiver-Location Preserving in Wireless Sensor Networks. In: Cheng, Y., Eun, D.Y., Qin, Z., Song, M., Xing, K. (eds.) WASA 2011. LNCS, vol. 6843, pp. 190–201. Springer, Heidelberg (2011)
6. Chaum, D.: Untraceable Electronic Mail, Return addresses, and Digital Pseudonyms. Commun. ACM 24(2), 84–88 (1981)
7. Chaum, D.: The Dining Cryptographers Problem: Unconditional Sender and Recipient Untraceability. Journal of Cryptology 1, 65–75 (1988)
8. Chen, H., Lou, W.: From Nowhere to Somewhere: Protecting End-to-End Location Privacy in Wireless Sensor Networks. In: 29th International Performance Computing and Communications Conference, IPCCC 2010, pp. 1–8. IEEE (2010)
9. Chen, J., Du, X., Fang, B.: An Efficient Anonymous Communication Protocol for Wireless Sensor Networks. Wireless Communications and Mobile Computing 12(14), 1302–1312 (2012)
10. Conner, W., Abdelzaher, T., Nahrstedt, K.: Using Data Aggregation to Prevent Traffic Analysis in Wireless Sensor Networks. In: Gibbons, P.B., Abdelzaher, T., Aspnes, J., Rao, R. (eds.) DCOSS 2006. LNCS, vol. 4026, pp. 202–217. Springer, Heidelberg (2006)
11. Deng, J., Han, R., Mishra, S.: Decorrelating wireless sensor network traffic to inhibit traffic analysis attacks. Pervasive and Mobile Computing 2(2), 159–186 (2006)
12. Deng, J., Han, R., Mishra, S.: Enhancing Base Station Security in Wireless Sensor Networks. Tech. Rep. CU-CS-951-03, University of Colorado (2003),
   http://www.cs.colorado.edu/~mishras/research/papers/tech03-1.pdf
13. Gómez, C., Paradells, J., Caballero, J.E.: Sensors Everywhere: Wireless Network Technologies and Solutions. Fundación Vodafone España (2010),
   http://fundacion.vodafone.es/static/fichero/pre_ucm_mgmt_002618.pdf,
   ISBN 978-84-934740-5-8
14. Jhumka, A., Leeke, M., Shrestha, S.: On the Use of Fake Sources for Source Location Privacy: Trade-Offs Between Energy and Privacy. The Computer Journal 54(6), 860–874 (2011)
15. Jian, Y., Chen, S., Zhang, Z., Zhang, L.: A novel scheme for protecting receiver's location privacy in wireless sensor networks. IEEE Transactions on Wireless Communications 7(10), 3769–3779 (2008)
16. Jiang, J.R., Sheu, J.P., Tu, C., Wu, J.W.: An Anonymous Path Routing (APR) Protocol for Wireless Sensor Networks. Journal of Information Science and Engineering 27(2), 657–680 (2011)

17. Kamat, P., Zhang, Y., Trappe, W., Ozturk, C.: Enhancing Source-Location Privacy in Sensor Network Routing. In: 25th IEEE International Conference on Distributed Computing Systems, ICDCS 2005, pp. 599–608 (June 2005)

18. Kazatzopoulos, L., Delakouridis, K., Marias, G.F.: A privacy-aware overlay routing scheme in wsns. Security and Communication Networks 4(7), 729–743 (2011)

19. Li, Y., Lightfoot, L., Ren, J.: Routing-Based Source-Location Privacy Protection in Wireless Sensor Networks. In: IEEE International Conference on Electro/Information Technology, EIT 2009, pp. 29–34 (2009)

20. Li, Y., Ren, J.: Providing Source-Location Privacy in Wireless Sensor Networks. In: Liu, B., Bestavros, A., Du, D.-Z., Wang, J. (eds.) WASA 2009. LNCS, vol. 5682, pp. 338–347. Springer, Heidelberg (2009)

21. Li, Y., Ren, J., Wu, J.: Quantitative measurement and design of source-location privacy schemes for wireless sensor networks. IEEE Transactions on Parallel and Distributed Systems 23, 1302–1311 (2012)

22. Lightfoot, L., Li, Y., Ren, J.: STaR: design and quantitative measurement of source-location privacy for wireless sensor networks. Security and Communication Networks (Online March 2012)

23. Mahmoud, M., Shen, X.: A Cloud-Based Scheme for Protecting Source-Location Privacy against Hotspot-Locating Attack in Wireless Sensor Networks. IEEE Transactions on Parallel and Distributed Systems 23(10), 1805–1818 (2012)

24. Mehta, K., Liu, D., Wright, M.: Location Privacy in Sensor Networks Against a Global Eavesdropper. In: IEEE International Conference on Network Protocols, ICNP 2007, October 16-19, pp. 314–323. IEEE, Beijing (2007)

25. Mehta, K., Liu, D., Wright, M.: Protecting Location Privacy in Sensor Networks Against a Global Eavesdropper. IEEE Transactions on Mobile Computing 11(2), 320–336 (2012)

26. Misra, S., Xue, G.: Efficient anonymity schemes for clustered wireless sensor networks. International Journal of Sensor Networks 1(1), 50–63 (2006)

27. Nezhad, A.A., Makrakis, D., Miri, A.: Anonymous Topology Discovery for Multihop Wireless Sensor Networks. In: 3rd ACM Workshop on QoS and Security for Wireless and Mobile Networks, Q2SWinet 2007, pp. 78–85. ACM, New York (2007)

28. Nezhad, A.A., Miri, A., Makrakis, D.: Location privacy and anonymity preserving routing for wireless sensor networks. Computer Networks 52(18), 3433–3452 (2008)

29. Ortolani, S., Conti, M., Crispo, B., Di Pietro, R.: Events privacy in WSNs: A new model and its applications. In: IEEE International Symposium on a World of Wireless, Mobile and Multimedia Networks (WoWMoM), pp. 1–9 (June 2011)

30. Ouyang, Y., Le, Z., Chen, G., Ford, J., Makedon, F.: Entrapping Adversaries for Source Protection in Sensor Networks. In: 2006 International Symposium on World of Wireless, Mobile and Multimedia Networks, WOWMOM 2006, pp. 23–34. IEEE Computer Society, Washington, DC (2006)

31. Ouyang, Y., Le, Z., Xu, Y., Triandopoulos, N., Zhang, S., Ford, J., Makedon, F.: Providing Anonymity in Wireless Sensor Networks. In: IEEE International Conference on Pervasive Services, pp. 145–148 (July 2007)

32. Ozturk, C., Zhang, Y., Trappe, W.: Source-Location Privacy in Energy-Constrained Sensor Network Routing. In: 2nd ACM Workshop on Security of Ad Hoc and Sensor Networks, SASN, pp. 88–93. ACM, New York (2004)

33. Pai, S., Bermudez, S., Wicker, S., Meingast, M., Roosta, T., Sastry, S., Mulligan, D.: Transactional Confidentiality in Sensor Networks. IEEE Security & Privacy 6(4), 28–35 (2008)

34. Pfitzmann, A., Hansen, M.: A terminology for talking about privacy by data minimization: Anonymity, unlinkability, undetectability, unobservability, pseudonymity, and identity management, v0.34 (August 2010),
http://dud.inf.tu-dresden.de/literatur/Anon_Terminology_v0.34.pdf

35. Pongaliur, K., Xiao, L.: Sensor Node Source Privacy and Packet Recovery Under Eavesdropping and Node Compromise Attacks. ACM Transactions on Sensor Networks 9(4), 50:1–50:26 (2013)

36. Proano, A., Lazos, L.: Hiding contextual information in wsns. In: IEEE International Symposium on a World of Wireless, Mobile and Multimedia Networks, WoWMoM, pp. 1–6 (June 2012)

37. Proano, A., Lazos, L.: Perfect Contextual Information Privacy in WSNs under Colluding Eavesdroppers. In: 6th ACM Conference on Security and Privacy in Wireless and Mobile Networks, WiSec, April 17-19. ACM, Budapest (2013)

38. Reiter, M., Rubin, A.: Crowds: Anonymity for Web Transactions. ACM Transactions on Information and System Security 1(1), 66–92 (1998)

39. Rios, R., Cuellar, J., Lopez, J.: Robust Probabilistic Fake Packet Injection for Receiver-Location Privacy in WSN. In: Foresti, S., Yung, M., Martinelli, F. (eds.) ESORICS 2012. LNCS, vol. 7459, pp. 163–180. Springer, Heidelberg (2012)

40. Rios, R., Lopez, J.: Exploiting context-awareness to enhance source-location privacy in wireless sensor networks. The Computer Journal 54(10), 1603–1615 (2011), impact Factor: 0.79

41. Shaikh, R., Jameel, H., d'Auriol, B., Lee, S., Song, Y.J., Lee, H.: Network Level Privacy for Wireless Sensor Networks. In: 4th International Conference on Information Assurance and Security, ISIAS 2008, pp. 261–266 (September 2008)

42. Shao, M., Hu, W., Zhu, S., Cao, G., Krishnamurthy, S., La Porta, T.: Cross-layer Enhanced Source Location Privacy in Sensor Networks. In: IEEE Conference on Sensor, Mesh, and Ad Hoc Communications and Networks, SECON 2009, pp. 1–9. IEEE Communications Society (June 2009)

43. Shao, M., Yang, Y., Zhu, S., Cao, G.: Towards Statistically Strong Source Anonymity for Sensor Networks. In: 27th IEEE Conference on Computer Communications, INFOCOM 2008, pp. 466–474 (April 2008)

44. Shao, M., Zhu, S., Zhang, W., Cao, G., Yang, Y.: pdcs: Security and privacy support for data-centric sensor networks. IEEE Transactions on Mobile Computing 8(8), 1023–1038 (2009)

45. Walters, J., Liang, Z., Shi, W., Chaudhary, V.: Wireless Sensor Network Security: A Survey. In: Security in Distributed, Grid, and Pervasive Computing, pp. 367–409. Auerbach Pub. (2007)

46. Wang, H., Sheng, B., Li, Q.: Privacy-aware routing in sensor networks. Computer Networks 53(9), 1512–1529 (2009)

47. Wang, H.J., Hsiang, T.R.: Defending Traffic Analysis with Communication Cycles in Wireless Sensor Networks. In: 10th International Symposium on Pervasive Systems, Algorithms, and Networks, ISPAN, pp. 166–171 (2009)

48. Wei-Ping, W., Liang, C., Jian-Xin, W.: A source-location privacy protocol in WSN based on locational angle. In: IEEE International Conference on Communications, ICC 2008, May 19-23, pp. 1630–1634. IEEE Communications Society, Beijing (2008)

49. Xi, Y., Schwiebert, L., Shi, W.: Preserving Source Location Privacy in Monitoring-Based Wireless Sensor Networks. In: 20th International Parallel and Distributed Processing Symposium, IPDPS 2006, p. 8 (April 2006)

50. Yang, Y., Shao, M., Zhu, S., Urgaonkar, B., Cao, G.: Towards Event Source Unobservability with Minimum Network Traffic in Sensor Networks. In: 1st ACM Conference on Wireless Network Security, WiSec 2008, pp. 77–88. ACM, New York (2008)

51. Yang, Y., Zhu, S., Cao, G., LaPorta, T.: An Active Global Attack Model for Sensor Source Location Privacy: Analysis and Countermeasures. In: Chen, Y., Dimitriou, T.D., Zhou, J. (eds.) SecureComm 2009. LNICST, vol. 19, pp. 373–393. Springer, Heidelberg (2009)

52. Yao, J.: Source-location privacy based on directed greedy walk in wireless sensor networks. In: 2010 6th International Conference on Wireless Communications Networking and Mobile Computing (WiCOM), pp. 1–4 (September 2010)

53. Yao, J., Wen, G.: Preserving source-location privacy in energy-constrained wireless sensor networks. In: Proceedings of the 28th International Conference on Distributed Computing Systems Workshops, ICDCSW 2008, pp. 412–416. IEEE Computer Society, Washington, DC (2008)

54. Yao, L., Kang, L., Deng, F., Deng, J., Wu, G.: Protecting source-location privacy based on multirings in wireless sensor networks. Concurrency and Computation: Practice and Experience (Online June 2013)

55. Yao, L., Kang, L., Shang, P., Wu, G.: Protecting the sink location privacy in wireless sensor networks. Personal and Ubiquitous Computing, 1–11 (2012), 10.1007/s00779-012-0539-9

56. Ying, B., Gallardo, J.R., Makrakis, D., Mouftah, H.T.: Concealing of the Sink Location in WSNs by Artificially Homogenizing Traffic Intensity. In: The First International Workshop on Security in Computers, Networking and Communications (INFOCOM Workshops), pp. 988–993 (April 2011)

57. Ying, B., Makrakis, D., Mouftah, H.T.: A Protocol for Sink Location Privacy Protection in Wireless Sensor Networks. In: IEEE Global Telecommunications Conference (GLOBECOM), December 5-9, pp. 1–5. IEEE Communications Society, Houston (2011)

Author Index